GENESIS

STEPHEN K. RAY

GENESIS

A Bible Study Guide and Commentary

IGNATIUS PRESS   SAN FRANCISCO

Printed with Ecclesiastical Permission.
Most Reverend Earl Boyea, March 3, 2023
Lansing, Michigan

Abraham's Sacrifice of Isaac
Aliense (Antonio Vassilacchi, 1556–1629)
S. Zaccaria/Venice/Italy
© Cameraphoto Arte, Venice/Art Resource, New York

Cover design by Roxanne Mei Lum

DEDICATION

To my father and mother, Charles and Frances Ray, who became Christians a year before I was born in 1954 and who instilled in me a love of Scripture from my youth.

To my beloved wife, Janet, who is ever at my side and sat with me untold hours, listening and advising, as I wrote this book. Many of the words and thoughts are hers. I could never have done it without her.

CONTENTS

PREFACE

My Purpose for Writing
This Commentary

This commentary is intended to encourage readers to believe in a personal and infinite God who superintends our lives and the universe he created. Hopefully it will provide a good companion to Genesis—answering questions, wrestling with conundrums, and revealing the beauty and eloquence of its literature, theology, and history. It presents Genesis as the inspired word of God, inerrant, trustworthy, and accessible. I hope it affirms the fullness of the Catholic faith and stimulates the study of Scriptures for both the novice and the scholar.

INTRODUCTION:
IN THE BEGINNING

Throughout history men have looked up at the stars and asked, "Who are we, where do we come from, do we have a purpose, what happens when we die?" The *Catechism of the Catholic Church* affirms this search for meaning: "It is not only a question of knowing when and how the universe arose physically, or when man appeared, but rather of discovering the meaning of such an origin: is the universe governed by chance, blind fate, anonymous necessity, or by a transcendent, intelligent and good Being called 'God'?" (*CCC* 284).[1]

The ancient book of Genesis provides answers to the big questions. Written under the inspiration of the Holy Spirit, it is especially relevant for modern times. It cries out to the world that there *is* meaning and hope. There is something—no, *someone*—bigger than we are and even bigger than the universe. There is a personal, infinite God. We *can* know where we came from! We *can* know who we are! We *can* know our destiny! And we are not alone in the universe!

Genesis is the beginning of God's written revelation. Through revelation, God tells us things we could never know with our five senses. Science can devise *theories* of how things began and how they work, but it can never go back and observe or recreate *the* beginning. Science can sometimes tell us the "how", but it cannot tell us the "why". Only God can tell us *how* and *what* and *why* he created. And this revelation is poetry for the soul—dripping with life and hope and truth and joy.

---

[1] Catholic Church, *Catechism of the Catholic Church*, 2nd ed. (Washington, D.C.: United States Catholic Conference, 2000), 74.

CLUES TO THE MEANING OF LIFE
AND EXISTENCE OF GOD

Genesis has, as I say, answers to big questions. But two of its key
answers should not come as a complete surprise. As detectives
sorting out a mystery, we can try to understand who we are and
attempt to make sense of the universe and our existence. Two clues
present themselves. First, using our senses and reason, we observe
the objective reality of an orderly universe around us; and second,
we contemplate mankind's unique personality, which separates us
from everything else on earth, with our ability to think abstractly,
to reason, communicate, create, love, make moral judgments, and to
search for the meaning of our own existence. What we conclude
based on these clues is confirmed by Genesis, namely, that the universe implies God as creator and that our experience of personhood
and the moral law within us point to our being in the image of a
personal God.

The first clue is mentioned by Saint Paul as he refers to our observation of the orderly universe in which we live. "Ever since the
creation of the world, [God's] invisible nature, namely, his eternal
power and deity, has been clearly perceived in the things that have
been made. So they are without excuse" (Rom 1:20; CCC 286).

"They are without excuse" refers to human being's awareness of
God and the problem of idolatry. It also points to the second clue
to the meaning of things—man's uniqueness and personal nature.
Human beings are accountable to God because he made us distinct
from the rest of his material creation, with our innate sense of personhood and significance. That is, with our sense of being made in the
image of God, with our ability to know, to choose, and to enter into
personal relationship with others. These aspects point to an immaterial dimension of man, as God is immaterial. And of course man also
has a conscience able to know, reject, or suppress the truth of the
moral law (Rom 1:18).[2]

---

[2] " '[T]he mannishness of man' draws attention to the fact that human beings are different
from all other things in the world. Think, for example, of creativity. People in all cultures of
all ages have created many kinds of things, from 'High Art' to flower arrangements, from silver ornaments to high-technology supersonic aircraft. This is in contrast to the animals about
us. People also fear death, and they have the aspiration to truly choose.... Human beings are
also unique in that they verbalize. That is, people put concrete and abstract concepts into

Saint Paul refers to the law of God written upon the hearts of all men. They have an internal witness to God and his law: "They show that what the law requires is written on their hearts, while their conscience also bears witness and their conflicting thoughts accuse or perhaps excuse them" (Rom 2:115). We have an innate inner moral compass by which we will be judged.

C. S. Lewis explains these two clues to meaning: creation pointing to God and the moral law within us:

> We have two bits of evidence about the Somebody. One is the universe He has made. If we used that as our only clue, then I think we should have to conclude that He was a great artist.... The other bit of evidence is that Moral Law which He has put into our minds. And this is a better bit of evidence than the other, because it is inside information. You find out more about God from the Moral Law than from the universe in general just as you find out more about a man by listening to his conversation than by looking at a house he has built.[3]

We begin with these two substantial clues: the objective world around us and the internal knowledge of our personality and humanity. Starting with absolutely nothing and ending up with this universe and our own human uniqueness is not a rational possibility—nothing comes from nothing, and it is hard to make sense of rational persons coming to be from a meaningless universe that came from nothing. As detectives, we boil things down to two real possibilities: (1) eternal and impersonal matter or energy, with time plus chance, gave rise to the complex life forms we encounter and are, or (2) a Being, both personal and eternal, created everything from nothing and intelligently designed it.

Atheistic materialists usually hold that the physical universe is eternal, and they usually claim that it is the sum total of all that exists. Or if they think there is more to existence than *this* physical universe, they usually point to the so-called multiverse, which is thought to be

---

words which communicate these concepts to other people. People also have an inner life of the mind; they remember the past and make projections into the future. One could name other factors, but these are enough to differentiate people from the other things in the world." Francis A. Schaeffer, *The Complete Works of Francis A. Schaeffer: A Christian Worldview*, vol. 5 (Westchester, Ill.: Crossway Books, 1982), 357.

[3] C. S. Lewis, *Mere Christianity* (New York: HarperOne, 2001), 29.

a collection of "universes"—in any case, a wholly physical reality.[4] Human existence is often thought to be the result of "random" biological mutations and to be without ultimate meaning. As the astronomer Carl Sagan once said, "The Cosmos is all that is or ever was or ever will be."[5] There is no God—only the physical cosmos. Man is reduced to a complex arrangement of biochemical molecules, made up of atoms and their particles. We have hormonal reactions and biological drives, but we are really only small biochemical machines inside a big, impersonal cosmic machine—all the result of eternal matter plus time plus random chance. Men and women do not really love each other; rather, they experience hormonal reactions caused by biochemistry and heredity.

The second option when it comes to understanding things is that there is something beyond and distinct from the universe—an Unmoved Mover, an Uncaused Cause, as the philosophers say. This *something* is really a Someone—a personal and intelligent being. This Artist or Creator created the universe and fashioned man for a purpose. The cosmos and our existence are the result of a Personal Being. We are made in the image of this Artist/Creator, which explains why the wondrous universe exists and why we are who we are within it. It takes far less faith to believe the second option than it does the first option, because a Creator answers all the big questions. As human persons, we know inside that we are more than merely complex meaningless machines with no ultimate purpose.

GENESIS AS REVEALING THE ARTIST

Setting aside the scientist's telescopes and microscopes, we ask, "What philosophy or world view best explains the clues?" In Genesis,

[4] Many atheists would see the Big Bang theory of cosmos origins as pointing to the beginning of *our* universe, but this universe, they would say, is only one of many universes or perhaps an infinity of universes, so the Big Bang would not be an absolute beginning of everything from nothing.

[5] Carl Sagan, *The Cosmos* (New York: Ballantine Books, 1980), 1. Sagan's opening statement is not a scientific assertion; rather, it is philosophical and religious. Sagan moved back and forth between the scientist that he was and the religio-philosopher that he was not. He used his credentials as a scientist to make religious or philosophical statements. In 1996, Joel Achenbach wrote an article in the *Washington Post* concerning Sagan's skepticism on the possibility of God existing (https://www.washingtonpost.com/news/achenblog/wp/2014/07/10/carl-sagan-denied-being-an-atheist-so-what-did-he-believe-part-1).

we find a personal and infinite God who created the world and man by an act of his will and for his pleasure (*CCC* 295). He is distinct from his creation, yet creation bears his imprint. He is an artist, and creation is his work of art. In Genesis we also find that God the artist made us—human beings—in his image. We are like him in profound ways: he loves, so we can love; he creates, so we can create; he communicates, so we can speak to one another; he is an artist, so we can enjoy and make beauty; he can choose, so we have been given free will to choose; he is intelligent, so we can reason and have abstract thoughts and understanding; he is infinite, so we, though finite beings, find complete fulfillment through communion with the infinite God (*CCC* 341).

There is a fit, then, between what we can find out through looking at clues in the universe and in human existence, and what Genesis tells us about God, creation, and our place in creation. Human reason reflecting on the world and human life comes to conclusions confirmed and clarified by revelation in the book of Genesis, the first book of the Bible.

TITLE AND PURPOSE OF GENESIS

The word *genesis* simply means *beginning*. Genesis' first words are *in the beginning* (in Hebrew, *bereshith*). The book of Genesis is the first book of the Bible, which is itself a book made of seventy-three "books" that form a unity, a whole story. Genesis begins the story.

As you might expect, the first book of the Bible is filled with beginnings, one right after another. First, we learn about *before* the beginning, so to speak; second, we learn about the beginning of the creation; then about the beginning of life and the beginning of mankind. These things are followed by another beginning—sin entered, and the fall of man took place. Then comes the first promise of restoration and the beginning of salvation history.

In Genesis, we see the first sacrifice to atone for guilty mankind when animal skins were provided as a covering for Adam and Eve. We see the beginning of the family, and the first murder. Then a new beginning with Noah, the beginning of nations and differing languages, and the beginning of God's salvation through Abraham

GENESIS

(*CCC* 1080). We also find in Genesis the beginning of the covenantal relationship between God and man with the first three major covenants—with Adam, with Noah, and with Abraham.

Genesis' purpose is to help us understand the origin of everything: God the Creator. It also presents God's plan for man, made in his image. It tells us how sin entered into the good creation and what God intended from the outset to do about it. It points to God's establishment of a people with a special mission among the human family, a people through whom the whole of the human family will be blessed and, ultimately, redeemed by a Savior.

Genesis begins the story; the book of Revelation, the last book of the Bible, completes it. In Genesis, the story begins with a garden; in the book of Revelation, at the culmination of human history, we find mankind dwelling in a city, in a new creation. In the beginning, we are naked; in the end, we are clothed with royal, heavenly garments; in Genesis we are driven from the earthly paradise, but in Revelation we enter the heavenly paradise forever. The beginning and the end call back and forth to each other, so to speak, so we can understand the whole epic of salvation history. God has a plan, and history is its fulfillment. You can divide history into two words: "His story." It all begins with Genesis.

The first book of the Bible is not only a sublime piece of literature; it is also an elegant, divinely revelatory story. God *wants* us to know who he is, who we are, what he created, and why. He wants us to know why things are not perfect today, the way he intended them to be. Consequently, he tells us in the book of Genesis. He reminds us that man rebelled against God, violated the moral law, and disrupted the order of the good creation. This is why man is exiled from Eden and why humanity experiences alienation from the natural world itself. Saint Paul says the whole of creation is groaning because of man's rebellion against the Creator (Rom 8:22).

C. S. Lewis described things brilliantly in his book *Out of the Silent Planet*. He said that the whole universe still sings and shimmers in the beauty of God's artistry and poetry, but Earth is quarantined as the "bent planet" due to the disease of sin, until the work of salvation is fully accomplished.

Genesis tells this story, and we have been gifted by God with this great treasure:

Among all the Scriptural texts about creation, the first three chapters of Genesis occupy a unique place. From a literary standpoint these texts may have had diverse sources. The inspired authors have placed them at the beginning of Scripture to express in their solemn language the truths of creation—its origin and its end in God, its order and goodness, the vocation of man, and finally the drama of sin and the hope of salvation. Read in the light of Christ, within the unity of Sacred Scripture and in the living Tradition of the Church, these texts remain the principal source for catechesis on the mysteries of the "beginning": creation, fall, and promise of salvation (*CCC* 289).[6]

Finally, we cannot discuss the purpose of Genesis without noting the importance of approaching the text with the understanding that Genesis reveals the answers to *theological* questions about the origin, purpose, and destiny of man. Science fails to answer questions of this type because they fall outside the scientific method. Science and Scripture both reveal truth; they are, however, distinct orders of knowledge: one reveals *scientific* truths about creation and physical realities; the other reveals *theological* truths about God and his creation, including immaterial realities and the ultimate meaning of things, even physical realities. Therefore, we should not expect Genesis to be a scientific textbook. That was not the intent of its divine author (or its human author, for that matter). To discover the truths revealed in Genesis, we must remember to ask the right questions—theological questions, not scientific ones.

AUTHOR AND DATE OF GENESIS

Genesis is part of a larger work known as the *Pentateuch*, the name of which comes from two Greek words meaning *five* and *scroll*; thus, *book composed of five scrolls*. In Hebrew it is known as the *Torah*, meaning *the Law*. The Pentateuch consists of the first five books of the Old Testament: Genesis, Exodus, Leviticus, Numbers, and Deuteronomy. The question of authorship is directed, not at Genesis alone, but at the entire Pentateuch. The book of Genesis does

---

[6] Catholic Church, *Catechism of the Catholic Church*, 75.

not specify its author, but traditionally Jews and Christians have attributed it to Moses.[7]

Scholars have pointed to both external and internal evidence to support Mosaic authorship, going back as far as Jewish tradition can be traced. The Fathers of the Church also maintained Mosaic authorship.

Internal evidence for Moses as the author comes from the frequent witness of the Pentateuch itself. This is pronounced in Deuteronomy 31:9, 24–26, "And Moses wrote this law, and gave it to the priests the sons of Levi.... When Moses had finished writing the words of this law in a book, to the very end, Moses commanded the Levites who carried the ark of the covenant of the LORD."

The writers of the Old and New Testaments, including Jesus, refer to the Pentateuch as the "book of Moses" or simply "Moses".

Most scholars today deny Mosaic authorship, though a minority still affirm his authorship. Another school of thought holds that most or at least some of the content of Genesis comes from Moses in some form or another, but that it has been edited and put in its final form by later editors. Others deny Mosaic authorship altogether, claiming that different authors wrote portions of the Pentateuch, and they were later combined into a unified document. It has become popular for various reasons to doubt or reject the convictions of past scholars, as though we are simply two thousand years smarter than the patriarchs, prophets, rabbis, apostles, Fathers, and sages of the past.

C. S. Lewis, one of the greatest Christian writers of the last century, sometimes used the phrase "chronological snobbery" to describe a prejudice against people, writings, and ideas of earlier times. Perhaps the term applies here. We should be careful of too easily rejecting the wisdom of the ancients and allowing, to use another phrase from Lewis, the "breeze of the centuries" to blow through our minds, as if simply because an idea was held in the past it must be wrong in the present.

Since the nineteenth century, it has been common to look within the Pentateuch for various source documents. The most popular of these approaches is called the Documentary Hypothesis. It proposes that the Pentateuch is the result of multiple documents, written

[7] Rabbi Dr. Charles B. Chavel, *Ramban Commentary on the Torah* (New York: Shilo, 1999), 7.

by a series of unknown authors, separated by time. Redactors or editors later wove these documents together to arrive at our Pentateuch. According to the classic formulation of the hypothesis, the variation in names used for God and other elements point to parts of the Pentateuch originating from four different sources: "J" for the source who used *Yahweh* for the divine name, "E" for the source who used *Elohim* for the divine name, "P" for an alleged source concerned with accounts and laws of special or particular interest to priests, and "D" for the source for Deuteronomy that added the details of Moses' death.

Many scholars still accept some form or other of the Documentary Hypothesis, also known as the "JEPD theory", but the theory is challenged or rejected by other scholars who are returning to the more traditional view of Moses' authorship, at least in seeing Moses as the primary author or major source for the Pentateuch, including the book of Genesis.

Although Genesis does not tell us who its author is, it seems we are in good company to hold that Moses is the primary author or source of the Pentateuch, even if it may have been redacted by other editors.[8]

Regardless of whether there was a single human author or more than one author of the Pentateuch, it should still be "read in its unity as a document inspired by God". For an excellent treatment on the history, on the reasons for and opposition to the Documentary Hypothesis, read Dr. Scott Hahn and Curtis Mitch's section *Author and Date* in the introduction to *Genesis: With Introduction, Commentary, and Notes*, which is part of the *Ignatius Press Catholic Study Bible*. The authors conclude their explanation and summary:

---

[8] Over a hundred years ago, the Pontifical Biblical Commission declared that Mosaic authorship does not "necessarily imply a production of the whole work of such a character as to impose the belief that each and every word was written by Moses' own hand or was by him dictated to secretaries". The commission elaborated further: "A legitimate hypothesis [is] that he [Moses] conceived the work himself under the guidance of divine inspiration and then entrusted the writing of it to one or more persons, with the understanding that they reproduced his thoughts with fidelity and neither wrote nor omitted anything contrary to his will, and that finally the work composed after this fashion was approved by Moses, its principal and inspired author, and was published under his name" (*Pontifical Biblical Commission*, "On the Authenticity of the Mosaic Authorship of the Pentateuch", June 27, 1906). While this judgment is not binding on Catholics today, it is worth noting.

In the final analysis, Catholic scholarship is not bound to espouse any particular view of the authorship and date of Genesis (or the Pentateuch). Scholars are free to investigate the historical background of the book within the doctrinal framework of Scripture's divine inspiration and without disparagement of the Church's tradition. A range of views, from the substantial Mosaic authorship of Genesis to the Mosaic origin of its sources and traditions to the notion that Genesis is indebted to Moses in a more indirect way, is allowable. Still, for reasons given above and elsewhere, it remains a defensible position that the Book of Genesis is substantially Mosaic, at least in the antiquity of its traditions and quite possibly in its authorship as well.[9]

What we *can* be certain of is that the final version of the Pentateuch, including the book of Genesis, was inspired by the Holy Spirit, and it is the inerrant, authoritative word of God (2 Tim 3:16; *CCC* 105–6). As Saint Theophilus of Antioch (second century), assuming the received tradition of Mosaic authorship to it, states, "And Moses ... or, rather, the Word of God by him as by an instrument, says, 'In the beginning God created the heavens and the earth'."[10]

When was Genesis written? We do not know. Most contemporary advocates of some form of documentary synthesis put the date of the Pentateuch in the fifth and fourth centuries B.C., although the traditions contained in Genesis would go back to the patriarchal period. Advocates of Mosaic authorship would (obviously) hold that Genesis dates from Moses' lifetime, even if he drew on various, older sources. Because Abraham and his descendants would have been a primary source, some of Genesis' material would have been collected and transmitted from the patriarchal period (around the year 1850 B.C.), until it was compiled into the book of Genesis in the time of Moses, after he led the Israelites out of Egypt (probably sometime around 1250 B.C.).

---

[9] Scott Hahn and Curtis Mitch, *Genesis: With Introduction, Commentary, and Notes*, Ignatius Catholic Study Bible, Revised Standard Version, Second Catholic Edition (San Francisco: Ignatius Press, 2010), 14.

[10] Theophilus of Antioch, *Theophilus to Autolycus* 2.10, in *Fathers of the Second Century: Hermas, Tatian, Athenagoras, Theophilus, and Clement of Alexandria (Entire)*, ed. Alexander Roberts, James Donaldson, and A. Cleveland Coxe, trans. Marcus Dods, The Ante-Nicene Fathers, vol. 2 (Buffalo, N.Y.: Christian Literature Company, 1885), 98.

THE STRUCTURE AND OUTLINE OF GENESIS

The structure of Genesis can be approached in one of two ways: according to its subject matter or according to its external form. The subject matter is presented in two basic sections: Primeval History (Genesis chapters 1–11) and Patriarchal History (Genesis chapters 12–50). Each section can be further subdivided by subject matter as follows:

GENERAL OUTLINE OF GENESIS

I. Primeval History (chaps. 1—11)
   A. Creation of the Cosmos (1:1—2:6)
   B. Anthropological Creation Account (2:7–25)
   C. Fall of Adam and Eve (3:1–24)
   D. Cain and Abel (4:1–26)
   E. Descendants of Adam (5:1–32)
   F. Wickedness of the World and the Flood (6:1—9:29)
   G. Table of Nations (10:1–32)
   H. Tower of Babel (11:1–9)
   I. Genealogy of Abraham (11:10–32)
II. Patriarchal History (chaps. 12—50)
   A. Abraham (12:1—25:18)
   B. Isaac (25:19—26:35)
   C. Jacob (27:1—36:43)
   D. Joseph (37:1—50:26)

Genesis provides its own divisions utilizing a framework "*of generations*" (in Hebrew, *tôledôth*). Each new division contains the phrase, "These are the generations of ..." and can be found in the following verses:

Genesis 2:4   These are the generations of the heavens and the earth
Genesis 5:1   [These are] the generations of Adam
Genesis 6:9   These are the generations of Noah
Genesis 10:1   These are the generations of the sons of Noah
Genesis 11:10 These are the [generations] of Shem

Genesis 11:27   These are the [generations] of Terah
Genesis 25:12   These are the [generations] of Ishmael
Genesis 36:1   These are the [generations] of Esau
Genesis 37:2   [These are the generations] of Jacob

THEMES OF GENESIS

Three themes permeate the book of Genesis. The first theme is God's intimate involvement with his people. He did not create and then abandon his creation. He comes down to visit his people, to communicate with them, and he even associates their names with his own. He communed with Adam and Eve in the garden and sought them out when they hid from him (Gen 3:8–9). Enoch and Noah walked with God (Gen 5:22; 6:9). He introduced himself to Moses by name: "the God of Abraham, the God of Isaac, and the God of Jacob has sent me to you" (Ex 3:15). God visited Abraham and called him "Abraham, my friend" (Gen 18:1; Is 41:8). God made covenants with men—bringing them into his very family. These covenants are key to understanding Genesis.

Second, God chooses according to his own will and winnows people on the threshing floor of history. He narrows down the family lines. Cain is set aside for Seth, Shem is chosen among the three sons of Noah. Abraham is selected from "beyond the River" to receive God's covenant (Josh 24:3). Ishmael does not receive the birthright and blessing—it goes to the younger son Isaac, whose youngest son Jacob wins out over his elder brother Esau.

Third, God draws straight with crooked lines. After Adam and Eve introduced sin into the world, sin became rampant. God used flawed men and brought good out of evil to fulfill his divine purposes. For example, Joseph's brothers wickedly sold him into slavery. But in God's providence, Joseph became the vizier of Egypt and saved the family. The great drama of God's salvation might be summed up best by Joseph, "You meant evil against me; but God meant it for good, to bring it about that many people should be kept alive" (Gen 50:20). Paul affirms this well in Romans, "We know that in everything God works for good with those who love him, who are called according to his purpose" (Rom 8:28).

NEW TESTAMENT CONCEALED IN
GENESIS—TYPOLOGY

We have identified three themes of Genesis, but we should speak more about something we have already touched on: Genesis as the book of beginnings *for the whole Bible*. We noted how Genesis is part of the five-part work called the Pentateuch or Torah, the first five books of the Old Testament. But of course Genesis is also the beginning of all of Scripture. The Old and New Testaments form a unified whole. Together they recount, in a divinely inspired way, the work of God in human history. Unfortunately, Christians often disregard the Old Testament in preference to the New. "Why desire the old when the new is already in hand?", some reason. But the Old and New Testament should be seen respectively as *foundation* and *fulfillment*.

Before any proper edifice can be built, it needs a foundation. The Old Testament is foundational to the New Testament. Jesus is the center and pinnacle of both. Here we might change the image a bit. Imagine an orchestra—the Old Testament presenting a theme that the New Testament picks up and develops. Violins and oboes elevate the themes that swirl into beautiful harmonies and melodies. Jesus is like the conductor in the middle.

Jesus, as the incarnate Word of God, appears on the scene in history in the New Testament. But he is revealed in both Old and New, and each is understood and defined through him. Genesis is the beginning of the Old Testament foundation for the edifice that will be brought to completion or fulfillment in the New Testament: the Redemption of Christ and the establishment of his Church. Genesis begins, again to shift the image, the orchestra performance, to be completed in the New Testament and its fulfillment at the end of history, conducted by Jesus from the center.

One key element of seeing the foundation of the New Testament, and indeed Jesus Christ, in the Old Testament is typology. Typology is invaluable to understanding the relationship of the Old Testament to the New. A *type* is a person, event, or thing in the Old Testament that prefigures or points forward to fulfillment in the New Testament. Typology is a form of prophecy—which can include foreshadowing things to come. It involves a theme or prefiguration of a future reality. For example, the ark of Noah represents the Church, and passing through the waters of the flood with the dove circling above prefigures the New Testament sacrament of baptism—new birth with water and Spirit (1 Pet 3:18–21; Jn 3:3–5). The Passover lamb's blood on the door frames in Egypt prefigures the blood of the ultimate Passover Lamb on the wood of the Cross. Moses is a type or image of Christ, the New Moses.

Genesis is loaded with types, as we shall see!

Saint Augustine said that the Old Testament is the New Testament *concealed*; the New Testament is the Old *revealed* (*CCC* 128–30). We will be watching for these nuggets of Old Testament types of New Testament gold as we progress through Genesis.

On the road to Emmaus, Jesus said, "'O foolish men, and slow of heart to believe all that the prophets have spoken! Was it not necessary that the Christ should suffer these things and enter into his glory?' And beginning with Moses and all the prophets, he interpreted to them in all the Scriptures the things concerning himself" (Lk 24:25–27).

Jesus shows the disciples how his story was anticipated in the Old Testament, to which he refers when he speaks of "beginning with Moses and all the prophets". "Moses" here means the books of Moses, the Torah, the first book of which is Genesis.

READ IN THE HEART OF THE CHURCH

Thus, the Old Testament and the New Testament fit together. And they must, in some ways, be read together. Which brings us to how we shall be interpreting the Bible in general and Genesis in particular. The Bible is not a random story to be read and interpreted by anyone without regard for its source, context, and author's intention. The Scriptures were intended to be read in a community. In a way, they are a "family story" to be read and understood within the context of the family and its tradition.

In reading Genesis, we will constantly refer to the tradition of the Church, the Fathers of the Church, the magisterial teachings, and the *Catechism of the Catholic Church*. We will interpret Genesis from the heart of the Church and within the unity of the whole of Scripture as it was meant to be read. This approach is different from how some other Christians generally approach Genesis. While they may draw on the opinions or judgments of other commentators, they have little or no role for the authoritative teaching of the magisterium or the long-standing tradition of the Church.[11] A Catholic approach integrates Scripture, tradition, and the Magisterium.

We will also use Jewish sources to enrich our study within the wider context of our "elder brothers" in the faith. Saint Paul reminds us that the Jews were "entrusted with the oracles of God" (Rom 3:2). Most Christians know little of Jewish liturgy and life in the synagogue. We have much to learn from our older brothers, the Jews, especially in liturgy and understanding of Scripture (see CCC 839–40, 1096).

BIBLE TRANSLATIONS AND VERSIONS

Several translations of the Bible will be used in our study. Our primary text is the *Revised Standard Version, Second Catholic Edition* (RSV-2CE) published by Ignatius Press. We will also refer to the *New American Bible* (NAB), the only translation approved for liturgical use in the Roman Catholic dioceses of the United States, and the *English Standard Version* (ESV-CE). The *New Jerusalem Bible* (NJB) and *Douay-Rheims Bible* (D-R) are two additional Catholic translations. A few Protestant translations are mentioned, including the *King James Version* (KJV), the *New International Version* (NIV), and the *Amplified Bible* (AMP).

Frequent reference to the original language texts will help clarify certain passages. We will refer to the *Hebrew Masoretic* text, used as the textual basis for the Old Testament. The *Greek Septuagint* is a translation of the Old Testament from around 250 B.C. for the Greek-speaking Jews. It is the translation most quoted by Saint Paul. Lastly, we will refer to the *Vulgate*—the official Latin text of the Catholic Church—and in a few cases the Syriac translation.

---

[11] Martin Luther broke from the Catholic Church in the sixteenth century and promoted a new way to read the Bible. He called it *sola Scriptura*, or "the Bible alone". He advocated a novelty—interpreting the Bible without regard for the Church's Magisterium or Sacred Tradition. This, of course, has spun off thousands of competing Christian denominations and sects that have arrived at their own interpretations of Scripture.

CHAPTER I

THE CREATION OF THE WORLD

INTRODUCTION

We are almost ready to begin at the beginning. There are two things to keep in mind as we proceed. We have already touched on one of the points, but it bears repeating, given the history of use and misuse of Genesis: the distinction between a scientific account of the beginning of the cosmos and the biblical narrative as given in story form in Genesis. The biblical author uses ideas and images from his time and culture to express theological truths, not to give a scientific report.

The second point is this. Today we have the benefit of the fullness of divine revelation through Jesus Christ. We also have the development of Christian tradition, the Spirit-guided Magisterium of the Catholic Church, and the serious reflections of the great doctors and theologians. The human author of Genesis, though he was divinely inspired, writes earlier in the unfolding of God's word to us.

The developed theological understanding we possess includes things that the human author of Genesis did not yet fully understand or know about—for example, the Trinity. What we *now* see as divinely guided statements of the human author anticipating the Trinity (e.g., the use of "us" by God in Genesis 1:26 and 3:22) we cannot suppose he understood when he wrote. This means at least two things. We should not read into the human author's writing things that God at that point had not revealed. And we should not suppose God is limited the way a human author is. Although the human author wrote to address his time and place, God is able to use what he wrote to prepare for his people's deeper, fuller understanding later, including the fullness of revelation to come in Jesus Christ.

FROM THE BEGINNING

God is, as many have said, like an artist; creation is his work of art. When considering a human work of art, we can always ask what the artist was doing *before* he created it. Can we say, "Before the beginning there was the divine Artist"? Then, "'in the beginning' the Artist created the heavens and the earth"?

It is hard to make sense of talking about a time *before* the beginning. We can talk about before this or that existed. But it does not make much sense to talk about *before* creation existed because time itself is part of creation. Apart from creation, there is no time. For God is not subject to time; he created it, along with space, matter, and finite spiritual beings (angels and human souls).

God's being "before" the beginning of creation really means God existing apart from or transcending creation. That is, God existing eternally, timelessly, not limited by his creation. Thus, it is better to say, as Genesis 1:1 says, "In the beginning God created the heavens and the earth." God made everything in creation. It was all conceived in the mind of the Artist and brought into being by his workmanship (cf. 2 Mac 7:28).

The Artist created the heavens and the earth out of nothing and "outside" himself—as related to himself but still distinct from himself. The Artist chose to create by an act of his will and for his good pleasure. Because he himself is love, creation was to express the superabundance of his love (*CCC* 235, 257).

Saint Paul of the Cross reflects on God as Artist: "[Listen] to the sermon preached by the flowers, the trees, the meadows, the sun, the sky, and the whole universe. You will find that they exhort you to love and praise God; that they excite you to extol the greatness of that Sovereign Architect Who has given them their being."[1]

Joseph Ratzinger (Pope Benedict XVI), stressing the Mind of the Artist, wrote:

Out of that "Let there be" it was not some haphazard stew that was concocted. The more we know of the universe the more profoundly

---

[1] Saint Paul of the Cross, *Flowers of the Passion: Thoughts of St. Paul of the Cross*, trans. Ella A. Mulligan (New York: Benziger Brothers, 1893), 89.

we are struck by a Reason whose ways we can only contemplate with astonishment. In pursuing them we can see anew that creating Intelligence to whom we owe our own reason. Albert Einstein once said that in the laws of nature "there is revealed such a superior Reason that everything significant which has arisen out of human thought and arrangement is, in comparison with it, the merest empty reflection." In what is most vast, in the world of heavenly bodies, we see revealed a powerful Reason that holds the universe together.[2]

God was not compelled to create. He was not deficient or lonely, nor did he need to create for reciprocal love (*CCC* 295). God is a Trinity—Father, Son, and Holy Spirit. The Persons of the Trinity eternally love one another (*CCC* 221, 315–16). God is fully self-sufficient. He is *Elohim* (not a proper name but the general Hebrew word for deity). His name is YHWH, "I am who I am" (Ex 3:13–15; *CCC* 206). No, God did not create out of some need. The Triune God's love was so abundant it bubbled over so that the Father, the Son, and the Spirit created the human race to share in the joy and love of the Trinity (*CCC* 221).

On January 2, 1980, Pope John Paul II spoke on creation as a fundamental and original gift:

> The Creator is he who "calls to existence from nothingness," and who establishes the world in existence and man in the world, because he "is love" (1 *Jn* 4:8). Actually, we do not find this word in the narrative of creation. However, this narrative often repeats: "God saw what he had made, and behold, it was very good." Through these words we are led to glimpse in love the divine motive of creation, the source from which it springs. Only love gives a beginning to good and delights in good (cf. 1 *Cor* 13).... The first chapters of Genesis introduce us to the mystery of creation, that is, the beginning of the world by the will of God, who is omnipotence and love.[3]

Saint John Paul II focuses on the first chapters of Genesis because they are the primary texts that reveal our origin—who we are and

---

[2] Joseph Ratzinger (Pope Benedict XVI), *'In the Beginning ...', A Catholic Understanding of the Story of Creation and the Fall* (Grand Rapids, Mich.: Eerdmans, 1986), 23.

[3] John Paul II, *Audiences of Pope John Paul II (English)* (Vatican City: Libreria Editrice Vaticana, 2014).

how we got here. These chapters are not just about history or the
process of creation; they also tell us about our purpose, condition,
and destiny. As we shall see, they provide the beginning in the great
story of salvation—the drama of creation, then of sin, and then the
hope of redemption and eternal life with God (*CCC* 289).

GOD BEGINS TO CREATE

"In the beginning God created the heavens and the earth", the opening sentence of the Bible declares. Then: "The earth was without
form and void, and darkness was upon the face of the deep...." (Gen
1:2). In the initial stage of creation, the world is said to have been in
primeval chaos, covered with water and engulfed in darkness. It was
"without form and void"—the closest thing the biblical author could
come to describing "nothing". There was no light and no life, and
darkness covered the surface of the deep. Then God began to form
things into the world we know today.

We read how "the Spirit of God was moving over the face of
the waters." In Hebrew, the word for "spirit" is *ruach*, which is
also the word for *wind* or *breath*. The *ruach* here was not an impersonal force or a movement of air molecules. It was the Spirit of
God. Christians understand the Spirit to be the third Person of the
Trinity—the Holy Spirit of God. The Spirit of God was moving over
the face of "the waters", the formlessness from which God brought
forth an ordered creation.

God spoke, and creation was. We know from the New Testament
that Jesus, the Son, is the "Word", the second Person of the Trinity.
"In the beginning was the Word", according to the Gospel of John,
"and the Word was with God, and the Word was God. He was in the
beginning with God; all things were made through him, and without
him was not anything made that was made" (Jn 1:1–3). Referring to
Jesus Christ, the book of *Hebrews* proclaims, "but in these last days he
has spoken to us by a Son, whom he appointed the heir of all things,
through whom also he created the ages" (Heb 1:2).

Thus, God, his Word (the Son), and his Breath (the Spirit) were
at work to bring about creation, including living beings (*CCC* 703).
The work of creation is a common work of the Holy Trinity as the
Divine Persons cooperate in the action of creating (*CCC* 291–92, 316).

Of course the human author of Genesis did not have all of this in mind, but the divine author did. While the Father had a message for his people when Genesis was first written, he came to reveal a fuller message over time—through the events and record of God's revelation in the Old Testament and ultimately when he spoke through his Son, Jesus Christ. The Church, meditating on Genesis, understands it more deeply, in the light of Christ.

That covers the topic of who created: the Triune God. What of the activity of creation itself? The Hebrew word for *create* is *bara* and means to "create a new thing". It differs from another Hebrew word, *yasar*, which primarily means to fashion or shape an object.[4] Throughout the Bible, including in Genesis 1, *bara* is used for an action performed by God. This powerful theological term expresses the utter newness of this creation. At one moment *nothing* (or at least its ancient Hebrew equivalent), the next moment *something* (*CCC* 290, 296, 338). Psalm 33 affirms this, "By the word of the LORD the heavens were made, and all their host by the breath of his mouth.... For he spoke, and it came to be; he commanded, and it stood forth" (vv. 6, 9).[5]

Later theology will refer to *ex nihilo* creation—creation "from nothing". God created everything—he is the cause of the being of everything. He did not need to use preexisting things to fashion the heavens and the earth, the way a painter requires paints, a canvas or something on which to paint, and ideas he acquired through experience of the world. Or the way a woodworker requires wood, a plan, and tools to make a cabinet.[6]

Still, the way creation is described—remember, the author of Genesis is giving us a nonscientific account and using, while also correcting, popular ideas from his culture—God creates the heavens and the earth, and he gives proper form to things. Creation comes from God, and the various aspects of creation are "shaped" or "formed" by God to be the kind of things they are.

---

[4] Cf. R. L. Harris, G. L. Archer, and B. K Waltke, *Theological Wordbook of the Old Testament* (Chicago: Moody Press, 1980), 127.

[5] Here we see another allusion to the trinitarian nature of God. God the Father creates with his *word* (the Son) and his *breath* (the Holy Spirit).

[6] "From Creation in the proper and strict sense (*creatio prima*) is to be distinguished the so-called *creatio secunda*, by which is understood the modeling of formless material and the bestowal of life upon it." Ludwig Ott, *Fundamentals of Catholic Dogma* (St. Louis: B. Herder, 1957), 79.

There is a well-known pattern in the Genesis account of creation. It uses the figure or image of a six-day "work week", with God "resting" or ceasing from his creative activity on the seventh day (*CCC* 337), and with each successive day reflecting a hierarchical order from the less perfect to the more perfect (*CCC* 339). Within the six-day "work week", there is a further pattern: two days then one, two days then one. On days one and two, God performed one creative act each day; on day three, he acted twice. On days four and five, God performed one act each day; on day six, he acted twice. On day three, his second act brought life from the ground; on day six, his second act again brought life from the ground—mankind. We will examine this pattern in detail as we study the first chapter of Genesis.

DAY ONE: BEGINNING OF THE FIRST CYCLE (1:1–5)

God's first act of "forming" is to say, "Let there be light" (Gen 1:3). Since the sun, moon, and stars are created on day four (Gen 1:14–16), this new light on day one has been a matter of much discussion. How can there be light without the sun or the other stars? It seems to be a light independent of the sun! The ancient Hebrews did not have a scientific view of the cosmos. Evidently, the human author thought of God creating light as a general phenomenon, we might say, to distinguish light from darkness, and then only later does the author describe God creating a specific place or places for light to reside— the sun, moon, and the stars.

Many Jewish rabbis considered this initial light to be the splendor of the Divine Presence. "The source of this supernal, nonsolar light of creation became a subject of rabbinic and mystical speculation. Genesis Rabba 3:4 expresses the view that this light is the effulgent splendor of the Divine Presence. Psalm 104:2, with its theme of creation, describes God as 'wrapped in a robe of light'."[7]

We are told that there was evening and morning the first day (Gen 1:5). The evening and morning references have led many Christians

_____
[7] Nahum M. Sarna, *Genesis*, The JPS Torah Commentary (Philadelphia: Jewish Publication Society, 1989), 7.

to believe the work of creation occurred over a period of six literal days. Indeed, in prescientific ages, this was how Genesis was generally understood and how it is still understood by a minority of believers today. Others interpret "days" to refer to periods of time, perhaps epochs or ages, but not literal twenty-four-hour days. Still others see the six-day pattern as a figurative or symbolic way to describe God's act of creating, a sort of divine work week. According to the *Catechism*, the work of creation is symbolically represented as a succession of six days of work with a seventh day taken for rest. This is by far the majority opinion today (*CCC* 337).[8]

Saint Augustine presented an alternative view to the literal six-day interpretation. He believed that God "created all things at once". Through Scripture, God presented his divine artistry as a series of days to be better understood by the less capable or as for the "weaker souls".[9] But Augustine remained uncertain about details, holding different views over the course of his life as a Christian. At one point he declared, "What kind of days these were it is extremely difficult, or perhaps impossible for us to conceive, and how much more to say!"[10]

Genesis was written in a prescientific age, before telescopes and microscopes, before our modern understanding of gravity, atoms, black holes, or the formation of galaxies. If God provided a scientific account of how he created, if such a thing is even meaningful to finite minds such as ours, who throughout most of history would even have understood it? Only in modern times would we have even

---

[8] "Modern readers must recognize that the author's world view is one of his cultural assumptions, not one of his inspired assertions; thus, the cosmological presuppositions of the author should not be taken as revealed propositions to be accepted by faith. The Church, following the wisdom of St. Augustine (*On the Literal Interpretation of Genesis* 2, 9), maintains that the Bible does not contain any properly scientific teaching about the nature of the physical universe (Leo XIII, *Providentissimus Deus* 39)." In Scott Hahn and Curtis Mitch, *Genesis: With Introduction, Commentary, and Notes*, Ignatius Catholic Study Bible, Revised Standard Version and Second Catholic Edition (San Francisco: Ignatius Press, 2010), 18.

[9] Augustine of Hippo, *On Genesis: Two Books on Genesis against the Manichees; And, on the Literal Interpretation of Genesis: An Unfinished Book*, trans. Roland J. Teske, The Fathers of the Church, ed. Thomas P. Halton, vol. 84, chap. 7 (Washington, D.C.: Catholic University of America Press, 1991), 164–65.

[10] Augustine of Hippo, *The City of God*, in *St. Augustin's City of God and Christian Doctrine*, bk. 11, chap. 6, ed. Philip Schaff, trans. Marcus Dods, A Select Library of the Nicene and Post-Nicene Fathers of the Christian Church, First Series, vol. 2 (Buffalo, N.Y.: Christian Literature Company, 1887), 208.

begun to make sense of it. The exact "how" of creation is not the point of Genesis 1. The "story" of Genesis gives us the truth *that* God created without it being a scientific treatise: everything that exists owes its existence to God, who created in an orderly, rational way, with man as his final creation.

On day one, light is created; light and darkness are separated, with light called "day" and darkness called "night". God then declares the result of his first day of creation good. He will repeat this appraisal after each day until he makes man. He will then say of man's creation that it is *very* good (Gen 1:31; *CCC* 299, 1604).

DAY TWO (1:6–8)

On day one, God differentiated light from darkness, day from night. Now he differentiates or separates two great bodies of water, the water covering the earth and the water "above the earth". Again, the biblical author thinks of the cosmos with a prescientific understanding. The "firmament" or expanse of the heavens, known now as our atmosphere, divides two expanses of water—a dome of water above the earth and the water covering the earth. The Hebrew word for *firmament* originally meant to "stamp or spread" as used in Exodus 39:3, to hammer and flatten a piece of metal to cover an extended area. This barrier of separation between the vast bodies of water was perceived as a dome.[11] The author later explains that this water above the earth was used by God to flood the earth in the days of Noah (Gen 7:11–12; Ps 148:4).

DAY THREE (1:9–13)

Differentiation continues. The surface of the earth is completely covered with waves breaking over the deep waters. God commands the water under the sky to be gathered into "one place", causing the land to appear. As it turns out, the surface of the earth is roughly

---

[11] William Lee Holladay and Ludwig Köhler, *A Concise Hebrew and Aramaic Lexicon of the Old Testament* (Leiden: Brill, 2000), 347.

71 percent water and 29 percent land—not exactly an even division. Still, water actually makes up a tiny part of the earth's mass, some 0.05 percent. But Genesis' point is that God made both the land and the seas.

Again, there is no *new* creation from nothing, only the "shaping", or at least relocating, of existing created material. One can imagine continents and islands rising out of the ocean, volcanos erupting, and the waters receding into the seas (v. 10). God calls the land *earth*, and the waters he calls *seas*. God again sees that it is good.

But God does not stop here. He commands the earth to produce vegetation. Here we *do* see a new creation. He creates plants that produce seeds for their own propagation, according to their own species—vegetation, plants, and trees all bearing seeds that reproduce according to their kind or species. In the Greek *Septuagint* translation of the Old Testament, the word used for *kind* is γένος (*genos*), from which we get the biological word *genus* or group of species. And for the second time on day three, "God saw that it was good."

Many pagan religions held that gods inhabited the earth and that they were the potent forces that made trees grow, springs gurgle, and rains fall. But when God reveals that he imbues the earth with the ability to produce plants, he essentially pulls back the curtain on pagan beliefs, illustrating that it is he, not some mythical beings, who animates nature. And, unlike pagan gods believed to exist *within* nature, the God of Genesis transcends his creation. Nature is nature, and God is God.

DAY FOUR: BEGINNING OF THE SECOND CYCLE (1:14–19)

As we noted earlier, Genesis presents God making the sun, moon, and stars *after* creating light. It also depicts him creating the vegetation on day three, as we have seen, before creating the sun, vegetation that needs sunlight to survive. This again suggests the days are symbolic. God creates places or spaces and then "furnishes" them appropriately.

The "great lights" of the sun and the moon are created, and they now mark days and months and years and determine the yearly cycles for the agrarian life-style (Gen 1:14–19).

In ancient cultures, the Egyptian for example, the celestial luminaries were considered deities. In Egypt, the head god was Ra, the Sun God. In Genesis, the great lights are not gods but are servants of God. The Israelites knew that the sun, moon, and stars were God's creation (not gods themselves). Israel was warned against worshipping the sun, moon, and stars like the neighboring nations (Deut 4:9; 17:3).

As the Navarre Bible commentary on the Pentateuch notes:

> Against the neighbouring religions, which regarded the heavenly bodies as divinities exerting influence over human life, the biblical author, enlightened by inspiration, teaches that the sun, moon and stars are simply created things; their purpose is to serve man by giving him light by day and night, and to be a way of measuring time. Put in their proper, natural place heavenly bodies (like all the rest of creation) lead man to appreciate the greatness of God, and to praise him for his awesome works: "The heavens are telling the glory of God; and the firmament proclaims his handiwork ..." (Ps 19:1; cf. Ps 104). It follows that all forms of divination are to be rejected—consulting horoscopes, astrology, clairvoyance etc. (cf. *Catechism of the Catholic Church*, 2116).[12]

God made the lights and set them in the firmament of the heavens, and "it was so", and "God saw that it was good." The earth is now sufficiently prepared to sustain animal life.

DAY FIVE (1:20–23)

Given the rhythm of the creation story, we can expect a single creative act on day five, the second day in the second cycle of three days, to correspond with day two, in the first set of three days. And, in fact, God creates the creatures of the air and of the sea. After Genesis 1:1, God has been shaping and making (*yasar*), but now we again see the word *bara* (*create*) used in reference to the creatures.

At God's command, the seas bring forth swarms of living creatures, including great sea monsters. No doubt these included whales, shrimp and lobsters, fish and sea turtles. If you have ever watched

---

[12] James Gavigan, Brian McCarthy, and Thomas McGovern, eds., *The Pentateuch*, The Navarre Bible (Dublin and New Jersey: Four Courts Press; Scepter Publishers, 1999), 40.

nature documentaries, you would have probably been amazed at the staggering variety of sea creatures with their brilliant colors, bizarre shapes, and eccentric behaviors. Many new species continue to be discovered every year.

God also created (*bara*) the winged creatures of the air. Our family, like many other amateur ornithologists, enjoy the hobby of bird-watching, and we know the thrill of sighting a new bird for the first time and enjoying the different behavior of the vast variety of birds. How God must have enjoyed creating these aeronautical masterpieces for his own pleasure, with their great diversity and the technology of flight. Imagine the delight of the Creator watching a tiny iridescent hummingbird, with wings buzzing at up to seventy wingbeats per second, dipping his pointy bill into a flower.

He commanded these creatures of sea and air to "be fruitful and multiply", to fill the waters and the sky. They have certainly obeyed; the desire to survive, reproduce, and fill the earth is built into their natural instincts.

Again, God saw that what he had created was good. It was now the end of the fifth day.

DAY SIX AND THE CREATION OF ANIMALS AND MAN (1:24–31)

We come now to consider day six. Corresponding to day three in the first cycle of creation, the sixth day involves God performing two distinct actions: the creation of land animals and the creation of man to have dominion over all the creatures.

First, God makes the land animals in distinct categories according to their kind. There are mammals, reptiles, amphibians, insects, spiders, and every other creeping, walking, crawling, climbing, hopping, and slithering creature. Once again, the great Artist produces a stunning array of creative brilliance and diversity.

According to God's original plan in the Garden, man would not kill animals or eat meat. Men and animals would have lived in a harmonious state, without the shedding of blood. Both were given the plants to eat; our original state was that of vegetarians. God said, "I have given you every plant ... you shall have them for food.... [To] everything that has the breath of life, I have given every green plant for food." After the flood, men were specifically granted permission to eat meat (Gen 1:29–30; 9:3).

With man we reach the summit of the creation drama. Creation to this point was in preparation for the appearance of man (Gen 1:28; *CCC* 343). Mankind is unique on earth, for God willed to make man in his own image and likeness (Gen 1:27; *CCC* 2331). Man is capable of relating to the heavenly (spiritual) and the earthly (corporeal) because he is a combination of both—a physical body like the animals, but also a spirit like the angels. Nevertheless, it is the *whole* man that is made in the image of God (*CCC* 327).

We sometimes speak of man having a body and a spirit, but this can be problematic. It is more accurate to say man does not *have* a body so much as he *is* his body. Man does not *have* a spirit so much as he *is* his spirit. Our bodies are not extraneous to what we are; they are aspects of who and what we are. "The central dogmas of the Christian faith imply that the body is an intrinsic part of the human person and thus participates in his being created in the image of God."[13]

In the ancient world, an *image* was often believed to carry the essence of that which it represented, so that actions of a deity were thought to be carried out through its image. Similarly, man, who was made in the image of God, was understood to have something of God in him (Gen 1:26–27; 9:6). God is personal; man is personal. God is spirit; man is spirit (as well as corporeal). God is love, and man is created with the ability to love. God creates, exercises his will, communicates, thinks rationally—all attributes possessed by man precisely because man is made in the image of God. God chose to delegate to the man made in his image a share of responsibility for the material creation. As God has dominion over the universe, so man has been given dominion over the earth. Being in the image of God affords man great meaning and dignity.

The Psalmist meditates on the mystery of mankind:

> When I look at your heavens, the work of your fingers,
>   the moon and the stars which you have established;
> what is man that you are mindful of him,
>   and the son of man that you care for him?

---

[13] Catholic Church, *Communion and Stewardship: Human Persons Created in the Image of God* (Vatican City: Libreria Editrice Vaticana, 2004), chap. 2, sec. 1, par. 29.

Yet you have made him little less than the angels,
   and you have crowned him with glory and honor.
You have given him dominion over the works of your hands;
   you have put all things under his feet,
all sheep and oxen,
   and also the beasts of the field. (Ps 8:3–7)

SEVERAL ISSUES RELATED TO MAN
CREATED IN THE IMAGE OF GOD

A. Foreshadowing of the Revelation of the Most Holy Trinity

Earlier we discussed the nature of the Most Holy Trinity: one God in three Persons and noted that the word for *God* is the plural noun *elohim*. Now we consider God's use of plural pronouns on the sixth day: "Let *us* make man in *our* image, after *our* likeness" (Gen 1:26). We know *us* and *our* in this passage do not refer to multiple gods. To what then do they refer?

One suggestion is that God employs here the "plural of majesty", as a king issuing a decree by his authority might say, "We decree ...". The trouble is, we do not find this a common way God speaks in the Old Testament. Such a usage occurs in only a few other places (Gen 3:22; 11:7), as we shall see. If it were simply a matter of the plural of majesty, we would expect this to be more common.[14]

Another explanation suggests the language here reflects a "plural of assembly", in which God, surrounded by his celestial court of angels, includes them in the divine "us". Some of the Jewish sages held to this position. But while there is no doubt that a heavenly host surrounds the throne of God, there is nothing in Scripture or tradition that suggests the angels were consulted or that they co-created with God.

A third explanation is that God refers to himself in a kind of "plurality of deliberative action". God has no equal with whom to deliberate, so he is presented as speaking with himself as if he had another with whom to consult and as exhorting himself to act. Of course, there is a similar problem with this idea as with the "plural

---

[14] Dianne Bergant and Robert J. Karris, *The Collegeville Bible Commentary: Based on the New American Bible with Revised New Testament* (Collegeville, Minn.: Liturgical Press, 1989), 39.

of majesty": we might expect to see this more frequently when God's deliberative action is described.[15]

Whatever the human author had in mind in Genesis 1:26, many Christian commentators see here an anticipation of the dogma of the Trinity. As the primary author of Scripture, the Holy Spirit communicates truth and may reveal more through the writer than even the writer may himself comprehend. Many, including the Fathers of the Church, see this plurality of *Elohim* and God's use of "our" and "us" as a preparation for the full revelation of the Holy Trinity.[16]

B. Man: Male and Female—in His Image

The Hebrew word for *man* is *'adam. Man* is a generic term for *mankind*, encompassing both male and female human beings. It was noted earlier that the image of God bestowed on man must be understood as being manifest in man as a whole: a creature that is at once both physical and spiritual. The importance of rejecting any suggestion of dualism in the nature of man becomes clearer when one considers the Trinitarian nature of God.

Cardinal Joseph Ratzinger referred to the human person as a being created in the image of God when he wrote, "the mystery of man cannot be grasped apart from the mystery of God"[17] (see *CCC* 1602,

---

[15] See, for example, Is 6:8 and Gen 11:7.

[16] Saint Augustine comments, "For God said, 'Let us make man in our image, after our likeness;' and a little after it is said, 'So God created man in the image of God.' Certainly, in that it is of the plural number, the word 'our' would not be rightly used if man were made in the image of one person, whether of the Father, or of the Son, or of the Holy Spirit; but because he was made in the image of the Trinity, on that account it is said, 'After our image.'" Augustine of Hippo, "On the Trinity", bk. 12, chap. 6, in *Augustin: On the Holy Trinity, Doctrinal Treatises, Moral Treatises*, ed. Philip Schaff, trans. Arthur West Haddan, A Select Library of the Nicene and Post-Nicene Fathers of the Christian Church, First Series, vol. 3 (Buffalo, N.Y.: Christian Literature Company, 1887), 157. Saint Irenaeus, the great theologian of the second century, concurs, "Angels did not make us or fashion us. Angels could not have made the image of God, nor could any other have done this but the Word of God, nor a power much less than the Father of all. In carrying out his intended work of creation, God did not need any help from angels, as if he had not his own hands. For he has always at his side his Word and Wisdom, the Son and the Spirit. Through them and in them he created all things of his own free will. And to them he says, 'Let us make man ...' [Gen 1:26]." *Adversus Haereses*, iv. xx. 1. Henry Bettenson, ed. and trans., *The Early Christian Fathers: A Selection from the Writings of the Fathers from St. Clement of Rome to St. Athanasius* (Oxford; New York: Oxford University Press, 1969), 84.

[17] Catholic Church, *Communion and Stewardship: Human Persons Created in the Image of God* (Vatican City: Libreria Editrice Vaticana, 2004), chap. 1, sec. 1, par. 7.

2331). God as Trinity is a communion of Persons: the Father, the Son, and the Holy Spirit. The Divine Persons exist "in relation" with one another. Given that man is made in the image of God, it makes sense that he, too, is a relational being, though not in exactly the same way as the infinite Triune God is. The creation of man as male and female points to a fundamental way in which human beings are relational. It demonstrates that man was created, not as an isolated being, but as a "person", someone who is in relation with other persons (*CCC* 383). What is more, human beings are made to be either male or female, and male is understood with reference to female, while female is understood with reference to male. And their union is the means by which new human beings, also made in the divine image, come to be. Like God, man—male and female—is both relational and fecund.

Man, as an "image" of God, makes visible the invisible, since an image reflects or manifests in some way what it "images". Although God is not a physical being, the physical aspect of man's nature reflects or images the spiritual, invisible God (*CCC* 299, 1604, 2501).

Additionally, by revealing that "God created man in his own image, in the image of God he created him; male and female he created them" (Gen 1:27), it is revealed that male and female are equal in dignity and complementary to one another, respectively, in their masculinity and femininity (*CCC* 372). As Pope John Paul II said, "Man, whom God created male and female, bears the divine image imprinted on his body 'from the beginning.' Man and woman constitute two different ways of the human 'being a body' in the unity of that image."[18] God made two sexes, male and female, to complement each other. The celebration of gender confusion, same-sex sexual activity, and related things by the LGBTQ movement, along with other sexual practices outside of marriage between a man and woman, are grave offenses against God and the natural order of his creation (*CCC* 1603, 2333, 2357).

Can we imagine anything more glorious for humanity than that human beings are made in the very image and likeness of the loving, all-powerful God? Contemplate the dignity and value this affords us. We are not accidents of random, impersonal processes. We are the pinnacle of God's creation and made to reciprocate his love and esteem. We are made by love, to love, and for love.

---

[18] Pope John Paul II, *Theology of the Body* (Boston: Pauline Books and Media, 1997), 58.

C. Be Fruitful and Multiply

The first command God imposed on man was that he "be fruitful and multiply, and fill the earth and subdue it; and have dominion" over all the creatures God had created. The Jews have concluded that in the *Torah* God imposed 613 laws. The first and primary law is found here in verse 28—we are to be fruitful and multiply (*CCC* 1652, 2331). This command constitutes the plan for marriage and family. Men and women are to marry and have children. As families and a society, they are then to extend the bounds of the garden and expand over the earth. If you have ever looked down on the earth from the window of an airplane, you have seen evidence that man has done just that. You have seen cities, towns, and neighborhoods, and the patchwork quilt of fields and farms.

But our dominion does not give us license to abuse, exploit, or raze the earth. We are here on earth as God's stewards. He has entrusted us with responsibility for his creation and to care for it according to his design (*CCC* 226, 373, 2415). Saint Francis of Assisi understood the relationship between God, his creation, and man. In his famous *Canticle of the Sun*, he praises God for Brother Sun and "for Sister Moon, for Mother Earth, for fruits, flowers, grass and even Sister Death"[19] (*CCC* 344).

Physical labor is not a result of the fall of mankind but part of God's original plan (*CCC* 2427–28). "God took the man and put him in the garden of Eden to till it and keep it" (Gen 2:15). Adam was responsible to tend and care for the earth as an agent of God. Only after the fall did work become onerous and difficult (*CCC* 378).

God does not speak to the plants or the animals directly and personally like he does with man. Man is created in God's image and can communicate directly with the Almighty. God is transcendent, but he is also personal and condescends to have communion with us. When God is finished creating everything on day six, he does not see that it is just good; rather, he sees that it is *very* good! There was evening and morning on the sixth day. Creation was complete.

[19] Marie Paul Curley and Mary Lea Hill, *Saints Alive!: The Faith Proclaimed* (Boston: Pauline Books & Media, 2013), 7.

CHAPTER 2

THE SEVENTH DAY;
MAN AND WOMAN IN THE GARDEN

DAY SEVEN: GOD CEASES FROM HIS WORK (2:1–3)

The chapter and verse divisions placed within the text of the Bible are not part of the inspired text. They are relatively modern additions to help readers locate things. Prior to their addition, it was not unusual to find a citation such as "Somewhere it says ..." (Heb 2:6; 4:4). Sometimes it seems a particular chapter break is not suitably placed. The division between Genesis chapters 1 and 2 is a good example. The first three verses of chapter 2 would better fit as part of chapter 1 with the *cosmological* creation account. They provide the natural conclusion of the seven days of creation—six days of work and one day of rest. The second account of creation, the *anthropological* account, begins in verse 4 of chapter 2.

We read, "And on the seventh day God finished his work which he had done, and he rested on the seventh day from all his work which he had done" (Gen 2:2). Did God need to rest? Did the six days of creation exhaust him? No, God did not need a rest, nor does the text say he did. The Hebrew word *shabbat* ("sabbath") means to *cease or desist from labor.*[1] The idea of "rest" is only secondary and was given more prominence starting in Exodus 23:12 and 31:17. God did not need a nap; he simply finished his creation and ceased the process—he ceased the work of creating.

Consider Jesus' words in John 5:17: "My Father is working still." Jesus was referring to the fact that God not only brings all things into

---

[1] Defined as "1. cease, stop, be at a standstill.... Gen 2:2; 2. Stop working, take a holiday." William Lee Holladay and Ludwig Köhler, *A Concise Hebrew and Aramaic Lexicon of the Old Testament* (Leiden: Brill, 2000), 360.

being; but *after* the act of creating, he sustains and holds his creation together. Yes, even on the Sabbath! At all times the Son is "upholding the universe by his word of power" (Heb 1:3; *CCC* 320) and "in him all things hold together" (Col 1:17). Seven days a week God blesses, answers prayers, saves souls, provides grace in the sacraments, heals, and otherwise supports his two "masterpieces"—his physical creation and his spiritual creation, the Church. In his encyclical *Dies Domini*, Pope John Paul II elaborated:

> It would be banal to interpret God's "rest" as a kind of divine "inactivity". By its nature, the creative act which founds the world is unceasing and God is always at work, as Jesus himself declares in speaking of the Sabbath precept: "My Father is working still, and I am working" (Jn 5:17). The divine rest of the seventh day does not allude to an inactive God, but emphasizes the fullness of what has been accomplished. It speaks, as it were, of God's lingering before the "very good" work (Gen 1:31) which his hand has wrought, in order to cast upon it *a gaze full of joyous delight*. This is a "contemplative" gaze which does not look to new accomplishments but enjoys the beauty of what has already been achieved. (*Dies Domini*, 11)[2]

On the sixth day God finished; on the seventh he ceased from his labors. "So God blessed the seventh day and hallowed it, because on it God rested from all his work which he had done in creation" (Gen 2:3). The word "hallowed" (Hebrew *qadash*) can also be translated "sanctified", "set apart" or "made holy". It is the first time the word *holy* is used in the Bible and the only time it is used in Genesis (though it shows up over 170 times in the Old Testament). The seventh day of the week is set apart from the others. The day is blessed—God imbues it with an extraordinary quality. God's people will be required to follow God's example by working for six days and ceasing from work on the seventh day (*CCC* 2184). This obligation to rest from work on the seventh day became memorialized in the Ten Commandments. The Third Commandment says, "Remember the sabbath day, to keep it holy" (Ex 20:8). It should be noted that the Sabbath rest imposed on God's people

---

[2] Pope John Paul II, *Apostolic Letter Dies Domini* (Chicago: Liturgy Training Publications, 1998), 11, https://www.ewtn.com/catholicism/library/jp2--dies-domini-lords-day-8153.

was not imposed or hinted at here; that started after the Exodus from Egypt with the giving of the Law.

Notice that the command in Exodus 20:8–10 is first to "remember" and then to "keep it holy." The connection between the remembrance of the wondrous works of God and the Sabbath rest is continued in the book of Deuteronomy (5:12–15). There is the same command to "remember" and "keep holy", but here the Israelites are to remember their slavery in Egypt, where they worked seven days a week. Now God is imposing a day of rest each week. These two descriptions of the Sabbath demonstrate a connection between creation and salvation. Pope John Paul II elaborated:

> What God accomplished in Creation and wrought for his People in the Exodus has found its fullest expression in Christ's Death and Resurrection, though its definitive fulfilment will not come until the *Parousia*, when Christ returns in glory. In him, the "spiritual" meaning of the Sabbath is fully realized, as Saint Gregory the Great declares: "For us, the true Sabbath is the person of our Redeemer, our Lord Jesus Christ" (*Epist.* 13, 1: *CCL* 140A, 992). (*Dies Domini*, 18)[3]

SEVERAL ISSUES RELATED TO THE ANTHROPOLOGICAL CREATION IN GENESIS 2

A. God Seeks a Relationship with His Creation

In Genesis chapters 2 and 3, God is referred to with the rare combination of two connected names: "Lord" (*Yahweh*, his name) and "God" (*Elohim*, what he is). *Lord God* is the only way God is addressed in these two short chapters, and this expression is used an amazing twenty times. This points to God's supreme power *and* his personal, intimate love for his creation. God is both the absolutely transcendent God of creation (*Elohim*) and, at the same time, the loving personal God (*Yahweh*), who deigns to care for and interact with man, who was made to have fellowship with his Creator. We are told an intimate detail about God—his walking in the garden in the cool of

[3] Ibid.

the day calling out to the man. Only from the mouth of the serpent is God referred to three times only as Elohim. Could it be that the serpent is trying to de-emphasize the personal and loving aspect of God to emphasize only his transcendent and powerful nature, suggesting that God is "aloof" and less than honest with Adam and Eve?

"Jewish tradition interprets the names Elohim and Adonai [YHWH] as explanations of the two sides of the nature of God, the former representing the quality of justice, the latter reflecting the quality of mercy. The Midrash says that the world was originally created by God as Elohim (Gen. 1), but that afterward He is called Adonai [YHWH] Elohim (Gen. 2) because He saw that without the added quality of mercy creation could not have endured."[4]

B. The Anthropological Account of Creation

So, if Genesis 1 is the account of creation, then why does Genesis chapter 2 present *another* creation story? Some people claim these two stories contradict each other. Do they? Are they two opposing stories of creation possibly written by two different authors and then redacted together? We cannot answer all the questions here, but we accept the Church's teaching that Scripture is a unity and that these accounts are both parts of the unified inspired Word of God and therefore do not present a contradiction but two accounts, each accurate in its own way, that complement one another.

These two accounts of creation, both inspired by the Holy Spirit, brilliantly reveal different yet complementary aspects of the *one* creation. They can be described, respectively, as the *cosmological* and the *anthropological* creation account. The *cosmological* perspective is the big picture, the massive expanse of the whole creation that includes man as one part of the cosmic *Poem*. At the same time, while man is part of the creation, he is also its crown and glory, the masterpiece. Thus, it is appropriate to zero-in, so to speak, on man's particular and personal beginning to understand how and why he is unique. This is an *anthropological* perspective. Genesis 1 gives the cosmological perspective of creation; Genesis 2 provides the anthropological account of creation. As John Bergsma and Brant Pitre observe:

---

[4] W. Gunther Plaut, "Genesis", *The Torah: A Modern Commentary* (New York: Union of American Hebrew Congregations, 1981), 31.

The account that begins in Genesis 2:4b is often called "Another Account of Creation", "The Second Creation Story", or a similar title. Modern source criticism identifies it as the "Yahwistic" creation account (J), as opposed to the "Priestly" account of Genesis 1:1—2:3 (P). The differences between the accounts could be explained as the result of different sources, but they can also be explained as the result of a shift in perspective by the sacred author. In any event, the interpreter must attempt to understand the relationship of the two accounts as we have them now, joined together. Genesis 1 and 2 should be viewed, not as competing, but as complementary scenes. Just as many movies begin with a "panoramic" shot that scans the horizon in order to establish the mood and the environment, followed by a "close-up" on the main character of the story, so Genesis 1:1—2:4a functions as a *panorama* or overview of the creation of the entire cosmos, while Genesis 2:4b–25 functions as a *close-up*, focusing the reader's attention on the creation of man and woman in the Garden of Eden.[5]

Or another way of looking at it. Imagine for a moment that you visit a famous art museum. You begin with a tour of the exceptional works of art throughout the centuries, but within the heart of the museum is *the* masterpiece that excels all the others. Admirers from around the world visit the museum to see it all, but the *real* draw is the masterpiece! You have seen the spectacular overview of art history, but then—*voila!* The masterpiece takes center stage!

The modern materialistic, atheistic, or "scientific" view of the universe belittles man, relegating him to an accident of random processes, an unplanned mutation whose primordial ancestors crawled out of the muck. But from the biblical and historic view, we understand man as the center and glory of God's creation, not random molecules emerging from slime, but a glorious creature with a soul made in the image of God. God formed man from the dust and breathed into him the breath of life, and he became a living soul with a divine purpose and majesty. We wake up in the morning knowing we have value and significance, but this can only be true if we have been purposely and lovingly created by a personal and infinite God. A finite reference point only has meaning in relationship to an

---

[5] John Bergsma and Brant Pitre, *A Catholic Introduction to the Bible*, vol. 1, *The Old Testament* (San Francisco: Ignatius Press, 2018), 100–101.

infinite reference point.[6] If we reject an intelligent designer, then we are merely a cog in the gears of a huge, meaningless machine.

FROM THE DUST OF THE GROUND (2:4–7)

In verse 2:4 we read, "These are the generations of the heavens and the earth." This is a heading that informs us of a new section or division in the narrative. It is the transition point between the two accounts of creation. The words *heavens* and *earth* are each mentioned twice, though the order is reversed the second time: earth and the heavens. God and his action in creating the various elements of the heavens and the earth are the focus of Genesis 1. God's creating man and his vocation are the focus of Genesis 2, hence the earth gets priority over the heavens. You can see the lenses of the telescope refocusing from the immensity of the cosmos down to the singular focal point of man in a garden. We were told that man was created; now we are told the details about *how* man was created.

The second creation account, like the first one, uses images and figurative language to describe the historical reality of man's creation by God. Since both accounts have figurative elements, we should not try to pit them against one another, as if one has to be true at the expense of the other. As if Jesus' references to a lost sheep, a lost coin, and a prodigal son are incompatible. Creation is a historical reality, like Jesus' saving mission to seek what was lost. But also like Jesus' mission, the account of creation can be described in figuratively different ways. Two accounts of a real, historical process of creation that both use figurative language, images, and analogies should not be treated as if they are incompatible. As we have seen, they are complementary, not contradictory.

---

[6] "The Greeks long before understood that there was a dilemma between the particulars and the universals. It was not only Plato who wrestled with this, but he especially understood exactly what Jean-Paul Sartre has said in our generation: a finite point has no meaning unless it has an infinite reference point. He is right. Unless the particulars have a universal over them, the particulars have no meaning. Whether a particular is an atom, or a chair, or you, there must be a relationship to something which gives it meaning, or these things all become a zero." Francis A. Schaeffer, *The Complete Works of Francis A. Schaeffer: A Christian Worldview*, vol. 4 (Westchester, Ill.: Crossway Books, 1982), 7.

The second creation account, as noted above, focuses on God's creating man. Thus, man's creation is described first. It has not rained yet, but a mist or flow came up from the ground to water the earth. The English translations usually use the word *mist*, whereas the Hebrew word is uncertain but suggests water coming from the ground, possibly a *stream* or a *flow*. It could be translated as water springing from the ground to make the earth wet.

It would be hard to find a verse more foundational and crucial to the whole understanding of man and salvation than Genesis 2:7. God takes dust or clumps of dirt[7] from the ground, and, like a potter, he fashions a human being. The description is figurative—human flesh and bone are not "dirt" or "clay". "Breathe" is a bodily image for life and, thus, for spiritual life or the soul. Likewise, God does not himself "breathe". To speak of God breathing into man's nostrils the breath of life is a figurative way of saying that God created the human soul, which made the material form of a man into a living human being.

Ever since Darwin published his *Origin of Species* in 1859, there has been great discussion among Christians (and others) about how the idea of biological evolution affects our understanding of the creation accounts in Genesis. The Catholic Church perceives no conflict between science and religion because both involve the truth. God is Truth, and truth will never contradict truth or the Truth. In other words, since both creation (sometimes referred to as "natural revelation") and Scripture (sometimes called "supernatural revelation") have God as their author, things we know from them cannot contradict each other. Catholics are therefore free to believe that an evolutionary process was used by God (and they are not obliged to adhere to a literal six twenty-four-hour-day creation). These theories relate to the *process* of creation, not the *origin* of creation. Even a process of evolution would require God to bring the universe into being and to establish the biological laws and conditions for that process of evolution to occur.

---

[7] "*Dust from the ground:* dust translates a word that is more appropriately rendered 'clods, lumps of earth, soil, or dirt.' *Dust* in English refers to dirt that has become like fine powder, easily carried by the wind or floating in the air." William David Reyburn and Euan McG. Fry, *A Handbook on Genesis*, UBS Handbook Series (New York: United Bible Societies, 1998), 63–64.

What Catholics *must* believe is that in the beginning God created everything *ex nihilo*, out of nothing (*CCC* 296–298, 318). Catholics are obliged to believe that God created life and that man's spiritual soul is created immediately by God (*CCC* 382). A Catholic cannot hold that matter existed eternally or that it was a matter of sheer chance that brought about a process of evolution. Additionally, Catholics cannot hold that the *soul* of man evolved or was derived from the parents. Human souls, being spiritual, cannot be subject to a material process such as evolution; Catholic teaching holds that man's spiritual soul was and is a direct and conscious creation of God and is eternal (*CCC* 366). God infuses an immortal soul into man, and as a result, man is created in the image of God. Whether you consider that man is created instantly or by a process of divine evolution, in either case, God directly creates the soul and infuses it into each person, and thereby confers wondrous dignity on mankind.

God did not form a "machine" or a mere animal. In the figurative account of Genesis 2, he took this incomprehensible body he had fashioned from dirt, and then with his own "breath" he breathed into the nostrils the breath of life—like divine CPR, except where CPR revives or resuscitates, God's breath bestows life. This was face-to-face, warmly personal, almost an intimate "kiss" of God. The body of clay came alive; it was animated. The created being was now a man with body and soul; he became a living, spiritual being.

The *Catechism* says that the human person is a being at once corporeal and spiritual (*CCC* 362–63, 703–4). Or, like the Baltimore Catechism says, "Man is a creature composed of body and soul, and made to the image and likeness of God."[8] The body and soul are related to earth and heaven (1 Cor 15:45–47).

The Divine Potter has made a man for glory out of the clay of the earth! Man is the crown of the creation!

Saint Ambrose wrote:

> Therefore the soul is not blood, because blood is of the flesh; nor is the soul a harmony, because harmony of this sort is also of the flesh; neither is the soul air, because blown breath is one thing and the soul something else.... the soul is living, for Adam "became a living soul,"

---

[8] Third Plenary Council of Baltimore, *Baltimore Catechism*, vol. 2 (Baltimore: Saint Benedict Press and Tan Classics, 2010), 7.

since the soul rules and gives life to the body, which is without life or feeling.[9]

Remember what Jesus does to the apostles in the Upper Room (Jn 20:22)? How does this signify the creation of another new being—the Church? Remember also that the wind of the Holy Spirit blew on Pentecost at the birth of the Church! You can already see a pattern forming. This is an act of self-giving as well as of making; God invests himself in his new creation with his own breath, his own life.

The Hebrew word for "man" is 'adam and the word for "ground" is 'adamah. This is a Hebrew play on words. "In modern terms, this is an assonance rather than correct etymology. Like-sounding words were thought to hint at a special association of concerts. An English equivalent might be: God fashioned an earthly from the earth."[10]

Animals live and breathe, but only man is directly "inspirited" by the very breath of God himself. The breath of God imparts to man that quality uniquely his in the universe—he is a spiritual soul, made in the image and likeness of God, with one foot on earth and one foot in heaven. He is made of dirt but only a little lower than the angels (Ps 8:5). He is material and spiritual at the same time.

Although we share being both material and spiritual with the first human beings, they possessed more than a spiritual soul—they possessed the life of grace, the very life of God himself. Thus, we can see that it is not unthinkable for God to make Mary the Mother of God "full of grace"—he had already made others "full of grace" before. With Mary, he would be starting a "new creation", in light of the Father's plan to being about a new humanity, led by his Son, the new Adam, and his mother, the new Eve

We can speak of man's two aspects or dimensions—body and soul, matter and spirit. But these aspects or dimensions involve a unity, the whole person. When God "breathes" into the form he has "shaped" from the "dirt", man becomes a "living being". Only later, after man's fall, will death encroach on this magnificent being, splitting asunder his unity—the soul being "ripped" from the body in death. Death is separation (CCC 624, 997, 1008).

[9] Isaac, or the Soul, 2.4, in Ambrose of Milan, Seven Exegetical Works, ed. Bernard M. Peebles, trans. Michael P. McHugh, The Fathers of the Church, vol. 65 (Washington, D.C.: Catholic University of America Press, 1972), 13.

[10] Plaut, "Genesis", in The Torah, 29.

Gregory of Nazianzus, Doctor of the Church, comments, "The soul is the breath of God, a substance of heaven mixed with the lowest earth, a light entombed in a cave, yet wholly divine and unquenchable.... He spoke, and taking some of the newly minted earth his immortal hands made an image into which he imparted some of his own life. He sent his spirit, a beam from the invisible divinity."[11] Saint Basil the Great explains how this breath of God is an inestimable honor:

> "And he breathed into his nostrils," that is to say, He placed in man some share of His own grace, in order that he might recognize likeness through likeness. Nevertheless, being in such great honor because he was created in the image of the Creator, he is honored above the heavens, above the sun, above the choirs of stars. For, which of the heavenly bodies was said to be an image of the most high God?[12]

Early theologian Tertullian explains how this breath of God, as with Adam, creates a living being in the womb with the conception of each new person, "Accordingly you read the word of God which was spoken to Jeremiah, 'Before I formed thee in the belly, I knew thee.' Since God forms us in the womb, He also breathes upon us, as He also did at the first creation, when 'the Lord God formed man, and breathed into him the breath of life.' "[13] Think of this quotation of Tertullian in light of rampant abortion in our time. Each human being, at the moment of conception, becomes a living soul, personally receiving the breath of life from God.

THE GARDEN OF EDEN (2:8–15)

Like a new baby placed in a specially prepared crib in a newly painted room, so man is placed in a perfectly prepared environment—a garden in Eden planted by God. Ezekiel 28:13 refers to Eden as the

---

[11] *Dogmatic Hymns*, 7, Andrew Louth and Marco Conti, eds., *Genesis 1–11*, Ancient Christian Commentary on Scripture, OT 1 (Downers Grove, Ill.: InterVarsity Press, 2001), 50.

[12] *Homily on Psalm 48*, Basil of Caesarea, *Exegetic Homilies*, trans. Agnes Clare Way, The Fathers of the Church, vol. 46 (Washington, D.C.: Catholic University of America Press, 1963), 325.

[13] Tertullian, "A Treatise on the Soul", chap. 26, in *Latin Christianity: Its Founder, Tertullian*, ed. Alexander Roberts, James Donaldson, and A. Cleveland Coxe, trans. Peter Holmes, The Ante-Nicene Fathers, vol. 3 (Buffalo, N.Y.: Christian Literature Company, 1885), 207.

"garden of God". In both the Greek *Septuagint* translation of the Old Testament and the Latin *Vulgate* translation, the word *garden* is translated as "paradise". The word *eden* is usually defined as a *luxurious* or *pleasurable place*—and *garden* implies an enclosed or at least dedicated park of pleasant grounds. Eden was "in the east", which would refer to Mesopotamia and was the wider geographic area into which the garden was placed. The garden was lush with every tree that was "pleasant to the sight" and "good for food" (Gen 2:9).

Even as I write, the birds are singing and the breeze is wafting in my window with the indescribable fragrance of lilacs and summer showers. My senses are overwhelmed—imagine the "garden of God"!

We are told that a river ran through Eden that watered the garden, and from this one unnamed river there branched four other rivers. The Tigris (1,200 miles long) and Euphrates (1,700 miles long) are well known today, but the Pishon and Gihon rivers are unknown. The modern occupants living at the junction of the Tigris and Euphrates Rivers in Iraq point to an ancient tree they claim was planted by Abraham to remember the place Adam lived in the garden. The rivers and the surrounding environs indicate that the human author of Genesis thought of "paradise" as a real state or condition on the earth. Adam, we may suppose, was not limited to Eden's original boundaries but had territory to expand and "subdue".

Adam was to "till" the ground and to "keep" the garden (Gen 2:15). In other words, Adam was a farmer, and agriculture was the oldest profession, contrary to the popular maxim. Work was not a result of the curse of the fall or due to sin, but was part of the unblemished original creation. Man was intended to work the land—to be the royal steward of God's creation (*CCC* 378, 2415). Although physical labor is often thought to be a result of sin and the fall, work was part of God's original plan for man.

"Several truths of creation are expressed here. Before sin entered the world, work was not a burden but a joyful activity derived from human nature. When placing human beings in the garden to till and maintain it, God explicitly entrusted them to be stewards of his creation and to share, albeit in a finite way, in his creative power" (*CCC* 373–79).[14] This was God's garden, and man was entrusted "to till it and keep it" for God.

---

[14] Jeffrey Cole, ed., *The Didache Bible* (San Francisco: Ignatius Press, 2014), 5.

TWO TREES, ONE RESTRICTION (2:16–17)

Genesis mentions two special trees in the garden: the tree of life and the tree of the knowledge of good and evil (Gen 2:9). Man was permitted to eat from any tree in the garden including the tree of life, but he was forbidden to eat from the tree of the knowledge of good and evil. According to theologian Ludwig Ott, "The Fathers regarded bodily immortality as being transmitted through the tree of life (Gen 2:9; 3:22)."[15] Scripture informs us, "God created man for incorruption, and made him in the image of his own eternity" (Wis 2:23). Even though man's nature is mortal, God has destined him not to die (*CCC* 1008). In Revelation, the tree of life appears again in the new paradise (Rev 2:7; 22:1–5). Immortality is also promised through the Body and Blood of Christ in the Eucharist. Jesus promises, "He who eats my flesh and drinks my blood has eternal life, and I will raise him up at the last day" (Jn 6:54). Through Christ, the bonds of mortality are burst and we obtain, not just immortality, but eternal life and share in the life of the Trinity (2 Pet 1:4; *CCC* 1265, 1988).

Adam was forbidden to eat of the tree of the knowledge of good and evil. Eating from that forbidden tree would not make him omniscient, but it seems that it would somehow expand his intellectual and moral knowledge. In Deuteronomy 1:39, Moses says, "Your children, who this day have no knowledge of good or evil, shall go in there, and to them I will give it, and they shall possess [the Promised Land]." This implies that lacking the knowledge of good and evil involves a certain innocence, maybe as a child who has not yet reached the age of reason or accountability.

Death was a new concept introduced in contrast to all the life and living and growing and multiplying in Genesis until now. The threat of death is imposed on Adam if he disobeys and rebels against the Creator. The tree was a test of Adam's freedom. Pope John Paul II discusses this in his catechesis "Sin Involves the Misuse of God's Gift":

> The presence of original righteousness and perfection in the human person ... did not mean that man as a creature endowed with liberty like the other spiritual beings, was exempted from the testing of his

---

[15] Ludwig Ott, *Fundamentals of Catholic Dogma* (St. Louis: B. Herder, 1957), 104.

freedom.... In Genesis, this test is described as the prohibition to eat of the fruit "of the tree of the knowledge of good and evil".... The tree ... recalls symbolically the absolute limit which man as a creature must recognize and respect. Man depends on the Creator and is subject to the laws by which the Creator has established the order of the world ... therefore, man is also subject to the moral norms which regulate the use of freedom. The primordial test is, therefore, aimed at the person's free will, at his freedom. (Pope John Paul II, *Sin Involves the Misuse of God's Gifts*, Sept 3, 1986).[16]

A SUITABLE HELPMATE (2:18–25)

God sees that the man is alone without a helper—a mate corresponding to him. Adam can walk in friendship with God, but God is not flesh and blood. God created man for communion with himself but also for human beings to be in relationship with one another. Genesis 2:18 indicates the divine mind when it declares, "It is not good that man should be alone." Human beings need others like themselves.

Like themselves are key words here. Genesis 2:19 describes God's creation of animals and his presenting them to man as if God were looking for a suitable companion for man. This account is figurative and somewhat anthropomorphic—describing God's action as if he were trying various options to see what would work for man. The creation of the animals, though pointing to a value in these things in their own right because they were made by God, is ultimately ordered to human good.

The Lord God (*Yahweh Elohim*) brings animals to Adam "to see what he would call them; and whatever the man called every living creature, that was its name" (Gen 2:19). In this way, God makes Adam the "vice regent" or "steward" of the earth. You do not have the authority to name your neighbors' children—that is their responsibility. You do have the authority to name your children because they are your responsibility. God delegated to man the responsibility to name the animals, because man has responsibility for and authority over the animals on God's behalf.

[16]John Paul II, *Audiences of Pope John Paul II (English)* (Vatican City: Libreria Editrice Vaticana, 2014).

The animals all passed before Adam, and he named the giraffes, gazelles, foxes, camels, lions, and bears. He assigned names for the pelicans, ostriches, ravens, turtle doves, and vultures. He named all the multitudes of walking, flying, and hopping creatures both large and small. Imagine the smile on his face when the baboons and hippopotamuses were presented. The animals all had mates, males and females corresponding to each other, "but for the man there was not found a helper fit for him" (v. 20). As the parade of animals passed before him, I like to imagine Adam looking down the line to see if a beautiful woman was approaching. But no such luck. Adam was alone.

In *Theology of the Body* Pope John Paul II wrote:

> His body, through which he participates in the visible created world, makes him at the same time conscious of being "alone".... Through it [the body], man is distinguished from all the *animalia* and is separated from them, and also through it he is a person. It can be affirmed with certainty that man, thus formed, has at the same time consciousness and awareness of the meaning of his own body, on the basis of original solitude. All this can be considered as an implication of the second narrative of the creation of man.[17]

God had seen his creation was *very good*. But now he sees something that is not good. God says, "It is not good that the man should be alone; I will make him a helper fit for him" (v. 18). So God provides a woman for the man. With the forming of the woman, creation is complete. God did not create the woman from the dust of the ground, like he did the man. He formed her from the man's own body (Gen 2:21–22; *CCC* 371).

After causing Adam to fall into a deep sleep, like an anesthesiologist before a serious operation, God removed a rib from Adam's side, and from the rib God fashioned the woman. It has been said that God used a rib because it was close to Adam's heart. The rib from the chest near the heart of man helps explain the intimacy—a rib from his side is appropriate for one who will walk by his side and be his partner and companion. "Eve's formation out of a rib, the place

---

[17] Pope John Paul II, *Theology of the Body* (Boston: Pauline Books and Media, 1997), 38–39.

closest to Adam's heart, is a parable about the attraction between male and female, and their intention to be reunited in marriage as a single personality (2:18–25)."[18]

Sometimes in jest it is said that Eve was formed after Adam because an artist creates the rough draft first before making the final masterpiece. Humor aside, the word *fashioned* literally means *to build*. It is the only time this word is used in the creation accounts. In the rest of Scripture, it is used of building structures like cities or altars. In the creation accounts, the word is unique, the fashioning is unique—Eve is unique. She is *built* using a part of the man's own body. God's conception of Eve is brilliantly conveyed in Michelangelo's masterpiece in the Sistine Chapel. In the most famous lunette in the center of the ceiling, God is reaching down from heaven with his finger creating Adam. Interestingly, many people interpret the reddish-colored oval behind God as being in the shape of the human brain portraying artistically the "mind of God".[19] If so, we see Eve already conceived in the mind of God and looking longingly at Adam. "Eve is already present in the background in the circle that surrounds God, as a foreshadowing of the completion of the story; man and woman together as two modes of being human, together imaging God. Among the beings next to God we also find a child who looks out at us and who has been interpreted as the anticipated depiction of Jesus, the New Adam. From this perspective the Incarnation here appears as the 'horizon' of Man's creation in the history of salvation."[20]

There are other creation accounts in ancient history, but not one account includes the woman's creation. The biblical account is unique in this regard, especially since man's creation is told in one verse, whereas the forming of woman covers six verses! The text emphasizes the importance of the woman. She inspired a poetic response! After Eve is presented to Adam, we find the first utterance

[18] Prosper Grech, *An Outline of New Testament Spirituality* (Grand Rapids, Mich.; Cambridge, UK: Eerdmans, 2011), 4–5.

[19] "In a provocative article published in 1990, F. L. Meshberger, M.D. made the surprising but cogent argument that in the *Creation of Adam* (the first and arguably the most famous of the final four panels), Michelangelo illustrated a human brain. Over time, Meshberger's argument has gained the cautious support of art scholars." *Neurosurgery*, vol. 66, issue 5, May 2010, pages 851–61, https://academic.oup.com/neurosurgery/article/66/5/851/2556584.

[20] Elizabeth Lev and José Granados, *A Body for Glory* (Città del Vaticano: Edizioni Musei Vaticano, 2014), 67–68.

of the man and find the first poetry in Scripture. Inspired by the dramatic presence of the woman, Adam sings out:

> This at last is bone of my bones
>   and flesh of my flesh;
> she shall be called Woman [Hebrew: *ishshah*]
>   because she was taken out of Man [Hebrew: *ish*].

Therefore, as a result, "a man leaves his father and his mother and clings to his wife, and they become one flesh" (Gen 2:24; *CCC* 1605). In Hebrew, it is expressed as *Ishah* from the *Ish*—"woman from the man". In the Hebrew, the expression "this one" is used three times. We lose this detail in the English, which translates it: *This at last*—*she*—and *she*. But the Hebrew says each time "this one". The three repetitions emphasize the utter love and pleasure Adam experiences as he looks at Eve:

> Here the man gives her a generic, not a personal, name, and that designation is understood to be derived from his own, which means he acknowledges woman to be his equal. Moreover, in naming her 'ishah, he simultaneously names himself. Hitherto he is consistently called 'adam; he now calls himself 'ish for the first time. Thus, he discovers his own manhood and fulfillment only when he faces the woman, the human being who is to be his partner in life.[21]

After "building" the woman from the rib of the man, God brings the woman to the man. Think for a moment of a wedding. What does the father of the bride do? He brings his daughter up the isle and presents her to the man. God himself establishes and sanctions the institution of marriage by giving the bride to her new husband. Untouched by the results of sin and the ravages of time, they must have made a stunning couple. The man loves the woman like himself, because she is one with him, part of his very being, a gift of God. There is complementarity of masculine and feminine. They are one, yet two; two, yet one. The mystery of holy matrimony (*CCC* 372, 1624, 1627).

[21] Nahum M. Sarna, *Genesis*, The JPS Torah Commentary (Philadelphia: Jewish Publication Society, 1989), 23.

Taking the woman from the man and the two being one flesh forms the foundation of marriage and the reason a man leaves his father and mother and cleaves to his wife and they become one flesh (*CCC* 372, 2335). There is so much about this in the New Testament but more than we can discuss here. Suffice it to say, Jesus refers to this passage more than once (e.g., Mt 19:4–6). The man and the woman were innocent, naked, and unashamed (Gen 2:25). Like a toddler running naked in the backyard without giving it a thought, Adam and Eve wandered in the garden unclothed. They were as innocent as children, because up to this point they had obeyed the command of God and refrained from eating the forbidden fruit.

SPIRITUAL MEANING: *Foreshadowing a New Bride*

As always, we glean deep truths from the Old Testament in light of the New. Consider the "forming" of Eve with another important bride. Saint Paul refers to Jesus as "the last Adam" (1 Cor 15:45), and Saint John makes us aware that the Cross and the tomb are in a garden (Jn 19:41). In the first garden, Adam is cast into a deep sleep, and God cuts open his side to remove a rib from which he made the woman. The woman is then presented to Adam as his bride, and she is named Eve "because she was the mother of all living" (Gen 3:20). Jesus, the new Adam, in another garden, is "put to sleep" on the Cross; his side is opened by a lance, and from his side flow blood and water, signifying baptism and the Eucharist. From his Son's body, God forms the Bride of Christ, the Church—Mother of those in Christ (*CCC* 169). Adam and Eve prefigure Christ and the Church (Eph 5:22–33; *CCC* 796, 1602).

God's creation is complete. Adam and Eve are partners made in the image of God. It is not Adam who is the image of God; rather, it is Adam and Eve together who are made in God's image (Gen 1:27). They stand apart from the rest of creation. Before the fall, they had fellowship with God and walked in communion with him in the cool of the day (Gen 3:8). The saga of salvation is off and running, but the "happy fault of Adam" is right around the corner. Things are about to change.

CHAPTER 3

THE FALL OF ADAM AND EVE

INTRODUCTION

More than a decade before he presented readers with the magical world of Narnia, C. S. Lewis released *Out of the Silent Planet*, the first book in his acclaimed Space Trilogy. In it, Lewis introduced a solar system in which Earth was just one of many planets that were filled with life. Each planet enjoyed membership and participation in a great rotating planetary society, all, that is, save one—the "silent planet". This planet was ruled by an evil spirit, referred to as the "Bent One", who had caused the planet to be isolated from the rest of the solar system. This "silent planet" could no longer hear from, or be heard by, those outside its orbit; it was in a sort of quarantine. The term "bent" was used by the beings from the other planets to describe the silent planet because they had no word for "evil", knowing only "good". The isolated world was created "straight", but now was "bent". "Bent creatures are full of fears.... It is the Bent One, the lord of your world, who wastes your lives and befouls them with flying from what you know will overtake you in the end. If you were subjects of Maleldil [God] you would have peace" (C. S. Lewis, *Out of the Silent Planet*).[1]

Mankind's condition reveals that we also are "bent". The earth is magnificent, yet it can be very harsh and unforgiving. Mankind is capable of great nobility and love, yet there is cruelty and depravity. We experience joy and compassion, but also sorrows, suffering, and death (*CCC* 1008). Given these paradoxes, mankind has always sought an explanation for evil and suffering. If there is a God, it seems as if two options present themselves. First, either God is all-powerful, but arbitrary and capricious to allow suffering and death—in other words,

[1] C. S. Lewis, *Out of the Silent Planet*, EPub edition, Space Trilogy, vol. 1 (HarperCollins, 2012), 121, 138–39.

not all-good; or, second, he is merciful and kind, yet weakly incapable of rectifying the problems—in other words, not all-powerful. Either one is a disturbing option. In the historical reality of man's rebellion and fall, however, we are presented with a third alternative, which God has revealed to us in Genesis. It reconciles these apparent contradictions and solves the dilemma. God is both all-good and all-powerful, not arbitrary or weak.

The third chapter of Genesis informs us that suffering and death entered the world as a consequence of a freely chosen act of disobedience committed by our first parents (*CCC* 1008). The Church refers to this primeval abuse of freedom as *original sin*, the result of which is the "bent" reality we experience today. Man's nature, and the world, was wounded and made subject to death and decay. Yet traces of creation's original beauty and grandeur still shine through, and there is the hope of a promise that everything will someday be restored.

God solved the dilemma, so to speak. He loved his creation and set a plan in motion to restore and "re-create" his creation. God is not weak or capricious. Rather, he has earth in "quarantine" while he himself steps in to redeem and restore his creation through a New Adam and a Second Eve.

SATAN ENTERS THE GARDEN; ADAM AND EVE SIN (3:1–6)

Adam and Eve were enjoying their paradise and friendship with the Lord God. Lurking in the garden was an adversary seeking to twist and destroy everything God loved. In the form of a serpent, this adversary takes aim at God's creation, especially man, who has free will. His goal is to deceive Adam and Eve into using their freedom to choose to destroy themselves.

THEOLOGICAL NOTE: *Who or What Is Satan?*

"Satan" means *adversary*. He was originally created as one of God's most powerful and beautiful heavenly creatures, a great angelic being. But he became proud and envious and was joined by other angels in his sin (Wis 2:24). He rebelled against God and was cast out of heaven (Lk 10:18; *CCC* 391–92). "In John's vision [of Revelation], a third of the angels, along with their leader, the great dragon, are thrown down from the heaven [Rev 12:9]."[2] Satan is "going back and forth on the earth, and ... walking up and down on it" (Job 1:6–7). He is not infinite but is a finite, created spiritual being. He is powerful, hateful, and full of wickedness (*CCC* 395). He is a murderer, a liar, and the father of lies (Jn 8:44). He is the deceiver, dragon, and the serpent of old (Rev 12:9). He is called Satan (2 Cor 11:14), Abaddon and Apollyon (Rev 9:11), Beelzebub (Mt 12:24), the god of this world (2 Cor 4:4), along with many other names. In the *Our Father* prayer, "evil is not an abstraction, but refers to a person, Satan, the Evil One, the angel who opposes God" (*CCC* 2851).

The Fathers of the Church point to biblical passages for clues about who Satan is and what he does. In one of these passages, God speaks to King Nebuchadnezzar of Babylon in words often regarded as referring also to the career of Satan.

> "How you are fallen from heaven,
> O Day Star [Latin Vulgate, *Lucifer*], son of Dawn!
> How you are cut down to the ground,
> you who laid the nations low!
> You said in your heart,
> 'I will ascend to heaven;
> above the stars of God
> I will set my throne on high;
> I will sit on the mount of assembly
> in the far north;
> I will ascend above the heights of the clouds,
> I will make myself like the Most High.'
> But you are brought down to Sheol,
> to the depths of the Pit." (Is 14:12–15)

Referring to this passage, Saint Jerome said, "Lucifer, who fell from heaven, has once more set his throne above the stars" (*Letter* 15).[3]

---

[2] Scott Hahn and Leon J. Suprenant, Jr., eds. *Catholic for a Reason II: Scripture and the Mystery of the Mother of God*, 2nd ed. (Steubenville, Ohio: Emmaus Road, 2004), 65.

[3] Jerome, "The Letters of St. Jerome", in *St. Jerome: Letters and Select Works*, ed. Philip Schaff and Henry Wace, trans. W.H. Fremantle, G. Lewis, and W.G. Martley, A Select Library of the Nicene and Post-Nicene Fathers of the Christian Church, Second Series, vol. 6 (New York: Christian Literature Company, 1893), 18.

Saint Thomas Aquinas, quoting Saint Augustine wrote, "[A]s Augustine says (*De Civ. Dei* xi. 13) ... for it is said of the devil under the figure of the prince of Babylon (Isa. 14:12): *How art thou fallen ... O Lucifer, who didst rise in the morning!* and it is said to the devil in the person of the King of Tyre (Ezech. xxviii.13): *Thou wast in the pleasures of the paradise of God.*"[4]

Jesus said, "I saw Satan fall like lightning from heaven" (Lk 10:18). Banished from his former glory, along with many angels who rebelled with him, Satan now wanders the earth with his wicked attempts to destroy everything that is important to God. What better target to poison and kill than the innocent couple newly placed in the garden to rule the earth and to populate the planet as God's regents? They were the crown of God's creation, and they were the target of the flaming darts of the devil (cf. Eph 6:10–17).

The opening words of chapter 3 introduce the serpent, who in later Christian revelation and theological understanding represents Satan (Rev 12:9). Genesis warns of the serpent's subtlety and craftiness. The warning is well-founded; doubt is interjected by the very manner in which he frames his questions. "'Did God say' is introduced in Hebrew by an intensive particle that gives the sense 'Is it really so that God said ...?' The expression shows that the serpent sows a seed of doubt regarding what God has said.... We may render 'Is it actually so that God said ...?' 'Did God really say ...?' or 'Is it true that God said ...?' ... [S]ome may find it natural to translate 'God didn't really say....'"[5]

Possibly the serpent approached Eve rather than Adam because Adam had heard directly and knew exactly what God had commanded and would have been more hesitant to disobey. Eve, however, received the words secondhand from Adam, so the serpent hoped she would be easier prey. Eve fell right into the serpent's trap; he framed the question in a fashion that successfully engaged her in conversation. Eve unhappily entertained the devil's distortion of God's words and added her own "neither shall you touch it" (Gen 3:3).

[4] Thomas Aquinas, *Summa Theologica*, trans. Fathers of the English Dominican Province (London: Burns, Oates & Washbourne, n.d.) (STh., I, q. 63, a. 5 resp.).

[5] William David Reyburn and Euan McG. Fry, *A Handbook on Genesis*, UBS Handbook Series (New York: United Bible Societies, 1998), 81–82.

Eve, we may suppose, now begins to question the limits that
God placed on her and Adam. The serpent has convinced her
that God may be withholding something from her: "You will not
die. For God knows that when you eat of it your eyes will be opened,
and you will be like God, knowing good and evil" (Gen 3:4–5). Was
this not the temptation that caused Lucifer to fall—did he not envy
and desire to be like God?

He lied to Eve, casting doubt on God's words and motives. Saint
Paul says, "[T]he serpent deceived Eve by his cunning" (2 Cor 11:3).
Eve looked at the Tree of the Knowledge of Good and Evil trusting
her own senses and impulses rather than thinking about it in the light
of the clear command from the Creator. Satan only needs a little
opening to slip in the seed of doubt. Once the camel gets his nose
under the hem of the tent, it is not long before the whole camel is
in the tent. From Eve's viewpoint, the tree seemed to be "good for
food" and a "delight for the eyes". If this serpent was correct, the tree
would also make her wise. So she took the fruit, ate it, and gave some
to Adam, who chose to eat it as well.

Why didn't Adam step in? Verse 6 says he was with her and that
when she gave some to him he ate also. Adam chose to be weak and
irresponsible; he did not protect his wife from the lies of the serpent,
and he failed God in his dominion of the garden. Eve was deceived,
not Adam (1 Tim 2:14). He was not deceived—he flat out disobeyed.
Maybe Adam loved the woman more than God—it is not infrequent
that God's good gifts draw us away from him. In any case, Adam
and Eve were now in a state of true moral guilt before the Maker and
Judge of the Universe.

Although Eve (and, no doubt, Adam) saw the goodness of the
fruit, she was not affected by concupiscence, as we are today due to
original sin. What is for us affected by the fleshy and fallen inclination
to sin that comes as an effect of original sin was for them a sheer sinful
choice, something they were more than adequately equipped by God
to reject, had they decided to do so. The first letter of John declares,
"For all that is in the world, the lust of the flesh and the lust of the
eyes and the pride of life, is not of the Father but is of the world"
(1 Jn 2:16). Corrupted by the sinful choice to disobey God, Adam
and Eve's desire for the fruit's goodness to eat becomes "lust of the
flesh". The attractive appearance becomes "lust of the eyes". And

the desire for becoming wise, good in itself, becomes "the pride of life". Sin distorts our desires for good things.

NOTE OF INTEREST: *What Was the Forbidden Fruit?*

We read nowhere of an apple, but art usually portrays the fruit of the Tree of the Knowledge of Good and Evil as such because it is such a common fruit. It is interesting that the Latin words for *apple* and *evil* are similar: in the singular form, *malus* is apple, and *malum* is evil; in the plural form, *mala* means both apple *and* evil. Perhaps this similarity played a role in influencing or perpetuating the association of the apple with the forbidden fruit. In any case, it looked delicious and was beautiful to behold, but ultimately the taste was as bitter as death.

The Jewish Rabbis have mulled over what kind of fruit was involved:

> The "fruit of the tree" from which Adam and Eve ate is not specified in the text. The Rabbis speculated that it was the fig (because it is subsequently mentioned, 3:7); or the grape (because its abuse leads one to forget his senses, 9:20 f.); or the *etrog* [citron] (because the word was seen as deriving from *ragag*, to desire); or wheat (because the Hebrew word for wheat, *chitah*, was seen as related to *chet*, sin); or that it was the carob, the Hebrew word suggesting destruction.[6]

Possibly Adam and Eve realized they were naked the moment they took the first bite and quickly grabbed the first leaves at hand—fig leaves—thus it is thought a fig may have been the forbidden fruit.

---

[6] W. Gunther Plaut, "Genesis", in *The Torah: A Modern Commentary* (New York: Union of American Hebrew Congregations, 1981), 42, quoting from *Legends of the Jews*. There is another suggestion in *Legends of the Jews* giving further reasons for the fig: "[Adam and Eve] stood there in their nakedness, and ashamed. Adam tried to gather leaves from the trees to cover part of their bodies, but he heard one tree after the other say: 'There is the thief that deceived his Creator. Nay, the foot of pride shall not come against me, nor the hand of the wicked touch me. Hence, and take no leaves from me!' Only the fig-tree granted him permission to take of its leaves. That was because the fig was the forbidden fruit itself." Louis Ginzberg, *Legends of the Jews*, trans. Henrietta Szold and Paul Radin, 2nd ed. (Philadelphia: Jewish Publication Society, 2003), 72.

THEOLOGICAL NOTE: *Original Sin*

Not only did Adam and Eve become guilty of sin, but all of their future progeny, including us, were affected by their disobedience. As Saint Paul says, "Therefore as sin came into the world through one man and death through sin, and so death spread to all men because all men sinned" (Rom 5:12; see also 5:13–19). It is a sin *contracted*, and not *committed*—a *state* and not an *act* (*CCC* 404). The *Catechism* paragraphs 386–89 and 397–409 provide an excellent summary of the Church's teaching on the sin of our human parents and the effects of original sin for all mankind.

The glossary in the *Catechism of the Catholic Church* defines *original sin* as follows:

> The sin by which the first human beings disobeyed the commandment of God, choosing to follow their own will rather than God's will. As a consequence they lost the grace of original holiness, and became subject to the law of death; sin became universally present in the world. Besides the personal sin of Adam and Eve, original sin describes the fallen state of human nature which affects every person born into the world, and from which Christ, the "new Adam," came to redeem us (*CCC* 396–412).

Think of original sin in this way. Imagine man created with the throbbing life of God in his soul. This life of God is called *grace of original holiness* (*CCC* 375–76), which is more than just "animal life" that is tied to the earth, or even simply the natural life of a rational free being, but an actual participation in the life of God (*CCC* 1997). God warned that disobedience would result in death. The devil said they would not die (Gen 3:4). They sinned but did not immediately die physically. At first glance, it seemed the devil was actually telling the truth and God had lied. But did they die? They did die—spiritually.

The life of God in their souls had died, and their bodies would later follow in death. The grace of original holiness and participation in the life of God was lost at the moment they sinned. In a manner of speaking, they now had a "genetic deficiency". Something they possessed in their innocence was gone. Sin killed the life of God in their souls. Their offspring, including us, inherited the "genetic deficiency" of original sin—the loss of the life of God we were created to possess.

Baptism grants sanctifying grace, which enables us to participate in God's own life through communion with Jesus Christ. New birth through baptism is a free and gratuitous gift of God whereby we are born again or anew spiritually, through the death and Resurrection of the Lord. Knowing this, you can certainly answer the riddle "Born once, die twice; born twice, die once" (Jn 3:3–5, CCC 405, 1213). The original holiness of which humanity was deprived as a result of the fall, God has graciously and freely restored and elevated through baptism.

SIN, NAKEDNESS, AND CURSE ON THE EARTH AND DEATH (3:7–24)

Death is a kind of separation (CCC 366, 400, 997). In the garden, a spiritual death took place instantly, a separation between man and his God; a second death also began to work in mankind, a physical death in which the body is separated from the soul (CCC 1005). Other "deaths" also were at work: separation of man from man—Adam blames Eve. Later, Cain kills Abel (CCC 1607, 2448), and a separation of man from himself so he now lies to and deceives himself; he has fear, loneliness, and psychological problems (CCC 379, 2448). Man is also separated from nature—harmony with creation is broken, and the physical world now turns a hostile face to mankind (CCC 400). As a result of man's sin, even the physical creation is cursed and suffers (Gen 3:17; 5:29; Rom 8:20–22; CCC 400).

God had truly warned them, and human death now entered God's creation; death like a plague ravages mankind. Why do we have evil, pain, suffering, alienation, loneliness, and death? God is not the author of moral evil and human suffering. Death was not in God's design for man. He did not make the world bent and broken in this way. Darkness descended as a result of Adam's sin. He was given dominion, and his disobedience had dire consequences. Choices have legs and walk around, so to speak. Satan sneered in wicked glee as he watched death overshadow what God had seen as "very good". As Wisdom says, "Through the devil's envy death entered the world, and those who belong to his party experience it" (Wis 2:24).

COVERING THE SHAME (3:7–10)

Adam and Eve were no longer innocent; self-consciousness and guilt racked their souls. Their eyes were opened, and they realized they were naked. They were now afraid of the Lord God who had walked with them in the cool of the day. They rushed to cover their newly discovered nakedness by sewing fig leaves together. They made aprons or loincloths to cover themselves, and they hid among the trees (Gen 3:7–8).[7]

Man's attempt to remedy his own sin backfired. We cannot cover our own sins—if we try, we only make matters worse. Only God can remedy our sin and shame. God had to kill an animal to cover the sins of our first parents. "And the LORD God made for Adam and for his wife garments of skins, and clothed them" (Gen 3:21).

GOD CONFRONTS SATAN; THE PROMISE OF A SAVIOR (3:11–15)

Instead of confiding in God, they hid from him. God had to come looking for them. Instead of acknowledging his guilt, Adam blamed his wife, implying somehow it was God's fault for giving her to him. Eve then passed the buck and blamed the serpent for her sin. God knew that all three were complicit in the disobedience, so he pronounced judgment on each one of them. Addressing first the serpent, God cursed it above all animals and condemned it to go about on its belly and to eat dust. Then in verse 15, God proclaimed one of the most amazing prophecies in all of Scripture. The following passage is known as the *Protoevangelium*—the "first good news".

> I will put enmity between you and the woman,
>   and between your seed and her seed;
> he shall bruise your head,
>   and you shall bruise his heel. (Gen 3:15)

[7] I asked myself, why does the Bible say specifically they used fig leaves—why not just leaves? So, I bought three books on biblical botany and was amazed to learn about the fig tree. "The latex in all parts of the fig tree is a skin irritant and may cause a kind of dermatosis." The sap contains furocoumarins that cause burning sensations and pain. Imagine Adam and Eve vigorously scratching because of the burning itch caused by their new fig leaf loincloths. Trying to cover their own sins only made their condition worse.

The colorful imagery foretells a future conflict between the devil and a man born of a woman. The image is of a man who comes upon a serpent. He raises his foot to stomp on the serpent's head. As the heel comes down, the serpent quickly strikes the man's heel. The man's heel is wounded, but the serpent's head is crushed. There will be an ultimate victory over this insidious power of evil, but the victor will not go unharmed. The scenario suggests a New Eve and a New Adam. The Church has always read this as a messianic prophecy, referring to Jesus Christ—the "seed" of the woman—as the "New Adam", and the Blessed Virgin Mary as the "New Eve" (*CCC* 410–11). Just as a woman played a key role in initiating the fall of mankind through disobedience, it will be a woman who will initiate the restoration of mankind through her obedience. Jesus, the fulfillment of Genesis 3:15, through his Cross and Resurrection destroyed the works of the devil (1 Jn 3:8; Col 2:15; *CCC* 394).

Here in a garden Adam and Eve brought about *death* at the tree of life through their disobedience. Someday in another garden (Jn 19:41), the Last Adam (1 Cor 15:45) and the New Eve will bring about *life* (1 Cor 15:22) at the tree of death (Gal 3:13) through their obedience. In Christian tradition we say with Saint Irenaeus, "[T]he knot of Eve's disobedience was loosed by the obedience of Mary. For what the virgin Eve had bound fast through unbelief, this did the virgin Mary set free through faith" (*CCC* 494).[8] Eve had tied the knot of disobedience, and it took a Second Eve in a second garden to loose the knot.

We see this combat played out in the book of Revelation where a woman and her son are in conflict with the same serpent of old (Rev 12:1–5, 9). The woman, it is often suggested, is a symbol of Israel or the Church, which is true as far as it goes, but primarily and literally the Woman is the Holy Mother of God (*CCC* 1138). Her son who will "rule all the nations with a rod of iron" is obviously Jesus Christ (Rev 12:1, 5). Victory over the devil will be brought about by a descendant of the woman, the Messiah. The Church has always read these verses as being messianic, referring to Jesus Christ; and she has seen in the woman the mother of the promised Savior; the Virgin Mary is the new Eve.

---

[8] *Against Heresies*, bk. 3, 22, 4, in *The Apostolic Fathers with Justin Martyr and Irenaeus*, ed. Alexander Roberts, James Donaldson, and A. Cleveland Coxe, The Ante-Nicene Fathers, vol. 1 (Buffalo, N.Y.: Christian Literature Company, 1885), 455.

The earliest documents, as they are read in the Church and are understood in the light of a further and full revelation, bring the figure of the woman, Mother of the Redeemer, into a gradually clearer light. When it is looked at in this way, she is already prophetically foreshadowed in the promise of victory over the serpent which was given to our first parents after their fall into sin (cf. Gen 3:15).... Comparing Mary with Eve, they call her "Mother of the living" (Saint Epiphanius, *Adv. haer. Panarium* 78, 18) and still more often they say: "death through Eve, life through Mary" (Saint Jerome, *Epistula* 22, 21; etc.). (Vatican II, *Lumen gentium*, 55–56).[9]

GOD CONFRONTS EVE (3:16)

God turns from the serpent to Eve and spells out the consequences of her disobedience. Sirach tells us, "From a woman sin had its beginning, and because of her we all die" (25:24). Her pain in childbearing would be greatly increased, and her husband would rule over her (Gen 3:16). Procreation was now a burden and painful or laborious. The relationship of mutual communion and attraction originally shared by man and woman would now be distorted by mutual recriminations, dominance, and lust (*CCC* 1607). Her desire would now be to her husband, and their relationship would change, for now he would tend to dominate in the home and in the social order.

It is interesting the words *pain* used of the woman in verse 16 and *toil* used of the man in verse 17 are the same Hebrew word *issabon*, meaning pain, toil, labor, hardship. They will experience this pain or toil in their own spheres of life, although the pain of childbirth is specific to woman, while the pain of toil applies to both men and women—though men tended to do the heavier field work. Woman's anguish in giving birth is equivalent to man's backbreaking labor in the fields. The curse is not childbirth or work—both of which were expected blessings before the fall—but now both have become *issabon*—laborious, difficult, and painful.

GOD CONFRONTS ADAM (3:17–19)

It is significant that though the serpent and the earth were cursed directly, men and women are not cursed as such. The curse of sin fell on "the ground" (Gen 3:17; 5:29). Saint Paul tells us that the "creation was subjected to futility" and that "creation itself will be set free from its bondage to decay" (Rom 8:20, 21). God does not love man alone; he loves his whole creation and "saw everything he had made, and behold, it was very good". God speaks of significant changes when he addresses Adam, changes that also affect Eve. The ground will resist them, and both will experience toil in their own specific functions, and they will both eventually return to dust.

The fall of man changed the *nature* of work, but not the *fact* of work. Tilling the soil will now be accompanied with sweat, and man will be resisted by thorns and thistles (Gen 3:17–19). Though the Hebrew word *issabon* is used for both the man and the woman, it is translated very differently for each, *pain* and *toil*, respectively. Because of sin, pleasurable experiences and tasks would become difficult and laborious, but these punishments also provide remedies that limit the damaging effect of sin (*CCC* 1609).

Because of sin, Adam was expelled from the garden and worked by the sweat of his brow. Isn't it interesting that the New Adam would enter a garden to reverse the result of the First Adam's sin and there sweat drops of blood from his brow (Lk 22:44). The medical term for this condition is hematidrosis.

But the most horrific words are spoken to Adam. It is bad enough that working the ground will now be laborious, painful, and hard, but after his toil to produce food, he will eventually die and himself return to the dirt from which he came. Mankind was created to be immortal, but now death has entered, and their physical bodies will decay and go back to dust, the very ground Adam tilled.

Ecclesiastes reminds us, "All go to one place; all are from the dust, and all turn to dust again" and "the dust returns to the earth as it was, and the spirit returns to God who gave it" (Eccles 3:20; 12:7). At funerals we often hear, "Ashes to ashes and dust to dust." On Ash Wednesday, we are reminded of this again, "Remember that you are dust, and to dust you shall return." Such a terrifying pronouncement; the man created immortal with great dignity now realizes he will die and return to the dust from whence he came (*CCC* 400, 1008).

ADAM NAMES HIS WIFE EVE (3:20)

After the dust settled (no pun intended), Adam "called his wife's name Eve", because she was "the mother of all living". When she was made from his rib, Adam called her "woman", but he now names her "Eve", meaning *life* or *living*. The Septuagint uses the word *zoe*, which means *life* or *life-giver*. She will become the primordial mother of us all. Giving her the name *life* implies he is looking with hope to the future and not fixating on their impending death.

THEOLOGICAL NOTE: *Why Did God Allow Adam to Sin?*

Why did God allow Adam to sin knowing the dire consequences? God created Adam with free will—God did not want a puppet or a robot. What is more, God allowed Adam's abuse of freedom so that God could bring about great good from the results. God created man with the dignity of freedom, but God's providence did not leave the matter wholly in the hands of human determination. Saint Leo the Great comments, " 'Christ's inexpressible grace gave us blessings better than those the demon's envy had taken away.' And St. Thomas Aquinas wrote, 'There is nothing to prevent human nature's being raised up to something greater, even after sin; God permits evil in order to draw forth some greater good. Thus, St. Paul says, "Where sin increased, grace abounded all the more [Rom 5:20]" ' " (*CCC* 412). God knew "Plan B" was even better.

God had a plan. Through a woman he would become the ultimate man, the new Adam, and as a man, he would crush the serpent's head. And because God became man, he could now raise man up with him to truly be like God—to share in the life of the Trinity (*CCC* 460). Saint Peter reminds us that we can now become partakers of the divine nature (2 Pet 1:4). Satan had tempted our first human beings with the promise of being "like God"; now God, because of the fall and his infinite love, has dramatically "upped the ante" and raised us up really to be like God! (*CCC* 460). This is why in the Easter liturgy we recite the words, "O happy fault that earned so great, so glorious a Redeemer!" (*CCC* 412).[10]

EXPULSION FROM THE GARDEN (3:20–24)

The fig leaves dried, and its rash spread. The Lord God steps in to provide adequate garments of skin—which did not come without a cost. Skins come from animals, and to acquire skins an animal must die. Here we see the first sacrifice to cover sin. As the caretaker of the animals, did Adam see God prepare the garments—had he seen death for the first time, the slaughter of the innocent to cover the sin of the guilty? The garments covered their shame, reminded them of their sin, and provided protection from the harsh world that was now their new reality. There is evidence that God made them special garments, with a significant implication of their continued roles as vice-regents and stewards over God's creation. "The garment given them is special, however. A *kuttōnet* is always worn by one in authority showing that, however diminished their standing, they still act with divine authority."[11]

Death was now man's destiny. Adam and Eve were banished from the garden and from the tree of life. He blocked them from eating of the tree of life. He sent them out of their garden paradise. The poignancy of the next statement is rich with irony—"to till the ground from which he was taken", knowing that as dust he would return into the ground. God placed the cherubim (angels) and a flaming sword to prevent access to the garden and the tree of life. However, we see after the redemption, the tree of life is again accessible in the new paradise of heaven (Rev 2:7; 22:2, 14).

---

[10] "Thus original sin refers to our human solidarity in sin and common call to the supernatural life in Christ. The *Exsultet* or proclamation sung during the Easter Vigil names original sin as a *felix culpa* (Lat., 'happy fault'), since it brought the Son of God to come and rescue us." Gerald O'Collins and Edward G. Farrugia, *A Concise Dictionary of Theology* (New York and Mahwah, N.J.: Paulist Press, 2013), 180.

[11] David W. Cotter, *Genesis*, in *Berit Olam: Studies in Hebrew Narrative and Poetry*, ed. Jerome T. Walsh, Chris Franke, and David W. Cotter (Collegeville, Minn.: Liturgical Press, 2003), 35–36.

A final consideration: Consider that Adam was naked in the garden in his innocence but due to sin he had to be clothed and ejected from the garden. Corresponding to that, the New Adam entered the garden clothed but was stripped of his garments to restore man's innocence.

CHAPTER 4

CAIN AND ABEL

If it were not for leaven or yeast, we would not have delicious bread. When yeast is added to flour and water, the process is called fermentation. The gas forms air pockets resulting in the soft, spongy texture. Adding fermented dough to new dough as the "starter", an original strain of yeast could continue to leaven new loaves of bread for decades.

Leavening is mentioned seventeen times in the New Testament, and it is usually *not* a good thing (e.g., Mt 16:6, 11). Saint Paul says, "A little leaven leavens all the dough" (Gal 5:9). Mostly it is used as a symbol of the spreading and corrupting influence of evil. When sin was introduced into human society, it was like the leaven or yeast that permeates the whole lump of dough.

Like leaven that was passed on from year to year, so the leaven of sin passed on through the generations of men. God promised to remedy the situation, but, in the meantime, the "leaven" of sin, a potent "starter", was well underway, fermenting within the hearts of men (Gen 4:7). "And even after Christ's atonement, sin raises its head in countless ways among Christians" (*CCC* 401). Adam was created in the image of God, and his offspring were in the image and likeness of Adam (Gen 5:3). Like Adam, they were imprinted with the image of God, but they were born with original sin, the "genetic deficiency". They lacked the grace of original holiness that God originally infused into their parents' souls. The world became inundated with sin and universal corruption (*CCC* 401).

In Genesis 1:26, God declares, "Let us make man in our image, after our likeness." This has led some commentators to distinguish the "image of God" from the "likeness of God", with the image of God in man being retained (if obscured or marred) after the fall, while the "likeness of God"—the Glory of God—was lost because of sin (*CCC* 705). Adam's sons bore the *image* of God, but the sinful *likeness* of their father Adam.

ADAM AND EVE ARE FRUITFUL AND MULTIPLY (4:1)

"Adam knew Eve his wife." *Knew* is a biblical euphemism for sexual relations, and the result was Eve's conceiving. Sexual relations between a man and his wife is a gift of God to unify a man and his wife and for procreation. The family reflects God in his creation (*CCC* 2335). The sacred writings often refer to sexual relations as a husband "knowing" his wife (Gen 4:1, 17). This terminology is not Victorian prudishness; rather, it reflects the depth of the relationship between husband and wife as they become "one flesh". The union of husband and wife is not merely physical and emotional; it is also spiritual. Their communion is intended to include a free act of will to give completely of themselves to one another and to God. In being open to new life, the dignity of the married couple is elevated to sharing in the creative process with God.

God created man as a whole—spiritual soul and physical body within one nature. Only in this way can man's dignity be recognized. When Adam and Eve looked at each other, they saw, not just a body, but the whole person. This mutual recognition of the inherent unity and dignity of the other made the conjugal act between them an expression of love and self-giving. Because of sin, this gift of sexual love between a husband and wife has often been separated from the intended union of persons in a most destructive manner. Disordered desires make it difficult for the man to recognize the woman as a "person", someone to be valued in her own right. Instead, men are often inclined to see women as objects of pleasure. Likewise, the reverse is often true with women and men. We will see this evil root bear much fruit as we move through Genesis and even into our modern world.

ABEL'S OFFERING IS ACCEPTED;
CAIN'S IS REJECTED (4:2–6)

Adam and Eve's first son was named Cain, which means "get" or "gotten" because Eve exclaimed, "I have gotten a man with the help of the LORD" (Gen 4:1). Another son was born named Abel, which could mean *breath* or *vanity*. This may refer to the shortness of his life. With these two sons, we see the origins of two main livelihoods of the time: shepherds and farmers. Civilization was beginning outside the garden in obedience to God's command to be fruitful and multiply, subdue the earth and fill it. Expelled from paradise, Adam's son Cain tilled the ground and gathered produce by the sweat of his brow, and Abel raised flocks.

Because everything came from God, our first ancestors offered back to God part of their bounty. Cain, for his part, brought to the Lord a portion of his harvest, and Abel offered a sacrifice from the firstlings of his flock. The Scripture tells us that the Lord was pleased with Abel's offering, but not with Cain's. Much ink has flowed over why God accepted Abel's sacrifice but rejected the sacrifice of Cain. Did God like dead animals better than bushels of produce? Not likely, since throughout the Old Testament, God required and accepted offerings of both animals and produce.[1]

God is not as concerned with the offering as with the heart of the one that offers—his disposition (1 Sam 15:22; Is 1:11–17; Mic 6:6–8). God says to Cain, "If you do well, will you not be accepted? And if you do not do well, sin is lurking at the door; its desire is for you, but you must master it" (Gen 4:7). This implies that Cain's disposition was disordered, and sin got the best of him. It is not the sacrifice that is the problem; it is Cain himself. Saint Gregory the Great concurs the problem is in the heart of Cain: "Thus it is plainly shewn that the offerer was not acceptable by reason of the gifts, but the gifts were so by reason of the offerer."[2] Church Father Origen (ca. 185—ca. 254)

---

[1] At least one Jewish sage, Rabbi David Kimhi (A.D. 1160–1235), considers the sacrifice of Cain as inferior, not in keeping with his brother's example, and thus rejected by God. "His sons learned from [Adam] what to do, and each brought an offering of thanks to God from what his particular line of work had produced. Our verse does not say what particular kind of plant Cain's offering was, but apparently it was of a lesser grade, or perhaps it was what was left after he himself had eaten—in either case, somewhat insulting. That is why his offering was not accepted. He also did not bring the 'first' fruits, because the text would have told us so, as it does with Abel." Michael Carasik, ed. and trans., *Genesis: Introduction and Commentary, The Commentators' Bible* (Philadelphia: Jewish Publication Society, 2018), 48.

[2] Gregory the Great, "Selected Epistles of Gregory the Great, Bishop of Rome (Books IX–XIV)", in *Gregory the Great (Part II), Ephraim Syrus, Aphrahat*, ed. Philip Schaff and Henry Wace, trans. James Barmby, A Select Library of the Nicene and Post-Nicene Fathers of the Christian Church, Second Series, vol. 13 (New York: Christian Literature Company, 1898), 35.

taught that the wickedness of Cain was in his heart from the beginning. "In the case of Cain his wickedness did not begin when he killed his brother. For even before that God, who knows the heart, had no regard for Cain and his sacrifice. But his baseness was made evident when he killed Abel" (*On Prayer* 29.18).[3]

In Old Testament history, including the book of Genesis, we often see God choosing the younger sibling over the firstborn, which often brings great resentment and conflict. God accepted the younger's sacrifice, rejecting that of the firstborn. "In this text, the emphasis falls, however, not on the reasons for God's preference, but on Cain's fatal and culpable refusal to reconcile himself to it."[4]

The New Testament sheds light on the rejection of Cain's sacrifice. "[W]e should love one another, and not be like Cain who was of the Evil One and murdered his brother. And why did he murder him? Because his own deeds were evil and his brother's righteous" (1 Jn 3:11–12). This confirms the point that Cain was already of the Evil One and that his deeds were evil. Abel had faith, and God rewarded his virtue. Hebrews mentions Abel's righteousness, "By faith Abel offered to God a more acceptable sacrifice than Cain, through which he received approval as righteous, God bearing witness by accepting his gifts" (11:4). Abel had faith and a heart for God. Cain was the opposite; sin and the devil became his master, and therefore his offerings were polluted and rejected. Cain's evil played out in murder.

CAIN KILLS ABEL (4:7–8)

Cain's face screwed up in an angry scowl after God disregarded his sacrifice. With hope of his reformation, God gave Cain a catechesis on the nature of sin by saying, "If you do well, will you not be accepted? And if you do not do well, sin is lurking at the door; its desire is for you, but you must master it." God's first warning about sin after the fall is very instructive.

[3] Andrew Louth and Marco Conti, eds., *Genesis 1–11*, Ancient Christian Commentary on Scripture, OT (Downers Grove, Ill.: InterVarsity Press, 2001), 104–5.

[4] Adele Berlin, Marc Zvi Brettler, and Michael Fishbane, eds., *The Jewish Study Bible* (New York: Oxford University Press, 2004), 19.

Giving his passions the steering wheel, Cain brushed aside God's warning. With premeditation, Cain drew his brother Abel into the field away from the eyes of the family.[5] Thinking no one saw him, Cain murdered his brother Abel, but Abel's blood cried out to God as it soaked into the ground (CCC 1867). Cain had refused to reconcile with God and, in that way, with his brother, Abel.

Jesus referred to Abel as "innocent" and mentions his "righteous blood shed on the earth" (Mt 23:35) and even places Abel among the prophets (Lk 11:50–51). The book of Hebrews concurs with the statement, "[Abel] died, but through his faith he is still speaking" (Heb 11:4). Jesus' blood is compared to the blood of murdered Abel: "And to Jesus, the mediator of a new covenant, and to the sprinkled blood that speaks more graciously than the blood of Abel" (Heb 12:24). Maybe more gracious because the blood of Abel cried out for vengeance, whereas the blood of Jesus cries out for forgiveness and reconciliation.

CAIN'S PUNISHMENT FOR MURDER (4:9–15)

God asked Cain, "Where is Abel your brother?" Like a cocky teenager, Cain plays dumb and lies to God. "I do not know; am I my brother's keeper?" If Cain had fallen on his face before God with contrite repentance, things might have been different. Scripture calls Cain "an unrighteous man" who departed from wisdom and "perished because in rage he slew his brother" (Wis 10:3).

God pronounces judgment on Cain; the consequences are severe. The ground was cursed by the fall, but now Cain is "cursed from the ground" because his brother's blood is crying out from the ground. Not even by the sweat of his brow will the earth yield produce for him. He is destined to be a fugitive, roaming the earth. Cain still does not repent but complains about his punishment. God puts a mark on Cain to warn anyone against killing him. What the mark

[5] Excluded by the Hebrew Masoretic text, but included in the Aramaic Targums, the Samaritan, Septuagint, Syriac, and Latin Vulgate are the words, "And Cain said to Abel, his brother, 'Let's walk through the fields.'" This reveals forethought for the premeditated murder.

was, is unknown. From the beginning of human history, the ugly consequences of original sin are made evident as men have become enemies with their fellow men, even their brothers (*CCC* 2259).

CAIN TAKES A WIFE AND HIS DESCENDANTS (4:16–22)

Cain went away from the presence of the Lord—which is a horrifying thought. He went to Nod, which means "wandering", a location unknown today. As Adam "knew" his wife, now Cain "knew" his wife, and she conceived and bore a son named Enoch, though not the Enoch who walked with God (Gen 4:17). Skeptics love to ask, "Where did Cain get his wife?" God had commanded Adam to "be fruitful and multiply", and since he lived 930 years, you would expect more children than just Cain, Abel, and Seth! Genesis 5:4 states that Adam had "other sons and daughters". In the ancient Jewish *Book of Jubilees*[6] we read, "And Cain took his sister, 'Awan, as a wife, and she bore for him Enoch at the end of the fourth jubilee."[7]

LAMECH'S "SONG OF THE SWORD" (4:23–24)

With Lamech and his family, the seventh in Adam's line, we complete the known family line of Cain. Lamech boasted about his murderous exploit to his wives in a poem. His is the first recorded instance of polygamy, which is a clear violation of God's intended design for marriage. His poem is an excellent example of Hebrew poetry using parallel thoughts rather than rhyming. Lamech's poem is referred to

[6] "An apocryphal Jewish work, also called 'The Little Genesis'. The original Hebrew text survives only in fragments found at Qumran.... The fact that the surviving Hebrew fragments are from at least 12 different [manuscripts] and that they were found in three different caves indicates that the Book enjoyed considerable popularity among the Qumran community.... The Book, which certainly appears to stem from priestly circles, is generally dated to the 2nd cent. B.C." F. L. Cross and Elizabeth A. Livingstone, eds., *The Oxford Dictionary of the Christian Church* (Oxford and New York: Oxford University Press, 2005), 910.

[7] James H. Charlesworth, *The Old Testament Pseudepigrapha and the New Testament: Expansions of the "Old Testament" and Legends, Wisdom, and Philosophical Literature, Prayers, Psalms and Odes, Fragments of Lost Judeo-Hellenistic Works*, vol. 2 (New Haven and London: Yale University Press, 1985), 61.

as *The Song of the Sword*—a fierce declaration of revenge. He admits to murder, though showing no sign of guilt or remorse. Sin was having a cancerous effect.

Jesus seems to allude to Lamech's poem. Lamech said that he will avenge himself seventy-sevenfold. Peter asks Jesus how many times he should forgive an offense. Jesus replied, "I do not say to you seven times, but seventy times seven" (Mt 18:22). "The phrase surely echoes the saying of Lamech in Gn 4:24, in which a limit is denied to the satisfaction of blood revenge. The Gospel inverts the old dispensation."[8] Tertullian (ca. 160–ca. 225) commented on Peter's question, "And when Peter had put the question whether remission were to be granted to a brother seven times, 'Nay,' saith He, 'seventy-seven times;' in order to remould the Law for the better; because in Genesis *vengeance* was assigned 'seven times' in the case of Cain, but in that of Lamech 'seventy-seven times.' "[9]

Regarding Cain and his descendants, we are told no more. God was already choosing the family line through which the "seed of the woman" would come. Cain's family line was not chosen, and he is dropped off the radar.

BIRTH OF SETH (4:25–26)

Adam knew his wife again. Eve gave birth to Seth, whose name is a wordplay off Eve's comment that God had "appointed" a son to replace Abel. Seth married and had a son named Enosh. Seth will be the line of Adam from which comes the Messiah, as promised by God in Genesis 3:15. We are told that "at this time men began to call upon the name of the LORD" (Gen 4:26; *CCC* 2569).

So we see the two faces of fallen man: the sinful, corrupt side; and the side that calls on the name of the Lord. Though sin had infected human beings, not all were completely corrupt, and the image of God remained. Aleksandr Solzhenitsyn once said, "If only

[8] Raymond Edward Brown, Joseph A. Fitzmyer, and Roland Edmund Murphy, *The Jerome Biblical Commentary* (Englewood Cliffs, N.J.: Prentice-Hall, 1968), 2:95.

[9] *On Prayer*, 7, Tertullian, "On Prayer", in *Latin Christianity: Its Founder, Tertullian*, ed. Alexander Roberts, James Donaldson, and A. Cleveland Coxe, trans. S. Thelwall, The Ante-Nicene Fathers, vol. 3 (Buffalo, N.Y.: Christian Literature Company, 1885), 684.

there were evil people somewhere insidiously committing evil deeds, and it were necessary only to separate them from the rest of us and destroy them. But the line dividing good and evil cuts through the heart of every human being. And who is willing to destroy a piece of his own heart?"[10]

---

[10] Aleksandr I. Solzhenitsyn, *The Gulag Archipelago*, part 1 (New York: Harper & Row, 1974), 168.

CHAPTER 5

ADAM'S DESCENDANTS TO NOAH AND HIS SONS

PURPOSE OF "THESE ARE THE GENERATIONS OF . . ." AND SUMMARY OF MAN CREATED AS MALE AND FEMALE (5:1–2)

In Genesis we repeatedly find the phrase "These are the generations of . . ." used as a heading that divides the book into sections. Chapter 5 begins with "This is the book of the generations of Adam" (or "these are the generations of Adam"). These introductory phrases announce new chapters, so to speak, in the narrative. Families and the genealogical lines keep narrowing down to one individual until we reach the coming of the Messiah. The drama was opened with the "generations of the heavens and the earth" (2:4). It now continues with "this is the book of the generations of Adam".

In chapter 5 we have a quick recap of Adam's creation progressing forward through the line of Seth. Adam lived 930 years and left behind a large family (Gen 5:4–5). Divine revelation follows Seth's line through his descendants leading to Noah, then Abraham.

THEOLOGICAL NOTE: *Genealogy, Not Chronology*

From Adam to Noah we have ten generations. This is to be taken, not as a strict chronology, but as a family genealogy. Like the genealogies of Jesus in Matthew's and Luke's Gospels, this genealogy is selective and incomplete. There are generational gaps. As a footnote in the RSV-2CE states, "It should be noted that these genealogies are selective and schematic, and the numbers, as often in the Old Testament, are symbolic." The longevity of these antediluvian descendants of Adam have been the matter of much discussion. Some see the extraordinary ages as symbolic, while others hold that they are actual ages and that the subsequent decline in life-spans represents sin's effects on fallen human beings as we get farther from the original state of man. (Of course, one thing the extraordinarily long life-spans declining in length over time would represent is precisely the increase of sin's effects on mankind.)[1]

The family line of Seth is provided in Genesis 5:6–32, extending to Seth's famous descendant, Noah, and his three sons. Along this line of descendants, only one son per father is mentioned, but this does not imply that each father had only one son. The sacred author is concerned with the godly line through whom the covenant people of Israel will come and, ultimately, from which the messianic lineage flows.

THEOLOGICAL NOTE: *Emphasizing Death as a Result of Sin and Promise of Redemption*

Notice the short but ominous phrase used eight times for each man mentioned in Genesis 5:3–31—"and he died." Like the doleful dong of a funeral bell, we are reminded over and over again—what sin has done. For Saint Paul, Genesis 5 was the lamentable evidence of sin through Adam. "Therefore as sin came into the world through one man and death through sin, and so death spread to all men because all sinned ... death reigned from Adam to Moses" (Rom 5:12–14). Christ is Adam's antitype and the antidote for sin. "As sin reigned in death, grace also might reign through righteousness to eternal life through Jesus Christ our Lord" (Rom 5:21; CCC 1009).

ADAM'S DESCENDANTS (5:3–32)

Seth's name appears in the genealogy of Jesus (Lk 3:38). His line introduces a few interesting characters, like Enoch, who lived for 365 years. "Enoch walked with God; and he was not, for God took

---

[1] For more discussion, see Scott Hahn and Curtis Mitch, *Genesis: With Introduction, Commentary, and Notes*, Ignatius Catholic Study Bible, Revised Standard Version and Second Catholic Edition (San Francisco: Ignatius Press, 2010), 25.

him" (Gen 5:22–24). The New Testament informs us that, "By faith Enoch was taken up so that he should not see death; and he was not found, because God had taken him. Now before he was taken he was attested as having pleased God" (Heb 11:5). Saint Irenaeus wrote, "Enoch, pleasing God, was even translated in the body ... and [Elijah] was taken up, as he was, in the substance wherein he was formed ... and the body was no impediment to them in regard of their translation and assumption."[2] And Sirach testifies: "No one like Enoch has been created on earth, for he was taken up from the earth" (44:16; 49:14).

This provides a precedent for future "assumptions" of body and soul into heaven. One might think of the resurrected Jesus ascending into heaven. Often, though, a distinction is made between the risen Lord who himself *ascends* into heaven and others who are *assumed* into heaven, including the Old Testament prophet Elijah and the Blessed Virgin Mary in the New Testament. In any case, the Greek word for "took him up" in Hebrews 11:5 is translated as *assumption* in the *New Jerusalem Bible*. In his book *The Mystery of Mary*, Paul Haffner writes, "In the Old Testament, there were some mysterious departures from this life. God granted a special privilege of not dying to Enoch and Elijah.... Significantly the word *assumption* is adopted [by the author of Hebrews]." He emphasizes this in a footnote, "The expression used in Greek is μετατίθημι which carries the sense of being transposed or carried over."[3]

Another noteworthy figure in Seth's lineage is Methuselah, son of Enoch and grandfather of Noah, who lived longer than any biblical figure—to the ripe old age of 969 years. His name likely means "Man of God".

INTRODUCTION OF NOAH AND HIS SONS (5:28–32)

Genesis chapter 5 ends with Noah and the birth of his sons Shem, Ham, and Japheth (Gen 5:32). Noah's name is phonetically similar

---

[2] *Against Heresies*, bk. 5, chap. 5, in St. Irenaeus, Bishop of Lyons, *Five Books of S. Irenaeus against Heresies*, trans. John Keble, A Library of Fathers of the Holy Catholic Church (Oxford, London, and Cambridge: James Parker and Co.; Rivingtons, 1872), 458.

[3] Paul Haffner, *The Mystery of Mary* (Chicago: Liturgy Training Publications, 2004), 208.

with the Hebrew *to comfort*. His father, Lamech, commented, "Out of the ground which the LORD has cursed this one shall bring us relief from our work and from the toil of our hands" (Gen 5:29). Adam's *toil* is certainly referenced here as it is the same Hebrew word *issabon*, and it references the ground that was cursed (Gen 3:17). How Noah will "bring us relief from our work" is unknown, though at least one Jewish sage suggests it is actually a prayer, and others suggest it is through the introduction of winemaking.

CHAPTER 6

CORRUPTION OF MANKIND
AND NOAH BUILDS AN ARK

THE SONS OF GOD AND THE DAUGHTERS
OF MEN (6:1–4)

In Genesis 6:1–4, we encounter one of the most enigmatic passages of the Bible, causing much speculation about the identity of the "sons of God" and what are called the "Nephilim". In short, the "sons of God" saw the "daughters of men" and took them as wives. The result of their sexual unions were the Nephilim, who were colossal giants called the mighty men of old.

Who and what were these Nephilim, the "sons of God", and "the daughters of men"? Some Bible translations render Nephilim as "giants", including the Septuagint. Scripture confirms they were giants: "And there we saw the Nephilim ... and we seemed to ourselves like grasshoppers, and so we seemed to them" (Num 13:33).

There are two main interpretations of this passage. First, the sons of God were men from the line of Seth who crossed over to take the daughters of men from the line of Cain. But how would this result in giants? Second, the sons of God were fallen angelic beings who lusted after the daughters of men and fathered giants by them. But how would incorporeal angels have sexual relations with women and father giants by them?

Jewish commentators differ among themselves in their interpretation of this passage. Some suggest they are the sons of Seth. But the *Jewish Study Bible* translates this passage "It was then, and later too, that the Nephilim appeared on the earth—when the divine beings cohabited with the daughters of men, who bore them offspring." In the footnote, "It records yet another breach of the all-important boundary between the divine and the human (vv. 1–2) and explains why human beings no longer attain to the great ages of their primordial forebears (v. 3). It also explains the origin of the Nephilim (v. 4), the preternatural giants that Israelite tradition thought once dwelt in the land (Num. 13:31–33)."[1]

Even among the Fathers of the Church there were a variety of opinions. Saint Augustine denied angelic involvement. He wrote, "Before the flood there were many giants, all of whom belonged to the earthly city in human society, and that there were sons of God descended from Seth who abandoned their holiness and sank down into this city of men" (*City of God* 15, 23).[2] This is also the explanation of Saint John Chrysostom (*Homiliae in Genesim*, 22, 4), Saint Cyril of Alexandria (*Glaphyra in Genesim*, 2, 2), and others.

On the other hand, Saint Augustine's mentor, Saint Ambrose, also a Doctor of the Church, writes, "The author of divine Scripture does not mean that those giants must be considered, according to the tradition of poets, as sons of the earth but asserts that those whom he defines with such a name because of the extraordinary size of their body were generated by angels and women."[3]

Some Catholic scholars explain it this way, "The *sons of Seth* interpretation, adopted here, is the common view of the Catholic tradition.... In the narrative of Genesis, the 'sons of God' are Sethites, heirs of the covenant of adoptive divine sonship from Adam. The 'daughters of men' would be the women descended from Cain, the line that has turned its back on the presence of God (Gen 4:16)."[4] However, we never find the descendants of Cain referred to as "daughters of men", nor do we find descendants of Shem referred to as "sons of God".

However, the plural term "the sons of God" is used elsewhere in the Old Testament, and each time it refers to angelic beings. The Book of

[1] Adele Berlin, Marc Zvi Brettler, and Michael Fishbane, eds. *The Jewish Study Bible* (New York: Oxford University Press, 2004), 21.

[2] Saint Augustine, *City of God*, bks. VIII–XVI, trans. Gerald G. Walsh, S.J., and Grace Monahan, O.S.U. Fathers of the Church, vol. 14 (New York: Catholic University of America Press, 2010), bk. xv, chap. 23, p. 475.

[3] *On Noah* 4, 8, in Andrew Louth and Marco Conti, eds., *Genesis 1–11*, Ancient Christian Commentary on Scripture, OT 1 (Downers Grove, Ill.: InterVarsity Press, 2001), 126.

[4] John Bergsma and Brant Pitre, *A Catholic Introduction to the Bible*, vol. 1, *The Old Testament* (San Francisco: Ignatius Press, 2018), 111.

Job applies the term to the angels who come before God accompanied by Satan: "Now there was a day when the sons of God came to present themselves before the LORD, and Satan also came among them" (Job 1:6; 2:1; 38:7). Certainly, this refers to nonhuman, angelic beings. Again, in Psalm 29:1: "Ascribe to the LORD, O sons of God, ascribe to the LORD glory and strength." The NAB, which we read at Mass, renders this "you heavenly beings". Since Nephilim are mentioned in this context as the result of the union between the "sons of God" and the "daughters of men", it would seem that we should understand this reference to mean that such giants resulted from angelic involvement with women rather than human sexual relations between men and women. As far as we know, the "angelic view" is the older view. It is held by many modern scholars.[5]

Still, it is a mysterious passage that will continue to be discussed and debated. Genesis includes this strange account to emphasize the rapid increase of sin and wickedness in the world, involving the crossing of many boundaries. Men's sinfulness and pride, their abuse of relationships, and the righteousness of God are preparing the way for God to cleanse the world through the upcoming flood.

WICKEDNESS INCREASES ON THE EARTH (6:5–7)

In the section of Genesis involved with the Nephilim (Gen 6:1–4), God expresses exasperation with the human race: "Then the LORD said, 'My spirit shall not abide in man for ever, for he is flesh, but his

---

[5] "The 'angel' interpretation is at once the oldest view and that of most modern commentators. It is assumed in the earliest Jewish exegesis (e.g., the books of 1 Enoch 6:2ff.; Jubilees 5:1), LXX, Philo, *De Gigant* 2:358), Josephus (*Ant.* 1.31), and the Dead Sea Scrolls (1QapGen 2:1; CD 2:17–19). The NT (2 Pet 2:4, Jude 6, 7) and the earliest Christian writers (e.g., Justin, Irenaeus, Clement of Alexandria, Tertullian, Origen) also take this line." Gordon J. Wenham, *Genesis 1–15*, Word Biblical Commentary, vol. 1 (Dallas: Word, Incorporated, 1987), 139. Scripture scholar Raymond Brown speaks of the passage related to Jude 6, "The second example [in Jude 6] probably refers to the 'sons of God' who took to wife the daughters of men (Gen 6:1–4). This seems implied in v. 7, since the Sodomites sinned 'in a similar manner' to the angels. Furthermore, *Enoch* (quoted in vv. 14–15) gives great emphasis to this sin of the angels (or heavenly 'Watchers') and to its punishment, in terms very similar to those used here by Jude." Raymond Edward Brown, Joseph A. Fitzmyer, and Roland Edmund Murphy, *The Jerome Biblical Commentary* (Englewood Cliffs, N.J.: Prentice-Hall, 1968), 2:379.

days shall be a hundred and twenty years'." After the flood, human life-spans decrease dramatically.

Looking at the world he created, the Lord laments that evil fills men's minds and hearts. The writer of Genesis says that God's heart was grieved and he was "sorry" he had made man. So the Lord decided to blot out humans and animals (Gen 6:5–7). Animals, too, would suffer because they were linked to the fate of man under his stewardship (cf. Rom 8:19–22). The earth was created for the benefit of man and is directly tied to his destiny. Including the animals and birds in punishment emphasizes the magnitude of the judgment God is about to exact.[6]

God does not get emotional, as people do. He does not grieve or change his mind, as we sometimes do. In punishing wickedness, God is not reacting in an emotional state. God's "anger" reflects his goodness, holiness, and justice "violently" contradicted by evil—sin. The author of Genesis describes God's attitude toward his wayward creation as akin to a father's grief or sadness in seeing his child go gravely astray. God's regret in making man is likened to the regret a human maker would have in finding some deep flaw or defect in the thing he made and wanting to start over.

God inspired the human author of Genesis to describe God as reacting to evil using the language of human emotions. This approach helps us "relate" to God; it is called *anthropomorphism*—a literary device in which God is presented with human emotions, thoughts, or feelings.

Of course, while we should not take such language literally, that does not mean the language reflects nothing true about God. Behind the human language of grief, regret, and anger there is the reality of God's goodness, holiness, and justice, as well as his love, which desires the best for mankind.

NOAH PLEASES GOD; BUILDING THE ARK (6:8–17)

God saw the earth was corrupt and filled with violence (Gen 6:11–12; *CCC* 401). But Noah stood out in stark contrast as a righteous and blameless man who walked with God (Gen 6:8–9). God found a

---

[6]See Saint Augustine's *City of God*, 15, 25.

clean remnant to tear from the contaminated cloth—and Noah found favor with God (6:8). Scripture recalls, "Noah was found perfect and righteous; in the time of wrath he was taken in exchange; therefore a remnant was left to the earth when the flood came" (Sir 44:17). Saved along with Noah were his wife, his sons Shem, Ham, and Japheth, and their three wives (Gen 6:10).

Noah's name is used over fifty times in the Bible, fourteen times outside the book of Genesis. He shows up in the genealogy of Jesus (Lk 3:36), and in both Matthew and Luke he is a reminder of the coming judgment. God blessed him and through him blessed all of creation (*CCC* 2569). Hebrews records his great faith: "By faith Noah, being warned by God concerning events as yet unseen, took heed and constructed an ark for the saving of his household; by this he condemned the world and became an heir of the righteousness which comes by faith" (Heb 11:7). Jews tend to think of Noah as the new Adam and the start of a new humanity.

God confided in Noah; he told him the plan to put an end to all flesh. The violence had gone too far and cried out to be judged by God (6:13). He commanded Noah to do the most outlandish thing. On dry land, far from any body of water, Noah was to build a huge boat called an ark. The local people must have thought he was crazy. How would Noah get this huge vessel to the sea? Think of how it seems when religious people today say or do odd things claiming they are preparing for the coming wrath of God. You can begin to see how odd Noah appeared to his neighbors. We do not know if Noah was a carpenter, but those whom the Lord calls, he equips. Starting with God's command, Noah would become an engineer, woodworker, building contractor, warehouse manager, navigator, and zookeeper!

Let's clarify a few terms to understand this vessel Noah was to build. The *ark* was a large floating warehouse. It was roughly 450 feet long (1½ football fields) by 75 feet wide and 45 feet high (roughly four stories high). It was about three million board feet of lumber with a storage capacity equal to about 450 standard semitrailers. The measurements were given in *cubits*, which was the length of a man's forearm from fingertip to elbow, roughly eighteen inches or a foot-and-a-half. *Gopher wood* is only mentioned once in the Bible; not found in Hebrew or similar languages. The Latin *Vulgate* renders it "planed wood", and the Greek *Septuagint* translates it "squared beams". The majority opinion of scholars seems to be that gopher wood is a kind of common Cyprus tree frequently used for ship-building. The *pitch* might better be called bitumen, a natural product of crude petroleum, which is readily found in Mesopotamia. It was a gooey tar-like substance to waterproof the ark. In Hebrew, the word *rooms* is *ken*, meaning *nest*, and the plural used here, *kinnom*, is taken to mean compartments for animals.

The boxy shape of the ark and the tremendous size would have prevented any form of steering or sailing. It was merely to stay afloat unguided. According to the *Catholic Encyclopedia*, "The form, very likely foursquare, was certainly not very convenient for navigation, but, as has been proven by the experiments of Peter Jansen and M. Vogt, it made the Ark a very suitable device for shipping heavy cargoes and floating upon the waves without rolling or pitching."[7]

GOD GETS NOAH TO BUILD AN ARK (6:18–22)

God promises to establish a covenant with Noah and to preserve his family and a male and female pair of all the living creatures (Gen 6:18–19). Noah and his sons are to build this huge wooden structure, collect food, and fill the floating warehouse with supplies. God would supernaturally guide male and female of every animal and bird and creeping thing onto the ark. Of clean animals (those useful for sacrifice), seven pair of each boarded the ark (Gen 8:20). Each species would be preserved for a fresh start after the flood. Noah is appointed steward of God's creatures and responsible for their care during the flood, and they are "delivered into his hands" after the flood (Gen 9:2; *CCC* 2417).

Noah was no fool. Movies show the people mocking Noah for building a large boat on the land. They taunted him—until the flood waters started to fall from the sky and burst forth from the earth (Gen 7:11). The ridicule did not faze Noah: "he did all that God commanded him" (Gen 6:22).

[7] Charles Souvay, "Ark", in *The Catholic Encyclopedia*, vol. 1 (New York: Robert Appleton Company, 1907), 720.

CHAPTER 7

THE GREAT FLOOD

As a young boy I lived on a small farm. Every morning my alarm rang at 5 A.M., and I would drag myself out of bed, dress, and put on my boots. Boots were important due to the muck involved. We had horses, goats, a cow, chickens, ducks, turkeys, pigeons, rabbits, guinea hens, dogs, and cats, and even ten hives of bees.

I broke the ice in the drinking buckets and brought hay and straw from the barn, corn and oats from the bins. I collected the freshly laid chicken eggs and milked "Mama Goat", who yielded about a gallon of milk each day. That was just for starters. With shovel and pitchfork, I removed their stinking manure. In the winter, it was still steaming, and the ammonia fumes burned my eyes. The animals were all bleating, whinnying, mooing, clucking, barking, and even buzzing for my immediate attention.

Recalling my boyhood days, I can relate to life on the ark. This was a floating farm, zoo, warehouse, and factory. Eight people would be worn ragged. But it was far better than the alternative. Knowing the others were floundering and drowning in the rising water, Noah realized that his obedience to God and his life of holiness were the smartest things he had ever done, for himself, his family, and God's creation.

NOAH'S FAMILY AND ALL THE ANIMALS
ENTER THE ARK (7:1–9)

Noah was six hundred years old when the flood waters came upon the earth. He had done all that the Lord had commanded. The animals were all now in their appropriate stalls, nests, and cages. Food was stored, pitchforks and shovels ready. After Noah entered the ark

with his family, "the LORD shut him in" (Gen 7:16). The long ordeal
was about to begin. Divine judgment was about to fall on the earth.

HISTORICAL NOTE: *Universality and Reality of the Flood*

Was the flood a historical reality or merely a fable to provide spiritual
lessons? Skeptics regard the story of the flood as a legend borrowed
from other civilizations and detached from history. Yet Jesus refers to
it as a historical event (Mt 24:37–39; Lk 17:27). Throughout history,
Jewish and Christian scholars have affirmed the historical reality of
the great flood. Scripture itself assumes it.

Precisely when the flood took place is not known; the Bible does
not provide dates. All ancient cultures have a flood story pointing
back to an ancient event. The Babylonian Gilgamesh Epic is probably the most famous, and it tells a similar story.[1] What is unique to
the biblical account is the relationship between God and the hero.
The biblical God is singular and not arbitrary and capricious like the
other gods. With Noah we are told *why* life on earth was destroyed
and that righteousness was the reason he was delivered.

According to the *Catholic Bible Dictionary*:

> In the nineteenth century, cuneiform tablets were discovered that
> narrated a Babylonian flood legend obviously based on the same tra-
> dition as the story of Noah. Since the cuneiform tablets were much
> older than the book of Genesis as we have it now, many scholars
> jumped to the conclusion that the Hebrew story was based on the
> Babylonian story—an unjustified conclusion, since both written ver-
> sions were almost certainly based on already ancient oral traditions.
> Anthropologists point out that a story of a great flood, with one
> family surviving it in a boat, is found in cultures throughout the Near
> East and Europe, suggesting that the tradition goes back to some real
> cataclysmic event.[2]

---

[1] "The flood as a primeval event is a motif found all over the world.... Riem advances texts
from the Indogermanic peoples, the near east, Europe, non-Indogermanic peoples, north,
south and east Asia, Malaysia, Australia, the south sea islands, Africa, North America, Central
America, and South America." Claus Westermann, *A Continental Commentary: Genesis 1–11*
(Minneapolis, Minn.: Fortress Press, 1994), 49.

[2] Scott Hahn, ed., *Catholic Bible Dictionary* (New York, London, Toronto, Sydney, and
Auckland: Doubleday, 2009), 292.

Widespread ancient stories of a great flood do not themselves prove there is a historical reality behind the stories or to the story of Noah and the flood in Genesis. But they lend credibility to it and provide us with reasonable grounds for supposing there is a historical basis for it.

THE FLOODGATES OPEN UPON THE EARTH (7:10–24)

We are presented with a vivid and terrifying sight, something we might only expect to see on the wide screen. With devastating force, the massive waves of water swirl and pile up upon the earth. To dramatize the cataclysm the text tells us fountains from the deep burst forth and windows from the sky were opened. Movies sensationalize the scene with gasping people pounding on the ark shrieking for entrance only to be engulfed by the angry waves as they scream in terror before being sucked under the billows. The great ark creaks and groans as it begins to rise.

The rains fell for forty days and forty nights. Noah and his family, the crew, had no control over the navigation of the ark. The water prevailed upon the earth for 150 days. Except for what was in the ark, all animal and human life on earth perished. This is mentioned repeatedly to emphasize the profound judgment being executed. Considering the times described from entering the ark to waiting for the rains and the flood to recede, most estimates are that Noah and his family were on the ark about a full year.

THEOLOGICAL NOTE: *Noah and the End Times*

Jesus recalls this period of human history, saying that the time preceding the Second Coming of Christ will resemble the corruption and sin before the flood. People lived in sin, ignorant of the calamity about to befall them. They were not prepared for the flood and were all swept away. "For as in those days before the flood they were eating and drinking, marrying and giving in marriage, until the day when Noah entered the ark, and they did not know until the flood came and swept them all away, so will be the coming of the Son of man" (Mt 24:38–39).

Unfortunately, some Christians misunderstand the comparison between the flood and the Second Coming of Christ. They refer to a theological novelty never taught before the mid-1800s called "the Rapture". Christ will supposedly return secretly *before* the Second Coming to snatch his people away. Catholics are challenged, "Do you want to be left behind?" This question is based on a misunderstanding of Jesus' words about the days of Noah, that "one is taken and one is left" (Mt 24:40–41). Proponents of the Rapture theory assume that the "saved" will be raptured into heaven and the "lost" will be left behind. However, in the days of Noah, the ones "taken" were the sinners swept away by the flood (Mt 24:39) and those "left behind" were Noah and his family. When asked if *I* want to be left behind, I say, "Absolutely, just like Noah and his family were."[3]

Scripture frequently refers to "the remnant". A remnant is a small portion of fabric that remains after the main cloth ceases to exist. No matter how wicked the world becomes or a people become, God always preserves a remnant that survives to carry on the purpose of God.[4] Mankind has fallen under the fearsome judgment of God, but a righteous remnant remains. We see it over and over again in the story of salvation; in fact, the word *remnant* is used over eighty times in the Bible. Saint Paul writes: "So too at the present time there is a remnant, chosen by grace" (Rom 11:5). It should be our desire and goal to be part of that remnant prepared for "the Day of the Lord".

[3] For more on the false teaching on the Rapture and the truth about the end times, see Carl E. Olson, *Will Catholics Be "Left Behind"?* (San Francisco: Ignatius Press, 2003).
[4] See Gen 45:7; 2 Kings 19:30; Is 10:20; Rom 9:27.

CHAPTER 8

THE FLOOD SUBSIDES

ARK SETTLES ON MOUNT ARARAT (8:1–5)

In chapter 8, the great flood gates close and the water subsides. The
ark came to rest on Mount Ararat located in what was known as
Armenia. Due to the Ottoman Empires' genocide and annexation
of Armenia, it is now located in eastern Turkey, in an area that is
covered with mountain ranges that run parallel to the Caucasus
Mountains on the north. The snow-covered "holy mount" of Ararat
lies northeast of Lake Van.

Some Armenian, Jewish, and early Christian traditions claimed
knowledge of the ark's resting place on Mount Ararat. "The first
Christians of Apamea, in Phrygia, erected in this place a convent called
the monastery of the Ark, where a feast was yearly celebrated to commemorate Noah's coming out of the Ark after the Flood."[1] However,
though there has been an ongoing debate about whether the remains
of the ark still rest in the snows of Mount Ararat, most scholars conclude that, "There is no reason, then, to believe that remnants of
Noah's ark are to be found anywhere in the world (regardless of one's
decision about the historicity of the biblical account of the flood)."[2]

THE RAVEN AND THE DOVE (8:6–12)

The water receded, and the ark rested on dry land. Noah opened
the window and sent a raven out first, and it flew "to and fro" until

---

[1] Charles Souvay, "Ark", in *The Catholic Encyclopedia*, vol. 1 (New York: Robert Appleton
Company, 1907), 721.
[2] Lloyd R. Bailey, "Noah and the Ark: Noah's Ark", in *The Anchor Yale Bible Dictionary*,
ed. David Noel Freedman (New York: Doubleday, 1992), 1131.

the water had dried up. It never returned to the ark. Then Noah released a dove, but the dove returned to the ark finding no place to land. Seven days later, Noah sent the dove out again, and this time she returned with an olive leaf in her beak. This indicated that the waters had receded, and it was soon time to exit the ark. The olive branch is used symbolically for peace, prosperity, and reconciliation (cf. Ps 52:8; Jer 11:16; Hos 14:6; *CCC* 701, 755).

THEOLOGICAL NOTE: *Typology of Noah, the Ark, the Flood, and the Raven and Dove*

In Scripture, Noah's ark prefigures salvation by baptism. Saint Peter informs us the ark saved Noah's family "through water", an event that corresponds to baptism which "now saves you" (1 Pet 3:20–21; *CCC* 1219). After the flood, the white dove returns to the ark with an olive branch prefiguring the water and Spirit by which we are born again (Jn 3:5).

The ark is popular in typology representing the Church (*CCC* 845). Saint Jerome writes:

> Noah's ark was a type of the Church.... [In] the ark there were all kinds of animals, so also in the Church there are men of all races and characters.... The ark had its rooms: the Church has many mansions.... The raven also is sent forth from the ark but does not return, and afterwards the dove announces peace to the earth. So also in the Church's baptism, that most unclean bird the devil is expelled, and the dove of the Holy Spirit announces peace to our earth.... The ark was in peril in the flood, the Church is in peril in the world.... The daylight would fail me if I were to explain all the mysteries of the ark and compare them with the Church.[3]

Justin Martyr argues that only those who had been prepared by water, faith, and wood, as forecast in the story of the deluge, would be

---

[3] *Dialogue against the Luciferians*, 22, in Philip Schaff and Henry Wace, eds., *St. Jerome: Letters and Select Works*, A Select Library of the Nicene and Post-Nicene Fathers of the Christian Church, Second Series, vol. 6 (New York: Christian Literature Company, 1893), 331.

spared God's judgment. According to Justin, the waters of the flood represent waters of baptism, the righteousness of Noah symbolizes the faith of the candidates, and the wood of the ark signifies the wood of the Cross (Justin, *Dialogues* 138.2–3; see also *1 Clem.*, 9.4).[4]

The Fathers of the Church saw in the raven and the dove many types and symbols. Saint Ambrose wrote: "The dove is that in the form of which the Holy Spirit descended, as you have read in the New Testament, Who inspires in you peace of soul and tranquillity of mind. The raven is the figure of sin, which goes forth and does not return, if, in you, too, inwardly and outwardly righteousness be preserved."[5]

Jewish tradition sees Noah as the new Adam, the man chosen to start a new humanity after the cleansing of the flood: "In Gen. ch 8, too, the world is, as it were, being created anew from the watery chaos that had undone God's original work of creation. A new beginning is at hand, with Noah as the new Adam."[6] Christian tradition also sees the covenant with Noah as a renewal of the blessings of fruitfulness that had originally been given in the Garden of Eden. God was starting over despite man's sinfulness and the cursed condition of the earth (*CCC* 1080).

When read in light of the New Testament, we can see the event of the flood pointing to future salvation through another "re-creation" in Jesus Christ (*CCC* 1094). After the flood and the start of the "re-creation", the dove found a place to light on earth; so, in the same way, a dove descends upon Jesus when he emerges from his baptism in the River Jordan and upon those who are baptized in the name of the Father, the Son, and the Holy Spirit. Shortly after his baptism, Jesus tells us that we must be "born again" and that "unless one is born of water and the Spirit, he cannot enter the kingdom of God" (Jn 3:5). Just as sin necessitated the cleansing flood, it is sin that requires the cleansing action of baptism.

---

[4] Robin M. Jensen, *Baptismal Imagery in Early Christianity: Ritual, Visual, and Theological Dimensions* (Grand Rapids, Mich.: Baker Academic, 2012), 17–18.

[5] Ambrose of Milan, "On the Mysteries", in *St. Ambrose: Select Works and Letters*, ed. Philip Schaff and Henry Wace, trans. H. de Romestin, E. de Romestin, and H. T. F. Duckworth, A Select Library of the Nicene and Post-Nicene Fathers of the Christian Church, Second Series, vol. 10 (New York: Christian Literature Company, 1896), 318.

[6] Adele Berlin, Marc Zvi Brettler, and Michael Fishbane, eds., *The Jewish Study Bible* (New York: Oxford University Press, 2004), 24.

LIFE AFTER THE FLOOD (8:13–22)

After the earth had dried, God told Noah to leave the ark: "[E]very-thing that moves upon the earth, went forth by families out of the ark" (Gen 8:19). God then renewed his command to the New Adam, so to speak. He reaffirmed that all the creatures should "breed abundantly on the earth, and be fruitful and multiply upon the earth" (Gen 8:17), and he also commanded Noah to "be fruitful and multiply" (Gen 9:1). Noah built an altar to the Lord and killed some of every clean animal and bird to offer them as a burnt offering to God. When God smelled the pleasing odor, he said, "I will never again curse the ground because of man, for the imagination of man's heart is evil from his youth; neither will I ever again destroy every living creature as I have done" (Gen 8:21). More specifically, he promised never to destroy the earth again with a flood (Gen 9:11).

We are at a disadvantage reading the Hebrew Scriptures in English because we lose many of the subtleties of literary techniques, such as wordplay. For example, a play on words is used in Genesis 8:21 expressing God's pleasure with Noah and his sacrifice. The Hebrew word for "pleasing" is *nihoah* which is a wordplay on *noah*. *Noah* and *pleasing* would resonate with a reader of the original Hebrew. God was pleased with Noah and his family for obeying him and fulfilling his plan during the flood. Now God blesses the family and swears a covenant with Noah.

CHAPTER 9

GOD'S COVENANT WITH NOAH; NOAH'S SONS

PERMISSION TO EAT FLESH; EATING BLOOD
PROHIBITED; CAPITAL PUNISHMENT (9:1–6)

The corruption of the old world has been wiped out, and the new order has begun. New norms are instituted. Chapter 9 is divided into two sections: first, the repopulation of the world and reaffirmation of man as God's vice regent of the new creation, and, second, the assurance that God will never again cause such a flood to cover the earth.

God blessed Noah and his sons Shem, Ham, and Japheth, and reaffirmed their stewardship over the earth and the animals, as he had done before with Adam. Now, however, the animals would fear man—man's kingship would be exercised no longer in an atmosphere of peace, but through fear. Whereas in Eden man had been given only the plants to eat, Noah is told that now "every moving thing that lives" shall be food for him, with the exception of "flesh with its life, that is, its blood". Man is no longer limited to vegetarianism but can now eat flesh, but not the blood (vv. 3–4). The ban on eating blood was enshrined in the Mosaic Law. In Leviticus 17:14, it reads, "For the life of every creature is the blood of it; therefore I have said to the sons of Israel, You shall not eat the blood of any creature, for the life of every creature is its blood; whoever eats it shall be cut off."

Verse 5 introduces a new prohibition that incorporates the word "accounting" or "reckoning" three times for emphasis. In making this prohibition, God illustrates the stark contrast between his gift of human life and the violence of a man or animal that would take a human life. If someone commits violence against man and sheds his blood, retribution must be imposed. "For your lifeblood I will surely require a reckoning." In both Scripture and tradition, blood is considered a sacred sign of the gift of life (*CCC* 2260).

The general rule is: if human life is violated by either man or animal, the life of the offender is required. This imposes a death penalty on man or animal that sheds the blood of (kills) a human being. "Whoever sheds the blood of man, by man shall his blood be shed; for God made man in his own image" (9:6). It should be noted that the phrase, "by man shall his blood be shed", refers to justice carried out by the society, not God. Society requires respect for human life and is empowered to take the life of an offender (*CCC* 2260). Murder was a problem before the flood (e.g., Cain and Lamech), and to curtail such disregard for human life God imposes retribution. Capital punishment is required as a prohibition and a penalty.

The Mosaic Law developed the requirement of capital punishment: "He who kills a man shall be put to death" (Lev 24:17, Ex 21:12–14). Saint Paul explains that civil governments have an obligation to maintain justice: "For rulers are not a terror to good conduct, but to bad.... But if you do wrong, be afraid, for he does not bear the sword in vain; he is the servant of God to execute his wrath on the wrongdoer" (Rom 13:3–4). There has recently been much discussion on the use and legitimacy of capital punishment. The Catholic Church, based on Scripture and tradition, has generally maintained the legitimacy, at least in principle and often in practice, of capital punishment. According to the 1997 Catechism, in civilized societies where justice can be protected through incarceration, the practical justification for capital punishment is diminished. Pope Francis altered the Catechism's wording on the point in 2019.[1]

After reaffirming the sacred value of human life, God makes a covenant with Noah, thereby weaving together the covenant reminders

---

[1] In their excellent book on capital punishment, *By Man Shall His Blood Be Shed*, Feser and Bessette conclude, "The Catholic Church stands as the world's preeminent advocate of human dignity and the culture of life against enormously powerful forces of modern secularism.... By saving innocent lives, by affirming the sacredness of the lives of murder victims, and by treating murderers as morally accountable creatures who deserve punishment proportional to their crimes, the death penalty plays a vital role in upholding human dignity and in promoting a culture of life. The solemn affirmation in Genesis 9:6 of both human dignity and capital punishment alike is as relevant today as it was to earlier generations: 'Whoever sheds the blood of man, by man shall his blood be shed; for God made man in his own image'." Edward Feser and Joseph Bessette, *By Man Shall His Blood Be Shed: A Catholic Defense of Capital Punishment* (San Francisco: Ignatius Press, 2017), 384.

of God's gift of life and the reality of man's murderous violence (*CCC* 2260).

GOD'S COVENANT WITH NOAH (9:7–17)

The Hebrew word for "covenant" is *berit*, and it is one of the most important concepts in salvation history. There is a significant distinction between *berit* and a simple contract. Scott Hahn explains it this way:

> Contracts usually exchange property, goods, and services. But covenants exchange persons. Contracts set the terms for a business transaction. But covenants create a family bond. Every covenant is based upon a contract, since all interpersonal relationships involve some sharing of property and obligations of service. Still, a covenant extends far beyond the limits of any contract. When people enter into a covenant, they say, "I am yours, and you are mine." Thus, marriage is a covenant, and adoption is a covenant. To the biblical authors (and to most ancient peoples), the difference between covenant and contract was like the difference between marriage and prostitution, or between adoption and slavery.[2]

God made a covenant with Adam and Eve and brought them together in the covenant of marriage. In that covenant, Adam represented all mankind. Now another covenant is made, this time with Noah, his descendants, and all flesh (*CCC* 56, 71). Never again would God flood the earth to destroy all flesh.

The rainbow reveals the mathematical precision and grandeur of God's creation. The arched bow in the sky is not an object to be touched. The seven-banded color spectrum appears when the sun's light penetrates rain drops and reflects back from the backside of the drop. As the light exits the rain drop, the light refracts, or is "bent", and the white light is dispersed into its various colors. The human eye sees seven bands of color when one has his back to the sun at a 42°

---

[2] Scott Hahn, *Swear to God: The Promise and Power of the Sacraments*, first ed. (New York, London, Toronto, Sydney, and Auckland: Doubleday, 2004), 61.

angle from the sun's rays. Someone standing off in another direction sees a "different" rainbow at 42° from his relative position.

The word "rainbow" is not used in the Bible. It is simply "bow"—the same word used elsewhere for the warrior's bow, a sign of war and death (Gen 48:22; 1 Chron 12:2). Both are curved arches—one of wood and one of light. Ezekiel uses the rainbow to describe the glory of heaven (1:26, 28; see also Rev 4:3; 10:1).

The relation of the rainbow and the warrior's bow was known in other cultures.

> The rainbow is YHWY's immense bow of War ("my bow"). This idea may be compared with the conception of the flashes of lightning as YHWH's arrows (Ps. 7:13 et seq.; Hab. 3:11). If YHWH lays aside His bow and hangs it in the clouds, it is a sign that His anger has subsided; on beholding it men may feel assured that the storm is past and that no flood will come. These mythological conceptions are of course very ancient. They are found in India, where the bow is Indra's weapon, which he lays aside after his battle with the demons. The Arabs also regard the rainbow as Ḳuzaḥ's bow, which he hangs in the clouds when he has finished shooting.[3]

It is not coincidental that the rainbow is seen after the flood, since it was given as a sign of God's covenant with man and all living creatures on earth not to destroy "all flesh" with a flood (Gen 9:8–17). Although the rainbow represents a new start for the world, it also serves as a reminder of divine punishment for sin that preceded it. The biblical author clearly sees the rainbow as representing a new chance for man following God's punishment in the flood unleashed on the world.

The shape of this sign in the sky is that of a bow, the instrument for hunting and combat. In the rainbow, God has "hung up his bow", so to speak. In his "Noahic" covenant, he has brought peace with man and the great diversity of other life on earth.

It is sadly ironic, then, that today the rainbow is used as a symbol to celebrate a "diversity" that is egregiously at odds with God's purpose

[3] Isidore Singer, ed. *The Jewish Encyclopedia: A Descriptive Record of the History, Religion, Literature, and Customs of the Jewish People from the Earliest Times to the Present Day*, 12 vols. (New York and London: Funk & Wagnalls, 1901–1906), 10:311.

for human beings—a celebration of sexual actions and relationships contrary to God's creation of human beings as male and female.

Paradoxically the symbol used to celebrate a diversity that includes immoral and sexual iniquity was the very sign God gave to remind men of the punishment for great sin and the exquisite sign of God's promising never to destroy with a flood again. The sign given in relationship to the order of the natural law is now co-opted to promote the exact opposite—a symbol celebrating people's acts against nature and nature's God, whether they realize it or not.

NOAH'S VINEYARD AND DRUNKENNESS (9:18–24)

After disembarking from the ark, Noah was apparently ready for a career change; he became a farmer. This is the Bible's first mention of vineyards and wine. Noah planted a vineyard and enjoyed the fruits of his labor, but on one occasion, he enjoyed the wine too much. Noah became drunk and "lay uncovered in his tent". Obviously making and drinking wine was not a sin. Jesus made over 120 gallons of wine in Cana (Jn 2:1–11). But drunkenness *is* a sin (cf. Rom 13:13; Eph 5:18; *CCC* 1809, 2290). Drunkenness often causes uncomely behavior; Noah lay uncovered in his tent, and his son Ham "saw the nakedness of his father" (vv. 21–22). In Hebrew, "exposing his nakedness" literally means exposing one's *genitalia* (Hab 2:15; Lam 4:21). Noah's nakedness was in the privacy of his own dwelling and not a public spectacle.

Lying drunk and naked can be associated with shame and a loss of human dignity. We see this with Adam and Eve in the garden when they realized they were naked after they ate of the forbidden fruit (Gen 3:7, 21). The prophets use this imagery to express degradation and humiliation (e.g., Is 20:4; 47:3; Ezek 23:29). When Ham entered the tent and saw the nakedness of his father, instead of acting nobly as his brothers subsequently did, Ham responded with disrespect for his father and told his brothers. Noah's sons Shem and Japheth walked in backwards to avoid gazing upon their father's nakedness, and they respectfully covered him with a garment. When Noah awoke, he knew what Ham had done, though we are not told how he knew. As a result, Noah cursed Ham's son Canaan to perpetual servitude.

HAM'S SIN; CANAAN'S CURSE; SHEM AND JAPHETH'S BLESSING (9:25–29)

What exactly did Ham do to merit such a curse upon his son, Canaan? Noah was aware that Ham had done something. The exact nature of Ham's offense is unclear, causing speculation. It seems wise to accept the text in its most natural reading on the face of it. Respect for parents is hugely important in Eastern societies, so viewing and ridiculing a father's debasement could incur a harsh response. If the proper response was the respectful covering of the father with eyes averted, then it seems the crime was the improper gazing upon the father and inappropriately discussing it.

While many believe that Ham's sin was disrespect for his father—looking upon his nakedness and then mocking his father in the presence of his brothers—others suggest a more nefarious crime.

> Both Jewish and Christian interpretation speculated that Ham's deed was a sexual offense since the same language is found in the Pentateuch describing sexual transgressions. Further support was garnered from v. 25, which refers to what Ham "had done to him." Many suppose that the original story contained the sordid details but that they were excised for reasons of propriety when later placed in the Torah. Castration was thought to have been the crime by some Jewish and Christian interpreters, and others argued for a homosexual act.[4]

But these scenarios do not explain why Ham's offspring, Canaan, was cursed, and not Ham himself.

The *Catholic Bible Dictionary* suggests another scenario, "The expression 'saw the nakedness of his father' is likely a euphemism; the meaning would be that Ham had incestuous relations with his mother (cf. Lev 18:7–8; 20:17). As a result, Noah cursed Ham's son, Canaan (Gen 9:25–27), who would have been the offspring of that incestuous union; that would explain why the curse fell with such severity on one of Ham's four sons."[5] However the text says Noah

---

[4] K. A. Mathews, *Genesis 1–11:26*, vol. 1A, The New American Commentary (Nashville: Broadman & Holman, 1996), 418.

[5] Scott Hahn, ed., *Catholic Bible Dictionary* (New York, London, Toronto, Sydney, and Auckland: Doubleday, 2009), 135.

was drunk and lay uncovered himself; his wife is never mentioned in this narrative. Plus, the text implies Canaan was already present at the time of the event since the flow of the story has Canaan cursed immediately after the event.

Tradition is not definitive on this issue, nor is there general agreement among commentators. We do know that Shem and Japheth acted honorably by respectfully covering their father with eyes averted, and they were blessed by Noah. If the remedy was covering the father, it seems to follow that the gazing upon, disrespect of, and talking about his father's nakedness was probably the crime. Michelangelo's painting of Noah in the Sistine Chapel portrays the less sordid perspective. He portrays Noah naked and drunk. Ham brings his brothers in to see the sight with finger pointed at Noah's uncovered loins, but his brothers approach with a garment to cover their father respectfully.

Saint Jerome is not alone among the Church Fathers to explain the story of Noah's drunkenness in terms of typology.

> See there is a mystery.... After the deluge, [Noah] drank and became drunk in his own house and his thighs were uncovered and he was exposed in his nakedness. The elder brother came along and laughed; the younger, however, covered him up. All this is said in type of the Savior, for on the cross He had drunk of the passion: "Father, if it is possible, let this cup pass away from me." He drank and was inebriated, and His thighs were laid bare—the dishonor of the cross. The older brothers, the Jews, came along and laughed; the younger, the Gentiles, covered up His ignominy.[6]

Even with a new beginning, mankind is plagued by sin, including Noah and his family. The Holy Spirit is reminding us that man must be vigilant in his spiritual battle against evil. God loves man and offers him a fresh start, but he still respects man's dignity by allowing him to choose freely whether or not to return that love through the obedience of faith. There is one, however, who never tires of tempting

---

[6] *Homily 13 on Psalm 80*, Jerome, in *The Homilies of Saint Jerome (1–59 on the Psalms)*, ed. Hermigild Dressler, trans. Marie Liguori Ewald, The Fathers of the Church, vol. 1 (Washington, D.C.: Catholic University of America Press, 1964), 94–95.

man to turn from God. Just as evil lay in wait in the first garden, it was just waiting to present itself in the new *vineyard* garden.

Chapter 9 ends with Noah's blessings and curses upon his sons and grandson, which will be discussed in chapter 10, where we deal with the "the generations of Noah". "All the days of Noah were nine hundred and fifty years; and he died", declares Genesis 9:29.

CHAPTER 10

NATIONS DESCENDED FROM NOAH

INTRODUCTION

A man worked studiously all his life, invested carefully, and reaped a great fortune. He called his two sons before he died and read his will. They were both delighted to hear that the fortune would be split equally between them. When the father died, each son received his share. The older son quickly followed his father's example by investing his money, working hard, and practicing thrift. He married a wise woman who bore him two sons, and together they increased his fortune from millions to billions of dollars.

The younger son, on the other hand, decided on a life of pleasure and luxury. He bought expensive cars, big houses, and fine clothes. He purchased gifts to impress his friends with no thought for the future. He married a foolish girl, and together they squandered the rest of his money until they were destitute and deep in debt. They had two sons.

Both brothers died. The sons of the wise father inherited untold riches; the sons of the foolish father inherited squalor, debt, and poverty. The sons of the older brother did nothing to earn or deserve the vast wealth they inherited, nor did the sons of the younger brother do anything to deserve the poverty and destitution that was their lot. Their fathers had made choices, and the consequences fell on their future generations.

In Scripture we are told "The LORD is slow to anger, and abounding in mercy, forgiving iniquity and transgression, but he will by no means clear the guilty, visiting the iniquity of fathers upon children, upon the third and upon the fourth generation" (Num 14:18). We have already seen that Adam's sin affected all his children, polluting the whole human race. It was not our fault—we were born into his family and contracted original sin without our prior consent. Due to his sin, Cain's offspring suffered from the choices of their father. Sin continues to flourish, and its effects continue to slither through every generation. Ham sinned against his father Noah, and now his son Canaan and all his descendants would suffer the consequences of their father's sin. As we study the *Table of Nations* and the distribution of humanity subsequent to the flood, we will see that choices have consequences. Ideas and choices have legs; they get up and walk around.

HISTORICAL NOTE: *The Seventy Nations*

The inspired Scripture now pauses from the narrative to demonstrate that Noah's sons were obedient to the command to be fruitful and multiply. Chapter 10 is important to understand the flow of history; it is often called the *Table of Nations*, for it maps out the rapid expansion of the families of Noah's sons as they branched out over the known world and formed the seventy nations. It begins with the dividing formula: "These are the generations of the sons of Noah, Shem, Ham, and Japheth." A chapter of history is closing, and a new chapter in the saga of salvation is opening.

According to the text and the tradition of the Jews, seventy nations sprang from Noah's loins. "The number seventy in the Bible is usually meant to be taken as typological, not literal; that is, it is used for the rhetorical effect of evoking the idea of totality, of comprehensiveness on a large scale. Thus, in Genesis 10 precisely seventy nations issue from the three sons of Noah, and these constitute the entire human family."[1] The *Jewish New Testament Commentary* adds, " 'Rabbi El'azar said, "To what do these seventy bulls correspond? To the seventy nations" (Sukkah 55b). In rabbinic tradition, the traditional number of Gentile nations is seventy; the seventy bulls are to make atonement for them.' "[2] In Luke 10:1, Jesus sent out seventy to prepare his way as he preached throughout the

[1] Nahum M. Sarna, *Exodus*, The JPS Torah Commentary (Philadelphia: Jewish Publication Society, 1991), 4.
[2] David H. Stern, *Jewish New Testament Commentary: A Companion Volume to the Jewish New Testament*, electronic ed. (Clarksville: Jewish New Testament Publications, 1996), Jn 7:2.

land. This number could very well indicate the universality of the ultimate mission to "make disciples of all nations" (Mt 28:18–20).

As the families of Shem, Ham, and Japheth spread across the land, we will see names that are familiar, but most of the names are unfamiliar, not names you would give your kids today. There are names like Riphath and Togarmah, Havilah and Dedan, Lehabim and Naphtuhim. We will not discuss each one, but we will point out a few notable personages and the overall expansion of humanity and the regions of the earth where they settled (*CCC* 56). Then we will key in on the family line of Shem, from which comes the nation of Israel and the future Messiah. The word *semite* comes from the name Shem.

THE LINE OF JAPHETH (10:1–5)

There is some confusion regarding the birth order of Noah's sons.[3] The scriptural list of names—the *Table of Nations*—begins with Japheth, even though he is considered the youngest son. The meaning of the name Japheth is uncertain. A reasonable explanation is given in the *Anchor Yale Bible Dictionary*: "A possible meaning of Japheth is hinted at in the Hebrew pun *yapt elohim leyepet*, 'May God make wide for Japheth' " (Gen 9:27). Thus the name may mean "spacious", an allusion, at least in Genesis, to an expanded inheritance of land by Japheth.[4]

The territories inhabited by Japheth's descendants were north and west of the Middle East, namely, Anatolia (modern-day Turkey) and the Aegean Sea, and into Europe. They eventually inhabited what

---

[3] "The birth order of Noah's sons is not clear from Genesis. Genesis 6:9 and 9:18 imply that Shem was the oldest. However, Gen. 10:21 is ambiguous; it could be understood as saying that Shem was either 'the older brother of Japhet' or 'the brother of Japhet, the oldest.' The latter reading would be strengthened by Gen. 10, in which Noah's descendants are listed in the order: Japhet, Ham, and Shem. Nonetheless, *Jubilees* here asserts that Shem was the oldest brother; cf. *Gen. Ap* 12:10, '[to Shem,] my eldest son'; also Vulg.; B. *Sanh.* 69b." James L. Kugel, "Jubilees", in *Outside the Bible: Ancient Jewish Writings Related to Scripture: Commentary*, ed. Louis H. Feldman, James L. Kugel, and Lawrence H. Schiffman, vol. 1 (Philadelphia: The Jewish Publication Society, 2013), 306.

[4] Ephraim Isaac, ed. David Noel Freedman, *The Anchor Yale Bible Dictionary*, s.v. "Japheth (Person)" (New York: Doubleday, 1992), 3:641.

is known today as the West. They are associated with the Indo-European languages. Noah's blessing on Japheth contains a Messianic prophecy (adding a new promise in addition to the promise of Genesis 3:15). The blessing of Japheth reads, "God enlarge Japheth, and let him dwell in the tents of Shem; and let Canaan be his slave" (Gen 9:27).

The Israelites from the line of Shem dwelled in the Middle Eastern regions. God would work through Shem's line (from whom Israel springs); but Japheth would be brought back to "dwell in the tents of Shem", back into connection with the faith of Shem's descendant, Jacob, and share in its promises. With the coming of the Jewish Messiah, the preaching of the Jewish apostles, and the establishment of the Church, the Gentiles from the lands of Japheth came back to the faith and promise of Abraham "in the tents of Shem". The Church is built on Jewish foundations and to believe in Christ and join the Church is to enter figuratively the tents of Shem (*CCC* 60). In a few chapters, God promises Abraham that "by you all the families of the earth shall bless themselves" (Gen 12:3).

Saint Augustine wrote:

> The occupation of all the world by the Church among the Gentiles was exactly foretold in the words: "Let God enlarge Japhet, and let him dwell in the tents of Shem." ... Is He not dwelling in the tents of Shem?—that is, in the churches built by the apostles, the sons of the prophets. Hear what Paul says to the believing Gentiles: "Ye were at that time without Christ, being aliens from the commonwealth of Israel, and strangers from the covenants; having no hope of the promise, and without God in the world." In these words there is a description of the state of Japhet before he dwelt in the tents of Shem. But observe what follows: "Now then," he says, "ye are no more strangers and foreigners, but fellow-citizens with the saints, and of the household of God, being built upon the foundation of the apostles and prophets, Jesus Christ Himself being the chief corner-stone." Here we have Japhet enlarged, and dwelling in the tents of Shem.[5]

---

[5] Augustine of Hippo, "Reply to Faustus the Manichæan", in *St. Augustin: The Writings against the Manichaeans and against the Donatists*, ed. Philip Schaff, trans. Richard Stothert, A Select Library of the Nicene and Post-Nicene Fathers of the Christian Church, First Series, vol. 4 (Buffalo, N.Y.: Christian Literature Company, 1887), 191.

THE LINE OF HAM (10:6–14)

Next, we follow Noah's middle son, Ham, and all of his descendants and lands (Gen 10:6–20). The etymology of Ham's name is unclear, though many suggest it derives from words meaning *warm* or *hot* from the Egyptian word meaning "the black land", which was a name for ancient Egypt.[6] Supporting this view, the Hamites did occupy the warmer lands in Egypt and farther south.

Ham's descendants dwelled in the territories of Canaan, Put, Cush (Ethiopia), and Egypt, thus presumably the rest of Africa as well. Egypt was later called the "land of Ham" (Ps 105:23, 27; 106:22). The portion assigned to Canaan was later called Israel—now the State of Israel, but it was originally called Canaan (Gen 12:5).

Nimrod is highlighted in Ham's family line. His name could mean *rebellious* or *valiant*. "[Ham's son] Cush became the father of Nimrod; he was the first on earth to be a mighty man. He was a mighty hunter before the LORD; therefore it is said, 'Like Nimrod a mighty hunter before the LORD'" (Gen 10:8–9). This passage mentions the impressive list of kingdoms and cities he established including Babel in Shinar (Babylon) and Nineveh in Assyria (cf. Mic 5:5). He is the subject of innumerable legends. Ham's son Cush fathered Egypt, who became the ancestor of the Philistines that fill the pages of the Old Testament, including their champion, Goliath (Gen 10:13–14).

HAM'S CURSED SON, CANAAN (10:15–20)

With the expansion of Ham's son Canaan, we see names that reappear frequently in the Bible, such as Canaan the land given to Abraham, Sidon (visited by Jesus; coastal city in today's Lebanon), Jebusite (conquered by King David), Amorite (enemy of Israel), Girgashite, and even Sodom and Gomorrah. The sons of Shem through Abraham's line eventually conquer Canaan and take possession of the land, renaming it Israel.

[6] See Isaac, "Ham (Person)", *The Anchor Yale Bible Dictionary*, 31.

Of Ham's four sons, we are most concerned with Canaan. Ham gazes on his father's nakedness and fails to receive a blessing from Noah; rather, his son Canaan receives a curse, "Cursed be Canaan; a slave of slaves shall he be to his brothers" (Gen 9:25). Throughout history the enslavement of Africans was often justified by the use of this biblical passage. Most of Ham's sons settled in Egypt, spreading down into Africa. For European and American proponents of slavery, the dark skin of Africans became associated with this *curse of Ham* and was used to justify the egregious institution of slavery.[7] Such justification can be seen in documents like *A Dialogue Concerning the Slavery of the Africans* in which the American abolitionist Samuel Hopkins debated against slavery and one of his interlocutors justified the institution with these words, "Therefore while we, the children of *Japheth*, are making such abject slaves of the blacks, the children of *Ham*, we are only executing the righteous curse denounced upon them."[8]

Of course, using Ham's curse to promote slavery is a heinous evil and utter nonsense, but it shows how Scripture can be twisted even to justify evil deeds and how deeply sin has infected the human race— to the point of exploiting and enslaving other human beings and justifying it by misappropriating Scripture. Depriving human beings of freedom and property is deplorable, and popes as early as 1435 condemned it (*CCC* 2414).[9]

[7] For more on the history of Ham and slavery, see Daniel G. Reid, Robert Dean Linder, Bruce L. Shelley, and Harry S. Stout, "Curse of Ham", in *Dictionary of Christianity in America* (Downers Grove, Ill.: InterVarsity Press, 1990).

[8] Samuel Hopkins, *A Dialogue concerning the Slavery of the Africans*, Early American Imprints, 1639–1800; no. 19044 (New York: Norwich: printed by Judah P. Spooner, 1776; New York: reprinted for Robert Hodge, 1785), 27.

[9] Referring to a book entitled *The Popes and Slavery*, "Beginning with Pope Eugene IV in 1435, when the Portuguese launched the modern slave trade in the Canary Islands, popes condemned slavery in no uncertain terms, decreeing excommunication for all who participated in the practice." *First Things*, no. 107 (2000): 83. Another example, regarding the treatment of Indians in Mexico, we read, "Pope Paul III was concerned with affairs in Mexico, and in 1537 he declared that the Indians should not 'be treated like irrational animals and used exclusively for our profit and our service.... [They] must not be deprived of their freedom and their possessions ... even if they are not Christians, and on the contrary, they must be left to enjoy their freedom and their possessions.' He emphasized the Christian principle that 'every person is my brother or sister'." Diane Moczar, *Converts and Kingdoms: How the Church Converted the Pagan West—and How We Can Do It Again* (San Diego, Calif.: Catholic Answers Press, 2012), 143.

THE LINE OF SHEM (10:21–32)

And now we come to Shem, from the line of Seth through Noah. He comes last for emphasis—salvation will come through his family line. His sons were Elam, Asshur, Arpachshad, Lud, and Aram (Gen 10:21–22). Shem does not receive a paternal blessing from Noah—but something even better. His father blessed God on Shem's account. That is the literal reading in Hebrew. The NAB, like most translations, renders it, "Blessed be the Lord, the God of Shem!" (Gen 9:26).

The name Shem means *name*, which is often used in place of the divine name Yahweh or the Divine Presence. Religious Jews do not verbalize the name of God but refer to him as *HaShem*—"the Name" (see Lev 24:11). "In Jewish tradition the holy name of God is not pronounced, and the 'four letters' are written without vowels as YHWH. In Jewish texts today, the name of God is often represented either by 'G-d' or *HaShem*, 'the Name,' rather than by the four letters and is frequently pronounced as *Adonaî*, 'Lord'."[10]

Twenty six of the seventy nations from the loins of Noah belong to Shem's descendants. They settled in Arabia and areas of modern-day Syria, Iran, and Iraq. One of Shem's descendants, and an ancestor of Abraham, is named Eber (Gen 10:21–25; 11:14ff.). "These are the families of the sons of Noah, according to their genealogies, in their nations; and from these the nations spread abroad on the earth after the flood" (Gen 10:32). And so the seventy nations were distributed throughout the known world.

---

[10] Arthur G. Patzia and Anthony J. Petrotta, *Pocket Dictionary of Biblical Studies* (Downers Grove, Ill.: InterVarsity Press, 2002), 114.

CHAPTER 11

THE TOWER OF BABEL;
DESCENDANTS OF SHEM

THE TOWER OF BABEL (11:1–4)

Chapter 11 tells of the Tower of Babel. As background to the story, we should note that, according to Genesis 11:1, the whole of humanity at this time had "one language and few words". As men migrated from the east, they settled in the land of Shinar (Gen 11:1–2). Shinar is in the area of Mesopotamia, later known as Babylon, roughly modern-day Iraq. Mesopotamia means "between two rivers"—in this case, between the Tigris and Euphrates rivers. The land is extremely flat, and you can see for miles. There are few rocks or natural building materials, and today, as in ancient times, men make bricks for building. On our visit to Iraq, we saw brickmaking factories everywhere. Among the buildings in ancient times were the stepped pyramids, called ziggurats, erected to Mesopotamian gods and seemingly reaching into the heavens. Though eroded over the millennia, a ziggurat still stands in Ur, the city of Abraham, near Naziriyah, Iraq, which Abraham saw with his own eyes. These structures provide the context for understanding the story of the Tower of Babel.

Envy had been the downfall of Adam and Eve. They wanted to be like God. In the land of Shinar, men again pursued folly: "Let us build ourselves a city, and a tower with its top in the heavens, and let us make a name for ourselves, lest we be scattered abroad upon the face of the whole earth" (Gen 11:4). Men have always wanted to reach the heavens. In the Bible, the phrase "high place" is used over ninety times referring to lofty open-air sites of worship.

BIOGRAPHICAL NOTE: *Nimrod, the Builder of Babel*

We are given a hint as to the man behind the building project. In the previous chapter of Genesis, Nimrod, the grandson of Ham, is described as one who began his kingdom in Shinar; two recognizable cities he built are Babel and Nineveh (10:9). The Hebrew text says he was a mighty man, but the Greek *Septuagint* translation uses the word *giant*.

Genesis itself says relatively little about Nimrod. It does not explicitly tie him to the building of the Tower of Babel and the rebellion against God. Nevertheless, Jewish and Christian tradition do. Indeed, Jewish tradition has much to say about Nimrod, and none of it very flattering.

In the first century, Jewish historian Josephus wrote:

> Now it was Nimrod who excited them to such an affront and contempt of God. He was the grandson of Ham, the son of Noah,—a bold man, and of great strength of hand. He persuaded them not to ascribe it to God as if it was through his means they were happy, but to believe that it was their own courage which procured that happiness. He also gradually changed the government into tyranny,—seeing no other way of turning men from the fear of God, but to bring them into a constant dependence upon his power. He also said he would be revenged on God, if he should have a mind to drown the world again; for that he would build a tower too high for the waters to be able to reach! and that he would avenge himself on God for destroying their forefathers! Now the multitude were very ready to follow the determination of Nimrod, and to esteem it a piece of cowardice to submit to God: and they built a tower.[1]

Saints Jerome and Augustine seem familiar with this tradition:

> Nimrod the son of Cush was the first to seize tyrannical power, [previously] unused, over the people and he ruled in Babylon, which was called Babel because there the speech of those who were building the tower became confused.[2]

---

[1] *The Works of Josephus: updated edition, Complete and Unabridged*, trans. William Whiston (Peabody, Mass.: Hendrickson, 1987), 35.

[2] Jerome, *Hebrew Questions in Genesis* 10:8, quoted in James L. Kugel, *The Bible As It Was* (Cambridge, Mass.: Belknap Press of Harvard University Press, 1997), 127.

That city which was called Confusion is Babylon; and the marvel of
its construction has been recorded in secular history, too. Babylon, in
fact, means confusion. It would seem that its founder was the giant
Nemrod [Nimrod], as was noticed above. In mentioning him, the
Scripture tells us that Babylon was the head of his kingdom.[3]

The *Catechism* teaches that the unity of mankind was shattered by
sin: pride, perverse ambition, polytheism, and idolatry (*CCC* 56–57).
The men who built the Tower of Babel were arrogant and prideful,
thinking they could reach heaven and resist the rule of God, who had
commanded Adam and Eve, and Noah's descendants, to be fruitful
and multiply and to fill the earth. Instead, they disobeyed God's command, failing to spread over the earth; rather, they stayed together to
build a city and a tower to make a name for themselves—to be like
God. Medieval Jewish rabbi Rashbam puts it this way:

> According to the straightforward sense of the text, what was the sin of
> the generation of the Dispersion? If it was the "tower with its top in
> the sky," we read elsewhere about "cities with walls sky-high" (Deut.
> 1:28). Rather, it is that the Holy One commanded them to "be fertile
> and increase" and "fill the earth" (1:28), but they chose instead to
> settle in a single place in order *not* to "be scattered all over the world."
> That is precisely why He decreed that they be scattered.[4]

GOD INTERVENES AT BABEL (11:5–9)

After viewing the tower and seeing the evil thoughts and purposes
of men, God decided to thwart their efforts and scatter them. It is
interesting that the builders said, "Come, let us ... build" (vv. 3–4),
but God mocks their own words with, "Come, let us ... confuse"
(v. 7). The irony is palpable. They intend to build "in the heavens",
yet the Lord "came down" to see the city and the tower. The tower

[3] *City of God*, bk. 16.4, Augustine of Hippo, *The City of God, Books VIII–XVI*, ed. Hermigild Dressler, trans. Gerald G. Walsh and Grace Monahan, The Fathers of the Church,
vol. 14 (Washington, D.C.: Catholic University of America Press, 1952), 495.
[4] Michael Carasik, ed. and trans., *Genesis: Introduction and Commentary*, The Commentators'
Bible (Philadelphia: Jewish Publication Society, 2018), 102.

was so far from reaching the heavens that God had to come down to see it.

Of course, God does not need to "come down" from anywhere. He is everywhere. Nor does he need to get close to something to "see it". He is all-knowing. Still, the human author describes God's actions here as if God were a man, "coming down" from the heavens to inspect the scene. As noted elsewhere, this is anthropomorphism—describing God and his actions in human terms.

The sin of Babel was the sin of Eden—pride and lust for power, to be like God. Saint Josemaría Escrivá commented on this constant temptation:

> This is a subtle temptation, which hides behind the power of our intellect, given by our Father God to man so that he might know and love him freely. Seduced by this temptation, the human mind appoints itself the centre of the universe, being thrilled with the prospect that 'you shall be like gods' (cf. Gen 3:5). So, filled with love for itself, it turns its back on the love of God. In this way does our existence fall prey unconditionally to the third enemy: pride of life (*Christ Is Passing By*, 6).[5]

Again, God uses the plural, "Let *us* go down" (cf. Gen 1:26). As noted previously, we should not suppose the human author understood the dogma of the Holy Trinity and intended his readers to grasp it here. Still, as Saint Augustine wrote, "It is conceivable that here, too, there may have been an allusion to the Trinity, if we suppose that the Father said to the Son and Holy Spirit: 'Come, let us descend and confound their tongue.' The supposition is sound if there is anything to rule out the possibility that angels were meant."[6]

Imagine the scene for a moment. Day dawns, the whistle blows, and men wait for their work assignments. The construction supervisor shouts orders—but only a few men understand him. The others hear gibberish and look at each other puzzled. "What'd he say?" They are more dumbfounded when their fellow workers answer with what sounds like babbling. The work screeches to a halt. Workers who understand each other gather and look quizzically at

---

[5] James Gavigan, Brian McCarthy, and Thomas McGovern, eds., *The Pentateuch*, The Navarre Bible (Dublin and New Jersey: Four Courts Press; Scepter Publishers, 1999), 81.

[6] *City of God*, 16.6, in Augustine of Hippo, *City of God, Books VIII–XVI*, 14:498.

the other groups. Eventually small groups of those who understand each other leave and start their own communities, and the huge ziggurat project is abandoned.

Why did God scatter the people? Does he not desire unity and community? The *Catechism* reminds us that the division into individual nations was cosmic, social, and religious. God used this division to limit the pride and arrogance of fallen men. Sin led to idolatry, polytheism, and the worship of false gods, and it threatened societies with the perversion of paganism (*CCC* 57).

The abandoned city was called Babel (in the Septuagint Greek translation, "Babylon"), because the Lord confused the peoples' languages and scattered them over the earth (Gen 11:9). The word *babel* sounds like the Hebrew word *balal*, which means "to confuse", surely a Hebrew wordplay on the confusion of the languages.

THEOLOGICAL NOTE: *A Christian Perspective on the Tower of Babel*

The confusion of languages at Babel points forward to a milestone event in biblical history. Is there a time when scattered peoples of different languages were suddenly unified through language—kind of like a reversal of Babel? If you guessed Pentecost, you are correct (Acts 2:1–13)! Pentecost is God's gracious reversal of the scattering at Babel. At Babel, God confused a single language into many, creating confusion among the people and leading them to scatter. In Jerusalem, at Pentecost, God brought common understanding among Jews from various places and speaking various languages so the apostles could be understood by all, thus creating a kind of unity. At Babel, language was used to promote a human agenda; at Jerusalem, common understanding of various languages was used to announce the "mighty works of God". In both cases, the people were scattered: from Babel to populate the earth; from Jerusalem to populate the kingdom of God. Isaiah prophesies about Pentecost, saying "all the nations shall flow to [Jerusalem]" (Is 2:1–5).

In his homily on the Solemnity of Pentecost, June 12, 2011, Pope Benedict XVI nicely summarizes the relationship between Babel and Pentecost:

In reciting the *Creed* we enter into the mystery of the first Pentecost: a radical transformation results from the tumult of Babel, from those voices yelling at each other: multiplicity becomes a multi-faceted unity, understanding grows from the unifying power of the Truth. In the *Creed*—which unites us from all the corners of the earth and which, through the Holy Spirit, ensures that we understand each other even in the diversity of languages—the new community of God's Church is formed through faith, hope and love.[7]

DESCENDANTS OF SHEM (11:10–26)

Scripture now funnels the narrative down to one particular line within Shem's family tree. There were ten generations represented from Adam to Noah, followed by ten generations from Shem to Abraham, which are provided here to arrive in our story at a major milestone in the history of salvation—the great patriarch and "the father of us all" (Gen 10:10–26; Rom 4:16).

Again we see the formula used to start a new chapter or segment of the story: "These are the descendants of Shem" (v. 10). In Shem's line to Abraham we find the name Eber, which in Hebrew means "beyond" or "across", probably "on the other side of" (v. 15). Israel's ancestors "lived of old beyond the Euphrates [River]" (Josh 24:2). From *Eber* we get the name *Hebrew*, which is first used of Abraham in Genesis 14:13—"Abram the Hebrew". The title *Hebrew* refers to the family line, but also the language of Hebrew. In Acts 6:1 the title refers to Hebrew-speaking Jews as opposed to Greek-speaking Jews. Saint Paul boasted of being a "Hebrew born of Hebrews" like claiming to be "pure bred" (2 Cor 11:22; Phil 3:5).

In verse 27 we find again the formula "Now these are the descendants of. . . ." This time it is the family line of Terah, the father of Abram, that funnels us toward the line of the Redeemer. Terah was the fifth from Eber and the father of Abram, Nahor, and Haran. Terah's youngest son died in Ur, the land of his birth, leaving behind a son named Lot (Gen 11:27–28).

---

[7] Benedict XVI, *Homilies of His Holiness Benedict XVI (English)* (Vatican City: Libreria Editrice Vaticana, 2013).

DESCENDANTS OF TERAH; INTRODUCING ABRAM AND HIS HOMETOWN, UR (11:27–32)

We have arrived at a huge juncture on the road of salvation history—the man Abraham, though that is not the name he was born with. His given name was Abram, meaning "exalted father" in Hebrew. Only later, at the age of ninety-nine, would God change his name to Abraham. We must also remember that Abram was not a Jew, per se, since at this point Jews did not exist. The word *Jew* comes from *Judah*—one of the twelve sons of Jacob, son of Isaac, son of Abraham. Abraham was also not an Israelite, since Israel was a new name given to Abraham's grandson Jacob (Gen 32:28). To outsiders, Abram was referred to as a *Hebrew*.

Abram was born in the city of Ur in Mesopotamia, between the Euphrates and Tigris Rivers, also known later as the land of the Chaldeans (Gen 11:31; Acts 7:2). Even today Iraqi Christians are called Chaldeans. The ancient site of Ur is located at Tel el–Miqayyar in Iraq, about 250 miles southeast of Baghdad, near the Persian Gulf.

> The city of Ur is one of the oldest and most famous in Mesopotamia, with a recorded history of over two millennia.... Findings at the tell point to the Early Dynastic III period (2600–2500 B.C.) and the Third Dynasty (2111–2003 B.C.), especially under Ur-Nammu and Shulgi, the first two kings of the Third Dynasty, as the high points in the city's history. It was during Ur-Nammu's reign that the famous ziggurat began to be constructed.... Ur was the center of Mesopotamian worship of Nanna/Sin, the moon god, the same god who was said to reside in Haran, the city to which Terah and his family migrated when they left Ur.[8]

At the archaeological site of Ur are the remains of the massive ziggurat, a square-shaped, multileveled temple. While recently visiting Ur in Iraq, my wife, Janet, and I climbed to the top of this amazing ziggurat. Even after significant erosion over the last 4,000 years, it was not difficult for us to image the splendor that entranced the people of Abram's time. Mesopotamia is a flat land with no natural

[8] W. Osborne, "Ur", ed. T. Desmond Alexander and David W. Baker, *Dictionary of the Old Testament: Pentateuch* (Downers Grove, Ill.: InterVarsity Press, 2003), 875.

"high places" to ascend for the worship of the gods. The people of Mesopotamia made bricks to build their own "high places", *ziggurats*, derived from an Akkadian word meaning to "build higher". The ziggurat in Ur was dedicated to *Nanna-Sin*, the god of the moon, in the twenty-first century B.C. The massive step pyramid was 210 ft. in length, 150 ft. in width and 100 ft. in height. Saddam Hussein restored portions of the ancient ziggurat.

When God called Abram, Abram was a pagan—living in an opulent land a thousand miles east of Canaan. Abram's ancestors, and certainly Abram himself, would have worshipped Nanna–Sin, the patron god of the city.[9] The book of Joshua informs us that, "Your fathers lived of old beyond the Euphrates, Terah, the father of Abraham and of Nahor; and they served other gods" (24:2). The "they" includes Abram.

Ur was an upscale, wealthy, urban center. The musical instruments, pottery, jewelry, and other treasures discovered attest to the wealth and elegance of the city.[10]

Abram took a wife named Sarai (Gen 12:5), whose name meant *princess*. With a subtle preparation for the story ahead, the author of Genesis emphasizes that Sarai was barren (11:30). In the book of Acts, Saint Stephen says, "The God of glory appeared to our father Abraham, when he was in Mesopotamia, before he lived in Haran, and said to him, 'Depart from your land and from your kindred and go into the land which I will show you.' Then he departed from the land of the Chaldeans, and lived in Haran. And after his father died, God removed him from there into this land in which you are now living" (Acts 7:2–3).

Canaan was the land bordering the east coast of the Mediterranean Sea, known today as the State of Israel. Abram and Sarai could not travel directly west from Ur to Canaan due to the Arabian Desert. Their route followed the Euphrates River northwest to Haran (in modern-day Turkey) and then southwest toward the Mediterranean Sea. Known as the Fertile Crescent, this region was the "highway"

[9] See M. Stol, "Sin", ed. Karel van der Toorn, Bob Becking, and Pieter W. van der Horst, *Dictionary of Deities and Demons in the Bible* (Leiden, Boston, and Cologne; Grand Rapids, Mich.; Cambridge: Brill; Eerdmans, 1999).

[10] See Richard L Zettler and Lee Horn, *Treasures from the Royal Tombs of Ur* (Pennsylvania: University of Pennsylvania Museum, 1998).

between the great civilizations in Mesopotamia and Egypt. Abram
and Sarai traveled about 600 miles to Haran, where they resided until
the death of Terah, and then they journeyed about 400 miles southwest through Syria into Canaan.

"The days of Terah were two hundred and five years; and Terah
died in Haran", Genesis 11:32 states. The biblical account now cen-
ters on Abram and his descendants.

CHAPTER 12

THE CALL AND OBEDIENCE OF ABRAM

"GO FROM YOUR COUNTRY" (12:1–4)

Genesis 1–11 is usually considered pre-history, not because nothing included there really happened, but because it is difficult to know many specifics and to assign concrete dates to events. What is more, Genesis 1–11 covers a vast stretch of time, describing things well before the invention of writing, and it uses highly figurative language in many instances. Things that really happened—such as the creation of man and the fall of the human race—are described in symbolic language as occurring who knows when and exactly how.

With Abram, however, we enter a period of history that can be pinned down within specific time frames and even, at times, with something akin to actual dates. Abram journeyed into Canaan around 2000 B.C. God promised that Abram would become a great nation, that he would protect him, and that all the families of the earth would be blessed through him (Gen 12:1–3).[1]

God's command to "Go" was all that Abram had to go on. No other conversations on the subject between God and Abram are recounted—just pack and go! Putting myself in Abram's sandals, I

---

[1] The last line of God's command is a messianic promise looking forward to Abram's descendant Jesus Christ through whom all the families of the earth will be blessed, not just those in his own blood line (Acts 3:25; Gal 3:8). The RSV translates it "will bless themselves", but when it quotes these words of God in Galatians 3:8, it translates them: "In you shall all the nations be blessed." The *Catechism* confirms this rendering (*CCC* 59). "Paul also understands it in this way, reflecting a common Jewish interpretation of the verse of [Genesis]. Gentiles were to share in the blessings promised to Abraham, provided they would worship Yahweh and submit to circumcision. Paul, however, insists that Scripture foresaw their share in the blessings of Abraham, as the children of Abraham through faith in Christ Jesus." Raymond Edward Brown, Joseph A. Fitzmyer, and Roland Edmund Murphy, *The Jerome Biblical Commentary* (Englewood Cliffs, N.J.: Prentice-Hall, 1968), 2:242.

would ask: "Lord, where do you want me to go? I have a house and a career and family here. My ancestors are buried here. This is my homeland. What about my next house, health insurance, and my pension? What does it mean that you will *bless* me? I am already seventy-five years old—I have no sons. Here my family will care for us in our old age. Should I leave my other gods here, all the idols we have worshipped for generations, or bring them with me? Are you sure I can trust *you*? And where did you say we are going again?"

Genesis is replete with memorable people, but the figure towering above them all is Abram. It is impossible to overestimate the importance and significance of this wrinkled old shepherd with sandaled feet. He traveled over 1,000 miles in obedience to God without knowing where he was going.

We may wonder why Abram trusted in this God. Was it an interior sense or a voice? (see *CCC* 2570).

> God appeared to Abraham as a personal Being, in the manner of a man, and yet superior to him and to all that exists. That is why He could command and be instantly obeyed. Yahweh speaks about Abraham, which means that He was not within him, as an interior voice. Neither pantheism nor mysticism has the slightest place in this story.... Everything was sustained by a firm foundation, which the author does not evoke, but he is obviously well aware of it.[2]

In other words, Abram had good and sufficient reasons to trust God.

It appears that Abram was vocal about his newfound God and the rejection of his national pagan deities. His fathers had served the gods of Mesopotamia (Josh 24:2). He now abandoned these gods to follow "the God of glory" (Acts 7:2). In that era, allegiance to the gods of the land was a civic duty; rejection of the local gods was tantamount to treason. Scripture reports that the people of Ur drove Abram and his family from their home.

> This people is descended from the Chaldeans. At one time they lived in Mesopotamia, because they would not follow the gods of their fathers who were in Chaldea. For they had left the ways of their ancestors,

---

[2] Angel Gonzalez, *Abraham, Father of Believers* (New York: Herder and Herder, 1967), 21–22.

and they worshiped the God of heaven, the God they had come to know; *hence they drove them out from the presence of their gods*; and they fled to Mesopotamia, and lived there for a long time. Then their God commanded them to leave the place where they were living and go to the land of Canaan. There they settled, and prospered, with much gold and silver and very many cattle (Jud 5:6–9, emphasis added).

Abram's journey from Mesopotamia was paused in Haran in today's Turkey. When Abram was seventy-five years old, his father, Terah, died, and from Haran he embarked on the second leg of his journey to Canaan (Gen 12:4).[3]

The Call of Abraham is one of my favorite poems:

> Talk about imperious.
> Without a "may I presume?"
> No previous contact,
> no letter of introduction,
> this unknown God
> issues edicts.
>
> This is not a conversation.
> Am I a nobody
> to receive decrees
> from one whose name I do not know?
>
> I have worshipped my own god.
> To you I had addressed no prayers,
> but quick,
> like sudden fire in the desert,
> I hear "Go."
>
> At seventy-five,
> am I supposed to scuttle my life,
> take that ancient wasteland, Sarai, place my arthritic bones
> upon the road
> to some mumbled nowhere?

---

[3] Genesis 12:1–4 refers to Abram being called from Haran; Genesis 11:31; 15:7, and Nehemiah 9:7 inform us that Abram was called from Ur. It appears that two steps were involved: the original calling out of Ur and a subsequent calling out of Haran after the death of his father.

Let me get this straight.
I will be brief.
I summarize.
     In ten generations since the Flood you have spoken to no one.
Now, like thunder on a clear day,
you give commands:
pull up my tent,
desert the graves of my ancestors, leave Haran
for a country you do not name, there to be a stranger.

God of the wilderness,
from two desiccated lumps,
from two parched prunes, you promise all peoples of the earth
will be blessed in me.

You come late, Lord, very late,
but my camels leave in the morning.[4]

The writer of *Hebrews* expounds on the profound faith of Abram.
"And without faith it is impossible to please [God]. For whoever
would draw near to God must believe that he exists and that he
rewards those who seek him.... By faith Abraham obeyed when
he was called to go out to a place which he was to receive as an inheritance; and he went out, not knowing where he was to go" (Heb
11:6, 8; *CCC* 142–46).

SPIRITUAL NOTE: *Abram's Wealth Did Not Deter Him*

Abram was an accomplished businessman with many servants, flocks
and herds, and other possessions. We learn later that Abram had 318
trained men who had been born in his house (Gen 14:14). Preparing
to leave on such an arduous journey was no easy matter. They must
have comprised an impressive caravan with lumbering camels, bleating sheep, frisky goats, donkeys, cattle, not to mention the families
of all his servants. Large families with flocks and herds traveled an

---

[4] This poem is contained in the book *Swift Lord, You Are Not*, by Fr. Killian McDonnell,
O.S.B. (Collegeville, Minn.: Liturgical Press, 2003), 10. Copyright 2003 by Order of Saint
Benedict. Reprinted with permission.

average of six miles in a day. This gives you an idea of the great burden it was to follow God's command. We know they had accumulated great possessions because, shortly after they arrived in Canaan, Abram and Lot had to split up because the land could not support all their flocks together (Gen 13:6).

Rich folks with many possessions often feel invincible and self-sufficient. This is why Jesus said it was easier for a camel to get through the eye of a needle than for a rich man to get to heaven (Mk 10:25). Not so with Abram. He latched onto God and would not let go. God was Abram's inheritance, and nothing else could entice, scare, or push Abram away from his tight embrace of God.

GOD CALLS ABRAM; ABRAM TRAVELS TO CANAAN (12:5–9)

Many generations earlier, Canaan, the cursed son of Ham, had settled in the strip of land bordering the Mediterranean Sea that was now called Canaan (Gen 10:15–19). Abram journeyed hundreds of miles from Haran southwest into the land of Canaan. The Lord appeared to Abram in Shechem, at the oak of Moreh, and said, in effect, "OK, Abram, stop, you have arrived, and this is the land I will give to your descendants" (cf. Gen 12:7). Notice that the land was promised, not to Abram, but to his descendants. Abram's first response was to build an altar to the Lord. Today Shechem is located in the Palestinian West Bank in the city of Nablus. Nearby is Jacob's Well, where two thousand years later Jesus would ask for a drink of water from the Samaritan woman (Jn 4:4–7).

Abram traveled south a bit more and pitched his tent near Bethel, built another altar, and he called upon the name of the Lord (Gen 12:8). Here he stayed for a while with his considerable entourage. As I travel through the Holy Land today, there are many Bedouins, the people of the land, who still dwell in tents and makeshift dwellings in the wilderness. They live off the land and tend their flocks and herds akin to how Abram lived. By our Western standards, their life-style is primitive. On many occasions, I have stopped to visit them, and when I stepped into their tents or caves with flies buzzing around my head, I said to myself, "This is Abraham!"

In *Abraham, Father of Believers*, we read:

Abraham was a simple nomad, owning flocks of sheep, who lived like all the nomads of his class in the borderland between the cultivated regions of the settler and the broad, open desert. He was familiar with the settler's customs and laws, and had partly assimilated them. Wherever he wandered, he took them along as part of his inheritance. The traditions of Abraham and the other patriarchs continued to reflect these customs, intermixed with the ways and customs of the Bedouin.[5]

The patriarchs did not build houses—they lived in tents. They constantly pulled up their tent stakes, though the stone altars they had made remained. When Abram pulled up his tent pegs, it signifies for us that he ultimately had no earthly home of his own—he was *not* a citizen of this world. Altars represent the permanence of God. Tents come down, the altars remain. In other words, Abram had his eyes on God and on a heavenly city. Saint Paul reminds us that our citizenship is not of this earth but in heaven from which we are awaiting our Savior, Jesus Christ (Phil 3:20; see Heb 11:10).[6]

Abram was heading south toward the Negev Desert, which covers more than half the land mass of the modern State of Israel, roughly 4,700 square miles. Beersheba is on the northern edge of the desert, which extends to the southernmost tip at the Sea of Aqaba from which today you can see four countries: Israel, Saudi Arabia, Jordan, and Egypt. It is rugged wilderness territory. But Abram was on the northern edge of the Negev where it is still fertile and green in the spring, though it dries up with the summer's burning heat.

Imagine you had trusted God, traveled over a thousand miles to arrive in the Promised Land, only to find out there was a severe famine (Gen 12:9–10). This is exactly what happened to Abram and

[5] Gonzalez, *Abraham*, 24.

[6] "The 'urban' or 'civic' metaphors for the Christian life in the New Testament, and especially in St. Paul, are quite coherent. Heaven is like a city (*polis*); Christ is its sovereign (*Kyrios*), and it has its own laws and constitution (*politeia*), namely, the gospel. Christians are its citizens ... and are not treated as foreigners or sojourners there; they have the rights of citizenship (*politeuma*) and are fellow-citizens of the saints (*sympolitai*). Such a citizenship carries with it rights and privileges but also obligations and responsibilities. Each one is then required to 'live as a citizen' (*politeuomai*), i.e., according to the laws and the spirit of this city, conformably to its statutes." Ceslas Spicq and James D. Ernest, *Theological Lexicon of the New Testament* (Peabody, Mass.: Hendrickson, 1994), 124.

Sarai. Abram did not even have time to pitch his tents. Anyone else would have been tempted to accuse God: "This parched land is my inheritance—maybe I should go back to Mesopotamia?"

ABRAM AND SARAI TRAVEL TO EGYPT
TO AVOID THE FAMINE (12:10–20)

The famine forced Abram to leave the Promised Land and drive his flocks and herds about four hundred miles through the Sinai wilderness to Egypt, where there was food. Imagine thinking you had "arrived" when another forced journey lay ahead. This was one of Abram's first major tests—would his faith in God waver?

This brings us to a strange episode in Abram's life recorded in Genesis 12:10–20. Abram arrived in Egypt with the knowledge that his wife Sarai was a beautiful woman. To prevent the Egyptians from killing him to seize Sarai, he concocted a scheme for Sarai to announce she was Abram's sister. Though a lie, it was partly true because Sarai was his half-sister (Gen 20:12). And when the princes of Pharaoh saw Sarai, they praised her to Pharaoh. And she was taken from Abram into Pharaoh's house (Gen 12:15). To compensate Abram for his "sister", the Pharaoh gave him sheep, camels, oxen, donkeys, and male and female servants (Gen 12:16). But God's plans did not include her becoming one of Pharaoh's harem!

God protected Abram and Sarai by causing a plague to befall Pharaoh and his household (12:17). Pharaoh was scandalized that Abram had lied to him about his wife. To stop the plague, Pharoah sent Abram away with Sarai and all his possessions. One idea that comes from this account is that God is not simply a localized deity as was thought to be the case with the gods of the pagans. The true God could intervene and deliver his people anytime, anywhere, even in the foreign land of Egypt.

Abram again made the four-hundred-mile trip back up to Canaan. Saint Augustine provides an interesting perspective on this episode:

[Abraham] was compelled by pressure of famine to go on into Egypt. There he called his wife his sister, and told no lie. For she was this also, because she was near of blood; just as Lot, on account of the same nearness, being his brother's son, is called his brother. Now he did not deny that she was his wife, but held his peace about it, committing to God the defence of his wife's chastity, and providing as a man against human wiles; because if he had not provided against the danger as much as he could, he would have been tempting God rather than trusting in Him.... At last what Abraham had expected the Lord to do took place. For Pharaoh, king of Egypt, who had taken her to him as his wife, restored her to her husband on being severely plagued. And far be it from us to believe that she was defiled by lying with another; because it is much more credible that, by these great afflictions, Pharaoh was not permitted to do this.[7]

HISTORICAL NOTE: *Camels*

In this chapter, camels are first mentioned in the Bible (12:16). The Hebrew word *gāmāl* is used sixty-four times and refers to the one-humped camel common in the Middle East. Scholars have claimed that camels only arrived late in the second century B.C. and that their mention in Genesis is anachronistic.[8] However, others assert that it is possible and likely that camels were in use in the patriarchal age. The archaeological journal *Bible and Spade* concludes, "Although the patriarchal narratives, the Exodus, and the Judges accounts are often accused of being historically inaccurate, in light of the archaeological and textual evidence pertaining to early camel domestication, this alleged anachronism is instead an historically accurate detail."[9]

In *A History of Israel* we read, "There seems to be more than passing evidence that the camel already was domesticated by patriarchal times in the first half of the second millennium B.C. Support for this concept is gathered from archaeological evidence of skeletal remains along with illustrations of camels at excavation levels belonging to the

[7] Augustine of Hippo, *The City of God*, in *St. Augustin's City of God and Christian Doctrine*, bk. 16, chap. 19, ed. Philip Schaff, trans. Marcus Dods, A Select Library of the Nicene and Post-Nicene Fathers of the Christian Church, First Series, vol. 2 (Buffalo, N.Y.: Christian Literature Company, 1887), 322.

[8] For examples, see Ilse Köhler-Rollefson, "Camels and Camel Pastoralism in Arabia", *Biblical Archaeologist*, 56, no. 4 (1993) (Philadelphia: American Schools of Oriental Research, 2001).

[9] Titus Kennedy, "The Domestication of the Camel in the Ancient Near East", ed. Bryant G. Wood, *Bible and Spade* 23, nos. 1–4 (2010).

third and second millennia B.C."[10] A lengthy treatment of this subject in the six-volume *Anchor Yale Bible Dictionary* suggests, "[I]f we hold that the patriarchal stories are essentially historical in outlook, we would not be totally amiss in suggesting that domestic camels may have been known to the inhabitants of Syria–Palestine as early as the turn of the 3d millennium B.C."[11]

[10] Walter C. Kaiser, Jr., *A History of Israel: From the Bronze Age through the Jewish Wars* (Nashville, Tenn.: Broadman & Holman, 1998), 64.

[11] Juris Zarins, "Camel", in *The Anchor Yale Bible Dictionary*, ed. David Noel Freedman (New York: Doubleday, 1992), 826.

CHAPTER 13

ABRAM AND LOT SEPARATE

THE SEPARATION OF ABRAM AND LOT (13:1–13)

Upon returning from Egypt, Abram and Lot traveled north back to Bethel. The text assumes the altar was still there (remember the permanence of altars), and we see Abram again "call on the name of the Lord". By returning to his original altar, Abram renewed his physical and spiritual connection to the land. The altar had been a way of "planting his flag" or "staking his claim" (13:4). From this vantage point, thousands of feet above the Jordan Valley below, Abram and Lot came to an agreement to part ways because their flocks were great and the land could not support them both.

Abram had acquired great wealth, which was considered a sign of God's blessing (Deut 8:18). Wealth was measured in gold, silver, flocks, herds, and land. Abram had it all except the land, which had been promised by God but not yet realized. The land still belonged to the Canaanites (Gen 13:7). Some translations use the word "cattle" in verse 7, which in English we assume refers to cows, but the best translation of the Hebrew is "livestock", including domesticated farm animals like cows, sheep, and goats. We confront the word fifty-four times in Genesis, so it is helpful to understand its meaning.[1]

Abram allowed his nephew to choose even though Abram was the elder. Lot chose the Jordan valley for himself, moving his tents as far as Sodom, while Abram took for himself the hill country above the valley, settling in Canaan. Preparing us for an upcoming event,

---

[1] "מִקְנֶה (miq·ně(h)).... *Livestock*, i.e., large and small domestic mammals that are found in herds and flocks, with an associated meaning that the animals are someone's property (1 Sam 23:5), note: this can include cows, sheep, goats, horses, donkeys, etc." James Swanson, *Dictionary of Biblical Languages with Semantic Domains: Hebrew (Old Testament)* (Oak Harbor: Logos Research Systems, 1997), ref. no. 5238.

the author tells us "this was before the LORD destroyed Sodom and Gomorrah" (v. 10). Lot chose poorly, considering his new neighbors.

To understand the movements of the nomadic patriarchs, it is important to understand the land and the grazing movements in southern Israel.

> Upon his arrival in the land of Canaan, Abraham commenced a pastoral pattern of what is best described as transhumance pastoralism [following the seasonal cycles].... Their grazing patterns were dictated by the seasons: during the hot, dry summer months, they would graze up in the Hill Country, where temperatures were comparatively mild and there was plenty of stubble in the recently harvested grain fields. During the cold, wet winter, the herders would drive their flocks either 1) east towards the eastern slopes lying in the rain shadow (e.g., the Judean Wilderness), or 2) south into the region of the Negev, near Arad, Beer-sheba, and Gerar. Temperatures there were warmer than in the Hill Country, and these semi-arid zones were alive with marginal grasses, flowers, and thistles, which provided ample forage for the sheep and goats.[2]

GOD REAFFIRMS HIS PROMISE TO ABRAM (13:14–18)

The phrase "after Lot had separated from him" is significant (Gen 13:14) because God could now invest Abram and his seed *exclusively* with the promise of the blessing and the land. From the heights of Bethel, God told Abram to look in every direction to see all the land God would give to Abram's seed forever (*zera* in Hebrew, *sperma* in Greek, *semen* in Latin) (Gen 13:14–15). While Abram was looking down at the dust covering his feet, God said "lift up your eyes"; in other words, do not just look down at the dust, but look up and see as far as you can in every direction—it is all yours; I give it to you and your descendants. I will make your descendants as plentiful as the dust on the earth (Gen 13:14–17). From the mountains of

[2] Vernon H. Alexander, "The 'Good Shepherd' and Other Metaphors of Pastoralism", in *Lexham Geographic Commentary on the Gospels*, ed. Barry J. Beitzel and Kristopher A. Lyle, Lexham Geographic Commentary (Bellingham, Wash.: Lexham Press, 2016), Mt 25:31– Jn 10:15.

Samaria—on a clear day—you can see the Mediterranean to the west, the hills of Hebron to the far south, north into Galilee, and over the Jordan River into the mountains of Moab to the east. With Lot gone, God began a new chapter in the life of his friend Abram.

Five centuries later, Moses would stand on the mountains of Moab in modern-day Jordan and look west across the Jordan River and survey the same land shown to Abram. The Jews have always remembered God's promise and consider that promise to be unconditional and in perpetuity. Even if exiled, the land was still inextricably linked to the sons of Isaac through Abraham.

ABRAM MOVES TO HEBRON (13:18)

Abram moved his tent and dwelt by the oaks of Mamre in Hebron, and he built another altar to the Lord (Gen 13:18). On many occasions we have visited Hebron where Abram settled, which is now a large Palestinian city with industry and commerce. We drove a short distance from the city center to visit "the oaks of Mamre". The location can be visited today. King Herod built walls around the famous site to preserve it, and later Constantine built a church there in the fourth century. For many centuries there was a famous tree associated with Abram. Hebron is about twenty miles south of Jerusalem. It is surrounded by miles of fertile land. Its modern Arabic name is al-Khalil, short for "friend of God", which refers to Abraham.

CHAPTER 14

WAR TO RESCUE LOT;
MELCHIZEDEK BLESSES ABRAM

LOT'S CAPTIVITY AND RESCUE (14:1–17)

God had promised this land to Abram, but the land was not unpopulated. It was a fertile land and fiercely defended. Abram now found himself embroiled in a war with a coalition of the current occupants. Four kings from the east had exerted themselves over the kings of Canaan for thirteen years. The vassal kings had had enough, and they refused further subjugation by the foreign dictators. Lot and Abram were embroiled in the conflict.

The battle went poorly for the armies of Sodom and Gomorrah. They fled, and many fell into pits of tarry bitumen, the substance that was earlier used in the making of ziggurats in Mesopotamia (Gen 11:3) and would be later used to seal baby Moses' reed basket as he floated in the Nile River (Ex 2:3). Bitumen, or natural asphalt, is native to the Dead Sea area. Because of the bituminous products of the Dead Sea, Josephus informs us that it was called *Asphaltitis*—the "Asphalt Sea".[1] We are told the kings gathered in the Valley of Siddom, near the Salt Sea, which refers to the Dead Sea.

A fugitive informed Abram that Lot had been kidnapped from Sodom during the uprising of kings. With his 318 men, Abram pursued Lot's captors (Gen 14:11–16). They overtook the kidnappers in the region of Dan, which in the time of Abram was called Laish

[1] "These kings had laid waste all Syria ... and when they were come over against Sodom, they pitched their camp at the vale called the Slime Pits, for at that time there were pits in that place; but now, upon the destruction of the city of Sodom, that vale became the Lake Asphaltitis, as it is called." *Antiquities*, 1.174, in *The Works of Josephus: Complete and Unabridged*, trans. William Whiston, updated edition (Peabody, Mass.: Hendrickson, 1987), 39.

(Judg 18:27–29); it would not be called Dan until the Israelites
returned from Egyptian slavery. In the Old Testament, the land of
Israel is described as extending from Dan to Beersheba—Dan in the
north and Beersheba in the south (e.g., 2 Sam 24:2). The distance
from Hebron to Dan is about 140 miles as the crow flies. Assuming the men could cover twenty-five miles a day on foot, it would
have been a five-to seven-day journey through the Jordan Valley.
After conquering his enemy, Abram pursued the invading kings
north beyond Damascus. He returned victorious, not only with his
nephew, but with all the spoils of war.

An ancient Canaanite gate was excavated at the site of Dan (Laish).
It is popularly called "The Abraham Gate" and is generally dated to
the time Abram arrived in the area to rescue Lot. We read in Genesis
14:14 that Abram "went in pursuit as far as Dan". It is fascinating to
see a four-thousand-year-old gate that Abram surely saw with his
own eyes.[2]

Upon Abram's return, he was greeted by the king of Sodom at the
Valley of Shaveh, which was also called the "King's Valley". This is
the only biblical mention of the name Shaveh, but the "King's Valley" is mentioned again in 2 Samuel 18:18. The general opinion is
that the King's Valley is at the junction of the Kidron and Hinnom
Valleys, immediately southeast of today's Old City of Jerusalem.[3] It
is unclear what the significance is of the king of Sodom coming out
to meet Abram; Scripture does not say. Perhaps the sacred writer
intends to leave us in suspense to build up to the future conflict with
Sodom. It is instructive that the king of Sodom came out empty-
handed to meet his deliverer and the first word out of his mouth was
"give"; whereas Melchizedek, king of Salem, brought gifts and the
first word out of his mouth was a blessing.

---

[2] According to the excavator Avraham Biran, "The gate served as the main gate to Laish. . . .
But to my way of thinking, Abraham, no doubt, was invited to visit the city of Laish, and
for all I know they had gone through the gate before it was blocked." Interview at Hebrew
Union College Skirball Museum, Jerusalem (October 12, 1996), quoted in Randall Price with
H. Wayne House, *Zondervan Handbook of Biblical Archaeology* (Grand Rapids, Mich.: Zonder-
van Publishers and World of the Bible Ministries and H. Wayne House, 2017), 81.

[3] "The Valley of Shaveh can thus be definitely located as the little plain formed by the
junction of the valleys of Hinnom, Tyropoeon, and Kidron." Michael C. Astour, "Shaveh,
Valley of (Place)", in *The Anchor Yale Bible Dictionary*, ed. David Noel Freedman (New York:
Doubleday, 1992), 1168.

INTRODUCING MELCHIZEDEK AND SALEM (14:18–20)

Genesis contains so many significant, foundational passages of the Bible. Genesis 14:18–20 is one of them, especially in light of how this section is used in the New Testament (Heb 5:6, 10; 6:20; 7:1–21), though the Old Testament also draws on it again (Ps 110:4). A man named Melchizedek is the key figure, and a mysterious one at that. His importance cannot be overestimated. Genesis describes him as "the priest of God Most High" (Gen 14:18). This is the first use of the word "priest" in Scripture. As we shall see, Melchizedek's priestly identity is closely tied to the eternal priesthood of Jesus Christ and the Most Holy Eucharist.

We had the odd mention of the king of Sodom; now another king arrived on the scene, for Melchizedek was "king of Salem" (Gen 14:18) as well as a priest. According to James Kugel:

> Melchizedek is something of an enigma in the Bible. We are not told the name of his father or his mother, or anything about his family. He is not mentioned anywhere in the various lists of Noah's descendants. We are not told *when* he was born—nor even *that* he was born—and the Bible is equally silent about his death. Nor, for that matter, is the location of his kingdom, Salem, known for sure. Thus, almost everything about him was mysterious for ancient interpreters.[4]

Adding to the mystery, the book of Hebrews says he had neither mother nor father nor genealogy, neither beginning of days nor end of life (Heb 7:3).

The name *Melchizedek* means "Righteous King" and is probably a title as well as a name. He appeared from nowhere—with no introduction and no explanation—and then he disappeared just as quickly. He received a tithe from Abram, offered him bread and wine, blessed him, and then he is mentioned no more in Genesis. He was the "king of Salem". The word *salem* means "peace" (see Heb 7:2). Psalm 76:1–2 gives us a clue as to the location of Salem, thereby suggesting the nature of this kingdom and of whom Melchizedek was a type

---

[4] James L. Kugel, *The Bible As It Was* (Cambridge, Mass.: Belknap Press of Harvard University Press, 1997), 256.

or figure: "In Judah God is known, his name is great in Israel. His abode has been established in Salem, his dwelling place in Zion." This seems to indicate that Salem was what would later become the city of Jerusalem, "Zion" being another name for Jerusalem (e.g., Ps 51:18; Is 30:19; Joel 2:1; Zech 8:3). The geographical location also suits this interpretation.

This priest-king approached Abram in the King's Valley adjacent to the city of Jerusalem. There was no separation of religion and civic life; Melchizedek was both priest and king. In this dual role, we see a foreshadowing of King David, who would come onto the scene almost one thousand years later making Zion his capital. We see David as king, yes, but while not an Aaronic priest, he nevertheless wore the priestly ephod (vestment) and offered sacrifices (2 Sam 6:12–14). With both Melchizedek and King David, there is a foreshadowing of the person of Christ, of whom the *Catechism* says, "'Christ' comes from the Greek translation of the Hebrew *Messiah*, which means 'anointed.' It became the name proper to Jesus only because he accomplished perfectly the divine mission that 'Christ' signifies.... It was necessary that the Messiah be anointed by the spirit of the Lord at once as king and priest, and also as prophet" (*CCC* 436).

A thousand years after King David, the Messianic King-Priest Jesus offered bread and wine in Zion, the bread and wine becoming the Holy Eucharist, his Body and Blood. Jerusalem has a long Eucharistic history.

Melchizedek presented an offering to Abram, and, as a priest would be expected to do, he blessed Abram. Gordon Wenham notes in this regard, "What is being portrayed ... is the generosity of Melchizedek. Bread and water would have been the staple diet. Bread and wine is royal fare (1 Sam 16:20) and regularly accompanied animal sacrifice (Num 15:2–10; 1 Sam 1:24; 10:3). Melchizedek, who in traditional Near Eastern fashion combined the offices of king and priest, should have had ample supplies of bread and wine. Here he is portrayed as laying on a royal banquet for Abram the returning conqueror."[5]

In response, Abram recognized Melchizedek's priestly status and gave a tithe—10 percent of the spoils of war. This tithing seems to

[5] Gordon J. Wenham, *Genesis 1–15*, Word Biblical Commentary, vol. 1 (Dallas: Word, Incorporated, 1987), 316.

be a prerogative of Near Eastern kings who exacted a payment as evidenced by ancient texts and with an example found in 1 Samuel 8:15, 17.

HISTORICAL NOTE: *Jewish Thoughts on Melchizedek*

Jewish traditions say much about Salem and Melchizedek. Josephus, first-century Jewish historian, and medieval rabbi Nahmanides concur that Salem is Jerusalem and prefigured the Temple and the priesthood of Abram's descendants. Josephus comments, "But he who first built it was a potent man among the Canaanites, and is on our tongue called [Melchizedek], the Righteous King, for such he really was; on which account he was [there] the first priest of God, and first built a temple [there], and called the city Jerusalem, which was formerly called Salem" (*The Jewish War* 6.438).[6]

Nahmanides agrees, but adds an interesting tradition that Melchizedek is really Shem the son of Noah:

> Salem is Jerusalem, as is clear from "Salem became His abode; Zion, His den" (Ps. 76:3).... This lets us know that Abraham would not give a tithe to a priest of other gods. But knowing that he was a priest of God Most High, he gave him a tenth of everything in honor of the Holy One. This also provided Abraham with a hint that the future House of God would be there, where his descendants would bring their tithes and offerings and bless the Lord. The midrash that says Melchizedek was Shem implies both that he came to Jerusalem in order to serve God and that they readily accepted him as the honored brother of their own ancestor, Ham.[7]

THEOLOGICAL NOTE: *Psalm 110 and Hebrews on Melchizedek*

One Old Testament passage is more quoted in the New Testament than any other—it is Psalm 110:1–4, which reads:

[6] *Works of Josephus*, 750.

[7] Michael Carasik, ed. and trans., *Genesis: Introduction and Commentary*, The Commentators' Bible (Philadelphia: Jewish Publication Society, 2018), 126.

The Lᴏʀᴅ says to my lord:
"Sit at my right hand,
till I make your enemies your footstool."
The Lᴏʀᴅ sends forth from Zion
   your mighty scepter.
   Rule in the midst of your foes!
Yours is dominion
   on the day you lead your host
   in holy splendor.
From the womb of the morning
   I begot you.
The Lᴏʀᴅ has sworn
   and will not change his mind,
"You are a priest for ever
   according to the order of Melchizedek."

Jesus quoted this psalm when he said to the Pharisees: "If David thus calls him [the Messiah] Lord, how is he his Son?" (Mt 22:45). The Messiah is far superior to David, since David calls him "lord". In this way, Jesus showed the transcendent nature of the Messiah. The psalm therefore finds its fulfillment in Jesus Christ.[8] Peter used this on Pentecost (Acts 2:34–36; *CCC* 447).

The book of Hebrews has a great deal to say about the importance of the priestly order of Melchizedek and its relation to Jesus Christ. A few verses stand out: "[Jesus was designated by God] a high priest for ever according to the order of Melchizedek" and "He is first, by translation of his name, king of righteousness, and then he is also king of Salem, that is, king of peace" (Heb 6:20, 7:2).

THEOLOGICAL NOTE: *Fathers of the Church on Melchizedek*

The Fathers of the Church echo the scriptural testimony. Saint John Chrysostom writes, "Quite rightly, on the contrary, did [Abram] accept them from Melchisedek; after all, Sacred Scripture gave

---

[8] James Gavigan, Brian McCarthy, and Thomas McGovern, eds., *Psalms and the Song of Solomon*, The Navarre Bible (Dublin; New York: Four Courts Press; Scepter Publishers, 2003), 372.

indication of the man's virtue in saying, 'Now, he was a priest of God the most high.' In particular, these events were a type of Christ, and the offerings themselves prefigured a kind of mystery."[9] Saint Clement of Alexandria writes, "For Salem is, by interpretation, peace; of which our Saviour is enrolled King, as Moses says, Melchizedek king of Salem, priest of the most high God, who gave bread and wine, furnishing consecrated food for a type of the Eucharist."[10]

Saint Cyprian writes:

Also in the priest Melchisedech we see the Sacrament of the Sacrifice of the Lord prefigured, in accord with that to which the Divine Scriptures testify, where it says: "And Melchisedech, the King of Salem, brought out bread and wine, for he was a priest of the Most High God; and he blessed Abraham." That Melchisedech is in fact a type of Christ is declared in the psalms by the Holy Spirit, saying to the Son, as it were from the Father: "Before the daystar I begot You. You are a Priest forever, according to the order of Melchisedech [Ps 110]." ... And who is more a priest of the Most High God than our Lord Jesus Christ, who, when He offered sacrifice to God the Father, offered the very same which Melchisedech had offered, namely bread and wine, which is in fact His Body and Blood! (*Letter to Cyprian to a Certain Cecil* 63.4).[11]

St Jerome writes,

After the type had been fulfilled by the passover celebration and He had eaten the flesh of the lamb with His Apostles ... just as Melchisedech, the priest of the Most High God, in prefiguring Him, made bread and wine an offering, He too makes Himself manifest in the reality of His own Body and Blood (*Commentaries on the Gospel of Matthew*, 4, 26, 26).[12]

---

[9] Homily 36.7, in John Chrysostom, *Homilies on Genesis 18–45*, trans. Robert C. Hill, The Fathers of the Church, ed. Thomas P. Halton, vol. 82 (Washington, D.C.: Catholic University of America Press, 1990), 331.

[10] *Stromateis* 4.25, in Clement of Alexandria, "The Stromata, or Miscellanies", in *Fathers of the Second Century: Hermas, Tatian, Athenagoras, Theophilus, and Clement of Alexandria (Entire)*, ed. Alexander Roberts, James Donaldson, and A. Cleveland Coxe, The Ante-Nicene Fathers, vol. 2 (Buffalo, N.Y.: Christian Literature Company, 1885), 439.

[11] W. A. Jurgens, trans., *The Faith of the Early Fathers*, vol. 1 (Collegeville, Minn.: Liturgical Press, 1970–1979), 232.

[12] Ibid., 2:203.

The *Catechism* speaks of the king-priest of Salem as a "figure of Christ" (*CCC* 58) and a "prefiguration of the priesthood of Christ" (*CCC* 1544), of Christ as the definitive fulfillment of priest and king (*CCC* 436) and the offering of bread and wine to Abram as a prefiguring of the Church's own offering of the Body and Blood of Christ (*CCC* 1333, 1350). Paragraph 1544 summarizes, "The Christian tradition considers Melchizedek, 'priest of God Most High,' as a prefiguration of the priesthood of Christ, the unique 'high priest after the order of Melchizedek'." Patrick Reardon summarizes it nicely, "'Who had the bread and wine?' asked Ambrose of Milan. 'Not Abraham,' he answered, 'but Melchizedek. Therefore he is the author of the Sacraments' (*De Sacramentis* 4.10). The living memory of Melchizedek thus abides deeply in the worship of the Christian Church."[13]

LITURGICAL NOTE: *Melchizedek in the Church's Liturgy*

"The sacrifices offered by Abel, Abram, and Melchizedek are invoked in Eucharistic Prayer I (the Roman Canon): 'Be pleased to look upon these offerings ... and to accept them, / as once you were pleased to accept / the gifts of your servant Abel the just, / the sacrifice of Abraham, our father in faith, / and the offering of your high priest Melchizedek.' Melchizedek, though he appears only briefly in Genesis, is proclaimed in the readings at Mass on the Solemnity of the Most Holy Body and Blood of Christ (*Corpus Christi*) and for the Conferral of Holy Orders; he is hymned also in the Entrance Antiphon of the Votive Mass of Our Lord Jesus Christ, the Eternal High Priest."[14] (See *CCC* 58, 1333, 1544.)

THEOLOGICAL NOTE: *El Elyon, God Most High*

In these short five verses (Gen 14:18–22) God is referred to four times as "God Most High", which is a rare name for God. In fact,

---

[13] Patrick Henry Reardon, *Creation and the Patriarchal Histories: Orthodox Christian Reflections on the Book of Genesis* (Chesterton, Ind.: Ancient Faith Publishing, 2008), 73.

[14] *The Didache Bible, Ignatius Press Edition* (San Francisco: Ignatius Press, 2016), 19.

in Scripture it is only used twice elsewhere—Psalm 78:35 and Sirach 50:17. In Hebrew it is *El Elyon;* a very ancient name, probably derived from a Canaanite creator god. "If '*elyon* was once the name of a pagan deity, there is no consciousness of this in the Bible and, like '*el*, it is simply an epithet of the One God."[15] This is certainly how Abram used the name in verse 22, to signify Yahweh the God of Glory.

ABRAM REJECTS COMPENSATION FROM THE KING OF SODOM (GEN 14:21–24)

Genesis 14 ends with Sodom's king making a demand of Abram, as though he had any right to do so after Abram had just delivered him. Abram rejected his demand and offer, not wanting to be entangled in his affairs or be obligated in any way. Whether Abram knew of Sodom's wickedness at this point is unknown, but he wisely stayed aloof from a city and its king soon to be destroyed for its wickedness.

[15] Nahum M. Sarna, *Genesis*, The JPS Torah Commentary (Philadelphia: Jewish Publication Society, 1989), 381.

CHAPTER 15

GOD'S COVENANT WITH ABRAM
AND PROMISE OF A SON

INTRODUCTION AND ABRAM'S JUSTIFICATION

At one time or another most Catholics have been on the receiving end of a zealous Evangelical Protestant's attempt to "get you saved". Understanding the life of Abraham is great preparation. I received such a call from a man (let's call him Jerry), who claimed to be fascinated with my conversion from Baptist to Catholic and asked to meet. Always happy to share, we invited him for dinner. It became quickly apparent that he was an ex-Catholic, now Baptist, with a self-appointed "ministry" to evangelize Catholics.

Jerry quoted John 3:16 from the *King James Version* of the Bible, unaware that I had memorized that verse when I was seven years old. With great seriousness he leaned forward and recited, "For God so loved the world, that he gave his only begotten Son, that whosoever believeth in him should not perish, but have everlasting life." He emphasized that we are saved once-and-for-all the moment we believe in Christ. Jerry then turned his Bible to Genesis 15:6. I knew in advance where he was going since I used to do the same thing. He read, "And [Abram] believed in the LORD; and he counted it to him for righteousness." Jerry stated that at that precise moment, Abram was forever saved just like John 3:16 said!

I asked Jerry if he was aware that "believe" in John 3:16 was in the Greek present tense, which meant, "whoever IS believing IS having eternal life." Jesus said whoever is "now" believing—in the present—is being saved. Surprised but undeterred, Jerry quickly flipped back to Abraham, saying, "Abraham believed God at one point in time and was eternally saved, once and for all." I told Jerry that biblical salvation was a process, not only for Abraham, but for us as well.

148

I then took Jerry on a tour of Abraham's life as described in the Bible (especially in Genesis, Romans, Hebrews, and James), demonstrating how Abraham was "being saved" throughout his life. Abraham had saving faith when he left his homeland (Heb 11:8–10; *CCC* 145). He built an altar and twice "called on the name of the Lord" (Gen 12:8; 13:4). Saint Paul refers back to Abraham in Romans 10:13, telling us "every one who calls upon the name of the Lord will be saved." Was Abraham "saved" when he believed or when he called upon the name of the Lord?

Abraham believed and obeyed. But what if Abraham had said to God, "I believe with all my heart, but I will not obey everything you demand, especially not circumcising myself or offering my son Isaac?" James asks, "Was not Abraham our father justified by works, when he offered his son Isaac upon the altar?" (Jas 2:21). He also states that "a man is justified by works and not by faith alone" (Jas 2:24). Abraham was in the *process* of salvation before his God. At any point, had he said "No", his story would have been very different. Abraham believed God and was justified by his faith, his obedience, and his works.

Four hours later, our dinner guest left with his head spinning— with not a lot more to say. So, with Abraham's journey of salvation in mind, let's jump into the next phase in Abraham's life.

GOD APPEARS TO ABRAM AND
REAFFIRMS PROMISES (15:1–5)

Chapter 15 opens with the first occurrence of the word "vision" in the Bible. God describes this form of communication in Numbers 12:6, "Hear my words: If there is a prophet among you, I the LORD make myself known to him in a vision, I speak with him in a dream." Through a vision, God carried on a direct dialogue with Abram.

God promised to be Abram's *shield*, a poetic image of God's divine protection. In the Psalms alone, *shield* is used nineteen times in a similar manner. Abram had just returned from battle and knew the importance of a good shield. Abram had shunned the spoils of war (Gen 14:22–23), but God now promised exceedingly more—his protection and a very great reward. Following God's promise, we have the first recorded words of Abram speaking to God, and in his words, he falters.

In Eastern cultures, a son is generally considered more significant than we tend to think of a son in the West. We are familiar with calling a son by his father's name. But even today in the Arabic cultures, a father is known, not by his own name, but by the name of his first-born son. For example, my friend and local guide in Israel is named Amer. Our pilgrims call him Amer, as does everyone not privy to society in Nazareth. But, I and everyone in his family and hometown call him *Abu-Philippe*. Philippe is the name of his firstborn son, and the prefix *abu* means "father of". So, the Arab locals know Amer as *Abu-Philippe*. I was honored when the locals began calling me *Abu-Jesse*. A son carries on the family name and inheritance and cares for his mother and sisters. Throughout Scripture, there is no catastrophe worse than not having a son.

With a son being so crucial for him to become a great nation, Abram counters God's generous promise with a lament, saying in effect: "I am happy with your promise, God, but what is it to me if I don't have a son?" The veiled complaint is a reminder of God's implied promise earlier—that of a son to make of Abram a great nation (Gen 12:1–2; *CCC* 2570). Abram feared his servant Eliezer of Damascus, not his own son, would inherit the reward. God vows that Eliezer would *not* be the heir, but, as the Hebrew puts it, the heir would come from his own loins (see Gen 15:4).

God took Abram outside, telling him to count the stars. Abram's own descendants will outnumber the stars he can count. In many locations today the ambient lighting from cities makes it difficult to see the stars in the sky. On our many visits to Mount Sinai at night, where there is no "light pollution", we are stunned by the breathtaking Milky Way, which resembles milk splashed across the sky. *Compton Encyclopedia* informs us, "On a clear dark night, far from the artificial lights of a city, one can see as many as 3,000 stars with the unaided eye at a given time."[1]

GOD REAFFIRMS HIS PROMISES (15:6–8)

God reminds Abram that he brought him out of Ur of the Chaldeans and promised him the land of Canaan. "But God," says Abram,

---

[1] "Star", *Compton's Encyclopedia* (Chicago, Ill.: Compton's Encyclopedia, 2015).

"how do I know I'll possess it. I've been here ten years; I still wander around with my sheep. When? I am 85 years old and I *still* don't have a son!" (see Gen 16:3). Even after verse 6, where "he believed the Lord", he still questions how he will know. His questions and frustration are without an accusatory tone. You can sense the depth of his questioning soul with his first words to God: "O Lord God...." He has a tenacious faith in God even in the face of the improbable and impossible. The title *Lord God* expresses his utter recognition of the Creator as absolute Lord. But in this brief moment of reservation or anxiety, he humbly asks God to explain. Who among us does not recognize from experience this sentiment welling up within Abram?

In response, God swears an oath. In Hebrew it is referred to as *ha-berit bein ha-betarim*, which means "the covenant between the pieces".[2] More on that soon.

THEOLOGICAL NOTE: *Abraham, Father of Faith and Works*

"And [Abram] believed the LORD; and he reckoned it to him as righteousness" (Gen 15:6).

This statement stands in bold relief against the backdrop of salvation history. The text comes at a crucial moment in salvation history, profoundly significant for understanding our own salvation and the teaching of the Catholic Church. Nehemiah mentions it (Neh 9:7–8); Paul quotes it with great effect in Romans and Galatians (Rom 4:3, 20–22; Gal 3:6), and James records it as well (Jas 2:23–24). Paul refers to "the faith of Abraham ... the father of us all" and "the father of all who believe" (Rom 4:9–13; *CCC* 146). It is also mentioned at least three times in the *Catechism of the Catholic Church*. Abram is used as the prime example of one who was justified by faith and not by works of the law such as ritual circumcision, dietary restrictions, and ceremonial cleansings (see Acts 15).

When Abram believed, it was reckoned to him as righteousness. The word "reckoned" is a financial accounting term—as in adding or depositing money into an account, a term involving credits and

---

[2] For a full explanation of this covenant and the slaughter of the animals, see Nahum M. Sarna, *Genesis*, The JPS Torah Commentary (Philadelphia: Jewish Publication Society, 1989), 111–12.

debits. In response to his trust, God rewarded Abram by reckoning it to him as righteousness—he credited the righteousness into Abram's account. It has the meaning of "merit" in that Abram's faith "merited" him righteousness.

> *Tanakh* [Jewish OT], which has no stake whatever in Christian debates, renders v. 6, "And because he put his trust in the LORD, he reckoned it to his merit." This translation would be a stumbling block to certain eyes, but *tsedaka* can mean many things. In modern Hebrew it is a charitable gift, as to the United Jewish Appeal. It can also mean uprightness of conduct—justice by God's standard—or, as here, a reward for a good deed. That deed is an expression of total trust in the Lord. If the divine covenantal promise (whose ritual sealing is described below in vv. 7–20) is that Abram would yet have an heir by his true wife, he believes it.[3]

Saint Ambrose, a Doctor of the Church wrote, "Abraham believed, not because he was drawn by a promise of gold or silver but because he believed from the heart. 'It was reckoned to him as righteousness.' A reward was bestowed that corresponded to the test of his merit."[4]
Saint Paul comments on this passage in Romans 4:

> In hope [Abraham] believed against hope, that he should become the father of many nations; as he had been told, "So shall your descendants be." He did not weaken in faith when he considered his own body, which was as good as dead because he was about a hundred years old, or when he considered the barrenness of Sarah's womb. No distrust made him waver concerning the promise of God, but he grew strong in his faith as he gave glory to God, fully convinced that God was able to do what he had promised. That is why his faith was "reckoned to him as righteousness." (Rom 4:18–22)

Man can never merit eternal life on his own. The initial act of God's love and mercy, when responded to with faith like Abram's, is a gratuitous and free gift of God's grace based on the merits of Christ.

---

[3] Gerard S. Sloyan, *Preaching from the Lectionary: An Exegetical Commentary* (Minneapolis, Minn.: Fortress Press, 2003), 565.

[4] *On Abraham*, 2.8.48, in Mark Sheridan, *Genesis 12–50*, Ancient Christian Commentary on Scripture OT 2 (Downers Grove, Ill.: InterVarsity Press, 2002), 32.

It is "reckoned" to us by God as it was to Abraham. However, subsequent to God's bestowal of initial justification, and moved by the Holy Spirit, we can merit graces, cooperate with the Holy Spirit in our lives, and attain to eternal life (*CCC* 1843, 2009–2011).

The same accounting term is used of another Old Testament figure, but apparently for a different reason. Phinehas acted to defend God's honor in Numbers 25:6–13, and because of his actions the Psalmist writes, "Then Phinehas stood up and interposed, and the plague was stayed. And that has been reckoned to him as righteousness from generation to generation for ever" (Ps 106:30–31). Faith is not mentioned as the basis for the "accounting" here; rather, it was the actions or works of Phinehas that caused righteousness to be credited to his account. And the result of God's "reckoning" was righteousness and a special promise of God to Phinehas and his future generations.

Genesis 15:6 is celebrated in the liturgical life of the Church on Wednesday of the 12th Week in Ordinary Time, Year 1; the 2nd Sunday of Lent, Year C; and Holy Family, Year B.

GOD'S COVENANT WITH ABRAM (15:9–21)

In Genesis 15:7, God reminded Abram of his history, how the Lord had brought him out of Ur of the Chaldeans. The phrase "brought you out" is reminiscent of wording that would later be associated with the Israelites being "brought out" of Egypt. Like Mary believing the astounding words of an angel, Abram did not doubt God but wanted to understand how and when what God promised would come to pass. God answered with a sworn oath—a covenant. Abram was told to bring a heifer, a she-goat, a ram, a turtledove, and a young pigeon. He cut them in halves and laid them out; but he did not split the birds. Abram remained to chase off the birds of prey.

This is not the first time we have seen animals killed for spiritual purposes. In Genesis 3:21, animals were slain to provide skins to cover the shame of Adam and Eve's nakedness after they sinned. Abel sacrificed "firstlings of his flock" and was accepted by God (Gen 4:4). Animal sacrifice is alien as a practice to modern culture. Most of us would find it hard to imagine God commanding a believer today to slaughter animals to ratify a covenant. Someone would surely protest and demand that no animals be injured in any liturgical service. The sacrifice Abram offered involved real blood and guts, and even birds of prey swooped in to eat the carnage.

But this was not a sacrifice in the sense we usually see sacrifices elsewhere in the Bible. There are no altars, no sprinkling of blood, and no eating of the sacrificed animals. The slaughter and splitting of animals was the sign of a covenant. When two parties killed animals and passed between the carcasses, they were basically saying, "Let this happen to either of us if we fail to fulfill our pledge!" (cf. Jer 34:18). It was obviously a common practice since God did not have to tell Abram what to do with the animals. He knew to kill them and cut them in two.

Scott Hahn notes, "A covenant oath is solemnly sworn and then ritually enacted. Ancient Near Eastern texts offer many examples of such sworn oath rituals, like the one presented in an Assyrian text (754 B.C.): 'This head is not the head of a lamb, it is the head of Mati'ilu [the covenant-maker]. If Mati'ilu sins against this covenant, so may, just as the head of this spring lamb is torn off ... the head of Mati'ilu be torn off.' "[5]

Similar covenant oath rituals of self-malediction are attested in Scripture (Gen 15:7–21), where Abram cuts the animals in half for the Lord to pass between the pieces (see Jer 34:18). Other kinds of self-maledictory rituals are also found in Scripture, such as animal sacrifice and the sprinkling of blood (Ex 24:8; Ps 50:5), which seem to convey a similar message: "May our blood be shed as the blood of these victims."[6] Abram realized God was very serious if he was willing to put himself under such a covenantal oath.

The dramatic stage was set for a frightful, unexpected announcement. The slaughtered animals, the setting sun, and the approaching darkness only extenuated the scene as a deep sleep fell on Abram. Adding to the gloom a "dread and great darkness fell upon him" (Gen 15:12). The news was dire, but the end was the fulfillment of the promises to Abram. While deep in sleep, God explained to

[5] The source of this quote is James Bennett Pritchard, ed., *The Ancient Near Eastern Texts Relating to the Old Testament*, 3rd ed. with supplement (Princeton: Princeton University Press, 1969), 532–33.

[6] Scott Hahn, "Covenant", *The Lexham Bible Dictionary*, ed. John D. Barry et al. (Bellingham, Wash.: Lexham Press, 2016).

Abram how God's promises and the future would unfold regarding his descendants. Abram got the bad news first—his descendants would sojourn in a foreign land (we know to be Egypt) and would suffer subsequent slavery and oppression for four hundred years. They would not possess the land of Canaan until after this difficult period. Abram was finally getting some information from God, but it was ominous to say the least. Then he got the good news—after his descendants were slaves in the foreign country, they would come out wealthy and free and return to possess this land (vv. 12–16). Afterward, a smoking fire pot and a flaming torch passed between the animal carcasses as God ratified his covenant (v. 17).

Many Jews consider this possession of the land as an everlasting covenant between God and Abraham's descendants even to this present day. There is no suggestion that the covenant was limited by an expiration clause; rather, it was an everlasting covenant (Gen 17:7–8). The gifts and call of God are irrevocable (Rom 11:29; *CCC* 839). God had made promises to Abram, but now he had sworn an oath—the promise was now a covenant, and God had obligated himself to give the land to Abram's offspring—all of Canaan and from the Nile to the Euphrates (Gen 15:18–21).

The previously ambiguous promises of God were being clarified. Abram now knew that (1) he would have descendants, (2) they would sojourn in a foreign land (Egypt), (3) that he himself would live a full life and die in peace, (4) his descendants would be enslaved four hundred years, (5) his descendants would return to the Promised Land with great possessions, (6) their oppressors would be judged (referring to the plagues), and (7) during this time the wickedness of the Amorites in Canaan would ripen enough to justify their punishment (v. 16).

In verse 16, the promise of return would be "in the fourth generation", which must refer to whole life-spans. "*Generation (dôr)* denotes a 'cycle of time, a life span,' which is here calculated to be one hundred years (cf. Ps. 90:10; Isa. 65:20). In Egypt at the time of the patriarchs, 110 was the ideal life span (see Gen. 50:22)."[7]

This is the only time Scripture uses this unique description of death as God's promise "you shall go to your fathers in peace" (v. 15),

---

[7] Bruce K. Waltke and Cathi J. Fredricks, *Genesis: A Commentary* (Grand Rapids, Mich.: Zondervan, 2001), 244.

reassuring Abram he would not himself be exiled into Egypt. It also may have overtones of life after death, which would reunite loved ones, though at this point it is doubtful the author had any understanding of the resurrection of the dead. Since his ancestors were buried in faraway lands, "going to your fathers in peace" seems to imply more than just a physical entombment. Many centuries later, referring to the resurrection from the dead, Jesus chided the Sadducees that God was the God of Abraham, Isaac, and Jacob—not the God of the dead but of the living (Mt 22:31–32). The curtain of eternity was also pulled back so that they could see Abraham, Isaac, and Jacob feasting in the kingdom of God (Lk 13:28).

The trouble soon to engulf Abram's descendants was not because of any weakness or capriciousness in God or any failure on Abram's part. As Didymus the Blind wrote, "From this we learn that if God maltreats someone for a time, he does this not as a matter of indifference but only for some good purpose. Consider too whether this passage might also allude to the sojourn of the saints."[8] God governs all peoples and does so justly.

The peoples occupying Canaan, here referred to as Amorites (15:16), were notoriously sinful. The Amorites (and others listed in Genesis 15:19–21) were pagan people practicing wickedness including all sorts of idolatry, sexual perversions, and infant sacrifice. Their corruption had not reached a point where God would bring about judgment. Their iniquity was not yet complete, or, in other words, not yet ripe enough, but it would be in four hundred years (Lev 18:24–28; Deut 12:29–31). But on the flip side of the coin, Abram could never conceivably conquer the whole land with his 318 men. That would take a massive military force. Abram's offspring needed to grow in number to be capable of conquering and filling the land. Abram would have to wait for God's timing.

---

[8] *On Genesis*, 231, in Sheridan, *Genesis 12–50*, 36.

CHAPTER 16

SARAI AND HAGAR; BIRTH OF ISHMAEL

SARAI BECOMES IMPATIENT (16:1–6)

Abram is now about eighty-five years old and Sarai is seventy-five, but there is still no son. One day Sarai vents her frustration and suggests a shortcut to circumvent God's promise with an alternative method of acquiring a son. Sarai had an Egyptian servant, probably acquired when they fled to Egypt when Pharaoh had given Abram "menservants [and] maidservants" (Gen 12:16). In reality, they were slaves— people who were "owned", in other words. The temptation to "help God out"—and to placate her husband overwhelmed Sarai. She was shamed because infertility was usually attributed to the woman and not the man—so out of desperation she came up with an idea.

Sarai knew according to the laws and customs of the times that a child born to her slave girl from her husband's seed would be her child. She decided to utilize that custom and give Hagar to Abram to provide her a son. Remember that the promise, up to this point, had *not* specifically stated that Sarai would be the mother of this promised son of Abram—only that the son would be from the loins of Abram (see Gen 15:4). So Sarai gave her servant to Abram to produce offspring. This was common practice, even sometimes required, and well-documented in ancient Eastern cultures—well within the moral standards of the day. "As Sarah gave her slave Hagar to Abraham as a concubine (ch. 16:1–4), so at Nuzi [city in ancient Mesopotamia] a marriage contract obliged the wife, if childless, to provide her husband with a substitute. Should a son be born of such a union, the expulsion of the slave wife and her child was forbidden—which explains Abraham's reluctance to send Hagar and Ishmael away (ch. 21:10f.)."[1] Rachel would later do

---

[1] John Bright, *A History of Israel*, 3d ed., Westminster Aids to the Study of the Scriptures (Philadelphia: Westminster Press, 1981), 79. Also see Nahum M. Sarna, *Genesis*, The JPS

the same thing with her husband, Jacob, to secure her progeny (Gen 30:3). Abram had relations with Hagar at the request of Sarai, and in biblical parlance, Abram *knew* Hagar, and she conceived.

Sarai had contempt for Hagar since the slave girl slept with her husband and had provided him with a son, which she had failed to do, and now Hagar treated her mistress with disrespect and scorn. Sarai blamed Abram, even though Abram had done this at the insistence of his wife. Jewish commentator Ramban says that Abram did not hurry the matter; he did not act without permission and acted only at the request of his wife, not through selfish motives.[2]

Even though Sarai had given Hagar as a concubine, Abram told Sarai that Hagar was still under her power—granting her continued "ownership" and authority over Hagar. He told Sarai to do as she pleased. He wanted nothing to do with this squabble. Sarai dealt harshly with Hagar. The Hebrew words for "dealt harshly" imply physical and emotional abuse. Even though ancient Near Eastern laws recognized the right of the mistress to punish an insolent servant, Ramban further commented that "our mother did transgress by this affliction, and Abraham also by his permitting her to do so."[3] Hagar fled into the wilderness. Abram threw his hands up in the air. This whole drama takes on the aura of a soap opera!

THE BIRTH OF ISHMAEL TO HAGAR (16:7–16)

The angel of the Lord approached Hagar by a spring of water in the wilderness (*CCC* 332) and asked her why she was there. She explained, and the angel told her to return to Sarai and submit to her.

Torah Commentary (Philadelphia: Jewish Publication Society, 1989), 119. From another Mesopotamian source, the Lipit-Ishtar Lawcode of 1860 B.C., "If a man's wife has not borne him children (but) a harlot (from) the public square has borne him children, he shall provide grain, oil, and clothing for that harlot; the children which the harlot has borne him shall be his heirs, and as long as his wife lives the harlot shall not live in the house with his wife." *Collection of Laws from Mesopotamia and Asia Minor, Lipit-Ishtar Lawcode,* par. 27, in James Bennett Pritchard, ed., *The Ancient Near Eastern Texts Relating to the Old Testament,* 3rd ed. with supplement (Princeton: Princeton University Press, 1969), 160. For other examples, Victor P. Hamilton, *The Book of Genesis, Chapters 1–17,* The New International Commentary on the Old Testament (Grand Rapids, Mich.: Eerdmans, 1990), 444.

[2] Rabbi Dr. Charles Chavel, *Ramban Commentary on the Torah* (New York: Shilo Publishing House, 1999), 211.

[3] Ibid., 213.

This is the first time the word *angel* is used in the Bible. *Angel* simply means messenger. According to Saint Augustine, "'Angel' is the name of their office, not of their nature. If you seek the name of their nature, it is 'spirit'; if you seek the name of their office, it is 'angel': from what they are, 'spirit,' from what they do, 'angel.'"[4] An angel is a noncorporeal, purely spiritual being, a spirit, who is a messenger of God.

Hagar was on the road to Shur, meaning she was headed back toward her homeland in Egypt, when the angel of the Lord approached her. The title or description "the angel of the Lord" often refers to God himself (cf. Ex 3:1–6). Moses spoke with God at the burning bush, yet God was referred to as "the angel of the Lord" (Ex 3:2–6). Such instances are referred to as a theophany, which is a revelation or a visible representation of God (*CCC* 707). Hagar said she had seen God himself, "You are a God of seeing.... Have I really seen God and remained alive after seeing him?" (16:13). Therefore, the well was called Beer-lahai-roi, "the well of the Living One who sees me". This place would be mentioned twice again in relationship to Isaac.

The angel of the Lord promised to multiply Hagar's descendants greatly, beyond counting. Her child would be a son to be named Ishmael, meaning "God hears", to remind her that God had heard and given heed to her affliction. Then she was given an unsettling description of the son—he would "be a wild donkey of a man, his hand against every man and every man's hand against him; and he shall dwell over against all his kinsmen" (Gen 16:10–12). Hagar was vindicated in the midst of her distress. The promise of innumerable descendants was similar to the promise made to Abram (Gen 17:4–6). Ishmael would be blessed as a son of Abram, but he was not the son of the promise (see Gen 17:18–21).

It is generally recognized that the Arabs are the descendants of Ishmael, and they are an apt fulfillment of God's promise to Hagar. Ishmael's list of descendants can be read in Genesis 25:12–18:[5] "Ishmael

---

[4] St. Augustine (*CCC* 329); St. Augustine, *En. in Ps.* 103, 1, 15: PL 37, 1348, in Catholic Church, *Catechism of the Catholic Church*, 2nd ed. (Washington, D.C.: United States Catholic Conference, 2000), 85.

[5] "According to the Jewish historian Josephus, the Arabs are descendants of Abraham's son Ishmael (*Ant.* 1.220–221)." Scott Hahn, ed., *Catholic Bible Dictionary* (New York, London, Toronto, Sydney, and Auckland: Doubleday, 2009), 62. "Abraham's own descendants fall into three groups: those descended from Ishmael (Ishmaelites or Arabs), those descended

is regarded as the progenitor of the Arabs, who trace their ancestry back to Abraham, as do the Jews through Isaac. The character of Ishmael as represented in the Genesis narratives is amply illustrated by his descendants, the bedouin Arabs."[6] God certainly kept his promise to Hagar as well as to Abram. His description as "a wild ass of a man" implied that he would be fearless, rugged, and independent—a war-like nomad: "The pere' [wild ass] may refer to the Asiatic (Syrian) wild ass (*Equus hemionus*), known also as Syrian onager. Captured onagers were bred with domestic donkeys and horses to produce mules, but were never domesticated."[7] The wild ass was unafraid, tough, and agile. "The fierce, aggressive way of life of the sons of Ishmael, as depicted in such fine poetic manner in Gen. 16:12, is other than the peaceful nomadic life-style of the patriarchs."[8]

Jeremiah 2:24 describes a wild donkey whose passion is uncontrolled. When one views the history of the Arabs and the nomadic Bedouins, it is not without some similarity to the prophecy and description announced to Hagar.[9] Ishmael's dwelling "over against all of his kinsmen" can be seen today in the political situation between the Jews and Arabs—both sons of Abraham, but from different women.

---

from Isaac (Edomites and Israelites), and those descended from the various sons of Keturah (a collateral line of Arabs).... Abraham's other sons were the sons of concubines, Hagar and Keturah, and he sent them away 'to the east' (Gen. 25:6), i.e., to Arabia. Thus the 12 sons of Ishmael, the son of Hagar, bear the names of 12 peoples of northern Arabia (Gen. 25:13–15; 1 Chr. 1:29–31)." P. Kyle McCarter, Jr. "Abraham", in *Eerdmans Dictionary of the Bible*, ed. David Noel Freedman, Allen C. Myers, and Astrid B. Beck (Grand Rapids, Mich.: Eerdmans, 2000), 10.

[6] W. Baur and R.K. Harrison, "Ishmael", in *The International Standard Bible Encyclopedia, Revised*, ed. Geoffrey W Bromiley (Grand Rapids, Mich.: Eerdmans, 1979–1988), 905.

[7] Oded Borowski, *The New Interpreter's Dictionary of the Bible*, ed. Katharine Doob Sakenfeld (Nashville, Tenn.: Abingdon Press, 2006–2009), s.v. "Wild Ass".

[8] Claus Westermann, *A Continental Commentary: Genesis 12–36* (Minneapolis, Minn.: Fortress Press, 1995), 246.

[9] "Moreover when I had, in the course of this year, prepared three books of the *Commentary*, a sudden furious invasion of the barbarous tribes mentioned by your Virgil as 'the widely roaming Barcæi,' and by sacred Scripture in the words concerning Ishmael, 'He shall dwell in the presence of his brethren,' swept over the whole of Egypt, Palestine, Phenice, and Syria, carrying all before them with the vehemence of a mighty torrent, so that it was only with the greatest difficulty that we were enabled, by the mercy of Christ, to escape their hands." Augustine of Hippo, "Letters of St. Augustin", in *The Confessions and Letters of St. Augustin with a Sketch of His Life and Work*, ed. Philip Schaff, trans. J.G. Cunningham, A Select Library of the Nicene and Post-Nicene Fathers of the Christian Church, First Series, vol. 1 (Buffalo, N.Y.: Christian Literature Company, 1886), 522.

In an elegant example of biblical allegory, Saint Paul contrasts the two sons of Abraham through two women: one in bondage and the other free. "For it is written that Abraham had two sons, one by a slave and one by a free woman. But the son of the slave was born according to the flesh, the son of the free woman through promise. Now this is an allegory: these women are two covenants" (see Gal 4:21–31).

Abram was eighty-six years old when Hagar bore him Ishmael. Abram now had a son, but not the son of promise; Ishmael came as a result of impatience and a human attempt to implement God's plan. Abram was ready for a new phase in this continuing saga.

CHAPTER 17

GOD'S COVENANT SIGN OF CIRCUMCISION

GOD REAFFIRMS THE COVENANT (17:1–9)

Chapter 17 begins a new chapter for Abram. We fast-forward fourteen years from the birth of Ishmael. Abram was seventy-five when he left his homeland for Canaan (Gen 12:4), and Hagar was impregnated ten years later (Gen 16:3). He is now ninety-nine years old. He will soon receive a new name and mark on his flesh. After years of silence, God again speaks, and the covenant is reaffirmed with the promise to multiply his seed beyond number.

Scripture affirms God had a long-term agenda, describing Abraham as "the father of a multitude of nations" (Gen 17:5; *CCC* 59–60). God planned to bless Abraham's own ethnic descendants, but also through Abraham and his seed (offspring) to bless all the nations of the earth (Acts 3:25; *CCC* 706). Little did Abraham know the profound extent of these words—a future fulfillment. Saint Paul explains, "Now the promises were made to Abraham and to his offspring. It does not say, 'And to offsprings,' referring to many; but, referring to one, 'And to your offspring,' which is Christ" (Gal 3:16).

The word *covenant* is used thirteen times in chapter 17. It is referred to as an *everlasting covenant* four times (vv. 7, 8, 13, 19). Abram has persevered in faith and obedience, and God now reaffirms his everlasting covenant. For the first time it is now specified that the son of promise will come, not just through Abraham, but specifically through Sarah (Gen 17:16).

God states that the covenant is an everlasting covenant, not just between God and Abraham, but "your descendants after you throughout their generations for an everlasting covenant", and the covenant includes "all the land of Canaan, for an everlasting possession"

(Gen 17:7–8). The Jewish people considered this a permanent "deed to the land", and even though exiled for periods of time, they believed they would always return because it was their immutable possession. The relationship between God, the land of Canaan (later Israel), and the Jewish people is central and the foundation of the Jewish people. It is hard not to see the establishment of the State of Israel, 1900 years after the destruction of the temple and the resulting diaspora, as related to this promise of the God of Israel.

THEOLOGICAL NOTE: *God Almighty—El Shaddai*

In Genesis 17:1, we are introduced to a new name or title for God, who refers to himself as "God Almighty"—in Hebrew, *El Shaddai*. This term is used forty-eight times in the Old Testament, six times in Genesis. The meaning of the title is hotly debated. English Bibles tend to translate *Shaddai* as "the Almighty", as it was translated from the Hebrew into the Greek and Latin translations. From antiquity, it was translated as "all-powerful"—from *el* meaning "god" and *Shaddai* meaning "all-powerful" or "almighty". The Latin *Vulgate* uses *omnipotent* and the rabbinic tradition breaks *Shaddai* into two words: *who* and *enough*, in other words, "the one who is sufficient".[1] Some suggest that the name means "from the hills" or "the breasted one", since the Hebrew word *shad* means breast. This would portray God, *not* as feminine, but as the nourisher and sustainer of his people.[2] Others suggest that *Shaddai* is associated with the root word for *mountain*, thus "the one far exalted above all", but the ancient understanding seems most appropriate, and most modern translations render it as "God Almighty".

---

[1] R. Laird Harris, Gleason L. Archer, Jr., and Bruce K. Waltke, eds. *Theological Wordbook of the Old Testament* (Chicago: Moody Press, 1999), 907.

[2] "In these passages the combined ideas of God as the all-powerful, all-sufficient, transcendent, sovereign ruler and disposer are present. This meaning is generally accepted, but there are differences as to the exact meaning of the term *Shaddai*. Some have begun with *shad* as the first concept to be considered; its meaning is 'breast, pap, or teat,' and it is considered a 'precious metaphor' of God who nourishes, supplies, and satisfies." Gerard Van Groningen, "God, Names of", *Baker Encyclopedia of the Bible* (Grand Rapids, Mich.: Baker Book House, 1988), 882.

THEOLOGICAL NOTE: *Abram Becomes Abraham*

In Genesis 17:5, God reminds Abram of his covenant, and now he changes Abram's name! A name change is much more significant in Eastern cultures than it is for most of us in the West. It signifies a change in status or standing and usually accompanies a new dignity or calling. A name is integrally associated with a person's essence and character. Until now, Abram's name had been *Abram*, meaning, as we have seen, *exalted father*, but now his name was *Abraham*, which means *father of nations* or *father of a multitude*. From this point on, we will use his new name, Abraham. He had received a new dignity, a new purpose, and new role in salvation history. Abraham's grandson Jacob would also be renamed *Israel*, which would become the name of the new nation from Abraham's seed.

CIRCUMCISION GIVEN AS THE SIGN OF THE COVENANT (17:10–14)

I suspect Abraham was thrilled finally to receive a sign of the covenant—something worth all his efforts and patience. And then the news was dropped in his lap (pun intended) that the sign of the covenant was circumcision (Gen 17:11). Abraham must have thought, "I am almost 100 years old, and you want me to cut off *what*?" And that was not the worst of it. Abraham was required to circumcise all 318 trained men in his household (Gen 14:14). Imagine Abraham calling his men together for the news: "Hey men, God met with me yesterday. Do you want to hear the good news first or the bad news?"

From then on, circumcision was required for all male infants on the eighth day (Gen 17:12). Infants were brought into the covenant with God by their parents through circumcision, similar to the way infants today are brought into the New Covenant by their parents through baptism. At the inception of the Church, it was mainly adults converting to the faith, thus the prevalence of adult baptism. But after things settled down, and more and more children were born to Christian parents, baptisms came to be administered more often to infants, as circumcision had been applied to infants in the Old Covenant (*CCC* 1250–52).

In modern times, circumcision is a common procedure in the West mainly for medical or health reasons. Among Jews, circumcision is an everlasting sign of the covenant, applying to any males whether born Jewish, converts, or servants (17:12). Any male not circumcised would be cut off from the people (17:14). For the ancient Jews, circumcision was a mark on the flesh that branded them for God. Even today it remains a covenantal sign. While most non-Israelites considered it a mutilation, for the Jews it was a sign of honor—they uniquely belonged to God. This covenant was not merely a contract with God but was a family pledge or an oath passed down from a father to a son. God had adopted Abraham and his descendants for this covenantal and familial relationship.

CULTURAL NOTE: *Circumcision*

Whenever a Jewish boy is born, joyous shouts of "*Mazel tov*" resound through the neighborhood. The parents plan for the local *mohel* to circumcise their son on the eighth day. The circumcision is so important that it will take place even if the eighth day falls on the Sabbath (Jn 7:23). No matter how capable a physician might be in removing the foreskin of the penis, it is performed by a Jewish *mohel* trained in the laws of circumcision. The procedure is called *bris*. I visited a rabbi in Jerusalem, and he showed me his instruments used to perform the *bris*—disposable scalpels made of precision stainless steel. The operation today is performed under very sterile conditions, quite different from the flint knives used in antiquity (Ex 4:25; Josh 5:2–3).

According to the *Dictionary of Judaism in the Biblical Period*, "The rabbis explain circumcision's importance by describing the foreskin as a disgusting imperfection, the removal of which renders the body perfect (M. Nedarim 3:11). In line with this, only after circumcision did God tell Abraham, 'Walk before me and be perfect' (Gen. 17:1; see also Gen. Rabbah 46). In this same passage, circumcision is described as the primary purpose for which God created the world in the first place, the embodiment of the covenant that made creation worthwhile."[3]

[3] Jacob Neusner, Editor in Chief, and William Scott Green, ed., *Dictionary of Judaism in the Biblical Period* (Peabody, Mass.: Hendrickson, 1996), 121.

The ancient traditions continue among the Jews today:

> The father recites a formula in which he declares that he is ready to fulfill the mitzvah of circumcising his son according to the divine commandment (Gen. 17:12). He then delivers his son to the *sandek* [person designated to hold the baby during the circumcision ceremony], usually one of the infant's grandfathers, who holds the boy on a pillow placed on a table or on his lap during the procedure. In many communities, the *sandek* sits on a special "chair of Elijah"; in some traditions the chair remains unoccupied at his immediate right.
>
> As a surrogate for the father, the *mohel* then recites the blessing for the circumcision and preforms the procedure. The father, or both parents in some communities, recites a blessing entering the child into the covenant "of Abraham our father." All present then respond: "As he has entered the covenant, so may he be brought to *Torah, huppah, uma'asim tovim* [to the study of Torah, to the marriage canopy, and to the practice of good deeds]."[4]

Jews believe that Elijah the prophet is present at each *bris*. It is the traditional belief that Elijah will crown the Messiah when he appears. To accomplish this, Elijah must appear at each circumcision to ascertain if this boy is the promised one. The infant boy is also given a name at the ceremony (just as Jesus was named at his circumcision, Lk 2:21). And then the festivities begin!

As obedient Jews, the parents of John the Baptist, Jesus, and Paul made sure their sons were all circumcised like their ancestors before them on the eighth day (Lk 1:59; 2:21; Phil 3:5) in obedience to God (Ex 12:48; Lev 12:3). Circumcision was an extremely important *mitzvah* (command of God)—the divinely appointed sign of the covenant among the Jews; no uncircumcised male could partake in the life and liturgy of Israel. Even today, when a Jewish baby is circumcised, it is time for celebration because he has been incorporated into the "Covenant of Abraham, our patriarch", which is still a profound acknowledgment after four thousand years.

In the early Church, many Jewish Christians demanded Gentile converts be circumcised to become Christians. After all, in Greek the word *Christ* corresponds to the Hebrew word *Messiah*. A "Christian",

---

[4] Ronald L. Eisenberg, *The JPS Guide to Jewish Traditions* (Philadelphia: Jewish Publication Society, 2004), 10–11.

then, is literally one who follows the Jewish Messiah. It was claimed that Gentiles must become Jews first to appropriate the *Christ*. But at the Council of Jerusalem in A.D. 49 (Acts 15), the Church decreed that circumcision was unnecessary for Gentiles. Whereas Jewish babies were brought into the Old Covenant through circumcision, Christian baptism now replaced circumcision (Col 2:11–13; *CCC* 527).

Scripture provides a summary of this period in Abraham's life: "Abraham was the great father of a multitude of nations, and no one has been found like him in glory; he kept the law of the Most High, and was taken into covenant with him; he established the covenant in his flesh, and when he was tested he was found faithful" (Sirach 44:19–20).

FROM SARAI TO SARAH (17:15–16)

The promise included a son given to Abraham through his wife, Sarai, who was now brought fully into the covenantal oath: "As for Sarai your wife, you shall not call her name Sarai, but Sarah shall be her name. I will bless her, and moreover I will give you a son by her; I will bless her, and she shall be a mother of nations; kings of peoples shall come from her" (Gen 17:15–16).

Like Abraham, Sarai shared in the covenant and therefore also merited a name change from Sarai to Sarah—seemingly a "modernization" of the name—but both mean *princess*. The text gives us no explanation for the name change or what it signifies, but it is significant that Sarah is the only woman in the Bible who receives a new name. Abraham's heir would come from the womb of Sarah, even though she was beyond childbearing years (Rom 4:19). Sarah, the *princess*, would be a mother of nations, and kings would come from her: "By faith Sarah herself received power to conceive, even when she was past the age, since she considered him faithful who had promised" (Heb 11:11; *CCC* 145).

ABRAHAM LAUGHS AT THE PROMISE
OF A SON (17:17–22)

After hearing that Sarah would give birth, Abraham fell on his face and laughed, saying to himself, "Will I father a child at 100 years old with a wife who is ninety?" Abraham said this to himself, so we do not know the tone of his voice or his facial expression. But we get a hint of his attitude when he suggested to God that since this was so unlikely, why not just let Ishmael be his heir. God was not offended; rather, he reconfirmed his promise that the special son would come from the womb of Sarah. God even told him the name of his son would be Isaac, which means *laughter*. Sarah would also laugh later, and all this laughter would become their son's name.

Abraham had raised the issue of his son Ishmael so God now responded, telling Abraham that Ishmael would be the father of twelve princes and a great nation—his progeny would also be blessed beyond measure (v. 20), but the promise of the covenant would be established through the son Sarah herself would bear—and God pledged that the son of the promise would be in Sarah's arms by the same time next year. After twenty-five years, the promise was finally being realized.

ABRAHAM, ISHMAEL, AND ALL HIS MEN ARE CIRCUMCISED (17:23–27)

To fulfill his part of the covenant, Abraham immediately sharpened the flint knives. He and Ishmael and all the men of Abraham's house were circumcised. He did not hesitate, negotiate, or try to weasel out of the situation. Scripture twice says the flint knives cut the flesh "that very day"—twice to emphasize the immediacy of Abraham's obedience (Gen 17:23, 26). Abraham was ninety-nine years old, and Ishmael was thirteen. Abraham was now ready to receive the son of promise for which he had waited so long.

Those who claim that Christians are saved by "faith alone", in a once-saved-always-saved fashion, should ponder what the results would have been if Abraham, confronted with the flint knife, had said, "No, at my age; too painful, I won't be circumcised!" But he did not. He said, "Yes." His was an *obedient* faith.

CHAPTER 18

THE LORD VISITS ABRAHAM;
PROMISE OF ISAAC'S BIRTH

THE LORD VISITS ABRAHAM AND HOSPITALITY
TO STRANGERS (18:1–8)

Unlike urban life along the Euphrates River back in Ur, in Canaan, Abraham lived in a tent. And like a Bedouin, he was a nomadic shepherd following the seasons with his flocks on land he did not own. His tents were set up at the Oaks of Mamre, about a mile north of the modern city of Hebron (Gen 13:8). The site can be visited today. It is called *Ramat el-Khalil*, or, in English, the "High Place of the Friend" because Abraham was described as the friend of God (Is 41:8; 2 Chron 20:7; Jas 2:23). "The Septuagint refers to 'the oak of Mamre', which would imply that one of the oaks was already being venerated as Abraham's altar."[1] In the first century, Josephus wrote of an ancient oak tree outside Hebron (*War of the Jews*, 4.534). King Herod the Great built massive walls around the site, encompassing an area of 150 by 200 feet to preserve it, and Emperor Constantine built a church on the site in the fourth century to honor Abraham.[2]

In Hebron the temperature can hover around 95° in the summer. It is no surprise that chapter 18 opens with Abraham sitting in the door of his tent in the heat of the day. This would imply it was around the noon hour, when you would not expect travelers to be

---

[1] Avraham Negev, *The Archaeological Encyclopedia of the Holy Land* (New York: Prentice Hall Press, 1990), 313.

[2] To see the biblical site of the Oaks of Mamre, see our documentary *Abraham, Father of Faith and Works*, in the Footprints of God series produced by Ignatius Press.

out in the sun. Abraham lifted his eyes, and behold, he saw three men standing before him. The text does not say he watched them walk up; rather, it appears he was startled to see them just standing as though they suddenly appeared. In this encounter, the spiritual mysteries run deep (*CCC* 2571).

Abraham's instant response was dramatic. He jumped from his seated position, ran out to meet them, and bowed himself to the earth. Though there were three men, Abraham addressed them in the singular, saying, "My lord". He invited them to remain with the words "do not pass by your servant" and offered them his extraordinary hospitality (Gen 18:2–3).

On a personal note, years ago, when visiting the site commemorating Abraham's visitation in Hebron, the caretaker showed us what Abraham's hospitality must have looked like. We had never experienced such a welcome. He literally ran to open the gate, ebulliently invited us in with repeated bows. After opening the gate, he ran down the lane ahead of us to set up chairs in the shade of the huge oak trees. For the next hour, he rushed to and fro bringing us grapes from the vineyard, then rushing to make us tea before hurrying off to bring snacks. He even climbed up in trees to pick us fresh fruit. I remember saying to my wife, Janet, "This man reminds me of Abraham!"

THE MYSTERY OF THE TRINITY

In Christian tradition, the three men who appeared to Abraham are often taken as a theophany, a revelation or visible representation of God. The most famous image of this mysterious encounter is the Andre Rublev's icon entitled *Holy Trinity* (ca. 1410–ca. 1420), in the Tretiakov Gallery in Moscow. It pictures three angelic beings sitting at Abraham's table with the oak tree behind. In the *Septuagint* translation of this passage, it states that God (*theos*) was seen by Abraham at the oak of Mamre. In the Hebrew text, it says *Yahweh* visited Abraham. Most English translation use "the Lord", but the original languages provide more clarity with *theos* and *Yahweh*. It is clear these are not your average visitors! While many interpret this as simply three angels, or a self-revelation of the Lord with two angels, others have perceived the mystery of the Trinity.

Consider the perceptive words of Saint Ambrose:

Abraham, ready to receive strangers, faithful towards God, devoted in ministering, quick in his service, saw the Trinity in a type; he added religious duty to hospitality, when beholding Three he worshipped One, and preserving the distinction of the Persons, yet addressed one Lord, he offered to Three the honour of his gift, while acknowledging one Power.... He brings forth three measures of fine meal, and slays one victim, considering that one sacrifice is sufficient, but a triple gift; one victim, an offering of three.[3]

Saint Augustine echoes these thoughts:

I could put these questions, if it had been one man that appeared to Abraham, and if that one were believed to be the Son of God. But since three men appeared, and no one of them is said to be greater than the rest either in form, or age, or power, why should we not here understand, as visibly intimated by the visible creature, the equality of the Trinity, and one and the same substance in three persons?[4]

In John 8:56 Jesus seems to allude to this event when he replied to the Pharisees with a statement they considered to be blasphemous: " 'Your father Abraham rejoiced that he was to see my day; he saw it and was glad.' The Jews then said to him, 'You are not yet fifty years old, and have you seen Abraham?' Jesus said to them, 'Truly, truly, I say to you, before Abraham was, I am [I AM].' So, they took up stones to throw at him" (Jn 8:56–59).[5] "I am" is the name of God (Ex 3:14),

---

[3] Ambrose of Milan, "The Two Books on the Decease of His Brother Satyrus", bk. 2, sec. 97, in *St. Ambrose: Select Works and Letters*, ed. Philip Schaff and Henry Wace, trans. H. de Romestin, E. de Romestin, and H. T. F. Duckworth, A Select Library of the Nicene and Post-Nicene Fathers of the Christian Church, Second Series, vol. 10 (New York: Christian Literature Company, 1896), 189–90.

[4] Augustine of Hippo, "On the Trinity", bk. 2, chap. 11, in *St. Augustin: On the Holy Trinity, Doctrinal Treatises, Moral Treatises*, ed. Philip Schaff, trans. Arthur West Haddan, A Select Library of the Nicene and Post-Nicene Fathers of the Christian Church, First Series, vol. 3 (Buffalo, N.Y.: Christian Literature Company, 1887), 47.

[5] There is a diversity of opinions among the Fathers as to when it was that Abraham saw the day of the Lord and rejoiced. Some of the Fathers pointed to Genesis 18: "S. Jerome and S. Gregory say that it was the day when, by the three angels that appeared to him, only one of whom spoke to him, the mystery of the Trinity was by symbols revealed to him; he saw three but adored one (Gen. 18:2)." Cornelius à Lapide, *The Great Commentary of Cornelius à Lapide: S. John's Gospel—Chapters 1 to 11*, trans. Thomas W. Mossman, 3rd ed., vol. 5 (Edinburgh: John Grant, 1908), 332.

and the Jews clearly understood he was claiming to be the eternal I AM of the exodus.[6] "Of this vision our Lord spoke to the Jews in the Gospel when He said: 'Abraham rejoiced that he was to see my day. He saw it and was glad.' He saw my day, He says, because he recognized the mystery of the Trinity."[7] At other times the Jews tried to stone him because he infuriated them with his claims. "The Jews answered him, 'We stone you for no good work but for blasphemy; because you, being a man, make yourself God'" (Jn 10:33).

They could not accept that Jesus was God, that he was *before* Abraham and had seen and been seen *by* Abraham. "They answered him, 'Abraham is our father.' Jesus said to them, 'If you were Abraham's children, you would do what Abraham did, but now you seek to kill me, a man who has told you the truth which I heard from God; this is not what Abraham did'" (8:39–40). The Jewish leaders tried to kill Jesus.

When did Abraham treat Jesus differently from the way the Jewish leaders were treating him in John 8? Jesus is certainly referring back to Genesis 18. "The Lord" arrived at Abraham's tent. Instead of trying to kill him, Abraham extended the most outrageous hospitality. The contrast between Abraham's eager reception of the Lord and the Jewish leaders' reception of Jesus could not be more pronounced. Jesus chided unbelievers among the Jews of his time—if they were *really* the sons of Abraham, why did they not receive him the way Abraham did at his tent in Hebron? The *Catechism* comments on Abraham's actions. He was eager to show hospitality to the mysterious Guest(s) because he believed in God and walked in his presence and they had a covenantal relationship (*CCC* 2571).

ABRAHAM'S HOSPITALITY

Abraham showed hospitality with speed and alacrity—notice the action. As soon as he saw them, he *ran* to meet them, he *bowed himself*

---

[6] To emphasize this, the *New American Bible* specifically capitalizes I AM, making it clear the translators consider that Jesus and St. John here used the Divine Name, which nearly incites the Jews to stone Jesus for blasphemy.

[7] Sermon 83.5, in Caesarius of Arles, *Saint Caesarius of Arles: Sermons (1–238)*, ed. Hermigild Dressler and Bernard M. Peebles, trans. Mary Magdeleine Mueller, The Fathers of the Church, vol. 2 (Washington, D.C.: Catholic University of America Press; Consortium Books, 1956–1973), 14.

to the earth, then *hastened* to tell Sarah to make cakes *quickly*. He *ran* to get a calf and *hastened* to prepare it. Then he *stood* by them as they ate (17:2, 6–7). Abraham's hospitality to three strangers was remarkable and without limit. Of course his behavior showed he possessed the virtue of hospitality. Even so, perhaps Abraham had an inkling of the Divine Presence. The Christian reader may even detect Trinitarian and Eucharistic imagery in the words, "Make ready quickly three measures of fine meal, knead it, and make cakes" (Gen 18:6), although Abraham would not have understood it himself!

Hospitality was very important in biblical times as emphasized in the oral tradition of the Jews: "Extending hospitality to strangers is more important than communion with God [lit. 'receiving the *shekinah*'], for it is written: 'And he [Abraham] said: My Lord, if I have found favor in your sight do not pass away from your servant' (Gn 18:3)."[8] The Fathers of the Church often mention the virtue of hospitality, for example, in the first century, Pope Saint Clement of Rome wrote, "Because of [Abraham's] faith and hospitality a son was given to him in his old age."[9]

In coming down from heaven, God witnessed Abraham's hospitality. In her *Diary, Divine Mercy in My Soul*, Saint Maria Faustina Kowalska had a similar experience. As the Lord had come hungry and tired to the entrance of Abraham's tent, so the Lord came to Saint Maria Faustina at the entrance gate of her convent. In both cases, God had come down from heaven to see if what had reached his ears was true, and in both cases Abraham and Saint Faustina gave the best that they had.

> Jesus came to the main entrance today, under the guise of a poor young man. This young man, emaciated, barefoot and bareheaded, and with his clothes in tatters, was frozen because the day was cold and rainy. He asked for something hot to eat. So I went to the kitchen, but found nothing there for the poor. But, after searching around for some time, I succeeded in finding some soup, which I reheated and into which I crumbled some bread, and I gave it to the poor young man, who ate it. As I was taking the bowl from him, he

---

[8] Bernard McGinn, ed., *The Talmud: Selected Writings*, trans. Ben Zion Bokser, The Classics of Western Spirituality (New York and Mahwah, N.J.: Paulist Press, 1989), 94.

[9] Michael William Holmes, *The Apostolic Fathers: Greek Texts and English Translations*, updated ed. (Grand Rapids, Mich.: Baker Books, 1999), 41.

gave me to know that He was the Lord of heaven and earth. When I
saw Him as He was, He vanished from my sight. When I went back
in and reflected on what had happened at the gate, I heard these
words in my soul: My daughter, the blessings of the poor who bless
Me as they leave this gate have reached My ears. And your compassion, within the bounds of obedience, has pleased Me, and this is
why I came down from My throne—to taste the fruits of your mercy
(paragraph 1312).[10]

The New Testament is quick to exhort us to hospitality. Saint Paul
writes, "Love one another with brotherly affection; outdo one
another in showing honor.... Contribute to the needs of the saints,
practice hospitality" (Rom 12:10, 13). The writer of *Hebrews*, certainly referring to Abraham's experience with the three strangers,
writes, "Do not neglect to show hospitality to strangers, for thereby
some have entertained angels unawares" (Heb 13:2).

Abraham's reception of the three visitors is celebrated in the liturgy on Saturday of the 12th Week in Ordinary Time, Year C, and
the 16th Sunday in Ordinary Time, Year C.

THE PROMISE OF A SON TO BE
NAMED ISAAC (18:9–15)

Abraham watched over his guests as they ate under the tree, but
Sarah remained in the tent. Even today in Middle Eastern culture,
it is common for men to sit around talking with each other while
the women are discreetly in the background. The Lord, in the form
of one of the men, asked for Sarah's whereabouts almost as though
he wanted to give her a message. Since Sarah was not present, the
Lord announced the good news, presumably loud enough for Sarah
to hear. By this time next year Sarah would have a son. The text
again has an element Christian readers have often read in a spiritual
way as anticipating or hinting at the later revelation of the Trinity:
"*They said*, 'Where is Sarah your wife?'" After being informed she

---

[10] St. Maria Faustina Kowalska, *Diary, Divine Mercy in My Soul* (Stockbridge, Mass.: Marian
Press, 2009), 471–72.

was in the tent, we read, "*The LORD said, 'I . . .'*" (Gen 18:9). Plurality asked, and Unity responded.

Sarah had been eavesdropping on the conversation and laughed to herself, "After I have grown old, and my husband is old, shall I have pleasure?" (18:12). The Lord obviously has good ears and asked Abraham why Sarah laughed. Sarah was embarrassed at being overheard as we have all experienced at one time or other (like politicians with an unexpected "live microphone"). She was fearful and must have stepped out from behind the tent flap to deny she had laughed. But the Lord corrected her, "No, but you did laugh" (18:15).

There are two ways to interpret her laughter. First, the surprise and thrill of the announcement inspired her to burst out with joyful laughter. Or, second, and what seems the most natural reading of the text, she laughed in shocked incredulity. The fact that she was fearful and subsequently corrected by the Lord seems to indicate the latter. The Bible does not overlook the weakness of the saints, and we are encouraged by knowing that even saints have their momentary failings.

ABRAHAM INTERCEDES FOR SODOM (18:16–33)

The meal is over, the announcement has been made, and the men prepare to leave. The Lord has obviously come for two reasons. First, to meet Abraham and Sarah—he had a special announcement to make, and it is always nice to make such exciting announcements in person, so to speak. Second, the Lord was aware of the egregious sins of Sodom and Gomorrah so he came to determine if the situation was as bad as he had heard (18:21). The Lord came to bring judgment against the wickedness of those cities.

Again, we see anthropomorphism used to describe God's action among men. God is omniscient and omnipresent; he does not need to *go* anywhere to know the truth of the situation. But he speaks and acts as if he does so human beings can relate to him. Other things God says and does in Scripture balances out this anthropomorphic language to show that God is not limited as human beings are.

God decided to disclose to Abraham what he intended to do with Sodom and Gomorrah. He revealed his intentions to Abraham because Abraham would become a great and mighty nation, and secondly—and this is important—so that seeing the judgment for sin, Abraham would command his household and those coming after him to avoid sin and to live in righteousness and justice so that he might do for Abraham as he had promised (v. 19). God wanted Abraham to realize that this new covenant relationship is serious business. If you want this promise to be fulfilled, do not follow the example of Sodom and Gomorrah. This is not a "faith alone" covenant; it is faith, obedience, and deeds appropriate to the covenant. Notice the whole of verse 19 pivots on the verb "doing". The Lord was using this as a teaching moment—watch what happens to these sinful cities, and be warned!

Some sins are so abominable they cry out to heaven (*CCC* 1867, 1871). Abraham knows that God has not come just to *see*, but he has come to *punish!* Whereas earlier Abraham had bowed before the Lord, now he "stood before the Lord" almost as though he were blocking his way. His nephew Lot lived in Sodom, so Abraham boldly interceded for him. Abraham had also had favorable dealings with the King of Sodom (see Gen 14). He appealed to the goodness and mercy of God. He asked if God would destroy Sodom if there were fifty righteous in the city. He asked if God was so unjust as to sweep away the good with the evil. When God conceded that he would not destroy the city if there were fifty righteous, Abraham kept pushing the issue, acknowledging that he was only "dust and ashes". What about if there were only forty-five? What if there were only forty? What if there were only thirty? I can imagine sweat breaking out on Abraham's brow, appealing to God in such a bold manner. What if there were only twenty? Once more, he takes a deep breath—a pause. What if there were only ten righteous? Would you spare the city for ten? God answers in the affirmative, and Abraham returns to his tent.

It is hard to find a more exquisite example of intercessory prayer (*CCC* 2571, 2635). Abraham was humble, yet persistent. He knew God was just and merciful, so he appealed to God's divine attributes. He was bold but very deferential. The *Catechism* says that Abraham perceived that the Lord was compassionate toward men, and thus he dared to intercede for them with a bold confidence. Abraham courageously walked the tightrope and tactfully avoided toppling into impudence and imprudence. Our hearts stop just imagining this conversation. His humble courage demonstrated that Abraham had come to know his God. At moments like this, we understand why the Bible refers to Abraham as the friend of God. Friends can speak freely.

Saint James tells us, "The prayer of a righteous man has great power in its effects" (5:16). Abraham had hopefully saved his nephew Lot and his family. He dared not push God further. Abraham returned to his place, and the Lord proceeded to Sodom. We await the results of the divine visit to Sodom and Abraham's intercession.

CHAPTER 19

WICKEDNESS AND DESTRUCTION
OF SODOM; LOT RESCUED

INTRODUCTION

It was hot, and people were hiding from the sun under the olive trees. Folks hoped for a wisp of breeze in the doorways of their basalt stone houses. The elders sat in the shade along the Via Maris near Matthew's tax booth rendering judgments on legal matters and discussing current affairs. Today the conversation centered on the charismatic young rabbi wandering around Galilee. The calm was disrupted when a massive throng of people crested the hills to the northwest. They were surrounding the remarkable but troubling young carpenter from Nazareth. Tens of thousands of people followed him even in the heat of the day because he taught with great authority and healed the thousands of sick or possessed who came to him.

In Capernaum, Jesus performed more miracles than anywhere else. Despite his miracles and works of power, the elders and the majority of people did not heed Jesus' words. Therefore, he upbraided the city because they refused to believe and repent. He said, "Woe to you, Capernaum!" *Woe* is an exclamation predicting great sorrow or calamity. Jesus proclaimed that if Sodom had seen the miracles he performed, they would have repented in sackcloth and ashes. "But," says Jesus, "I tell you that it shall be more tolerable on the day of judgment for the land of Sodom than for you" (Mt 11:20–24).

Contrasted with the gravity of Sodom's immoral conduct, one would expect Capernaum to fare better on the day of judgment. Sodom practiced inhospitality with wanton sexual perversion, homosexuality, and gang-raping visitors with unlicensed abandon. They flaunted their defiance against the laws of nature and nature's God.

Their sin was such an abomination that the Lord came down from heaven to see if the reports were true.

But why would the citizens of Capernaum be judged more harshly than the Sodomites? After all, they did not rush en masse to demand sexual relations with Jesus as the men of Sodom had done with the heavenly visitors during Abraham's time (Gen 19:5). One would consider Capernaum's actions more benign. But Sodom had not witnessed the revelation of God in Jesus Christ, and its people were not eyewitnesses of Jesus' miraculous power. They never had the opportunity to see and believe as did Capernaum. As Jesus said, "Every one to whom much is given, of him will much be required" (Lk 12:48). Capernaum's culpable disbelief in the face of God's overwhelming love and power was damnable (*CCC* 678). This applies not only to Capernaum but even more to us who have the full revelation of Jesus Christ as taught by his Church. We have been given much more, and much more will be required of us on judgment day.

With that introduction, we now join the two mysterious sojourners as they left Abraham and arrived at the gates of Sodom as the sun was setting and as Lot greeted them in the city gates.

THE TWO ANGELS ARRIVE IN SODOM; LOT'S HOSPITALITY (19:1-3)

From ancient times, Sodom has traditionally been thought to have been located at the southern end of the Dead Sea, about twenty to thirty miles southeast of Hebron. There is an Israeli city there named *Sedom*, and the Arabs pointed to a rock formation they called "Jebel Usdum", or "Mount Sodom". Nearby is also Zoar, which lends credibility to the southern location of Sodom. The ancient sites and tradition are not to be easily dismissed, but there is some debate among scholars:

> The cities of Sodom and Gomorrah have, at times, been considered mythical, the invention of the biblical author. However, recent archaeological excavations have made a strong case for identifying Sodom and Gomorrah with *Tall-el-Hammam*, a site in what is now the state of Jordan, near the entrance of the river Jordan to the Dead

Sea. If the identification is correct, the archaeological record shows that Sodom and Gomorrah were extremely powerful and wealthy cities in the early second millennium B.C., but were destroyed suddenly by a natural disaster by mid-millennium and remained uninhabited for about 700 years.[1]

There are four theories as to the location of Sodom: (1) The traditional theory that Sodom was at the southern end of the Dead Sea; (2) the newer theory mentioned above that it is located at the northern end of the Dead Sea; (3) that Sodom is somewhere under the water of the Dead Sea; and (4) that it is a mythical city, which for those who trust in the credibility and trustworthiness of the Scriptures, has no credibility since it denies the historicity of the Bible and also considers the accounts of the patriarchs to be mythical as well.

When the "two angels" arrived in the evening, Lot was sitting in the gate, presumably with the leading men of the city. He saw the angels, and, like Abraham, he rose to meet them, bowing with his face to the ground. Sitting in the gates of a city was a common practice, which shows up about thirty times in the Bible. For example, "Her husband is known in the gates, when he sits among the elders of the land" (Prov 31:23). The city gates usually had benches and seats from which the important men of the city conducted business. Civic affairs and judicial rulings were discussed within the view of the people. It was here that news and gossip was peddled. That Lot was sitting in the gates of the city could imply that he was now one of the leading citizens of Sodom.

The three travelers were now two. Two of the men who had been among the "trinity" of travelers at Abraham's tent are now referred to as *angels*. The Hebrew word for angel is *malak*, which means "messenger". These men were divine agents visiting Sodom "disguised" in human form (*CCC* 332). The great mystery of the heavenly presence continues. Lot is certain to have known his neighbors' habitual aggressive sodomy, the very opposite of hospitality, and it is likely he greeted arriving strangers to offer the shelter of his home. There is no evidence the strangers had any special appearance or aura that evoked such a response from Lot, yet Lot, too, addressed them as "my Lords".

With great hospitality Lot invited them to his home to wash their feet, feed them, and give them a room for the night. They declined, preferring to spend the night "in the street", which meant outdoors, probably in a tent or under the stars. But Lot, knowing the immoral climate of his city, insisted they stay in his home. He prepared a feast for them, not unlike the hospitality of Abraham and Sarah. The Hebrew word used for *feast* denotes the drinking of wine. The unleavened bread was quick and easy to make and probably given to slack their hunger while the feast was being prepared.

Washing feet is a disgusting task reserved for the lowest of slaves. This is why Jesus washed his disciples' feet in the Upper Room as a lesson in humility and service. This is the first of over twenty times that the Bible mentions washing of feet. People walked on dirty paths littered with donkey and camel dung, and a good rain made it worse, filling the sandals with muck. I have walked in sandals on such paths. Even today in many Middle Eastern communities, it is considered rude to cross your legs in church or to expose the bottom of your feet. How interesting that the Bible says, "How beautiful are the feet of those who preach good news!" (Rom 10:15). Lot offered them the basic courtesy so they could wash their feet after a long journey.

THE WICKEDNESS OF SODOM (19:4–5)

At first the strangers refused Lot's offer of hospitality—either to test him or to see firsthand the moral condition of the city. They chose to spend the night outdoors. But Lot knew the wickedness of the local men and refused to take no for an answer. Earlier, in Genesis, Sodom's reputation is described, "Now the men of Sodom were wicked, great sinners against the LORD" (Gen 13:13). Before retiring for the night, all the men of Sodom, young and old, surrounded Lot's house and demanded he bring the visitors out.

The sinfulness of Sodom was not underestimated as the men approached to rape the visitors. Imagine the fear as a gang surrounded the house shouting lewd demands: "Where are the men who came to you tonight? Bring them out to us, that we may know them"

(Gen 19:5). The phrase "that we may know them" is clearly a euphemism for sexual relations (as when "Adam knew Eve, and she conceived") (cf. Gen 4:1). See Judges 19:22–25 for the same language describing a very similar vile situation.

THEOLOGICAL AND MORAL NOTE:
What Was the Sin of Sodom?

In the Law of Moses, the people of Israel were commanded not to live according to the conduct of Egypt or Canaan, whose inhabitants practiced perverse conduct such as homosexuality, considered an abomination in the eyes of God (Lev 18:3, 22–30). The Sodomites were prime examples of this forbidden behavior. The *Concise Oxford English Dictionary* defines *sodomy* as "anal intercourse" and then "from late Latin *peccatum Sodomiticum* 'sin of Sodom'".[2] Homosexual rape is the obvious intention expressed in verse 5. The city of Sodom became synonymous with brazen sin (Is 3:9; Lam 4:6; Jude 7).

The sexual sins of Sodom were all the more egregious because they were piled on top of the city's wicked treatment of these guests and the people's treacherous inhospitality. Ezekiel lists their sins as he compares Jerusalem with her "sister Sodom": "Behold, this was the guilt of your sister Sodom: she and her daughters [surrounding cities] had pride, surfeit of food, and prosperous ease, but did not aid the poor and needy. They were haughty, and did abominable things before me; therefore I removed them, when I saw it" (Ezek 16:49–50).

Homosexual rights activists sometimes claim that the crime committed in Sodom was not homosexual rape but the lack of hospitality, based primarily on the above passage in Ezekiel. But it is clear from Scripture and the constant teaching of both the Jews and the Church that the sin of Sodom is twofold: first, people engaging in homosexual acts, which are regarded as an abominable abuse of sexuality (Lev 18:22); and second, the men of Sodom intended to rape what they took to be visitors. Ezekiel says, as we noted, that the Sodomites "did abominable things before me". Although hospitality was highly valued, the mere lack of it among the men of Sodom can hardly be

---

[2] "Sodomy", Catherine Soanes and Angus Stevenson, eds., *Concise Oxford English Dictionary* (Oxford: Oxford University Press, 2004).

understood as warranting the label "abomination". The *Catechism* refers to this event in Sodom when it explains the disordered and grave sin of homosexual acts (*CCC* 2357).

First-century Jewish historian Josephus explains that the sins of the Sodomites were not just inhospitality or even homosexual actions, including rape, but a combination of sinful conduct. He wrote, "About this time the Sodomites grew proud, on account of their riches and great wealth: they became unjust toward men, and impious toward God, insomuch that they did not call to mind the advantages they received from him: they hated strangers, and abused themselves with Sodomitical practices."[3]

The New Testament also points to the vile sexual conduct of the Sodomites as the sin that brought about their destruction. According to 2 Peter 2:6–7, the burning of Sodom and Gomorrah made them an example to others considering an ungodly life, and God rescued righteous Lot, who was "greatly distressed by the licentiousness of the wicked". The word *licentiousness* is defined as "sensuality, debauchery, licentiousness, lewdness, i.e., be unrestrained in moral attitudes and behaviors".[4]

The rest of the New Testament also condemns homosexual acts (Rom 1:24–27; 1 Cor 6:9; 1 Tim 1:10). This is confirmed in Jude 7, "Just as Sodom and Gomorrah and the surrounding cities, which likewise acted immorally and indulged in unnatural lust, serve as an example by undergoing a punishment of eternal fire." The Greek words rendered "unnatural lust" are *sarkos heteras*, "(an idiom, literally 'to go after strange flesh') to engage in unnatural sexual intercourse— 'to have homosexual intercourse ... like the people of Sodom and Gomorrah' (Jude 7)."[5]

Some interpreters explain going after "strange flesh" as the desire to have sex with angels rather than humans.[6] While this may be a

---

[3] *Antiquities of the Jews* 1:11, in *The Works of Josephus: Complete and Unabridged*, trans. William Whiston, updated edition (Peabody, Mass.: Hendrickson, 1987), 40.

[4] James Swanson, *Dictionary of Biblical Languages with Semantic Domains: Greek (New Testament)* (Oak Harbor: Logos Research Systems, 1997), ref. no. 816.

[5] Johannes P. Louw and Eugene Albert Nida, *Greek-English Lexicon of the New Testament: Based on Semantic Domains* (New York: United Bible Societies, 1996), 771.

[6] See Donald P. Senior and Daniel J. Harrington, *1 Peter, Jude and 2 Peter*, ed. Daniel J. Harrington. Sacra Pagina Series, vol. 15 (Collegeville, Minn.: Liturgical Press, 2003), 196–97. Also Daniel Keating, *First and Second Peter, Jude*, Catholic Commentary on Sacred Scripture (Grand Rapids, Mich.: Baker Academic, 2011), 203–4.

legitimate understanding, it has the difficulty of assuming the men of Sodom *knew* the visitors were actually angels. In fact, it seems apparent the men had no idea the visitors were angels; rather, they appeared to be men (Gen 19:5). In other words, we do not see the men of Sodom saying, "Though these strangers appear to be men, they are really angels, so let us try to have sex with 'some strange flesh', namely, sexual relations with angels." It seems more likely that this passage is referring to homosexual desire as "strange flesh" and "unnatural desires".[7]

When it comes to same-sex attraction, sound moral teaching distinguishes three things: (1) the person, (2) the inclination, and (3) actions. Merely possessing a same-sex inclination is not sinful, nor does it make the person with such an inclination a sinner. The inclination or even a temptation itself is not a sin. Homosexuality is "disordered", which means here not ordered to the appropriate or proper end or goal. It involves a more or less strong inclination not ordered or directed to the proper end of sexuality, which is marital union—a union that involves two people of the opposite sex. Same-sex attraction disposes one to do something sinful.

As with all sins and inclinations to sin, the sin is one thing, the inclination, another. And even when we are talking about sin and not simply an inclination to a sinful action, Christians must "love the sinner and hate the sin". Charity must be exercised toward anyone with same-sex attraction, who, like opposite-sex attracted people, is called to live a chaste life (*CCC* 2358–59). While we must respect the dignity of every human being, including people with same-sex attraction, under no circumstances can homosexual conduct be approved of or condoned.

---

[7] "Verse 7 is an explicit condemnation of homosexual immorality (cf. Rom 1:24–27; 1 Cor 6:9; 1 Tim 1:10)", *The Navarre Bible: New Testament* (Dublin and New York: Four Courts Press; Scepter Publishers, 2008), 970. Also, "Likewise, Sodom and Gomorrah violate the biblical purity code by going after 'other flesh,' and so become polluted. Kashrut laws, which prohibit the mixing of things (Deut 22:9–11), emphatically insist on the separation of the sexes; men may not dress like women and vice versa (22:5). Yet in terms of sexual commerce, men may not have intercourse either with animals or men (Lev 18:22; 20:13), but only with women. Hence, Sodom and Gomorrah cause pollution by crossing the lines of acceptable sexual partners. Paul reflects the same pollution code in Rom 1:26–37, where he labels this pollution as 'shameful' (*atimia*)." Jerome H. Neyrey, *2 Peter, Jude: A New Translation with Introduction and Commentary*, Anchor Yale Bible, vol. 37C (New Haven; London: Yale University Press, 2008), 61.

THE SODOMITES' PERSISTENCE; LOT OFFERS
HIS DAUGHTERS (19:6–11)

The men continued to push against the door and demand the two
visitors be sent out. Lot begged them to leave the men alone. In
response to the demands of his neighbors, Lot did something quite
shocking. He offered his own virgin daughters in the place of his
guests (19:8). Accepting strangers into his home required a duty to
protect them. But did his duty require the relinquishing of his own
virgin daughters? Perhaps he knew they would be rejected and was
buying time. With no local police force to call with 911, Lot may
have been doing what he thought to be the lesser of two evils, but
we recoil at the idea of his giving preference to protecting his male
visitors over the safety of his own daughters. As one commentator
notes, "We are shocked by Lot's attempt to placate the townsmen
by offering to give them his two virgin daughters for their pleasure,
but it is unlikely that an ancient audience would have been as horrified. They would have seen in Lot's offer a noble attempt, even if
extreme, to fulfill the demands of hospitality."[8]

Abraham and Lot came from a pagan culture in Mesopotamia and
had very limited knowledge of God and morality, something we take
for granted with the full revelation we possess. As noted above, we
see this sort of thing happen again in Judges 19:22–25.

Lot was attacked by the mob threatening rape and worse! Pull-
ing Lot to safety, the angels struck the Sodomites with blindness.
Even *after* experiencing the angels' miraculous power, they did not
repent. Driven by their lust, they continued groping for the door.
Though earlier respected as a citizen "sitting in the gate", Lot was
now despised and accused of being a bossy newcomer. Lot became a
member of their community; he "dwelt in Sodom" (Gen 14:12). Did
these men so soon forget that Abraham had delivered Sodom from
foreign kings in a recent war (Gen 14:14)? Lot's daughters were even
engaged to marry men from Sodom (Gen 19:14). Yet Lot is scorned
because of his moral stand. The Lord had promised Abraham that if
ten righteous dwelled in Sodom he would spare them. With no need

---

[8] Dianne Bergant and Robert J. Karris, *The Collegeville Bible Commentary: Based on the New
American Bible with Revised New Testament* (Collegeville, Minn.: Liturgical Press, 1989), 58.

to count the righteous, the angels quickly gathered the family—it was only Lot, his wife, and their two daughters. The sons-in-law rebuffed Lot's attempt to save them. Judgment was imminent.

Lot's situation in Sodom brings to mind the present situation of Christians in aggressively neo-pagan, ethically revisionist, relativistic, post-Christian societies today. As we continue to teach and practice the Christian faith, how will society respond, especially considering issues such as abortion, the LGBT agenda and its efforts to promote same-sex activity and sexual relationships as equivalent to marriage, gender confusion and its ideology, and the loss of religious freedom? In many ways, Christian teaching is simply at odds with the larger culture. How will we Christians respond?

LOT ESCAPES SODOM (19:12–23)

Destruction was looming. Haste was essential, but Lot hesitated. Oh, how often we hesitate when God warns us and provides a way of escape! But God was merciful. Grabbing the four by the hand, the angels took them from the city. Run for your lives! Flee the wrath to come! (Cf. Mt 3:7.) The angels commanded they flee quickly to the mountains. But Lot again hesitated and challenged the Lord's command to run to the hills, and he asked instead to flee to the nearby city of Zoar. The Lord agreed, saying, "I grant you this favor also, that I will not overthrow the city of which you have spoken. Make haste, escape there; for I can do nothing till you arrive there." Saint Cyril of Alexandria wrote, "Great is the loving kindness of God. He who is all-powerful says, 'I can do nothing until you arrive there.' He accommodates even the weakness of his servant and tolerates his delay."[9]

The decisive authority of God can be seen in the Lord's answer. From now on the angels are not referred to as "men" but as the Lord (*Yahweh*). In fact, in verse 24 we read, "Then the LORD (*Yahweh*) rained on Sodom and Gomorrah brimstone and fire from the LORD (*Yahweh*) out of heaven."

---

[9] *Catena on Genesis* 3.1144, in Mark Sheridan, *Genesis 12–50*, Ancient Christian Commentary on Scripture OT 2 (Downers Grove, Ill.: InterVarsity Press, 2002), 78.

Lot's family walked all night since we are told the sun had risen when they arrived in Zoar after which the Lord rained down fire and brimstone on those cities, the valley, and the inhabitants. Zoar means "small" and is well-attested to in Scripture and extra-biblical sources right up until modern times. One scholar notes:

> The traditional location of the place is at the south end of the Dead Sea. Josephus says (*BJ*, IV, viii, 4) that the Dead Sea extended "as far as Zoar of Arabia," while in *Ant*, I, xi, 4, he states that the place was still called Zoar. Eusebius (*Onom*, 261) locates the Dead Sea between Jericho and Zoar, and speaks of the remnants of the ancient fertility as still visible.... The place has not been definitely identified by modern explorers, but from Gen 19:19–30 we infer that it was in the plain and not in the mountain. If we fix upon the south end of the Dead Sea as the Vale of Siddim, a very natural place for Zoar and one which agrees with all the traditions would be at the base of the mountains of Moab.[10]

This also gives credence to the traditional site of Sodom at the south end of the Dead Sea.

SODOM IS DESTROYED; TRINITY ALLUDED TO (19:24–25)

Judgment may be a bit of an understatement. We read, "Then the Lord rained on Sodom and Gomorrah brimstone and fire." If this were a Hollywood production, the conflagration would be exploited by special effects, surround sound, and shots from every conceivable angle. But that is not the intention of Scripture. The purpose is to learn of God's holiness and justice and how he deals with sin.

We mentioned something interesting a bit earlier in verse 24. Go back if you did not catch it. Did you notice the two mentions of "the Lord"? In Hebrew, the word for *Lord* is Yahweh. It is the name that God revealed to Moses at the burning bush—"Say this to the sons of Israel, 'I AM [Yahweh] has sent me to you'" (Ex 3:14). This is the

---

[10] George Frederick Wright, "Zoar", in *The International Standard Bible Encyclopaedia*, ed. James Orr et al. (Chicago: Howard-Severance Company, 1915), 3154.

name of God forever. The double use of the divine name could be a
literary device used to emphasize this catastrophe as no natural disaster but a specific judgment straight from the hand of God. But it also
suggests that someone named Yahweh is on the earth calling down
fire from someone named Yahweh in heaven.[11]

The mystery of the Trinity explains Yahweh being referred to as
on earth and Yahweh being referred to as in heaven. Mysteriously,
and certainly not in a way explained by the author of Genesis, the one
Yahweh seems to have something akin to what we will know from
later revelation and the teaching of the Church as more than one
personal reality. In the dogma of the Trinity, we recall, the Church
affirms one God in three Divine Persons.

By the way, this passage is effective when addressing groups such as
the Jehovah's Witnesses, who deny the doctrine of the Trinity.

Saint Justin Martyr, the great apologist of the second century, wrote:

> When Scripture says, "The Lord rained fire from the Lord out of
> heaven," the prophetic word indicates that there were two in num-
> ber: One upon the earth, who, it says, descended to behold the cry of
> Sodom; Another in heaven, who also is Lord of the Lord on earth, as
> He is Father and God; the cause of His power and of His being Lord
> and God.[12]

Eusebius (ca. 260–ca. 340) wrote:

> First then Moses expressly speaks of two divine Lords in the passage
> where he says, "Then the LORD rained from the LORD fire and brim-
> stone upon the city of the ungodly": where he applied to both the
> like combination of Hebrew letters in the usual way [YHWH]; and
> this combination is the mention of God expressed in the four letters,
> which is with them unutterable.[13]

---

[11] Kenelm Vaughan, in his *Divine Armory of Holy Scripture*, lists this verse along with other
"texts of Holy Scripture which vindicate the Catholic doctrine on the oldest and most august
of Mysteries" in the section of the book "On the Trinity of Persons in the Unity of Nature".
See Kenelm Vaughan, *The Divine Armory of Holy Scripture*, American Edition Revised (Public
Domain: Catholic Book Exchange, 1894), 31.

[12] Justin Martyr, "Dialogue of Justin with Trypho, a Jew", chap. 29, in *The Apostolic Fathers
with Justin Martyr and Irenaeus*, ed. Alexander Roberts, James Donaldson, and A. Cleveland Coxe,
The Ante-Nicene Fathers, vol. 1 (Buffalo, N.Y.: Christian Literature Company, 1885), 264.

[13] Eusebius of Caesarea, *Evangelicae Praeparationis Libri XV*, bk. 11, chap. 14, ed. E. H. Gif-
ford (Oxford: Oxford University Press, 1903), 573.

WICKEDNESS AND DESTRUCTION OF SODOM; LOT RESCUED   189

The word *brimstone* is "sulphur". It occurs naturally in volcanic regions like the Dead Sea basin. It burns easily, which is why sulphur is used on the heads of matches. It is often associated with the purging, judgment, and the wrath of God. In Scripture it is almost always used in conjunction with fire. We also hear it frequently in phrases like "That pastor sure preaches fire and brimstone!" On pilgrimages to Israel, we drive along the Dead Sea. Frequently, the passengers on the bus look askance at those sitting next to them. A foul odor has filled the bus, but it is not from a human source. It is the acrid smell of sulfur seeping from the ground. It is a constant reminder of the sulfurous destruction wrecked upon these cities in divine judgment.

Scripture repeatedly uses Sodom's judgment as a constant reminder (cf. Deut 29:23; Is 1:9; Jer 49:18; Lam 4:6; Amos 4:11; Lk 17:29; 2 Pet 2:6). Because of sin and debauchery, God purged this confederacy of cities. Jesus confirms this historical event and uses it to warn his own generation, and it certainly applies to ours as well.

LOT'S WIFE AND THE PILLAR OF SALT; SURVEYING THE DESTRUCTION (19:26–29)

In verse 17 the men told Lot and his family to flee with the specific command "Do not look back." Lot's wife couldn't resist—she looked back "and she became a pillar of salt" (Gen 19:26). In discussing the future judgment, Jesus referred to her misfortune:

> Likewise as it was in the days of Lot—they ate, they drank, they bought, they sold, they planted, they built, but on the day when Lot went out from Sodom, fire and brimstone rained from heaven and destroyed them all—so will it be on the day when the Son of man is revealed. On that day, let him who is on the housetop, with his goods in the house, not come down to take them away; and likewise let him who is in the field not turn back. Remember Lot's wife. Whoever seeks to gain his life will lose it, but whoever loses his life will preserve it (Lk 17:28–33).

At least one Church Father interpreted the account allegorically. Origen (ca. 185–ca. 253) said that Lot represented the rational understanding and manly soul, and Lot's wife represented the flesh that always looks back to vices and seeks after pleasure.[14] Why did Mrs. Lot look back? We can only speculate that Sodom had become her home after years of wandering. Maybe she was even attracted to some of its baser qualities or simply missing friends left behind or curious about the conflagration exploding behind them. Recall our Lord's response to a potential disciple, "Another said, 'I will follow you, Lord; but let me first say farewell to those at my home.' Jesus said to him, 'No one who puts his hand to the plow and looks back is fit for the kingdom of God'" (Lk 9:61–62).

The fiery destruction of Sodom became an archetype for future threatened judgments (e.g., Deut 29:23; Zeph 2:9). The author of Wisdom confirmed the historicity of the event, "Wisdom rescued a righteous man when the ungodly were perishing; he escaped the fire that descended on the Five Cities. Evidence of their wickedness still remains: a continually smoking wasteland, plants bearing fruit that does not ripen, and a pillar of salt standing as a monument to an unbelieving soul" (Wis 10:6–7).

The story then circles back to Abraham, who surveys the smoking ruins below and leads us to conclude that there must have been fewer than ten righteous (19:27–29). But God had kept his promise and had saved his nephew Lot.

THE INCEST OF LOT'S DAUGHTERS (19:30–38)

We were shocked and scandalized when Lot offered his daughters to the lustful mob in Sodom, but now we are scandalized again. After leaving Zoar, Lot and his daughters dwelled in a cave. The daughters had lost their betrothed and possibly despaired of future matrimony. They might have assumed the conflagration had consumed all mankind, like the destruction of the flood during Noah's time. To preserve the human race and their family line through their father's seed, they hatched a plan. The two daughters gave their father wine in abundance until he was drunk. Each in turn committed incest with their father.

---

[14] Origen, Homily 5.2, in *Homilies on Genesis and Exodus*, ed. Hermigild Dressler, trans. Ronald E. Heine. The Fathers of the Church, vol. 71 (Washington, D.C.: Catholic University of America Press, 1982), 14.

Saint Irenaeus (ca. 130–ca. 200), whether he is correct or not, and whether he shared the inspired author's viewpoint or not, expresses his interesting perspective on the daughters' thought processes.

Thus, after their simplicity and innocence, did these daughters [of Lot] so speak, imagining that all mankind had perished, even as the Sodomites had done, and that the anger of God had come down upon the whole earth. Wherefore also they are to be held excusable, since they supposed that they only, along with their father, were left for the preservation of the human race; and for this reason it was that they deceived their father.[15]

The incestuous relationships gave each daughter a son from whom proceeded two great nations: Moab and Ammon. The first son was named *Moab*, which means "from [my] father". Today if you fly into the country of Jordan, you will land in the capital city of Amman, the location of the capital city of the Ammonites. Moab's descendants dwelled on the Jordan side of the Dead Sea, south of the Ammonites. Ruth, who has her own book of the Bible, was a Moabitess; she was the great-grandmother of King David; and she is mentioned in the ancestry of Jesus Christ. She is listed in the *Catechism* as one of many holy women who prepared the way for the mission of Mary (Ruth 1:4; Mt 1:5–6; *CCC* 489). Again, we see God drawing straight with crooked lines.

The mountains of Moab overlook the Jordan Valley from the east where Jesus was baptized centuries later. Though related by blood to the Israelites, Moab and Ammon were usually hostile. However, King Solomon had wives from Ammon and Moab, who continued to worship their wicked national gods Milcom, Chemosh, and Molech (1 Kings 11:1, 5, 7, 33). Due in part to Solomon's idolatry with the gods of his wives, the kingdom of Israel was split.

So ends the episode involving Sodom and Abraham's nephew Lot. Nahum Sarna summarizes the tawdry end of Lot's story. "The two sons are born, and nothing more is heard of Lot. His story ends on an inglorious and ironic note. At the beginning of the chapter he

---

[15] Irenaeus of Lyons, "Irenaeus against Heresies", bk. 4, chap. 31, in *The Apostolic Fathers with Justin Martyr and Irenaeus*, ed. Alexander Roberts, James Donaldson, and A. Cleveland Coxe, The Ante-Nicene Fathers, vol. 1, 505.

was willing to let the virginity of his daughters be forcibly defiled, without even informing them, in order to save lives. Now, in order to 'maintain life,' his daughters have lost their virginity by forcing themselves upon him without his knowledge."[16]

[16] Nahum M. Sarna, *Genesis*, The JPS Torah Commentary (Philadelphia: Jewish Publication Society, 1989), 140.

CHAPTER 20

ABRAHAM, SARAH, AND ABIMELECH

ABRAHAM DECEIVES ABIMELECH (20:1–9)

Leaving Hebron, Abraham moved south into the harsh desert area
of the Negev, which encompasses more than half of today's State of
Israel. Kadesh, along with Shur, are in northern Sinai, which is expansive and rugged. Abraham the shepherd sought good grazing for
his flocks and herds. While in the area he visited the city of Gerar,
not to settle down, but only to sojourn there, maybe for trading or
the purchase of supplies. Gerar is about ten miles southeast of today's
Gaza, and Abimelech was its king.

Similar to an earlier situation (Gen 12), Abraham deceived Abimelech regarding his relationship with Sarah, saying, "She is my sister." Sarah joined in the deception (Gen 20:5, 13). This was only
half-true, as we learned before. Sarah was a half-sister of Abraham,
but he neglected the all-important fact that she was also his wife (Gen
20:12). Thinking he was well within his rights, the king "sent and
took Sarah". It can safely be assumed she was taken into his harem.

At almost ninety years old and pregnant, Sarah must have been
an extraordinary woman! A rabbinic tradition preserved in the *Babylonian Talmud* comments on Sarah's appearance after God's visit
in Genesis 18. "After the flesh got worn and the skin wrinkled,
the flesh became pleasurable, the wrinkles were smoothed out, and
beauty was restored."[1]

Other possibilities for Abimelech's desire might be that Sarah was
desired for her age and wisdom in the king's household and harem,
or possibly, as was often the case, she functioned to seal an alliance

---

[1] Jacob Neusner, *The Babylonian Talmud: A Translation and Commentary*, vol. 14 (Peabody,
Mass.: Hendrickson, 2011), 669.

between Abimelech and Abraham. King Solomon forged alliances from among the nations by marrying princesses from the surrounding kingdoms (1 Kings 11:3). As one scholar reminds us, "In biblical times marriage was viewed as a covenant between two families, and thus marriages often served the political function of cementing a treaty between two families or nations. Intermarriage with pagan nations was opposed by the prophets because it would lead to the worship of other gods, as it did with Solomon (1 K. 11:1–8)."[2]

Genesis 20:7 is unique—it introduces us to two common biblical words for the first time. God tells Abimelech in a dream that Abraham is a *prophet* (Hebrew *navi*) (20:7). This is the first time the word *prophet* is used in the Bible and the only time used of Abraham. A prophet is one who speaks God's word—God's mouthpiece. But it also seems to imply the knowledge of God's mind. Abraham is to pray for Abimelech according to the word of the Lord (20:17). Interestingly, this is also the first use of the word *pray* in the Bible, and Abraham is the first recorded person to *pray*. The sacred writer shows us that Abraham continued to be an intercessor. His intercession saved Lot, and now his prayer saved Abimelech. Abimelech and his men were fearful finding out the real identity of Abraham and Sarah.

ABRAHAM PRAYS FOR ABIMELECH (20:10–18)

Looking to preserve his long-term goals with Abraham and Sarah, God intervened in the predicament. He made up for Abraham's cowardice (20:11) and treachery by personally warning the king. God told Abimelech he was "a dead man" for taking a married woman. Imagine the shock when he awoke from the dream! Abimelech "had not come near her", so he proclaimed his innocence and appealed to God's sense of justice. Abimelech returned Sarah to Abraham as God commanded, and he was spared.

Is there a bit of irony or sarcasm in the words of Abimelech when he says to Sarah, "I have given your *brother* a thousand pieces of silver"? He gave Abraham riches as a lavish gesture of recompense

[2] Geoffrey W. Bromiley, ed., "Marriage Alliance", in *The International Standard Bible Encyclopedia*, rev. (Eerdmans, 1979–1988), 3:266.

and possibly to insure a friendship alliance. He invited Abraham to settle anywhere he pleased. Sarah was vindicated, and the prayers of Abraham healed Abimelech, his wife, and their female slaves whose wombs had been closed on account of Sarah.

One might logically ask, why is this story of Abimelech so important? Why does such a seemingly insignificant story take up a whole chapter? God is demonstrating his divine protection of Sarah, who is about to give birth to the son of promise. Twice God has preserved Sarah from certain harm or illicit sexual relations with foreign kings to safeguard her for Abraham alone and to eliminate any doubt that Isaac is truly Abraham's son through Sarah. This reason would justify the incident taking place immediately before the birth of Isaac. God has made a promise and intends to keep it. He will allow nothing, not even kingly lust or a treaty through marriage, to stand in the way of his promise of a son by the seed of Abraham through the womb of Sarah.

We now proceed to a pinnacle of Abraham's life—the long-awaited birth of his son and the heir of God's promises.

CHAPTER 21

THE BIRTH OF ISAAC;
HAGAR AND ISHMAEL SENT AWAY

INTRODUCTION

We turned our vehicle off the main road. The two-track led us mean-
dering through the desert hills and wadis. Scrubby acacia and tamarisk
trees spread over the rugged landscape, gripping the cracked ground
waiting for rain. Caves dotted the hillsides. We saw flocks of sheep in
the distance and a few camels wandering here and there. With bin-
oculars we could see the shepherd girls dressed in black scrambling
among the rocks tending their sheep. As we crested a rise, we saw our
destination. Black tents sprawled along the edge of the wadi, which
are bone-dry riverbeds that have rushing water only after the rare
downpour or when flash floods rush from the mountains.

But not everyone sees this as barren, inhospitable land. At first you
think the sheep and goats must be eating dirt. But on closer exam-
ination, there are scrubby plants sparsely distributed among the rocks.
This is why the flocks and shepherds keep moving. They need to
cover a lot of ground to find ample food for all their animals. Smoke
was rising from some of the tents. We were filming in the Wilderness
of Ziph, south of Bethlehem. To drive into this remote area is to step
back in time. Here before our eyes I imagined Sarah and Abraham—
their tents, their flocks, their primitive life-style. Children who have
never had a bath or shower watched us from a distance, only slowly
warming up to our presence. By our standards, one would be repulsed
by their dirty faces and the flies around their eyes. The leathery faces
of the older women were creased with lines and often tattoos, framed
by their matted hair.

The women sat together with the smaller children in the shade of
the tent that was in front of a cave they shared with the sheep and

goats. The men were gone, possibly caring for the flocks—or more likely, they were enjoying their favorite pastime—sitting in a group smoking cigarettes in the "city gates" away from the women. The women spoke Arabic and gestured for us to enter the tent and sit down. With great hospitality and toothless smiles, the women offered us hot *chai*. The Bedouin tea is always sweet with sugar, sometimes with a sprig of fresh mint. The sun was hot. There was no breeze that day. Unrelenting flies buzzed in our faces as we drank our *chai* and smiled. By Western standards, this was primitive living—tents with no electricity, crude rugs on the dirt with low platforms covered with blankets for sleeping. No running water, showers, toothbrushes, blow driers, washing machines, refrigerators, or any other conveniences.

Welcome to Abraham and Sarah's world. Visiting a Bedouin camp today is still in many ways like being transported in a time machine back four thousand years. Not a lot has changed for these nomadic shepherds. Every time we drive through the Judean Wilderness on a bus with our pilgrimage groups, I say, "Look at the Bedouin encampment on the left. There you see Abraham, Isaac, and Jacob!"

GOD VISITS SARAH (21:1)

At this point in Genesis, Sarah was about ninety years old. Every day and every night she lived in a tent with the heat, the flies, and the bleating animals. And now the joy of her life was finally arriving— she was with child. Resting in the tent, she was overjoyed, ecstatic finally to be bringing the promised son into the world. Finally, the shame and humiliation had vanished. She felt the baby squirming with life as he grew in her womb.

Their barrenness had haunted Abraham and Sarah for nearly a century. The suspense of waiting for the fulfillment of God's illusive promise had been building for over twenty–five years. For us it has only built up over the last nine chapters of Genesis. We have it easy—reading the story takes only a short time. We do not live with the drama and the tension day in and day out. We do not lie awake in the tent at night feeling age creep deeper into our bones. Time, the unrelenting enemy, had been wreaking its havoc on Abraham and Sarah for many years. The fertility of youth and the strength of middle age had long since passed, and had it not been for the hard-to-believe promise of God, a child would have been unthinkable. They had experienced their own "dark night of the soul". The stress had taken its toll, the waiting had worn thin their patience, and the humiliation and longing had been more than most could humanly endure. But God had promised, and Abraham believed. He had clung to God and the promise like a baby clings to his mother's neck.

The promise of a son had been made to Abraham, but to Sarah as well. We hear so much of God meeting with Abraham, but now God visited Sarah as he said he would, and Sarah conceived and bore Abraham a son in his old age. This remarkable event—the Lord announcing the birth of an exceptional and miraculous son—certainly anticipated the angel of the Lord coming to Mary in the caves of Nazareth with an extraordinary announcement and promise. The Annunciation is also a covenant of sorts between God and a woman. The *Catechism* reminds us that the holy women of the Old Testament prepared the way for Mary (*CCC* 489). Sarah is specifically mentioned as receiving a promise from God that was fulfilled in the birth of a son in spite of her age. Sarah, who was approached with a divine message and promise in the tent, prepares the way for Mary, who is later approached with a divine message and promise in a cave.

God had made two promises to Sarah, and he fulfilled them both (Gen 18:10). Notice how both promises are mentioned in one breath in Genesis 21:1. Notice similar language used with another woman initially unable to conceive (1 Sam 2:21)? The son was not born according to Sarah's timetable; God has his own schedule. He knows the appointed time. There is a famous Yiddish proverb, "Man plans and God laughs." Sarah bore a son at the appointed time of which God had spoken.

ISAAC IS BORN, NAMED, AND CIRCUMCISED (21:2–8)

It is interesting how precisely Genesis 21:3 is worded: "Abraham called the name of his son who was born to him, whom Sarah bore him, Isaac." Sarah is emphasized—this son "whom Sarah bore him". They had tried to convince God of servant Eliezer's suitability. Then they tried on their own to bring about the Lord's plan through Hagar. Twice Sarah was taken by other men but protected from sexual relations. No, this baby did *not* come into being through Abraham's relations with other women or Sarah's relations with other men. This child came about exactly as God had promised—a gift from God, "born to him [Abraham], through Sarah". Both Abraham and Sarah are emphatically mentioned for obvious reasons.

Of the three major patriarchs—Abraham, Isaac, and Jacob—Isaac is the only one never granted a name change by God. Only Isaac kept the name given at circumcision. Why is that? I suspect that it is because God himself named Isaac before he was even conceived (Gen 17:19). In Hebrew, Isaac is *Yitzhak*. If you are a lover of classical music, that name will ring a bell—the great Jewish violinist and conductor Itzhak Perlman. *Isaac* means "he laughs". Sarah laughed twice. Once when eavesdropping on a conversation, when her laugh seemed to indicate disbelief, and a second time, in verse 6, where she laughed with joy and invited everyone else to laugh with her. Isaac, *laughter* himself, is a powerful testimony to the faithfulness and power of the living God in the very face of human weakness and doubt.

Isaac was circumcised on the eighth day; from birth he was the son of promise. In Scripture, Isaac is the first recorded infant circumcision. The flint knife was again picked up and without antiseptic or anesthesia Abraham cut the foreskin from his son. Blood flowed, the wound healed, and Isaac was branded for God in his flesh. Abraham passed two milestones: first, he now had a son, and, second, he turned one hundred years old.

Sarah's two joyful exclamations may have been sung. According to Nahum M. Sarna, "This utterance of Sarah has the form of a song. It consists of three short clauses of three words each. The forms of the verbs as well as the rare stem *m-l-l* seem to indicate that the words of Sarah had their origin in an ancient poem."[1] Sarah bubbled over with joy. Another holy woman did the same. John Paul II wrote, "Samuel's birth was thus an experience of joy and an occasion for thanksgiving. The First Book of Samuel contains a hymn known as

[1] Nahum M. Sarna, *Genesis*, The JPS Torah Commentary (Philadelphia: Jewish Publication Society, 1989), 146.

Hannah's Magnificat, which seems to anticipate Mary's: 'My heart exalts in the Lord, my strength is exalted in the Lord' (1 Sam 2:1)."[2] You could say that Sarah set the precedent, and other holy women followed, including the Blessed Virgin Mary!

Breast-feeding fell out of fashion in the mid-twentieth century, when bottles and formula became popular, but many mothers now have returned to breast-feeding their babies. Sarah had no such options in the second millennium B.C.: "And the child grew, and was weaned; and Abraham made a great feast on the day that Isaac was weaned" (Gen 21:8). How old was Isaac when Abraham threw the big celebration party? Probably about three years old.[3] After circumcision and being named, the next significant stage in a baby's life was weaning. Infant mortality was high in the ancient times with some estimating that one in three babies died in childbirth or during infancy. Isaac survived the precarious first years, and Abraham prepared a great feast to celebrate!

HAGAR AND ISHMAEL ARE SENT AWAY (21:9–14)

At or soon after the great feast celebrating the weaning of Isaac, Sarah saw Ishmael "playing with her son Isaac" (21:9). The phrase describing the interaction between Ishmael and Isaac is ambiguous and rendered differently in other Bible translations. Some render it as "mocking", following the Greek *Septuagint*. Others prefer "playing with Isaac". According to *A Handbook on Genesis*, published to help translators correctly translate the original text into various languages,

---

[2] Pope John Paul II, *Theotokos: Woman, Mother, Disciple, A Catechesis on Mary, Mother of God* (Boston: Pauline Books & Media, 2000), 70–71.

[3] "The norm throughout the ancient Near East was to breastfeed a child from birth until the third (or fourth) birthday. The mother of the seven martyrs in the Second Book of Maccabees exhorts her youngest son to courage: 'My son, have pity on me. I carried you nine months in my womb, and nursed you for three years' (2 Mac 7:27). The legal requirements for priestly service seem to take this custom into consideration. A Levite child's duties began at age three (cf. 2 Chron 31:16); until then he was under the care of his mother. Similarly, Hannah turned her son Samuel over to tabernacle service 'when she had weaned him' (1 Sam 1:24); it is unlikely that she would have released an infant or a child of two to the care of the elderly priest Eli." Mike Aquilina, with Terri. "Milk and Mystery: On Breastfeeding and the Theology of the Body." In *Catholic for a Reason IV: Scripture and the Mystery of Marriage and Family Life*, ed. Scott Hahn and Regis J. Flaherty (Steubenville, Ohio: Emmaus Road Publishing, 2007).

The meaning is better taken as "playing".... The Hebrew verb expresses the intensive form of the root from which Isaac's name is derived [laughter]. This is another example of a play on the name Isaac. It is highly unlikely that this play on words can be reproduced in translation. It is the sight of young Ishmael playing as an equal with Isaac that causes Sarah to become jealous and angry.[4]

Aren't siblings supposed to play nicely together? But Sarah was upset, and her contempt was manifested by refusing even to mention Ishmael's name. Several things could have caused such animosity: (1) it would have been demeaning for Isaac to fraternize with a slave's son, or (2) playing as equals could have jeopardized her son's status, or (3) the sight of Ishmael recalled her earlier bad judgment and animosity toward Hagar, or (4) some rabbis interpret *play* as either a kind of immoral activity or the mocking of Isaac, or (5) a perception that Ishmael was asserting prerogatives as Abraham's firstborn son.

The second and fifth alternatives seem most likely. Sarah had arranged the union between her husband and Hagar expressly to provide a firstborn son. They were circumcised together, and Abraham recognized Ishmael as his son (Gen 16:15; 17:23, 25f.). Ishmael had legal standing as firstborn, and Sarah knew it. That was the law. But Sarah was determined to establish the privileged status of the son from her own womb. But there was another law, and Sarah knew this law, too. "According to the laws of Lipit-Ishtar, which antedate Hammurabi by 150 years, the slave-girl and her son may become free but are not then entitled to an inheritance."[5] In other words, if Hagar remained Sarah's slave, Ishmael had a right to an inheritance, but if she was granted freedom, his rights would be forfeited. Sarah demanded that Abraham exercise his rights, free the bondwoman, and send her away with her son. In doing this, Sarah secured Isaac the position of exclusive heir and safeguarded the family line through her son. As she said, "for the son of this slave woman shall not be heir with my son Isaac" (Gen 21:10).

---

[4] William David Reyburn and Euan McG. Fry, *A Handbook on Genesis*, UBS Handbook Series (New York: United Bible Societies, 1998), 467.

[5] W. Gunther Plaut, "Genesis", in *The Torah: A Modern Commentary* (New York: Union of American Hebrew Congregations, 1981), 139.

Abraham loved his son Ishmael and was dismayed by Sarah's demand to "cast out this slave woman and her son". Ishmael was at least fourteen years old (cf. Gen 16:16 and 21:5), and Abraham had a fondness for Ishmael and a sense of obligation. God instructed Abraham to comply with Sarah's wishes and send Hagar and Ishmael away—liberating them and severing any legal obligations. God softened the blow with a pledge, "I will make a nation of the son of the slave woman also, because he is your offspring" (Gen 21:13; see Gen 16:10; 21:18; 25:12–18). With only some bread and a skin of water, Abraham sent them away to wander in the wilderness around Beersheba.

Though we are again scandalized by this harsh treatment, God promised to bless them greatly and to protect Isaac's inheritance. He would intervene to keep his promise to Hagar, as he kept his promise to Sarah. From this Egyptian slave woman, through her son, would come a great nation because he was also an offspring of Abraham.

GOD PRESERVES AND BLESSES HAGAR AND ISHMAEL (21:15–21)

No one wants to see his child die. It is often said to be the worst of sorrows. Wandering until the water ran out, Hagar left her boy under a bush and went a bowshot away to avoid watching him die of dehydration. She wept, but it was the voice of the lad that God heard. Scripture says, "God heard." This is a clever play on words if you recall the meaning of the name Ishmael (Gen 16:11). God again reiterated his promise, though it was different from that given to Isaac. Isaac was promised the land and numerous descendants; Ishmael was promised nationhood, but not any particular land. Ishmael became the father of the Arabs. For more on the descendants of Ishmael, see Genesis 25.

God opened Hagar's eyes to see a well of water, giving Hagar confidence in God's providential care. The episode of Hagar and Ishmael ends with God being with the lad who grew up in the wilderness of Paran, which is in the Sinai Peninsula. His mother found him a wife from Egypt, and he became an expert with the bow (Gen 21:20–21).

ABRAHAM AND ABIMELECH MAKE A COVENANT AT BEERSHEBA (21:22–34)

The next thirteen verses revolve around a dispute over a well. That may sound insignificant to those who turn on a faucet to get a drink. But in the desert, water was scarce, essential, and an invaluable commodity. Wealth was measured by the size of flocks and herds, but animals do not survive long without water. Even today, battles are fought over water.

Abimelech was king of Shur (also in the northern Sinai Peninsula), though here his royalty remained unmentioned, perhaps to emphasize their equality, though Abraham still owned no land of his own. Abraham swore to deal fairly and truly with Abimelech. But subsequent to this agreement, Abimelech's men had confiscated a well used by Abraham, and Abraham had reproved him. The problem of no access to water needed an instant resolution since conflicts over water could easily end in bloodshed. Abimelech had surely heard of Abraham's military prowess and did not want trouble. So the two men made a covenant.

Abraham's actions anticipate the Christian gospel advocating love of neighbor and enemy, settling disputes quickly, and living at peace with all men. In its document *Gaudium et spes*, the Second Vatican Council says, "Motivated by this same spirit, we cannot fail to praise those who renounce the use of violence in the vindication of their rights and who resort to methods of defense which are otherwise available to weaker parties, too, provided this can be done without injury to the rights and duties of others or of the community itself."[6]

The number seven is creatively interlaced throughout the story of Abraham and Abimelech—certainly not by accident. The number *seven* is used to "swear" or make an "oath"—literally to "seven oneself".[7] The names Abraham and Abimelech are each used seven

---

[6] *Vatican Council II, The Conciliar and Post Conciliar Documents*, electronic ed. of the new revised ed., vol. 1, Vatican Collection (Northport, N.Y.: Costello Publishing, 1992), 987.

[7] "There are two Hebrew words to denote 'oath'. The first, *š bû'â*, derives from the triconsonantal root *šb'*, from which is formed the noun 'seven' (*šeba'*). This root, in the reflexive verbal formation (the *nip'al*), means 'to swear' (literally, 'to seven oneself')." Scott W. Hahn, *Kinship by Covenant: A Canonical Approach to the Fulfillment of God's Saving Promises* (New Haven and London: Yale University Press, 2009), 51.

times. Seven ewe lambs are offered. The verb "to swear" (vv. 23, 24, 31) and the name "Beersheba" both contain the root word "seven". The name of the city, Beersheba, is literally "the well of the oath" or "the well of seven".

Abraham and Abimelech made a covenant together at Beersheba (21:31). The modern name is Be'er Sheva, and it is the largest modern city in the Negev Desert, often referred to as "The Capital of the Negev", and is mentioned no less than thirty-four times in Scripture. Its name relates to the oath ratified at the well. Today, the Well of Abraham is a landmark in the center of the city. Isaac lived most of his life in Beersheba; Jacob offered sacrifices there; it was an inheritance of Judah; and there an angel fed Elijah. It was the southernmost city of Israel. The north-south limits of the Promised Land are often referred to as "from Dan to Beersheba" (e.g., Judg 20:1; 1 Sam 3:20).

We are not told why Abraham planted a tamarisk tree (Gen 21:33), but they are common in the Negev. Possibly it was to commemorate his covenant with Abimelech, to stake his claim as owner of the well, or to provide shade. This tree is the official emblem of modern Be'er Shevah. It has white flowers and offers good shade, rarely losing its foliage, which is why Bedouins plant these trees to provide protection from the sun. Their soft leaves provide food for their flocks. It thrives in hot, sandy desert areas, often in wadis where it puts down its wide-ranging roots to gather water. It can be seen as a symbol of Abraham's life in this arid desert since he was putting his roots down deep, providing shade and blessing for those who followed him, and he had learned to wait patiently for the blessings of God to rain down from heaven.[8]

Abraham sojourned many days in the land of the Philistines. Commentators have suggested the presence of Philistines at this time is an anachronism.[9] It is generally believed that the Philistines arrived

[8] Michael Zohary, *Plants of the Bible* (Cambridge: Cambridge University Press, 1982), 115. Also Allan A. Swenson, *Plants of the Bible and How to Grow Them* (New York: Citadel Press, 1995), 181–84.

[9] "'Land of the Philistines' is anachronistic, since the Philistines did not arrive in Canaan till about 1200 B.C. It could be viewed as proleptic, anticipating the later name of the area and its people (cf. Dan in Gen 14:14; Ur of the Chaldeans in Gen 15:7). But K.A. Kitchen has suggested that the Philistines of Genesis may, like the later real Philistines, have come from the Aegean area, a suggestion that gains added weight if Phicol is identified as an Anatolian name." Gordon J. Wenham, *Genesis 16–50*, Word Biblical Commentary, vol. 2 (Dallas: Word, Incorporated, 1994), 94. Recent archaeological discoveries

in Canaan about eight hundred years after the Patriarchs. There are two solutions to the mention of the Philistines. First, it could be an anachronistic reference, and second, it could be referring to "an earlier wave of Sea Peoples, which predated the 1200 B.C. large-scale migration".[10] However, there is no reason to doubt the author. "The Philistines, to whom Palestine owes its name, did not make their chief settlement in the country till ca. 1200 B.C., but from earlier times had smaller trading stations there."[11] *Archaeology of the Bible: Book by Book* confirms this:

> The Genesis accounts of the relations between Abraham, Isaac, and Abimelech, king of Gerar, are consistent with the conditions existing between the Israelite tribesmen of Judea and their subgroups in the Negeb and the Philistine kingdoms during the last quarter of the eleventh century. The background of Genesis is essentially the same as that of the books of Samuel. If Abraham belongs to the Late Bronze Age, there is no reason to consider the reference to the Philistines as a serious anachronism. The text may be more accurate than most modern scholars are willing to concede.[12]

It is certainly plausible that early Aegean seafarers established outposts along the Mediterranean coastline and assumed similar cultural traits as the Canaanites, before the swarm of war-faring Philistines occupied the coast in later centuries.

Abraham calls upon the Everlasting God (*El Olam*) who had given him an everlasting covenant. This is the only occurrence of this appellation for God in the Old Testament, and scholars suggest Abraham may have applied a Canaanite name to his God *Yahweh*, the God

---

in the Philistine city of Gath, of Goliath fame, demonstrate it was much larger and earlier than previously believed, a discovery that is changing the views of the Philistines in Canaan. "'It was assumed the city reached its large size during the 10th and 9th century B.C.E.... It now appears that the early Iron Age city—11th century B.C.E. and perhaps before—may have been even bigger and more impressive'" (https://www.jpost.com/Israel-News/New -archeological-findings-at-Goliaths-birthplace-recontextualize-history-600704).

[10] Douglas Mangum, Miles Custis, and Wendy Widder, *Genesis 12–50*, Lexham Research Commentaries (Bellingham, Wash.: Lexham Press, 2013), Gen 21:1–34.

[11] E. F. Sutcliffe, "Genesis", in *A Catholic Commentary on Holy Scripture*, ed. Bernard Orchard and Edmund F. Sutcliffe (Toronto, New York, and Edinburgh: Thomas Nelson, 1953), 196.

[12] Gaalyad Cornfeld and David Noel Freedman, *Archaeology of the Bible: Book by Book* (San Francisco: Harper & Row, 1976), 28.

of Abraham. Abraham had a son, he had a secure well, and he rested under his own tamarisk tree. He wandered in this land for many days, until Isaac was about fifteen years old. And then the frightful words of God thundered from heaven, and for a few days Abraham's whole life was turned upside down.

Chapter 22

God Tests Abraham; The "Binding of Isaac"

INTRODUCTION

When our son Jesse was two years old, my wife and I took him for a walk in the Swiss Alps near our chalet in Chesières, Switzerland. We were visiting a friend in the neighboring village. Night had fallen, and the snow was deep. When I set Jesse down, he sank into the snow up to his chest. I could see both excitement and apprehension in his red little face. I loomed large over my son. He wanted to push through the snow himself. He struggled and fell. He struggled to regain his feet. He whimpered, but was determined. I encouraged him, "Get up, Jesse; you can do it!" My instinct was to reach down and pick him up. But it was good for him to learn, to build his strength, and to know Dad was never far away.

The snow and darkness were no obstacles for me. I knew where we were going and had the strength to plow easily through the snow. He kept looking up to me as I held his hand. My little son had no idea where we were going; he only knew he was with Dad, so everything was OK. He knew that Dad was big, strong, smart, and would make sure everything went well. He always knew, though maybe not consciously, that I loved him, would always take care of him, and that in the end whatever I did was for his good. Many times during his childhood, I did pick him up and carry him, but many other times I let him push through on his own. I was always there.

The story is told of Saint Teresa of Ávila, who had been thrown from her carriage into some mud, that she looked up to God and said, "If this is the way you treat your friends, it's no surprise you have so few."[1] At times, little Jesse would have thought the same as I restrained my fatherly instincts, letting him struggle.

Abraham, the friend of God, must have had similar internal conflicts after all the waiting, toil, and questions. During his upcoming trial, it would be natural for him to say, "I don't understand; what can this mean? Should I do what he asks? Is God really going to come through as he promised?"

PREPARATION FOR GOD'S TESTING OF ABRAHAM

Isaac had passed the perilous infant years and was a strong young man and Abraham's constant companion—father and son together, still almost too good to be true. Then, one day out of the blue, God appeared to Abraham and shattered the tranquility. God had decided to test Abraham. God "said to him, 'Abraham!' And he said, 'Here am I.' He said, 'Take your son, your only-begotten son Isaac, whom you love, and go to the land of Moriah, and offer him there as a burnt offering upon one of the mountains of which I shall tell you'" (Gen 22:1–2).

What? Had he heard God correctly? Abraham had already "lost" his first son. That was bad enough. Now God wanted him to offer the son of promise as a burnt offering! His own son whom he loved. But he trusted God. In 1833, during a time of great physical, emotional, and spiritual despair, Cardinal Saint John Henry Newman penned this stanza to his famous hymn *Lead, Kindly Light*, pleading for divine guidance:[2]

> Lead, kindly Light, amid th'encircling gloom, lead Thou me on!
> The night is dark, and I am far from home; lead Thou me on!
> Keep Thou my feet; I do not ask to see
> The distant scene; one step enough for me.[3]

---

[1] See William A. Barry, *A Friendship Like No Other* (Chicago: Loyola Press, 2009), 127. Additionally, "I am familiar with the delightful tale of her chiding God when a cart in which she was riding flipped over into the mud. 'It's no wonder you have so few friends, Lord,' she is quoted, 'if this is how you treat them!'" Mary Lea Hill, "Foreword", *Peace in Prayer: Wisdom from Teresa of Avila*, ed. Mary Lea Hill, Classic Wisdom Collection (Boston: Pauline Books & Media, 2011), xiii.

[2] Kenneth W. Osbeck, *101 Hymn Stories* (Grand Rapids, Mich.: Kregel Publications, 1982), 151.

[3] H. D. M. Spence-Jones, ed., *Psalms*, The Pulpit Commentary, vol. 1 (London and New York: Funk & Wagnalls Company, 1909), 181.

SIX THINGS TO CONSIDER IN ADVANCE (22:1–2)

Before we dive into this gut-wrenching passage in Genesis, which in some ways can be thought of as the pinnacle of the whole book, let us set the stage with six initial considerations based on the first two verses of chapter 22, which are a masterpiece of composition.

First, do God's words "your only-begotten son Isaac, whom you love" remind you of a famous verse in the New Testament? Maybe John 3:16, "For God so loved the world that he gave his only-begotten Son"? There is a reason for this that we will touch on shortly. But just to prepare you a bit, I note that the story we are about to consider is a human drama that will be played out again as a divine drama with another father and his only begotten son, who became a sacrificial victim.

Second, while this passage is usually read as God commanding Abraham to offer his son, we should note something usually not indicated in the translation of the text. Accompanying the imperative "take your son" is a qualifier in Hebrew that softens things. The meaning is something akin to "Take, please, your son" or "Take, if you will, your son". Even so, God's will is clear. He is not saying, in effect, "Option 1 is to go on with your business as you like, and that's quite fine with me, or Option 2 is to take your only son and offer him as a burnt offering."

Many commentators understand God to be softening the blow of his command here, not leaving the matter to Abraham's discretion. He is *commanding* Abraham, but commands in a way that reflects God's respect for how Abraham hears the special commandment. Still, some interpreters think we should understand God's instruction as more of a *request,* something that could be declined without disobedience. On this view, Abraham could have said "No" without sinning. Abraham would have had freedom of choice regarding this test, and no guilt and condemnation would have been attributed to him if he had declined. Abraham's response would mean, "God, I will not only do what you *command* of me, but I will also do what you *wish* of me." Therefore, Abraham's response would be all the more poignant.[4]

---

[4] "The reader has been alerted by the verb 'test' that something difficult is about to be asked of Abraham, while he, of course, is quite in the dark. The way the command is put here tries to soften the blow for Abraham while maximizing our realization of its enormity. 'Please take.' The use of the enclitic נא 'please' is rare in a divine command and makes it more like an entreaty, another hint that the Lord appreciates the costliness of what he is asking."

Third, this is the first time the word *love* is used in Scripture. Is it significant that the Holy Spirit has waited until now to use the word *love* to emphasize the profound bond of love between a father and a son? Certainly, the immediate context is the relationship of Abraham to his son Isaac. But we can see that the Holy Spirit also gives us a glimpse into the mystery of the Trinity and the love God the Father has for his only begotten Son. In these short nineteen verses, the word *father* is used twice and the word *son* is used nine times to emphasize that this is personal, about a father and his son. We will soon discover that the second usage of *love*, the love of Isaac for his bride, Rebekah (Gen 24:67), is just as strategically placed in Scripture.

> We have here the first mention of the word "love" in the Word. Does it not suggest that the love of a godly father for his son is a miniature picture of the love existing among the persons of the Holy Trinity, and in particular the love of the Father for the Son of God (cf. John 17:24)? It is an interesting fact that in the New Testament the first occurrence of the word "love" is a clear expression of the love of the Father for the Son (cf. Matt. 3:17; Mark 1:11; Luke 3:22). If Abraham loved Isaac, how much more deeply and fully did the Father love the Son! In the gospel of John the first occurrence of the word "love" is found in the great verse of God's love for the world of Jews and Gentiles (3:16).[5]

Fourth, we notice a three-step escalation as God describes Isaac. Take your son, your only-begotten son Isaac, whom you love. Remember that the number three is used for emphasis, to put something over the top. He is not just Abraham's *son*, but he is Abraham's *only-begotten* son, he is Abraham's only-begotten son whom he *loves*.

Gordon J. Wenham, *Genesis 16–50*, Word Biblical Commentary, vol. 2 (Dallas: Word, Incorporated, 1994), 104.

"The command sounds more brusque in translation than the original (*qaḥ-nā'*) warrants. This is a polite request, something more like 'Would you take ...,' and a request, moreover, that at least according to some commentators could be declined without difficulty. Perhaps even the appearance of being able to avoid the test was part of the test, but Abraham might well have missed this subtlety, so shocking will the next words have been." David W. Cotter, *Genesis*, in *Berit Olam: Studies in Hebrew Narrative and Poetry*, ed. Jerome T. Walsh, Chris Franke, and David W. Cotter (Collegeville, Minn.: Liturgical Press, 2003), 153.

[5] S. Lewis Johnson, Jr., "The Sacrifice of Isaac, or the Old Testament's Greatest Scene", *Emmaus Journal* 18, no. 1 (2009): 23.

A very specific point is being made. God in heaven clearly understands how important this lad is to the old man.

> But of course Abraham has two sons, so what can God mean? Rashi, the great medieval Jewish commentator,[6] includes in his commentary on Genesis a famous midrash that this sentence is actually one half of a dialogue between Abraham and God, "'*Thy son*': (Abraham) said to Him, 'Two sons have I.' (God) said to him, 'Thine only son.' (Abraham) said to Him, 'This one is an only son to his mother and the other is an only son to his mother.' (God) said to him, 'Whom thou lovest.' (Abraham) said to Him, 'Both of them do I love.' (God) said to him, 'Isaac' (Sanh. 89)."[7]

Fifth, whereas Christians usually refer to this event as the "sacrifice of Isaac", many Jews refer to it as the *Akedah,* or the "binding of Isaac", because, they say, Abraham does not sacrifice his son; rather, he binds him in preparation for a sacrifice that is subsequently aborted by God.

Sixth, this chapter is a masterpiece, not only in its dramatic story and pregnant theology, but also in its inner structure and the way it relates to other episodes in the life of Abraham, not to mention parallels with the sacrifice of the ultimate Son of Promise. Reading the text as a story of great human tragedy and triumph is like rowing across a lake and enjoying what can be seen only from the surface. But, don scuba gear and flippers, and you will see a whole new world under the surface. Let me whet your appetite for diving into this passage by showing how the story is divinely inspired to correspond with other events in Abraham's life: (1) the first agonizing decision to follow God and leave his family and homeland, and (2) the last great test of Abraham when he sent away his other son, Ishmael. Here we chart a comparison between Genesis 22—first with Genesis 21 and then with Genesis 12 as gleaned from the *Word Biblical Commentary*.[8]

---

[6] Rabbi Solomon ben Isaac (Shlomo Yitzhaki) (A.D. 1040–1105), known as Rashi (based on an acronym of his Hebrew initials), is one of the most respected Jewish commentators of all time. This quote is from *The Pentateuch*, The Navarre Bible (Dublin and New Jersey: Four Courts Press; Septer Publications, 1999), 199.

[7] Cotter, *Genesis*, 153.

[8] Wenham, *Genesis 16–50*, 99–100.

Genesis 21	Genesis 22
Lost Ishmael	"Lost" Isaac
God orders expulsion of Ishmael	God orders the sacrifice of Isaac
Food and water taken for the journey	Supplies and sacrificial material taken for the journey
Journey into the wilderness	Journey into the wilderness
With agony, first firstborn son willingly given up	With agony, last firstborn son willingly given up
Ishmael almost dies	Isaac almost dies
Ishmael's life saved by divine intervention	Isaac's life saved by divine intervention
First time angel calls from heaven	Last time in OT an angel calls from heaven
"I will make him a great nation."	"Your descendants like the stars, sand."
Hagar opened her eyes and saw ...	Abraham raised his eyes and saw ...
Saved by fortunate discovery: well	Saved by fortunate discovery: ram

Notice also that in both cases the boy is referred to as "lad", both stories have "early in the morning Abraham took", both say "shall inherit", and more. There are also significant parallels between chapters 22 and 16.

Now notice the parallels between this passage and Abraham's leaving his homeland in Mesopotamia.

Genesis 12	Genesis 22
First great trial—agonizing decision	Last great trial—agonizing decision
God calls, asking Abraham to leave home, giving up his family	God calls, asking Abraham to leave home, sacrificing his son
Decision cuts him off from his past	Decision cuts him off from his future
"Go forth to a land I will show you"	"Go forth to Moriah, to a mountain I will show you"
Not told where he is going	Not told exactly where he is going
"your land, your homeland, your father's house"	"your son, your only son Isaac, whom you love"

Genesis 12	Genesis 22
Promise of a glorious future	Promise of a glorious future
Blessing received at Moreh	Blessing received at Moriah
Built an altar when arriving	Built an altar when arriving
Followed by a genealogy	Followed by a genealogy

The Hebrew phrase "go forth" is used nowhere else in Scripture, demonstrating its deliberate use and significance in these two incidents. See if you can find other parallels.

Genesis 22 is a climactic event that left an indelible mark on history. It was a watershed moment in Abraham's life that we can only appreciate from a distance. Without doubt, it is the pinnacle of Abraham's life, if not the whole book of Genesis. The agony, suspense, and grief resulting from God's "command" cannot possibly be fathomed. The aged patriarch had heeded every word of God, and now came the most difficult task of all—one that certainly earned Abraham the title "Father of Faith". This event colored all of salvation history and even prefigured the most crucial cosmic event ever to take place in space and time—the death of our Lord Jesus Christ.

LOGISTICAL NOTE: *Preparing for the Test*

Where to begin with such an agonizing and personal story? There are rivers of theology and drama running through this passage. We are told from the outset that Abraham was being tested. We could ask, "Hasn't he been tested enough? He left his homeland and family; he wandered in arid lands promised to him but not yet delivered; he was exiled to Egypt during a famine; he waited twenty-five years for a son; he believed against all odds and even circumcised himself in his old age; he sent away his oldest son; he never argued but always believed and obeyed God—what more need he prove?"

Of course, God is all-knowing. Thus, he does not need to "test" people to find out what they will do. But Scripture often describes divine things in human terms. The time had now come for God to give Abraham a final test to know if Abraham really feared him (Gen 22:12). God would later also test the Israelites in the wilderness,

"You shall remember all the way which the LORD your God has led you these forty years in the wilderness, that he might humble you, testing you to know what was in your heart, whether you would keep his commandments, or not" (Deut 8:2).

Later Jesus would be tempted or tested in the wilderness. "Jesus was led up by the Spirit into the wilderness to be tempted by the devil" (Mt 4:1). The Greek word used for "tempt" is more often translated as "test" in the New Testament. Frequently the Pharisees are said to "test" Jesus using the same Greek word (e.g., Mt 16:1; Mk 8:11). Hebrews recalls Abraham's tests with the same Greek word, "By faith Abraham, when he was tested, offered up Isaac" (Heb 11:17; CCC 145).

Using the same root word, though in a different form in the *Our Father*, where Jesus told his disciples to pray, "Lead us not into temptation", it is often translated "and do not subject us to the final test" (Mt 6:13; Lk 11:4) as in the NAB. The Spirit led Jesus out to be tested. God has tested many of the saints—look at righteous Job! Abraham now took center stage as he was tested.

We are privy to information that Abraham did not have. We are told up front about Abraham's test. We have the benefit of hindsight as the sacred writer shows us the production notes, so to speak. But having no clue why this was happening to him, notice Abraham's response. From his humble, obedient heart, he responded, "Here am I."[9] He heard and was ready to obey—to do from the heart whatever God asked. Even after God's shocking words "offer him there as a burnt offering", there was no hint of resistance or debate. Abraham arose early and headed out to do God's bidding. Imagine Abraham stretching out on his mat for sleep that night. Did he tell Sarah? Did he sleep at all? Did he have doubts?

GEOGRAPHICAL NOTE: *Where Is Moriah?*

One basic principle of Bible study is to ask as many questions as you can and then look up the answers. With this passage, you might ask,

[9] If you are ever called by God, this is the proper response, "Here I am, Lord" or "Here am I, Lord." It is used at least fourteen times in the Bible: twice by Abraham, once by Jacob, Moses, Tobias, Isaiah, Ananias, and five times by Samuel. God himself uses the phrase twice to show his accessibility to us.

Where is Moriah? Why is Abraham instructed to walk so far? And is "Moriah" mentioned elsewhere in Scripture? By researching these three questions, you discover again the unity of the Bible and the correspondence between Old and New Testaments.

Abraham was instructed where to make the sacrifice; he could not offer his son anywhere he pleased. It had to be the mountain in the land of Moriah. Mount Moriah is about fifty miles northeast of Beersheba, thus the three days' walk. The name Moriah is mentioned only twice in the Bible, here in Genesis 22 and again in 2 Chronicles 3:1. Meditate for a minute on these two passages, and you will not only discover where Moriah was, but also catch a glimpse into the mind of God and why he sent Abraham walking three days for the sacrifice! In 2 Chronicles we read, "Then Solomon began to build the house of the LORD in Jerusalem on Mount Moriah, where the LORD had appeared to David his father" (2 Chron 3:1).[10]

Moriah was at the center of the world! It is the Temple Mount in Jerusalem, the holiest place in the world for Jews. It was God's chosen place for his dwelling. The Temple was built on Mount Moriah over the site of Abraham's binding of Isaac. The Jerusalem Cross, used as the emblem and coat of arms of the Kingdom of Jerusalem from the 1280s, has a large cross in the center with four smaller crosses at the four corners. One of its symbolic meanings is Jerusalem as the center of the world, and the smaller crosses as the four corners of the earth.

Three pivotal events took place at Mount Moriah in Jerusalem roughly a thousand years apart: (1) Abraham offered the son that he loved on an altar on Mount Moriah; (2) a thousand years later, about 960 B.C., Solomon built his temple and offered animal sacrifices on Mount Moriah; and (3) a thousand years later Jesus was crucified near the Temple, just outside the city walls. Interestingly, the *Akedah*, the "Binding of Isaac", has been called the "Calvary of the Old Testament".[11] What stunning parallels and correspondences between Old Testament and New Testament—between an earthly father offering his only-begotten son whom he loved and a Heavenly Father sacrificing his only-begotten Son whom he loved.

---

[10] For a detailed discussion of the location of Moriah and the "Mount of the Lord", see Scott W. Hahn, *Kinship by Covenant: A Canonical Approach to the Fulfillment of God's Saving Promises* (New Haven; London: Yale University Press, 2009), 117–18.

[11] See John Bergsma and Brant Pitre, *A Catholic Introduction to the Bible*, vol. 1, *The Old Testament* (San Francisco: Ignatius Press, 2018), 142.

As the Hebrew Scriptures will later make clear, the "mount of the
LORD" here is the Jerusalem Temple mount.... In some streams of
later Jewish tradition, the animal sacrifices offered at the Jerusalem
Temple were regarded as memorials or re-presentations of the sacrifice of Isaac, the rationale being that the blood of bulls and goats was
not effective in itself but symbolized the truly meritorious self-offering
of the forefather of the entire nation.[12]

MORAL AND HISTORICAL NOTE: *Human Sacrifice—Did God Intend Abraham to Slay Isaac?*

We would be remiss to neglect the issue of human sacrifice presented
in the passage. How could God possibly ask Abraham to kill and burn
his son? That goes against everything we know as moral and ethical.
It is like fingernails scratching across a chalkboard! We live in a day
and age when killing an innocent human being is unthinkable, right?
WRONG! In our own Western societies, many find it acceptable
and convenient to kill human beings through abortion, infanticide,
euthanasia, mass shootings, and genocide. We live in a society where
"human sacrifice" for the convenience of others is quite common.

We can theorize that God did not actually intend Abraham to
sacrifice Isaac because he was the son of promise, and to fulfill the
promise of God, he had to live. And in the end, God clearly demonstrated that no sacrifice was intended. He stopped it before the knife
ever fell. But still, the command/request and subsequent obedience
to kill a human son must be addressed.

Let's examine a few possibilities. First, Abraham was no stranger
to human sacrifice since it was common in the ancient world. In
Abraham's hometown of Ur, human sacrifice was frequent. In the
early twentieth century, famed British archaeologist Sir Leonard
Woolley excavated Ur and found hundreds of tombs. Among them
were royal tombs that he called Death Pits because the royal personages were surrounded by the skeletons of their entourage carefully arranged to accompany them on their journey into the afterlife.
Some tombs had over eighty skeletons strategically arranged around

[12] Ibid.

the king or queen. "In the corridors and in the wells, funerary chariots are found with their teams of equids, their drivers and a whole group of servants and musicians that must have accompanied the king in death. Sometimes more than 80 bodies have been found, certainly sacrificed before the funeral."[13] Woolley drew illustrations showing those poor souls killed to join the king or queen in death. One diagram, drawn at the scene, shows how the skeletons were discovered carefully arranged around the royal personages.[14] The people of Ur practiced human sacrifice.

In Ur, Abraham's family served foreign gods (Josh 24:2). The patron god of Ur was Nanna, the god of the moon. The Law of Moses would later forbid infant sacrifice precisely because it was widely practiced in Canaan and surrounding countries—human sacrifice was not new to Abraham.

Maybe God was testing Abraham to see if he was willing to do for him what he had been willing to do for Nanna. Would Abraham do for the true God what he would have done for a false god? Had Abraham truly switched his loyalties to the God of Glory? Was he as loyal to Yahweh as to Nanna? Maybe that was the test.

Could it be that God was giving us a human story so we could understand in human terms the agony that he went through when he gave his Son Jesus as a sacrifice for us, kind of like a sneak preview of the ultimate sacrifice he would be making of his own Son. Or could it be that God, knowing that he was going to give his only Son for men, was seeing if there was a man who would be willing to do the same and give his son for God?

Saint Irenaeus writes, "Abraham, according to his faith, adhered to the command of God's Word, and with a ready mind delivered up, as a sacrifice to God, his only-begotten and beloved son, in order that God also might be pleased to offer up, for all his seed, His own beloved and only-begotten Son, as a sacrifice for our redemption."[15]

---

[13] Jean-Cl. Margueron, "Ur (Place)", in *The Anchor Yale Bible Dictionary*, ed. David Noel Freedman, trans. Stephen Rosoff (New York: Doubleday, 1992), 767.

[14] See *Treasures from the Royal Tombs of Ur*, ed. Richard Zettler and Lee Horne (Philadelphia: University of Pennsylvania, 1998).

[15] *Against the Heresies* 4.5.4, in Patrick Henry Reardon, *Creation and the Patriarchal Histories: Orthodox Christian Reflections on the Book of Genesis* (Chesterton, Ind.: Ancient Faith Publishing, 2008), 89.

Viewing the outcome, and with a few hints in advance, I am convinced God did not intend Abraham to sacrifice his son, nor did Abraham expect actually to sacrifice Isaac. Notice two hints. First, Abraham informs his two servants, "I and the lad will go yonder and worship, and come again to you" (Gen 22:5). Two of us will go up to worship God, and two of us will return. Second, Isaac knows wood, hot coals, and an animal are necessary for the sacrifice. He asks his father, "Behold, the fire and the wood; but where is the lamb for a burnt offering?" Abraham answers, "God will provide himself the lamb for a burnt offering, my son" (vv. 7–8). In other words, at the last minute, we will find a lamb provided by God. Lastly, Hebrews tells us that even if he *did* have to kill his son, Abraham "considered that God was able to raise men even from the dead" (Heb 11:19; *CCC* 2572).

THE JOURNEY TO MORIAH AND THE BINDING OF ISAAC (22:3–14)

Abraham started out the next morning, with Isaac, wood, fire, a donkey, and two servants. Leaving Beersheba "early in the morning" and walking until sunset, it is reasonable to calculate they could cover twenty miles a day over the rugged terrain. By the noonday sun on the third day, they could expect to arrive at Moriah. Consider the three-day journey with the burden of his task weighing heavy on his heart—but also his constant trust in God. Three days is a long time for sober contemplation.

Notice the unusual words spoken to the two young men when they arrived at Moriah: "I and the lad will go yonder and worship, and come again to you." Abraham seems to be lying or confused. If he kills his son, how will the lad return with Abraham after they have worshipped. Origen best describes the thought process in Abraham's mind:

Tell me, Abraham, are you saying to the servants in truth that you will worship and return with the child, or are you deceiving them? If you are telling the truth, then you will not make him a holocaust. If you are deceiving, it is not fitting for so great a patriarch to deceive.

What disposition, therefore, does this statement indicate in you? I am speaking the truth, he says, and I offer the child as a holocaust. For this reason I both carry wood with me, and I return to you with him. For I believe, and this is my faith, that "God is able to raise him up even from the dead [Heb 11:19]."[16]

The writer of Hebrews knew exactly what was at play here, "By faith Abraham, when he was tested, offered up Isaac, and he who had received the promises was ready to offer up his only-begotten son, of whom it was said, 'Through Isaac shall your descendants be named.' He considered that God was able to raise men even from the dead; hence he did receive him back and this was a symbol" (Heb 11:17–19; CCC 1819, 2572). Instead of the word *symbol* as used in the RSV-2CE, some translations use the word *type* or *figure*. Isaac coming back down the mountain alive is a type or symbol of the risen Christ.

Throughout human history, worship has always involved sacrifice. Abraham is going up the mountain to worship God through a sacrifice. "Abraham took the wood of the burnt offering, and laid it on Isaac his son. So they went both of them together" (Gen 22:6). We have Saint John's words ringing in our ears: "So they took Jesus, and he went out, bearing his own cross, to the place called the place of a skull, which is called in Hebrew Golgotha" (Jn 19:17). Isaac carried the wood of the sacrifice on his back; Jesus carried the wood of the Cross on his back. The father and son arrived at the place of sacrifice together. Origen comments on the parallels:

That Isaac himself carries on himself "the wood for the holocaust" is a figure, because Christ also "himself carried his own cross," and yet to carry "the wood for the holocaust" is the duty of a priest. He himself therefore becomes both victim and priest. But what is added also is related to this: "And they both went off together." For when Abraham carries the fire and knife as if to sacrifice, Isaac does not go behind him, but with him, that he might be shown to contribute equally with the priesthood itself.[17]

---

[16] Homily 8.5, in Origen, *Homilies on Genesis and Exodus*, ed. Hermigild Dressler, trans. Ronald E. Heine, The Fathers of the Church, vol. 71 (Washington, D.C.: Catholic University of America Press, 1982), 140.

[17] Homily 8.6., ibid., 140–41.

The *fire* they carried was a pottery vessel containing hot coals to start a fire in this remote location (cf. Is 30:14).[18] After the wood was placed on the altar and the victim slaughtered, the coals were placed in the pile of wood to ignite the flames for the burning or immolation of the victim. Abraham had the knife in one hand and the fire in the other—ready to kill and burn out of love and obedience to God. Jesus' words come to mind, "If any one comes to me and does not hate his own father and mother and wife and children and brothers and sisters, yes, and even his own life, he cannot be my disciple. Whoever does not bear his own cross and come after me, cannot be my disciple" (Lk 14:26–27).

Isaac was no longer an infant or young boy (Gen 22:5, 12). The Hebrew word *na'ar* means "lad" or "young man", implying a teenager near adulthood. Isaac was a strong young man, able to walk three days and carry the wood up the mountain. In a short dialogue with his father—the only recorded conversation between Abraham and Isaac—he asks his father about the lamb, since it is peculiar approaching a sacrifice without an animal for the holocaust. Abraham was either confident of God's provision, expected a resurrection of sorts, or was trying to postpone telling Isaac the bad news. Their dialogue added tension to the drama. Again, the same sentence was repeated, "So they went both of them together", which elicits great emotion, their togetherness, as the stress builds.

Something can be learned about the son. Abraham built the altar, laid the wood on the altar, bound Isaac and laid him on the firewood, and then raised his knife to slay his only son. The father had completely submitted to the will of God, and the son was completely docile to the wishes of his father. There is no indication that the strong young man resisted his elderly father. He could have resisted and fled for his life. But he willingly allowed himself to be bound and placed on the altar. How could the old man pick up the teenager to hoist him up onto the top of the altar? It would almost require the son's cooperation. Did not Jesus willingly obey the will of his Father and

---

[18] "The production of fire by artificial means was a skill known to man from Stone Age times, but then and in later times great care was taken to preserve a burning fire to avoid the necessity for rekindling. Abraham apparently carried a piece of burning fire with him when he went to offer Isaac (Gn. 22:6), and Is. 30:14 indicates that this was a usual domestic practice." T. C. Mitchell, "Fire", in *New Bible Dictionary*, ed. D. R. W. Wood et al. (Leicester, England; Downers Grove, Ill.: InterVarsity Press, 1996), 368.

submit himself to the crucifixion, stating, "not my will, but yours, be done" (Lk 22:42)? Isaiah prophesies of our Lord, "He was oppressed, and he was afflicted, yet he opened not his mouth; like a lamb that is led to the slaughter, and like a sheep that before its shearers is silent, so he opened not his mouth" (53:7).

Jewish historian Flavius Josephus (ca. 37–ca. 100) wrote:

> Now Isaac was of such a generous disposition as became the son of such a father, and was pleased with this discourse; and said "That he was not worthy to be born at first, if he should reject the determination of God and of his father, and should not resign himself up readily to both their pleasures; since it would have been unjust if he had not obeyed, even if his father alone had so resolved." So he went immediately to the altar to be sacrificed.[19]

> On Rosh Hashanah and Yom Kippur, when Jews pray for forgiveness for their sins, the focus is on the *Akedah*, the "Binding of Isaac," the Genesis 22 account of Abraham's willingness to sacrifice Isaac at God's request. Remarkably, some traditional prayers ask for forgiveness for the sake of Abraham, who was a father who had such great love for God that he was willing to sacrifice his own son. Others even petition for mercy for the sake of Isaac, who offered himself up as a willing sacrifice! (They point out that if Isaac was carrying enough wood to burn a sacrifice, he had to be a grown man and easily able to overpower his elderly father. His willingness to be a sacrifice is seen as a prominent theme of the story.)[20]

Isaac's willing cooperation is a poignant prefiguration of Jesus' own cooperation. In the Church of the Holy Sepulchre, at the very geographical location where Jesus was nailed to the cross, there is a darkened mosaic unnoticed by most people, and seldom is the typological connection made. The mosaic shows Abraham with arm uplifted and knife descending. This is the very place that two fathers each offered up their beloved sons as sacrifices (*CCC* 2572). But one son was spared; the other was not. Yet even with the prefigurement

---

[19] *Antiquities of the Jews* 1, 13, 4, in *The Works of Josephus: Complete and Unabridged*, trans. William Whiston, updated edition (Peabody, Mass.: Hendrickson, 1987), 43.

[20] Lois Tverberg, *Reading the Bible with Rabbi Jesus: How a Jewish Perspective Can Transform Your Understanding* (Grand Rapids, Mich.: Baker Books: A Division of Baker Publishing Group, 2018), 151–52.

of the Father's "sacrifice" of Jesus in Abraham's offering of Isaac, we can never really appreciate the love and ultimate price God demonstrated for us, as "they went both of them together", expressing their loving bond and firm intention.

The voice of God suddenly called from heaven with an urgency that was demonstrated by the double use of his name, "Abraham, Abraham!" Virtually all modern translations use an exclamation point here for emphasis. We are told the voice was that of "the angel of Yahweh", but as with the experience of Hagar, we discover in verse 12 that it was actually God himself commanding Abraham not to harm the lad, "for now I know that you fear God, seeing you have not withheld your son, your only-begotten son, from me" (22:10–12). God only intended to test Abraham—to see if he would obey at any cost. The test was complete. Abraham had passed with flying colors. *He* now knows what *we* have known all along—that it was just a test. Abraham had confidently told Isaac that God would provide a lamb, and he did. The language is poetic: "And Abraham lifted up his eyes and looked, and behold, behind him was a ram...." The word "behold" introduces a dramatic effect of suddenness and surprise. Abraham saw a ram caught in a thicket by his horns. He took the ram, and, with a certain sigh of relief, he offered it as the burnt offering instead of his son. Even though Isaac was spared, God the Father did not spare *his* own Son, as Saint Paul reminds us, God "did not spare his own Son but gave him up for us all" (Rom 8:32). "In fact, chapter 22 is the Bible's first instance of a 'substitution' made in the matter of sacrifice. This ram caught in the bush becomes the substitute for Isaac...."[21]

Why are we told the ram's head was stuck in a thicket? For one reason, because that is what happened. How to account for there being a ram available in the vicinity for sacrifice? One got stuck in the thicket. But there is more we can say about it.

First, as a result of Adam's sin, the ground was cursed (3:17; 5:29). Remember, the sign of the curse upon the ground was thorns and thistles (3:18). God loved man, but he also loved the whole world (Greek word *cosmos*). Might the thicket or bramble bush represent the sign of the curse of the earth? Jesus is the lamb of God provided for us (Jn 1:29). The ram on Mount Moriah had his head stuck in a

[21] Patrick Henry Reardon, *Creation and the Patriarchal Histories: Orthodox Christian Reflections on the Book of Genesis* (Chesterton, Ind.: Ancient Faith Publishing, 2008), 89.

thicket, and Jesus had his head stuck in a thorn bush, too—a crown of thorns (Jn 19:2–5). Second, a thicket brings to mind thorns. Might the crown of thorns worn by Jesus symbolize the curse of the earth being borne by Jesus with the ultimate goal of redeeming mankind and bringing restoration and re-creation, including a removal of the curse of the ground? (See Rom 8:19–22; *CCC* 400, 1043.)

Abraham named the place "The LORD will provide" (*Yahweh–yireh*). This led to the proverbial saying, "On the mount of the LORD it shall be provided".[22] But we may ask, *what* shall be provided, and on *what* mount? On the mountains of Jerusalem (Moriah), God had provided a substitute holocaust in the place of Isaac. Abraham's naming of the location and the proverbial saying at the time were prophetic words. We who have the fullness of Christ's revelation should be shouting, "Jesus, the true sacrificial lamb will be sacrificed on this same mountain for the sins of the world! The Lord will provide the savior on this mount!" When John the Baptist says, "Behold, the Lamb of God" (Jn 1:29), it is a correlation with this prophecy. Saint Paul reminds us, "But when the time had fully come, God sent forth his Son" (Gal 4:4). "[T]*he mount of Jehovah* is Mount Moriah, the Temple Mount, which also became known as Mount Zion. This will be the future place of the atonement, and so atonement on this mountain will be provided."[23]

This event in Abraham's life is commemorated in the Catholic liturgy five times: the 2nd Sunday of Lent, Year B; Thursday of the 13th Week in Ordinary Time, Year 1; Easter Vigil of Years A, B, and C.

THEOLOGICAL NOTE: *Abraham Was Justified by Faith and Works*

Some Christians hold that people are saved (justified before God) by "faith alone". They emphasize that the "finished work of Christ" is

---

[22] Some translations render this "On the mount of the Lord it will be seen" since there is ambiguity in translating this passage. Though much discussed, it actually has the same result. It will be provided on the mountain, or it will be seen on the mountain. The coming atonement through Christ will both be provided and seen on the mountain in Jerusalem.

[23] Arnold G. Fruchtenbaum, *Ariel's Bible Commentary: The Book of Genesis*, 1st ed. (San Antonio, Tex.: Ariel Ministries, 2008), 356.

sufficient for salvation, and no works or effort on our part are meritorious for our salvation. Catholics agree that we are saved by grace through faith and that no works of ours can impart or deserve the initial justification before God. What is more, no one will be able to stand before God on judgment day and rightly say, "You owe me!", as if his heavenly "reward" had been accomplished by himself. But do works of obedience and righteousness play any part in our salvation or our ongoing grace-filled relationship with God, subsequent to initial justification? Yes. And this is why Luther despised the book of James, because it insisted on works of Christian fidelity being part of our ongoing justification. Luther's understanding of justification "by faith alone" conflicted with James' teaching.

It is significant to look at the Epistle of James to see what he wrote about Abraham and our salvation:

> What does it profit, my brethren, if a man says he has faith but has not works? Can his faith save him? ... Was not Abraham our father justified by works, when he offered his son Isaac upon the altar? You see that faith was active along with his works, and faith was completed by works, and the Scripture was fulfilled which says, "Abraham believed God, and it was reckoned to him as righteousness"; and he was called the friend of God. You see that a man is justified by works and not by faith alone. (Jas 2:14, 20–24)

Actually, this is the only time in Scripture that the two words *faith* and *alone* are used together (*CCC* 162, 1815). Abraham's faithfulness and obedience, not "faith alone", is attested to elsewhere in Scripture, "Remember the deeds of the fathers, which they did in their generations; and receive great honor and an everlasting name. Was not Abraham found faithful when tested, and it was reckoned to him as righteousness?" (1 Mac 2:51–52).

COVENANT REAFFIRMED, AND THEY WALK HOME TOGETHER (22:15–19)

Abraham was justified before God again. In response to his obedient heart and actions, God reaffirmed his covenant and promises with Abraham. It was conferred upon Abraham and his seed without obligation on their part (cf. Ex 32:13). The angel of the Lord called to Abraham a second time from heaven. God again affirmed that in Abraham's offspring (*seed*) all the nations of the earth would be blessed (v. 18; *CCC* 706, 1819). The NAB has it, "In your descendants all the nations of the earth shall find blessing." The New Testament understands the seed to be Christ, who as the son of Abraham brings blessing to all the nations (see Acts 3:25; Gal 3:8–9, 16). And it is on this mount that the blessing would be realized even for the Gentiles.

Imagine the sense of relief as he mulled over these words and returned to the young men and the donkey with his son Isaac, just as he had promised. He had not known exactly *how* he would return with Isaac, but he had trusted God—and that was enough. He walked three days back to Beersheba, lighter in heart and load than when he left. Sarah undoubtedly was waiting in the doorway of the tent as they arrived home through the desert. Whether she knew of God's test or not, we are not told. Abraham dwelled in Beersheba presumably until he died. Over the long years, Abraham had proven faithful and obedient—*he was never again tested by God.*

THE FAMILY OF NAHOR (22:20–24)

Abraham's brother Nahor had remained in Haran after Abraham left for Canaan probably forty or more years earlier. Abraham was now updated on his brother's offspring. A genealogical list was necessary because Isaac needed a wife, and she had to come from Abraham's family. Isaac would not be allowed to marry a pagan Canaanite, nor would he be allowed to leave the Promised Land himself to find a bride. Abraham looked to his relatives to find a bride for his son. In the genealogical list, we see a familiar name—Rebekah.

CHAPTER 23

THE DEATH OF SARAH; PURCHASE OF MACHPELAH

PERSONAL NOTE: *Recalling the Faith of Sarah*

Following Abraham's monumental demonstration of faith and obedience on Mount Moriah, he and Sarah, with their only son, Isaac, lived for some twenty years in relative silence, enjoying quiet family life with hard work and faithfulness, tending their ever-growing flocks and herds in Beersheba in the Negev Desert. Looking back at the work of God in their lives is certainly easier than looking forward with unfulfilled expectations and uncertainties. Genesis 23 picks up with the death of faithful Sarah, who died at the ripe old age of 127 years, leaving behind her husband, Abraham, and son, Isaac, who was about thirty-seven years old at this time and still unmarried.

Sarah's prominence in Scripture is stellar. One is at a loss to find another Old Testament woman who was more honored than Sarah. Let's pause for a moment to contemplate her role in the history of salvation. Her name shows up fifty-four times in the Bible, three times in the New Testament. Sarah, like Abraham, was honored with a new name signifying her new status. Sarah was to be "a mother of nations", and kings and peoples would come from her (17:15–16). She is eulogized in the "chapter of faith" in Hebrews, "By faith Sarah herself received power to conceive, even when she was past the age, since she considered him faithful who had promised" (11:11).

The *Catechism* teaches that Sarah (who by her faith was "given to conceive the son of promise") helped to prepare the way for the mission of the Blessed Virgin Mary. Like Abraham, Sarah served to help keep alive the hope of Israel's salvation and, by extension, the salvation of all mankind (*CCC* 64, 145, 489). Sarah's son, Isaac—like Mary's Son, Jesus—was born of an undeniable supernatural intervention that transcended nature (Sarah's sterility, Mary's virginity). This was to realize, through a beloved son, the blessing God had promised to visit upon Abraham and his descendants. When Mary asked the angel Gabriel, "How can this be, since I have no husband?" the response was, "With God nothing will be impossible" (Lk 1:34, 37). When Sarah asked the Lord, "Shall I indeed bear a child, now that I am old", the response was: "Is anything too hard for the LORD?" (Gen 18:13–14). In his humanity, Jesus looked to Sarah as his ancestor and based on *Catechism* paragraph 61, she is certainly honored as a saint in the liturgical tradition of the Catholic Church.

DEATH OF SARAH (23:1–2)

Sarah died in *Kiriath-arba* (an earlier name for Hebron). She had been Abraham's constant and faithful companion, as half-sister and wife, from their youth in Ur, through decades in the wilderness of Canaan, and the drama of God's testing and blessings. Now his steadfast companion had died, and he mourned and wept for her. In ancient times, mourning the dead was usually a loud expression of grief. Mourning could not last too long, since the general practice was to inter the body quickly. Isaac is not mentioned until later when he takes a wife to assuage his grief at losing his mother (Gen 24:67).

PURCHASING THE CAVE OF MACHPELAH
FOR SARAH'S BURIAL (23:3–20)

God had promised Canaan to Abraham, yet after sixty years Abraham still did not own one inch of the land. After Sarah's death, he approached the local Hittites of Kiriath-arba to purchase land to bury his wife. Abraham was quite the diplomat as a "stranger and sojourner". It would have been imprudent to announce that God had already promised him their land.

Though the English texts refer to Hittites, in the original Hebrew text, the word is literally "the sons of Heth", who was a son of Canaan, a grandson of Noah (Gen 10:15; 23:3).

The Hittites were descendants of Heth, sons of Canaan, who was a grandson of Noah (Gen 10:15). Though the text names them as

Hittites, it is literally "the sons of Heth" (23:3). Abraham was a sojourner dwelling among the Hittites in the area of Hebron. The Hittites knew Abraham was wealthy, powerful, and a "mighty prince". He had dwelled among them for over sixty years, defeated kings in battle, and had made treaties and covenants. They offered him the best of the sepulchres for the burial of his wife. They were diplomatic, too. They certainly desired Abraham's favor to avoid treachery with him or his descendants in the future.

What follows is a detailed negotiation for property between Abraham and Ephron the Hittite. These are typical legalities illuminated by ancient documents disclosing many details of the Hittite Code of Law. Abraham proves to be a savvy negotiator with knowledge of the local laws and customs. They offered Abraham a choice sepulchre, but he appealed for a permanent family burial plot, knowing that his descendants would eventually inhabit this land. He offered to buy the cave of Machpelah. Ephron the Hittite offered to give the field and the cave to Abraham, saying, "My lord, listen to me; a piece of land worth four hundred shekels of silver, what is that between you and me? Bury your dead" (23:15). Notice how he hinted, through his suggestion, at the land's worth. So Abraham weighed out the four hundred shekels of silver. A shekel was not a coin per se, but a specific weight of pure silver, about 0.4 of an ounce. So, the price of the land was roughly 10 pounds of silver.

We read in verse 17 that the field of Ephron in Machpelah was just east of Mamre in the land of Canaan, which should sound familiar. It was there that the Lord, in the form of three travelers, had visited Abraham so long ago. The cave of Machpelah is today the predominant landmark in Hebron. The cave contains the bones of Abraham and Sarah, Isaac and Rebekah, Jacob and Leah (Gen 25:9; 50:13). Over the tombs King Herod built a massive structure that still exists today and is called the cave of Machpelah. It is divided into two distinct sections: half a Jewish synagogue and the other half a Muslim mosque. Security is very tight as can be imagined. The Tomb of the Patriarchs is the second most holy place in the world for the Jews, second only to Temple Mount where Abraham bound Isaac and where the Temple once stood.

Abraham now owned his first plot of ground in Canaan, bought from Ephron the Hittite, not for dwelling upon, but for burials. Sarah was placed in the cave (23:19).

THE MARRIAGE OF ISAAC AND REBEKAH

INTRODUCTION

Chapters 23 and 24 are meant to be read together. This can be seen by the way the author "bookended" them. One woman is lost; another one is found; a mother dies; a wife arrives. Chapter 23 begins with "Sarah lived a hundred and twenty-seven years;... and Sarah died at Kiriath-arba." Chapter 24 closes with the words, "Then Isaac ... took Rebekah, and she became his wife; and he loved her. So Isaac was comforted after his mother's death."

Chapter 24 is the longest story in Genesis and artistically composed to express the crucial significance of finding the right bride for the son of promise. At Sarah's death, Abraham was 137 years old and would live another thirty-eight years. These later years are quiet with no tests and no further communication from God that we know of. God blessed him beyond measure.

A BRIDE NEEDED FOR ISAAC; ABRAHAM SENDS HIS SERVANT (24:1–9)

Before the covenant could be fulfilled through Isaac, Isaac needed to marry and have children of his own. But there were no Hebrew girls for him to marry since Abraham had left his remaining family behind in Haran. Isaac could not marry a Canaanite girl. The Canaanites were corrupt and wicked and had forfeited the land. Abraham had to find a bride from among his own people over five hundred miles to the north. That may not seem like a big deal today, but that was a long trek by foot—like walking from Detroit to Washington, D.C.!

Turning his mind from the dead to the living, Abraham devised
a plan to find a suitable wife for his son. Many years earlier, he had
had 318 male servants in his household—enough to defeat kings
in battle (14:14–16). He certainly had accumulated more over the
years. He picked his oldest and most reliable servant and charged
him with this vital task. It was probably the trusted Eliezer from
Damascus (15:2), but in this episode the servant is left unnamed.
Notice the authority of this servant: (1) he was the oldest servant
in Abraham's household; (2) he had charge of everything Abraham
had; (3) he alone was trusted with the sensitive and monumental
task of finding a wife for Abraham's son.

Abraham sent his servant off on the time-sensitive journey. It was
so critical that the servant had to swear his absolute obedience to find
a wife from Abraham's own kindred and not from the Canaanites
(24:3–4) and never to take Isaac back to Haran—he had to stay on the
Promised Land. Before preparing ten camels laden with supplies and
gifts, Abraham made his servant swear an oath. The physical gesture
that accompanied the "swearing" would be considered strange today.
Abraham ordered him to place his hand under Abraham's thigh (vv.
2–3). Most scholars agree that "thigh" is a euphemism for the male
genitalia. This would be appropriate since the sign of the covenant
was applied to the male genitals and this organ is also instrumental in
the procreation of future generations. Gravity was added to this oath
by swearing by the organ that transmitted life.

> Now he entrusts [his servant] with the most important and delicate
> task in his career as Abraham's servant. The sacredness of this duty
> is underlined by the oath he is invited to swear.... It is no ordinary
> request that Abraham is making, so he couches it with some delicacy.
> By putting his hand under Abraham's thigh, the servant was touching
> his genitals and thus giving the oath a special solemnity. In the ancient
> Orient, solemn oaths could be taken holding some sacred object in
> one's hand, as it is still customary to take an oath on the Bible before
> giving evidence in court.... An oath by the seat of procreation is
> particularly apt in this instance, when it concerns the finding of a wife
> for Isaac.[1]

---

[1] Gordon J. Wenham, *Genesis 16–50*, Word Biblical Commentary, vol. 2 (Dallas: Word,
Incorporated, 1994), 141.

Abraham's servant swears that he will carry out Abraham's dying wish (Gen 24:2, 9), placing his hand under the "thigh" of Abraham. This is clearly a serious oath, sworn on the genitals, the source of life, and thus under threat of the loss of fertility.[2]

Saint John Chrysostom confirms this:

You see, since he had reached extreme old age, the text says, he wished to preserve Isaac from association with the Canaanites, lest he take a wife from among them; so he summoned the more prudent of his servants, the text says, and gave him the following instructions: "Place your hand under my thigh." In Greek the verse is written this way: "under my thigh," whereas in Hebrew it says "under my loins." Why did he speak in this fashion? It was an idiom of people in the past. But on other grounds it was also because the birth of Isaac takes its origin from there.[3]

Three possible scenarios present themselves: (1) find a local girl for Isaac among the Canaanites, (2) take Isaac back to the homeland, or (3) find a wife from Abraham's people to marry Isaac. Abraham was clear! In the last recorded words of Abraham in Scripture, he reaffirmed that the bride had to come from his own people to propagate the covenant. The promise of the land was tied directly to Isaac, and he must never leave it. Isaac's presence in the Promised Land represents and symbolizes the fulfillment of the covenant—to abandon the land or to marry a Canaanite would have been equal to renouncing God's promises. Abraham had experience with God's provisions and the work of angels; he promised his servant that God's angel would go before him. If his best efforts failed, he would be released from his oath. The servant placed his hand under Abraham's thigh, swore the oath, loaded ten camels with all sorts of choice gifts, and set out for Haran.

The servant went to "the city of Nahor", which probably is not the city's name, but a reference to the city in which Nahor lived. It

---

[2] John R. Spencer, s.v. "Thigh", in *Eerdmans Dictionary of the Bible*, ed. David Noel Freedman, Allen C. Myers, and Astrid B. Beck (Grand Rapids, Mich.: Eerdmans, 2000), 1301.

[3] Homilies on Genesis 48.7, in *The Fathers of the Church: St. John Chrysostom: Homilies on Genesis 46–67*, trans. Robert C. Hill (Washington D.C.: Catholic University of America Press, 1992), 28–29.

probably refers to Haran (where Abraham had lived before moving to Canaan), which was situated in northwestern Mesopotamia along the Balikh River, a tributary of the Euphrates. It was at the northern tip of the Fertile Crescent and was a stop along the major trade route. The ancient city is now a village named *Harran* in modern-day Turkey. Abraham's brother Nahor, who had remained behind in Haran, had eight sons with his wife, Milcah. One son was named Bethuel, who became the father of Rebekah, who was to become the wife of Isaac.

Abraham's servant needed ten camels and a group of men to carry the supplies for such a long trip and to transport the many gifts for Isaac's future wife and her family. Arriving with ten camels demonstrated Abraham's great wealth. The archaeological ruins of the city are visible today. This area often exceeds 100°. To avoid the heat, women drew water in the cool of the morning and evening. The servant arrived and had the camels kneel at the well, prepared for a drink after the long trek. (If you have not ridden a camel, especially as it drops to its knees, you have missed a momentous experience in life.)

THE SERVANT ARRIVES IN HARAN; REBEKAH WATERS HIS CAMELS (24:10–27)

The servant prayed to God. It was an astute prayer full of an expectation that God was providentially involved in human history and was ready to assist him. He made a bold request. Let the maiden of God's choice offer him a drink from the well and *also* offer to water his ten camels. Notice the girl had to offer to water the camels, not be requested or offered payment. This was way out of the range of possibility. Even in a culture known for hospitality, this was an outrageous expectation.

Rebekah was a young maiden, fair to look upon, who had never known a man, i.e., was a virgin. She was the daughter of Bethuel, the son of Nahor, the brother of Abraham—which made her Abraham's grandniece. As she approached the well, the servant ran to the girl and asked for a drink. After complying with his request, she willingly said, "I will draw for your camels also, until they have done drinking" (Gen 24:19).

Do you know how much water camels can drink after a long journey? Based on my own experience, a single camel can drink twenty-five gallons of water in ten minutes—up to fifty gallons in a day. The camels were thirsty after the journey, so these ten camels were expected to drink over 250 gallons of water. Jugs of water were carried either on the head or on the shoulder—in this case, it was the shoulder (v. 45). Each jug would contain two to three gallons.[4] This meant she ran to the spring and either descended down stairs into the well or dropped a bucket down with a rope to fill her jug before bringing the water back to pour into the drinking trough (v. 20). She was a very busy girl for well over an hour as she hoisted and lowered the jar and "quickly emptied her jar into the trough and ran again to the well to draw, and she drew [water] for all his camels." If calculations serve us correctly, Rebekah made at least one hundred trips back and forth.

Without any promise of reward, Rebekah voluntarily ran back and forth between the well and the watering trough until "the camels had done drinking." Remember Abraham's hospitality when the three strangers arrived at his tent? He rushed, he ran, he quickly cared for them! Rebekah is very much like her granduncle Abraham, rushing to show hospitality to strangers and also their animals. Imagine the look on the servant's face as he watched her—this must be the chosen maiden.

This is the first of the biblical marriages described as being initiated at a well. Jacob and Moses first met their wives at wells (Gen 29:6; Ex 2:16–21). Jesus also met the Samaritan woman at a well.

Abraham's servant "gazed" at the girl as she worked. He pulled a nose ring and bracelets from his treasures. Still not knowing if she was from the family of Abraham, he asked her two questions when she had completed the exhausting task. She answered, Yes, I am the daughter of Bethuel, and we have accommodations for you and your camels. Convinced this maiden was the girl of God's choice, he gave

---

[4] "Camels drink only as much water as they have lost and do not store it in the hump.... A camel that has gone a few days without water could drink as much as twenty-five gallons. In contrast, the jars that were used for water would usually hold no more than three gallons." Victor Harold Matthews, Mark W. Chavalas, and John H. Walton, *The IVP Bible Background Commentary: Old Testament*, electronic ed. (Downers Grove, Ill.: InterVarsity Press, 2000), Gen 24:19–20.

her the jewelry, and she rushed home to announce his arrival. The gold ring for Rebekah's nose weighed half a shekel, which was about .2 ounces. Rebekah wore a nose ring![5] The two gold bracelets were ten shekels, or about four ounces each. The emphasis here is in the extraordinary size and value of the gifts. The servant's next reaction was to bow and worship God.

MEETING REBEKAH'S FAMILY (24:28–51)

So far success. He had found the girl, and she was from the right family. Now to convince her to marry Isaac, the son of Abraham whom they had not seen for over sixty-five years. She *ran* all the way to tell her family. As Abraham's grandniece, she was Isaac's first cousin once removed. Her mother was Milcah—a wife, not a concubine. The servant was elated. Now we meet a new character who will loom large later in the story. Rebekah's brother Laban, impressed with the new jewelry adorning his sister and her excited words, rushed out to escort the servant to the house. He greeted him as "blessed of the Lord—Yahweh", indicating that the family acknowledged the God of Abraham. The camels were tended, feet were washed, and the servant and his men were brought in for dinner. Before dinner, the servant insisted on explaining his mission, how Abraham had become very rich and had sent him to find a bride for his only son, to whom he had given all that he had. From verses 33–49, he reiterated the whole story including his prayer and how he met Rebekah. This full recounting demonstrates how significant this link is to the whole saga of salvation. After narrating the facts in detail, he made the generous offer. Now Rebekah's family had to decide—remembering that marriages were arranged by the fathers. Even Abraham was arranging a marriage for his forty-year-old son! The family agreed that this whole affair was from the Lord and that Rebekah should return with the servant (24:50–51).

---

[5] "Nose rings were especially popular during the Iron Age (1200–600 B.C.), though there are examples from earlier periods. Made of silver, bronze, and gold, and often tubular in design, they were round with two ends for insertion and sometimes included a tiny pendant. The beka is the half-shekel measure of weight, equal to one-fifth of an ounce." Ibid. Gen 24:22.

PERMISSION FOR MARRIAGE IS GRANTED; REBEKAH TRAVELS TO WED ISAAC (24:52–67)

With permission to marry granted, the treasures were revealed—gold and silver, clothing for Rebekah, and costly ornaments for her brother and mother. Reluctantly, her family attempted to delay her departure, but the servant prevailed. His mission was complete, and he was anxious to return home with the prize. With a final blessing in poetic form, her family sent her off with her nurse and maids. They mounted the camels and began the long trek to Beersheba (v. 61). The camels served as moving vans as they started the long 500-mile trek for her to marry a man she had never met. Caravans traveled about twenty miles a day, so the trip back to Beersheba took roughly twenty-five days. There is no accounting for time in the narrative—they just arrived.

Isaac had returned from Beer–lahai–roi, mentioned earlier in Genesis 16:14, where God spoke to Hagar near the Egyptian border. It was a strategically located well in the Negev desert. Isaac settled there later (25:11). Many translations say that Isaac "went out to meditate in the field". But an obscure word is used, one with alternative meanings of strolling, chatting, walking, or even mourning the death of his mother (see v. 67). A popular Rabbinic tradition asserts that Isaac was praying.

Isaac "lifted up his eyes", and, behold, he saw camels coming. *Behold* amplifies the scene. Rebekah astride a camel at the same time "lifted up her eyes" and saw Isaac. The author has them noticing each other simultaneously by using the same language for each, surely meant to give the impression that it was an instant recognition, or, in modern language, love at first sight. The style of the story is very endearing. When Rebekah spotted Isaac, she alighted from her camel, confirmed it was Isaac, and instantly veiled her face. It was not customary for all Near Eastern women to have their faces covered. Rebekah's face was only covered at the meeting of her betrothed. "She covered herself with a *veil*, it being customary for the bride to be veiled in the presence of her betrothed till after the nuptial ceremony."[6] With the veil, Rebekah signaled Isaac without a word that she was ready and willing to be his bride. "Then Isaac brought

---

[6] E. F. Sutcliffe, "Genesis", in *A Catholic Commentary on Holy Scripture*, ed. Bernard Orchard and Edmund F. Sutcliffe (Toronto, New York, and Edinburgh: Thomas Nelson, 1953), 197.

her into the tent [of Sarah, his mother], and took Rebekah, and she
became his wife; and he loved her. So Isaac was comforted after his
mother's death" (24:67). As romantic as this love story is, the hero
remains Abraham's unnamed servant who trusted God and served his
master faithfully.

A SPIRITUAL INTERPRETATION: *The Marriage of Isaac and Rebekah*

When Isaac took her into his mother's tent, she formally became
Sarah's successor, the new daughter of the promise. The continuation
of the covenant and the family line was now assured. The term "Isaac
took" means that he formally wed Rebekah and took her as his wife.
This is the second time that the word *love* is used in the Bible. The
first time was to describe the bond between a father and his son (22:2).
Here is the first use of *love* between a man and a woman. Isaac missed
his mother, who used to live in this tent. But now he had a wife, and
after three years of Sarah's absence, we are told that because of his love
for Rebekah, he was comforted after the loss of his mother.

Looking back at this chapter we see marvelous parallels with the
life of our Lord. The typological depth is stunning. In Genesis 22, we
saw the death, Resurrection, and Ascension of our Lord prefigured in
Isaac, who was offered as a sacrifice on the same mountain, "raised"
from the dead, and taken back to his father's house. The typology is
fulfilled as we see Jesus and his Father on the same mountain. Jesus
was the sacrifice who was also raised from the dead, and like Abraham
with Isaac, God the Father took his son back home.

Now we see Isaac, the beloved son at the right hand of his father
Abraham, back at his dwelling. He held the position of firstborn son
and had inherited everything his father owned; but the father wanted
a bride for his son. The Father Abraham sent his unnamed servant
to his own people to find a bride. The unnamed servant found the
bride and gave her extravagant gifts as Abraham willed and brought
the bride back to the father and the son. The son took the bride into
his tent as his wife, and he loved her.

Think of our Lord Jesus. After his Resurrection, the Son returns
home to his Father. The only Son sits at the right hand of the Father,

who has given everything to the Son. Like Abraham, the Father desires a bride for his Son to perpetuate the covenant. In a certain sense, we can say that the Holy Spirit does not have a name—*Holy Spirit* is more a description, at least for us. He is, so to speak, the unnamed servant who has been with the Father and the Son from all eternity. After the Son "returns home" from the Sacrifice at Mount Moriah, the Holy Spirit is sent by the Father to God's people on the day of Pentecost to "find a bride" for the Son. The Church is the Bride of Christ. The Holy Spirit brings gifts, which he freely distributes as he wills (Rom 12:6; 1 Cor 1:7; 12:4, 11; *CCC* 1692). The bride, the Church, succeeds the synagogue, so to speak, as Rebekah succeeded Sarah. The Church submits to her Lord, and there is a great marriage feast (Rev 19:7–9; *CCC* 808, 1602). The bride comes into the tent of heaven to live with the Groom. As Isaac loved Rebekah, so Jesus loves the Church (Eph 5:31–33). No wonder the Holy Spirit waited until Isaac and Rebekah to use the word *love* for the second time. First, to show the love between a father and his only-begotten son fulfilled in the love of God the Father for his only-begotten Son. Second, to depict the love of a man for his wife to prefigure the love of the Son for his Bride, the Church.

Saint Caesarius of Arles (ca. 470–542) saw connections as well:

Isaac's servant found Rebecca at the well, and Rebecca in turn found Isaac himself at the well [well of Beer-lahai-roi]. It is true: Christ does not find the Church, nor the Church Christ, except at the sacrament of Baptism.... Isaac took Rebecca "and led her into the tent of his mother." Christ also took the Church and established it in place of the synagogue.... Moreover, dearly beloved, because from us Christ the Lord prepared for Himself a spiritual spouse which, as I said, He even redeemed with His precious Blood.[7]

---

[7] Sermon 85.4, in Caesarius of Arles, *Saint Caesarius of Arles: Sermons (1–238)*, ed. Hermigild Dressler and Bernard M. Peebles, trans. Mary Magdeleine Mueller, The Fathers of the Church, vol. 2 (Washington, D.C.: Catholic University of America Press; Consortium Books, 1956–1973), 23–24.

CHAPTER 25

DEATH OF ABRAHAM;
DESCENDANTS OF ISHMAEL; ISAAC'S SONS

ABRAHAM MARRIES KETURAH (25:1–6)

The life of Abraham comes to a close. Genesis 25 summarizes this final chapter: (1) Abraham's new wife Keturah and the sons born through her, (2) the descendants of Ishmael, and (3) the death and burial of Abraham.

Abraham took another wife, whose name was Keturah. The *Septuagint* simply states "Abraham added and took a woman" without using the word *wife*. The text does not tell us *when* he took Keturah or anything about her. The flow of the text suggests it was after the marriage of Isaac, but if Abraham considered himself beyond the age of fathering at one hundred years old (17:17), how would he have expected to father multiple children after the age of 140? Some suggest Keturah had actually been a wife or concubine from a much earlier time. Verse 6 (like 1 Chron 1:32) implies that Keturah was a "concubine", not a wife, and it also uses the plural for *concubine*, suggesting that Abraham may have had other concubines, unless the plural simply refers to Hagar and Keturah.

Keturah's name means *incense*, and, interestingly, her sons and grandsons settled along the "incense route" through western Arabia south of Edom and Moab. Midian stands out from the list of sons through Keturah whose descendants are mentioned as many as sixty-four times in Scripture. The Midianites would later sell Joseph into slavery (Gen 37:28, 36), and Moses married Zipporah, a Midianite whose father, Jethro, advised Moses (Ex 18). On the Feast of the Epiphany, celebrating the arrival of the magi, we read Isaiah, who prophesied, "A multitude of camels shall cover you, the young camels of Midian and Ephah; all those from Sheba shall come. They

shall bring gold and frankincense, and shall proclaim the praise of the
LORD" (Is 60:6).

Though later laws legislated the treatment of sons from different
wives (e.g., Deut 21:15–17), Abraham appointed Isaac as sole heir to
everything. He gave gifts to the other sons (to avoid claims after his
death) and sent them away. His separation from Lot and the expulsion of Ishmael insured no relative could threaten Isaac's claim to the
promises and covenant of God.

THE DEATH AND BURIAL OF ABRAHAM (25:7–10)

The death and burial of Abraham are covered briefly (25:8–10). He
was buried with Sarah in his purchased cave of Machpelah. The
phrase "gathered to his people" might imply the idea of life after
death, as even Jesus developed later when, referring to the patriarchs, saying that God is not the God of the dead but of the living
(Mk 12:26–27; CCC 632–34). Jesus also revealed that Abraham was
alive in the afterworld in Luke's Gospel: "The poor man died and
was carried by the angels to Abraham's bosom", where the curtain
is pulled back and we witness a conversation from beyond the grave
(Lk 16:19–31).

Isaac and Ishmael together buried their father, Abraham (25:9).
Abraham had been prudent according to the customs of the time, so
the two brothers could amicably bury their father together. They are
listed by importance, not by sequence of birth, Isaac first and then
Ishmael. Even today, almost four thousand years later, though with
much tension and security, the sons of Isaac and Ishmael still visit
the cave of Machpelah together—though separated in mosque and
synagogue at the "Tomb of the Patriarchs".

As the friend of God, Abraham died wealthy and "full of years" at
175.[1] His name is mentioned 326 times in the Bible and 59 times in
the *Catechism*. Hebrews summarizes his life well (Heb 11:8–19), and
Sirach gives him a well-deserved eulogy:

---

[1] Is 41:8; 2 Chron 20:7; Jas 2:23. Though we are told in Exodus 33:11 that "the LORD used
to speak to Moses face to face, as a man speaks to his friend", Scripture does not actually refer
to Moses as "the friend of God" as it does to Abraham.

Abraham was the great father of a multitude of nations,
  and no one has been found like him in glory;
he kept the law of the Most High,
  and was taken into covenant with him;
he established the covenant in his flesh,
  and when he was tested he was found faithful.
Therefore the Lord assured him by an oath
  that the nations would be blessed through his posterity;
that he would multiply him like the dust of the earth,
  and exalt his posterity like the stars,
and cause them to inherit from sea to sea
  and from the River to the ends of the earth. (Sir 44:19–21)

ISHMAEL'S DESCENDANTS (25:11–18)

The covenant God made with Abraham would now be realized through Isaac exclusively. God blessed Isaac, and he settled at Beer-lahai-roi, where God had promised to bless Ishmael. With the now familiar words, "These are the generation of. . .", the chapter on Ishmael ends with a list of his descendants before moving on through the family line of Isaac (vv. 13–16). God kept his promise—Ishmael became a great nation and the father of twelve princes, corresponding to the twelve tribes of Israel (Gen 17:20). Ishmael died at 137 years, and we are not told where he was buried.

Ishmael's descendants dwelt in the area from Havila to Shur near Egypt and in the direction of Assyria, possibly corresponding to present-day Saudi Arabia (v. 18). We are informed that "he settled over against all his people" (v. 18). Other translations suggest he settled in opposition or defiance to all his kinsmen, an apt fulfillment of God's word to Hagar, "He shall be a wild donkey of a man, his hand against every man and every man's hand against him; and he shall dwell over against all his kinsmen" (Gen 16:12).

THE BIRTH AND YOUTH OF ESAU
AND JACOB (25:19–28)

The story of Isaac and Rebekah now takes center stage as we begin a new chapter in the story of salvation. Again, the words "These

are the descendants of Isaac" are used to direct the narrative following a distinct family line as with Noah (6:9), Shem (11:10), Terah
(11:27), Ishmael (25:12), Isaac (25:19), Esau (36:1), and finally Jacob
(37:2). Isaac and Rebekah's family pedigrees are reiterated in verses
19–20. Isaac was forty years old when he wed Rebekah. Scholars
disagree on the meaning of *Paddam-aram* (v. 20), a name used only
in Genesis, though it probably means the area surrounding Haran.
Bethuel and Laban are referred to as Arameans, and later this appellation is applied to Israel (Deut 26:5). It probably refers to *Aram
Naharaim*, where Abraham's family lived and where he sent the servant to find a bride for Isaac. Aram, a grandson of Noah, is mentioned in Genesis 10:20 as a son of Shem.

Rebekah experienced infertility as did Sarah. The promise of
descendants would come through Isaac, and Rebekah's family had
blessed her, "Our sister, be the mother of thousands of ten thousands; and may your descendants possess the gate of those who hate
them!" (Gen 24:60). Yet now, *twenty years later*, she remained childless (25:20, 26). Imagine Isaac and Rebekah's anxiety! For the third
time in the Bible, we see the word "pray"; Isaac prayed to the LORD
for Rebekah and she "conceived" (Gen 25:21).

Even without ultrasound technology, they realized there were two
children struggling in Rebekah's womb—and so the Lord told her.
I remember the thrill of feeling our babies moving inside my wife's
womb. It was not always so for my wife, who often groaned when
kicked in the ribs. The two wrestlers in Rebekah's womb caused
her anguish. The Hebrew word "struggled" anticipates the future
rivalry between these boys. It means to "struggle together, jostle each
other, i.e., have a physical contest to gain a superior position over
an opponent, as in a wrestling match".[2] Sitting in her tent, in the
oppressive heat of the Negev Desert, she burst out, "If it is thus, why
do I live?" (v. 22). She inquired of the Lord, who responded, "Two
nations are in your womb, and two peoples, born of you, shall be
divided; the one shall be stronger than the other, the elder shall serve
the younger" (25:23). This was contrary to the customs in which
the youngest served the eldest. But Isaac and Rebekah should not

[2] James Swanson, *Dictionary of Biblical Languages with Semantic Domains: Hebrew (Old Testament)* (Oak Harbor: Logos Research Systems, 1997), ref. no. 4189.

have been scandalized; Isaac himself was the younger of two sons, yet he was the "firstborn", the son of promise and Abraham's heir. Saint Paul uses these brothers in Romans 9 to explain God's free election, which was not limited to Israel.

When Isaac was sixty years old, the twins were born, and they were very different—certainly not identical twins. The first was born red and hairy. Both characteristics are important to the story. He was named Esau, which means *red*, and his descendants would occupy Edom, which also means *red* and would become a name synonymous with Esau (v. 30). Ironically, the sandstone in that region has a decidedly reddish color. The Hebrew word for *red* is used twice again in Scripture, both times referring to David's handsome appearance and his ruddiness (1 Sam 16:12; 17:42). Edom extends south and east of the Dead Sea to the Gulf of Aqaba. King Herod was of Edomite heritage, though the territory was called Idumea under Roman rule.

Esau was not only red at birth, but his whole body was covered with hair "like a hairy mantle" (Gen 25:25).

Esau's shaggy hairiness has often been compared to Enkidu, a wild uncivilized man in the Gilgamesh epic, whose "whole body is covered with hair" (GE 1.36). Vawter observes "Hairiness or shagginess seems to have been *eo ipso* a mark of incivility.... Similarly, there was a prejudice against a ... redheaded person, which existed not only in the ancient Near Eastern world but well into the time of Western Christianity as well. Judas Iscariot was depicted in mediaeval art as a redhead!... In respect to Esau, therefore, the author's wordplays go beyond mere cleverness and insinuate a bias against him from the beginning."[3]

From the *Jewish Study Bible*, "To the ancient Israelite, Esau's hunting, like his hairiness, suggested uncouthness and even a certain degree of danger. The uncouthness is also apparent in his blunt speech and impulsive behavior in the ensuing tale (vv. 30–34)."[4] Jewish scholar Philo (ca. 20 B.C.–ca. A.D. 50) agreed, "The ruddy body and the hairy

[3] Gordon J. Wenham, *Genesis 16–50*, Word Biblical Commentary, vol. 2 (Dallas: Word, Incorporated, 1994), 176.

[4] Adele Berlin, Marc Zvi Brettler, and Michael Fishbane, eds., *The Jewish Study Bible* (New York: Oxford University Press, 2004), 53.

hide are a sign of a savage man who rages furiously in the manner of a wild beast."[5]

Emerging from the womb right on Esau's heels (literally, pun intended), Jacob was neither red nor hairy. He was smooth-skinned and fair. As the second one emerging from the womb, his hand tightly grasped his older brother's heel. How prophetic this was—even the prophets mention it (Hos 12:2–4). It earned him the name Jacob, which means "one who takes by the heel" or supplants; describing Jacob perfectly, as one who takes the place of, often by trickery or force. By grasping the heel, the youngest had set the stage—always conniving to overtake his brother. Interestingly, Jacob received a new name later in life also based on conflict. His new name would be *Israel*, those "who have striven with God" (32:28).

The boys could not have been more different. One hunted and roamed the fields; the other was mellow and stayed in the tents. "Momma's Boy" would not be an inappropriate description. But do not be deceived. Jacob was anything but placid and guileless. He lived up to his name as "supplanter" by being clever and deceitful. Isaac enjoyed red meat, so he loved his overtly masculine son, who loved to hunt. Mom loved the quiet, gentler boy. Her knowledge that Jacob would be the heir may have also been a factor in her special love for Jacob.

Saint Augustine explains precisely their differences:

> In the time of the ancient fathers, to speak concerning illustrious persons, there were born two twin brothers, the one so immediately after the other, that the first took hold of the heel of the second. So great a difference existed in their lives and manners, so great a dissimilarity in their actions, so great a difference in their parents' love for them respectively, that the very contrast between them produced even a mutual hostile antipathy.... One of these twins was for a long time a hired servant; the other never served. One of them was beloved by his mother; the other was not so. One of them lost that honor which was so much valued among their people; the other obtained it.[6]

[5] Philo, *Philo: Questions and Answers on Genesis and Exodus*, trans. Ralph Marcus, The Loeb Classical Library, vol. 1 (Cambridge, Mass. and London: Harvard University Press; William Heinemann, 1953), 445.

[6] Augustine of Hippo, *The City of God*, in *St. Augustin's City of God and Christian Doctrine*, bk. 4, chap. 4, ed. Philip Schaff, trans. Marcus Dods, A Select Library of the Nicene and Post-Nicene Fathers of the Christian Church, First Series, vol. 2 (Buffalo, N.Y.: Christian Literature Company, 1887), 86.

ESAU SELLS HIS BIRTHRIGHT (25:29–34)

One event sets in motion the prophecy of God to their mother that "the elder shall serve the younger" (v. 23). While hanging around the tents with his mother one day, Jacob was cooking some pottage. The Hebrew word *nazid* contextually means "thick boiled food" and doubtless refers to a thick red lentil stew (v. 34). It must have smelled delicious because it overwhelmed the senses—and the sensibilities—of the older brother. The English text renders the food as "red pottage", but in the Hebrew it is literally *red red*—in other words, idiomatically, Esau said, "Let me eat some of that red pottage." In parentheses we are informed, "Therefore his name was called Edom" (v. 30), which is another clever play of words. Esau used an uncommon word for *eat*, as in, "Let me *eat* some of that red stuff." The word is used only here in the whole Old Testament. It is a word that actually means to devour, gulp, or swallow greedily. It is a verb applied to animals eating, which further suggests Esau's crude manner. No wonder Rebekah had less regard for Esau than for the more genteel Jacob.

Always looking for an advantage, Jacob saw an opening. What he was denied at birth he might now steal back. Imagine the cunning smile as he held the steaming bowl of red lentil stew under Esau's nose and said, "First sell me your birthright!" The birthright was the most valuable possession of the oldest son. "The firstborn son inherits a double portion of his father's estate (Deut. 21:15–17; Isa. 61:7), the paternal blessing (Gen. 27), and succession to authority (Gen. 27:29, 37; 43:33; 2 Kings 2:9)."[7] In this case, he also inherited the covenantal family line.

Esau returned from the fields famished and dramatically declared "I am about to die; of what use is a birthright to me?" Taking nothing for granted, and wanting to seal the deal with an oath, Jacob said, "Swear to me first." Esau swore and sold his birthright to Jacob. His impetuous and foolish action became a famous by-word used when something of great value is traded away for a trifle—"to sell one's birthright for a mess of pottage!" Esau greedily gulped down the

---

[7] Paul J. Achtemeier, Harper & Row, and Society of Biblical Literature, *Harper's Bible Dictionary* (San Francisco: Harper & Row, 1985), 310.

"pottage of lentils" and bread. He rose and went his way. The chapter ends with the poignant and brief sentence, "Thus Esau despised his birthright" (v. 34).

Jacob had coveted the status of firstborn "from the womb". Esau was cavalier about such matters. Though the youngest, Jacob, was now the "firstborn", not by birth order, but by status. God had told Rebekah that the older would serve the younger, and now the transition had taken place—Jacob the "heel-grabber" had finally pulled ahead by deceit. Jacob watched Esau gulp his food and walk away. The writer of Hebrews recalls this event, "See to it that no one fail to obtain the grace of God ... that no one be immoral or irreligious like Esau, who sold his birthright for a single meal. For you know that afterward, when he desired to inherit the blessing, he was rejected, for he found no chance to repent, though he sought it with tears" (Heb 12:15–17).

BIBLICAL NOTE: *The Office of the Firstborn*

Esau sold his birthright, meaning his title of firstborn with all its rights and privileges. "The firstborn, through the birthright, shares in the father's authority and is given much property."[8] Firstborn can refer to "birth order" or to the *office* of firstborn—a position of rights, privileges, and the heir-apparent. Jacob, though the second born, received the title of *firstborn*, as was the case with Isaac over Ishmael. Jesus is "the image of the invisible God, the first-born of all creation; for in him all things were created ... all things were created through him and for him" (Col 1:15–16). This passage is not suggesting that Jesus was created or born first among many of more or less equal status. Jesus is eternally co-existent with the Father with no beginning. Scripture is assuming readers are culturally literate, knowing that *firstborn* was emphasizing Jesus' priority and supremacy over all of creation. The passage means that he is "preeminent", not that he is a mere creature, even if the most important one. He is preeminent as the Son; his status as such involves his eternal relationship with the Father.

---

[8] *Prōtotokos*, in Ceslas Spicq and James D. Ernest, *Theological Lexicon of the New Testament* (Peabody, Mass.: Hendrickson, 1994), 211.

With respect to Isaac's and Esau's status, birthright was not just financial and legal; it was also spiritual through the promise and covenant of God. God's covenant with Abraham, and to the world through Abraham's seed, would pass through the "firstborn". Had Esau not despised his birthright, God might have described himself as, "I am the God of Abraham, Isaac, and Esau!" Esau squandered, not only privilege and position, but also his standing before God and history. Jacob would now be the branch that led to the coming of the Messiah, Jesus Christ. Esau became a proverb—remembered as the fool who would "sell his birthright for a mess of pottage".

Jesus warns us, "For what does it profit a man, to gain the whole world and forfeit his life?" (Mk 8:36). Paul also warns us, possibly with Esau in the forefront of his mind, "For many ... walk as enemies of the cross of Christ. Their end is destruction, their god is the belly, and they glory in their shame, with minds set on earthly things" (Phil 3:18–19). One might see an analogy representing Jews and Gentiles. The Jews denied their Messiah and thus squandered their status as God's "firstborn", thus opening the door for the Gentiles to be grafted onto the tree in their place (see Rom 11:17). Saint Augustine warns:

> Now apply this. You have a Christian people. But among this Christian people it is the ones who belong to Jacob that have the birthright or right of the firstborn. Those, however, who are materialistic in life, materialistic in faith, materialistic in hope, materialistic in love, still belong to the old covenant, not yet to the new. They still share the lot of Esau, not yet in the blessing of Jacob.[9]

---

[9] Sermon 4.12, in Mark Sheridan, *Genesis 12–50*, Ancient Christian Commentary on Scripture, OT 2 (Downers Grove, Ill.: InterVarsity Press, 2002), 151.

CHAPTER 26

ISAAC AND ABIMELECH

ISAAC STAYS IN GERAR; GOD'S PROMISE
TO ABRAHAM (26:1–6)

Chapter 26 recounts a few episodes in the life of Isaac. Though over-
shadowed by his father, Abraham, and his son Jacob, the name Isaac is
nonetheless found 139 times in the Bible; he serves as the covenantal
link between his father and his son Jacob. He is one of the patriarchs,
certainly a saint in the Catholic Church's liturgical tradition (*CCC*
61), since we are told of his presence in heaven (Mt 8:11; Lk 13:28),
and he is included in God's description of himself: "I am the God of
Abraham, and the God of Isaac, and the God of Jacob" (Mt 22:32).

The agrarian life-style of ancient times was dependent upon the
vicissitudes of the weather far more than we are, with our technical
irrigation systems—though even we are not exempt from problems
with weather. Abraham had experienced a drought-induced famine,
and Jacob would experience the same, which would eventually send
the children of Israel into Egypt. There was bad news and good news
for Isaac. The bad news was that Isaac was now confronted with
a famine; the good news was that he stayed on the land, and God
renewed his covenant with Isaac. When famines crippled Canaan,
the occupants often fled to Egypt for refuge. Isaac was no exception
and was heading to the land amply supplied by water from the Nile
River. However, God stopped him, speaking to Isaac like he had
spoken to his father. He renewed the covenant with Isaac, who knew
of the promises of God only by word of mouth from his father. Now
he heard the all-important words of the covenant firsthand from God
himself. God told him to stay on the land, and there he would be
blessed, and the oath to Abraham would be Isaac's as well. So Isaac

obeyed God and dwelt in Gerar, which was a bit northwest of Beer-sheba toward the border with Egypt.

THEOLOGICAL NOTE: *Why Is Isaac the Beneficiary of the Covenant?*

Isaac's life was uneventful compared with his father's. What heroic faith, virtue, or deeds had he displayed? What great tests had he endured? God reminded Isaac that he was blessed *because of the obedience of his father Abraham* (26:5). There is no "faith alone" promoted here, if that means works of fidelity are irrelevant. Isaac was the beneficiary of Abraham's obedience. The choices of a father have consequences inherited by the son.

TROUBLES WITH KING ABIMELECH (26:6–17)

We experience a little *déjà vu* in Gerar. Abraham had lied to Abimelech about his marital relationship with Sarah (20:1–2). Twice he stretched the truth by saying that Sarah was his sister and hiding the truth that she was also his wife. In both Egypt and Gerar, he lied to two kings; now Isaac was doing the same. The difference was that Rebekah was *not* his half-sister. Fearing death, Isaac deceived the men of Gerar, claiming Rebekah was his sister.

> The account of Isaac's dealings with Abimelech, has perplexed scholars for at least two reasons. First, the narrative bears many similarities to earlier stories about Abraham. Second, the story interrupts the account of Jacob and Esau.... Furthermore, the events of Gen 26 appear to occur prior to the birth of Jacob and Esau, since the wife-sister ruse of Isaac and Rebekah would probably not have worked if their children had been with them.... Regardless of its compositional history, the chapter continues the theme of God's covenant with Abraham's descendants, as God appears twice to Isaac with covenant affirming words (26:2–5, 24–25). Like his father before him (12:7; 22:9–18) and like his son after him (35:3, 6–7), Isaac builds an altar and acknowledges Yahweh as his God.[1]

[1] Douglas Mangum, Miles Custis, and Wendy Widder, *Genesis 12–50*, Lexham Research Commentaries (Bellingham, Wash.: Lexham Press, 2013), Gen 26:1—27:40.

The name Abimelech was common, and this king was, perhaps, the first Abimelech's son. This king discovered the subterfuge before taking Rebekah to his harem. He looked out his window and "saw Isaac fondling Rebekah his wife" (v. 8). The Hebrew word incorporates a wordplay off the name Isaac, which means *laughter*. It is here used for what is proper between a husband and wife: fondling, sporting with, exchanging conjugal caresses.[2] A man and wife in love is a good thing, but the surprised king was scandalized by the deception. After being confronted, Isaac confessed his scheme. Abimelech who was fearful that one of his men might have unbeknownst lain with Rebekah, announced that anyone who touched Isaac or Rebekah would be put to death.

Against all odds, especially during a famine, God blessed Isaac, who sowed seed and reaped an incredible harvest of a hundredfold (v. 12). Remembering Jesus' parable about the sower, one could expect a hundredfold only in the best of times (Mt 13:8).

Isaac had inherited the wealth of his father in flocks and herds, gold and silver, servants and possessions. But now we see an additional source of wealth. This is the only time in Scripture that we find one of the patriarchs working the soil to grow crops. Isaac increased in wealth until he was in the category of "wealthy", or, in modern terms, he was the equivalent of a multimillionaire. But great wealth brings great envy. The Philistines in Gerar grew jealous and tried to sabotage him. They filled his wells with dirt. Consider the disaster of bringing huge flocks of panting sheep to the well for water only to find it filled with dirt.

QUARRELING OVER WELLS (26:18–25)

This was not a new problem. Abimelech's men had confiscated a well dug by Abraham (21:25, 30). The problem resurfaced again with the next generation. Abimelech asked Isaac to leave. He had grown powerful, and the Philistines were intimidated by his presence. Isaac did not argue or claim his rights to the wells as had his father. He left and encamped in the Valley of Gerar southeast of the city of Gerar, near modern-day Gaza and northwest of Beersheba.

[2] See R. Laird Harris, Gleason L. Archer, Jr., and Bruce K. Waltke, eds., *Theological Wordbook of the Old Testament* (Chicago: Moody Press, 1999), 763.

It can be difficult for us to comprehend the importance of wells in ancient times. In the kitchen we turn on the faucet. Bottled water is everywhere. Living in the Negev Desert four thousand years ago is foreign to us. Wells meant water, and water meant life. It is often said that a man can live three minutes without air, three days without water, and three weeks without food. When we travel through these areas with our pilgrimages, we constantly remind the pilgrims to drink lots of water to avoid dehydration. In the days of the patriarchs, wells meant life and survival.

The wells dug by Abraham had been filled in with dirt. Isaac went from one to the next, and the fighting continued with the Philistines—the men of Gerar. As soon as Isaac's men re-dug a well, the men of Gerar would claim it as their own and vindictively fill it with dirt. Unhappily, warring and fighting between the sons of Abraham and the Philistines would go on for centuries. Remember that David fought Goliath the Philistine from Gath, a short thirty-five miles from Gerar. Isaac went back to Beersheba. God again appeared to Isaac at this historical site of the "Well of the Oath", reaffirming his promise. Isaac's response was to build an altar and call upon the name of the Lord as his father, Abraham, had done.

COVENANT BETWEEN ISAAC AND ABIMELECH (26:26–33)

The fighting continued and came to a head. Abimelech realized it was better to work with Isaac than against him, especially since it was obvious that God was on Isaac's side. Abimelech and Isaac swore an oath together. Isaac triumphed, found a good source of water, and established *shalom* (peace). We recall that the land was promised, but would not be possessed until after the four hundred years in Egypt. He dug a well and called it *Shibah* (which sounds like the Hebrew word for oath), reviving the name his father had given the place.

ESAU MARRIES HITTITE WOMEN (26:34–35)

After this brief struggle over wells, Jacob and Esau return to the narrative. Bad news first. At forty years of age, Esau married two

Hittite women—which brought great distress and bitterness to Isaac and Rebekah. Remember Abraham's resolve about his son Isaac not marrying Canaanites? Maybe Isaac should have insisted on choosing Esau's bride like his father had done for him. Isaac seemed to lack the drive and resolve of his father and brought this misery upon himself. In any case, Esau made another monumental mistake. Jacob understood the situation and would eventually take the long journey to Haran to find his bride. Jacob now stood out as the future hope for God's covenant and promises.

CHAPTER 27

JACOB'S DECEIT AND ISAAC'S BLESSING

AGED ISAAC PREPARES TO BLESS
HIS SON ESAU (27:1-4)

Sitting in the tent with failing eyes and assuming his impending death, Isaac decided to get his house in order. Scripture says "his eyes were dim so that he could not see" (v. 1). This was probably a form of macular degeneration, glaucoma, or cataracts, which are three major causes of vision loss in the elderly. Isaac was forty years old when he married Rebekah (25:20) and sixty when the twins were born (25:26). Esau was forty when he married the Hittite women, making Isaac one hundred years old at the time. Isaac was between 125 and 135 when he eventually blessed his sons, and 45 to 55 years later died at 180 years of age (35:28).

It was customary in the Near East to call in the family, especially the older sons, to give a paternal blessing and instructions before death. Isaac's actions are troublesome on several counts: (1) why did he only call Esau at his impending death; (2) why bless the brutish son married to pagan Canaanites; (3) why bestow the paternal blessing on a reckless son who bartered his birthright for a gulp of stew; (4) why ignore God's prophetic word that the older would serve the younger; and (5) why think he was near death when he actually lived another forty years? The fact that Jacob was about forty years old and unmarried may have factored into Isaac's thinking. On the other hand, Esau had married pagan women, but God had not chosen Esau; he had chosen Jacob from the womb.

The story of Jacob's deception of his father, in complicity with his crafty mother, has seven distinct "chapters" or scenes. Only the parents and the sons were involved in the drama, and they only appeared as couples: Isaac and Esau in dramatic tension with Rebekah and

Jacob. Isaac and Rebekah came together only briefly when she intervened to keep the deception on track. Each couple stepped onto center stage twice. Isaac was *in* the darkness, and Rebekah connived *from*
the darkness of deceit in another room. The prize was the paternal
blessing even if obtained deceitfully. The Hebrew noun for "bless"
(*barak*) was used seven times as this drama played out. A blessing
from a dying father invoked divine favor and future blessing upon
the blessed son. Once given, it could not be retracted or transmitted
to another (27:33–37).

Expressing his desire for the savory meat dish that he loved, Isaac
summoned his oldest son, the hunter. The author avoids the obvious complications of using the *firstborn*, referring to Esau only as "his
older son". After disclosing to Esau his intention of giving him the
paternal blessing, Isaac sent him out with quiver and bow to hunt and
cook the meat before he died. His appetite had overcome his obedience; his belly took precedence over the prophecy of God. "Like
father, like son"—Isaac was swayed by his belly like Esau, when he
sold his birthright for a bowl of lentil stew. The Hebrew word for
savory food in this episode is used again only in Proverbs 23:3, 6. Saint
Paul referred to people whose "god is the belly" (Phil 3:19).

REBEKAH AND JACOB DECEIVE ISAAC (27:5–27)

Sarah had once eavesdropped on Abraham speaking with the Lord.
Rebekah now eavesdropped on Isaac since he had just summoned
Esau. Having overheard his intention to bless Esau, she conjured up
a plot to foil her husband's plan. She loved Jacob but also recalled
God's word to her while the boys were still in her womb. Jacob was
a deceiver and supplanter, but the dialogue between Rebekah and
Jacob also exposed the mother's cunning (traits shared by her brother
Laban as well—cf. 24:29–32). The old adage applied "like mother,
like son"—the fruit did not fall far from the tree. Esau was a good
hunter and would be back soon. She quickly directed Jacob to dress
in Esau's clothes.

It is questionable whether domesticated goat meat can be prepared cleverly enough to deceive a connoisseur of wild game. Isaac
loved Esau because "he ate of his game" (25:28). *Game* referred to the

wild animals that Esau hunted. The Law of Moses later listed the following animals as kosher: oxen, sheep, goats, harts, gazelle, roebuck, wild goats, ibex, antelope, and mountain sheep (Deut 14:4–5). This gives us an idea what Esau may have stalked for his father. Isaac had eaten wild and domestic animals for over a hundred years. But Rebekah also knew Isaac's favorite dishes, and she would prepare two young goats to compete with Esau's fare.

There was another problem for Rebekah and Jacob. Esau was a hairy man, whereas Jacob was smooth-skinned. How to trick the father if he reached out to touch the imposter Jacob? Esau must have *really* been hairy if Jacob could simulate Esau's skin by covering his own arms with the coarse hair of a goat! And not only did the two sons feel different, but they smelled different, too. Jacob was fearful of being detected and seen to be mocking his father, thus receiving a curse instead of a blessing. A father's curse was as devastating as a father's blessing was profitable. To mock a father, especially taking advantage of his blindness, was walking on very thin ice.[1] Rebekah was clever; willing to take every risk. She dismissed Jacob's fear by saying, "Your curse be on me, my son; only obey my voice."

Rebekah planned the whole thing. How could they trick all of Isaac's five senses? Sight was eliminated by Isaac's blindness. They had the sense of taste covered, but feel and smell posed a problem. We can only imagine the rank smell of Esau's clothing! Rebekah put Esau's pungent clothes on Jacob and put the skins of the goats on his arms and the smooth part of his neck (below and behind his beard). With the savory goat meat, she sent him in to his father pretending to be Esau. He lied through his teeth in obedience to his mother. He said, "My father." Isaac was immediately suspicious due to his voice and asked who he was. Jacob responded, "I am Esau your firstborn. I have done as you told me; now sit up and eat of my game, that you may bless me." Isaac's doubt increased, asking how he caught the game so quickly. Jacob lied, saying God had given him success (27:19–20).

---

[1] "The verbal root תעע 'mock,' used only here and in 2 Chr 36:16, seems a very strong one. It would certainly be a most inappropriate way to treat a blind man, let alone one's parent (cf. Lev 19:14; Exod 21:17). Indeed, Deut 27:18 invokes a curse on those who physically mislead the blind, so it is quite realistic for Jacob to envisage a curse falling on him for deceiving his blind father." Gordon J. Wenham, *Genesis 16–50*, Word Biblical Commentary, vol. 2 (Dallas: Word, Incorporated, 1994), 207.

Isaac insisted on feeling his son, knowing one was hairy and the other smooth-skinned. While feeling the deceptive hairiness, Isaac commented, "The voice is Jacob's voice, but the hands are the hands of Esau" (27:22). Isaac was conned. He gave his blessing. He ate the game and drank the wine. But second-guessing himself, he beckoned his son to come near to kiss him with the intent of smelling him. After eating the food, he asked again: Are you really my son Esau? Jacob lied again. Now the con was complete.

ISAAC DECEIVED AND BLESSES JACOB (27:28–29)

The hairy arms, the savory food, and the smell of the field—along with the blatant lie and his own corrupting appetite enabled the ploy to work. Isaac gave Jacob the final and binding paternal blessing.

> May God give you of the dew of heaven,
>   and of the fatness of the earth,
>   and plenty of grain and wine.
> Let peoples serve you,
>   and nations bow down to you.
> Be lord over your brothers,
>   and may your mother's sons bow down to you.
> Cursed be every one who curses you,
>   and blessed be every one who blesses you! (27:18–29)

The patriarchal blessing was one for a farmer, not for a hunter. The blessing was full of imagery and meaning to the people who lived on the land. The prayer for *dew from heaven* is significant since dew provided moisture even when rains were scarce. Dew was a symbol of prosperity and God's blessing; the word is used nearly forty times in Scripture. Isaac also blessed Jacob with *the fat of the land*, which refers to the finest produce and abundance from the soil. *Grain and wine* are indicative of settled farmers and symbolized fullness of joy, satisfaction, and success. Next were blessings with future national implications. He and his descendants would have military might, and nations would bow to him. He would rule over his family and siblings, which fulfills the prerogatives of the firstborn, echoing God's word to Rebekah as the twins were wrestling in her womb.

THEOLOGICAL NOTE: *Blessing in Spite of Sin and Deception*

Sirach provides an interesting perspective on who actually "made the covenant rest upon the head of Jacob". "To Isaac also he gave the same assurance for the sake of Abraham his father. The blessing of all men and the covenant he [God] made to rest upon the head of Jacob; he acknowledged him with his blessings, and gave him his inheritance; he determined his portions, and distributed them among twelve tribes" (Sir 44:22–23). The NAB adds clarity, emphasizing God's design working through the duplicity of Rebekah and Jacob, "The blessing rested upon the head of Jacob. *God acknowledged him as the firstborn*, and gave him his inheritance" (emphasis added).

In other words, Scripture affirms that God gave Jacob the blessing of the firstborn. If so, then God used the deception of Rebekah and Jacob to suit his own purposes. Isaac was disobeying the prophecy of God to Rebekah so God must direct the end result—God was drawing straight with crooked lines, as the proverb goes. It was deception, pure and simple, and Scripture states it so, without giving approval to it. God insured that Jacob received the blessing of the firstborn, though he was younger than Esau. Some Jewish writers claim Isaac did not recognize Jacob because of heavenly influences, as suggested in the *Book of Jubilees*, "Jacob came close to his father Isaac. When he touched him, he said, 'The voice is Jacob's voice, but the forearms are Esau's forearms.' *He did not recognize him because there was a turn of affairs from heaven to distract his mind*" (26:17–18, emphasis added).[2]

> Apparently even God must select imperfect instruments to fulfill His purposes. He must choose between Jacob—a man who desires the birthright so deeply he will cheat to secure it—and Esau, who so lightly esteems it that he forfeits the birthright for a bowl of lentils. Jacob's calculated cunning must be weighed against Esau's undisciplined craving for immediate self-gratification. Working with "human material" involved God in a difficult but inescapable choice, and God decides: It is better to care too much than too little.[3]

---

[2] James C. VanderKam, *Jubilees: A Commentary on the Book of Jubilees, Chapters 1–50*, ed. Sidnie White Crawford, Hermeneia—A Critical and Historical Commentary on the Bible, vols. 1 & 2 (Minneapolis, Minn.: Fortress Press, 2018), 742.

[3] Samuel E. Karff, as quoted in W. Gunther Plaut, "Genesis", *The Torah, A Modern Commentary* (New York: Union of American Hebrew Congregations, 1981), 192.

It is amazing (and comforting) that God was willing to be known as "the God of Jacob" (see Ex 3:6; 2 Sam 23:1). Abraham, yes; Isaac, maybe, though he did nothing heroic. But *Jacob?* Jacob the supplanter, deceiver, and liar? But Scripture testifies that God loved Jacob (see Mal 1:2; Rom 9:13). It is comforting to think that if God is willing to be closely associated with a man like Jacob, maybe he can love us, too, even with our sin and shortcomings.

THEOLOGICAL NOTE: *Blessing Realized by Future Generations*

Abraham never realized the promise of the land; it was deferred to his descendants. Similarly, even though the birthright had been purchased by Jacob and the paternal blessing bestowed, it was to be realized by his progeny because Jacob never really experienced the blessing himself. The Fathers of the Church had interesting takes on this blessing. Consider third-century saint and biblical scholar Hippolytus:

> If one believes that this blessing was accomplished in Jacob, he is mistaken. Nothing of this ever happened to Jacob. First we find him in Mesopotamia at the service of Laban for twenty years (Gen 31:38); then he prostrates himself before his brother Esau and tries to make himself pleasing to him by offering presents (Gen 33:3, 8, 10); after this he goes down to Egypt to avoid starvation with his children (Gen 42:2; 46:3). In whom then have the words "Ah, the smell of the clothes of my son is like the smell of a fruitful field that the Lord has blessed" been accomplished? In nobody else but Christ, Son of God. In fact, the field is the world, and the smell of his clothes are all those who believe in him, according to what the apostle says: "We are the aroma of Christ to God among those who are being saved and among those who are perishing; to the one a fragrance from death to death, to the other a fragrance from life to life" (2 Cor 2:15–16).[4]

The giants of faith in the Old Testament rarely experienced the full blessing themselves, but in faith they looked beyond this life for the "better country". In Hebrews 11:13–21, we read a summary of

---

[4] *On the Blessings of Isaac and Jacob*, 7, in Mark Sheridan, ed., *Genesis 12–50*, Ancient Christian Commentary on Scripture (Downers Grove, Ill.: InterVarsity Press, 2002), 174–75.

these saints, including Isaac who "invoked future blessings on Jacob and Esau". These saints of the past did not receive what they were promised, but they saw it from afar, accepting their status as strangers and exiles seeking a better and heavenly city.

ESAU RETURNS WITH ISAAC'S MEAL; LOST BLESSING (27:30–40)

Isaac trembled with great violence when Esau arrived with the savory food and identified himself as "your first-born, Esau".[5] The blind old man shuddered uncontrollably—with anger, fear, shock, distress, and a sense of betrayal. Esau's "great and bitter cry" must have been frightful to hear. Just as Esau had sold his birthright when coming in from the hunt (25:29–34), so he now lost the accompanying blessing arriving from another hunt. Esau retorts with anguish, "Is he not rightly named Jacob? He has supplanted me these two times!" This referred to the birthright and now the blessing. The word "supplanted" is a bitter pun on Jacob's name. "Jacob's overweening ambition was first manifested in the womb when he sought to supplant his brother Esau (12:3a). The word 'supplant' (ya⟨āqōb) here plays on the name of Jacob. Cf. Gen 25:26, where Jacob takes Esau by the heel (⟨āqēb), and ⟨āqab (supplant) is used rather in connection with Jacob's taking Esau's birthright and blessing in Gen 27:36."[6]

Isaac appropriately used the word "guile" in verse 35. Jacob became infamous for his guile, which means he acted with premeditated craftiness, subtle treachery, and deceit. Knowing that Jacob is later given the new name *Israel*, it is significant that Jesus uses this word when he meets Nathaniel in John 1:47: "Jesus saw Nathana-el coming to him, and said of him, 'Behold, an Israelite indeed, in whom is no guile!'" There is no doubt that Jesus is referring to this passage.

---

[5] "Then Isaac trembled violently is literally 'And Isaac was terrified with a very great terror.' Isaac knew the voice of Jacob in verse 22, and now Esau's words of identification caused his father to realize that he had been deceived, and the shock caused him to tremble. The word translated *trembled* is used of the quaking or trembling of a mountain in Exo 19:18. In 1 Sam 14:15 it is used of both people and the earth." William David Reyburn and Euan McG. Fry, *A Handbook on Genesis*, UBS Handbook Series (New York: United Bible Societies, 1998), 634.

[6] John Barton and John Muddiman, *Oxford Bible Commentary* (New York: Oxford University Press, 2001), Hosea 11:12.

In verse 47, what does Jesus say about Nathanael? Notice that the word "Israelite" is not common to the New Testament, being used only one other time (Rom 11:1). Whose name did God change to "Israel" (Gen 32:27–28)? What was the character of the man renamed "Israel"—why was he known for his guile and deceit (Gen 25:21–34, esp. 26; Gen 27:1–29)? Using the play on words, one could translate Jesus' pun as "An Israelite in whom there is no Jacob—no guile and cunning".[7]

Since Isaac's blessing cannot be reversed or transferred, the opposite is now bestowed on Esau. He will be deprived of the dew and the fatness of the earth, live by fighting, and will serve his brother. This is realized in the subsequent history of Esau's descendants who settled in Edom—a rugged, barren land. The only positive note is that Esau would become restless and throw his brother's yoke from his neck, which the Edomites did periodically, though for most of their history they were under the domination of Israel.

JACOB FLEES TO LABAN IN HARAN TO ESCAPE ESAU'S FURY (27:41–46)

Esau seethed with hatred for Jacob and vowed to murder his brother as soon as Isaac died. Everyone in the drama suffered for his own disobedience, weakness, and deceit. Isaac was punished through deception and "cursing" his loved son; Esau by losing everything, and now Rebekah and Jacob pay the price of their deceit since Jacob must flee for his life where *he* will *serve others*, and Rebekah loses her pet son for at least twenty years, probably never to see him again. Rebekah senses the danger and warns Jacob to flee immediately to her brother Laban in Haran (v. 43). Again, God's providence is at work, and in Haran Jacob will find wives from the family of Abraham and start his own family.

Rebekah complained about Esau's Hittite wives, whom she loathed, pejoratively calling them "women of the land". She said to Isaac, What good will my life be to me if Jacob also marries "one of

---

[7] Stephen K. Ray, *St. John's Gospel: A Bible Study Guide and Commentary* (San Francisco: Ignatius Press, 2002), 68.

the Hittite women such as these". This was said with the intention
of getting Isaac to bless Jacob's journey to Haran. God works even
in spite of their sins, for now Jacob, the blessed "firstborn", would
marry wives from the family of Abraham, actually Rebekah's nieces.
Rebekah expected Esau's anger to subside and that Jacob would be
gone only "a while", but in reality, he was gone over twenty years.

Human deception, trickery, and weakness are reported in Scripture without ever approving this conduct. The great mystery is how
God uses human failings and weaknesses for his own ends without
ever approving of such shortcomings or relinquishing his sovereign
choice. God had chosen Jacob above Esau from the womb (Rom
9:12–13), and when all is said and done, God had fulfilled his plans.

CHAPTER 28

JACOB FLEES TO HARAN;
VISION OF STAIRWAY TO HEAVEN

ISAAC FINALLY STEPS UP (28:1–5)

Until now Rebekah had been the driving force adhering to God's revealed plan. Now Isaac finally stepped up to the plate and did the right thing—having been forced to acquiesce to God's design, he blessed Jacob again, this time willingly. He commanded his son Jacob not to marry Canaanite women, knowing the line of the covenant would pass through Jacob. Jacob had to marry—and marry within the family. Why did Isaac wait so long? His father, Abraham, had been very specific on this matter, but Isaac seemed to be a weaker man without the strength of conviction and personality of his father.

Another blessing was bestowed on Jacob as he was sent on his journey to the house of Bethuel, son of Nahor and father of Laban and Rebekah. The blessing of Abraham was now bequeathed to Jacob—that he might take possession of the land, he and his descendants. Jacob did not yet understand the magnitude or the personal relationship with God that was involved. Isaac knew the blessing had not been granted on his account but because of his father Abraham's obedience and friendship with God. This was now bequeathed to Jacob as he set off on the arduous journey to Paddan-aram, which is in northern Mesopotamia, the area surrounding Haran. The family line shifted to Jacob, who now took center stage, and what a character he was, with nary a dull moment. He was now a personality and patriarch in his own right.

ESAU MARRIES ISHMAEL'S DAUGHTER (28:6–9)

Esau was certainly aware of his parents' contempt for his Canaanite wives. He took note of his brother's obedience to Isaac and Rebekah to find a wife from the family of Abraham. He had been a big disappointment, so he tried once again to gain their favor. He went to the people of Ishmael, also Abraham's son, and added a new wife named Mahalath. He hoped this would please his parents. But this was too little, too late. Plus, Ishmael had already been removed from the blessed family line.

JACOB FLEES TO HARAN (28:10–11)

Jacob fled from his brother's wrath and embarked upon a very long and rugged trek from Beersheba in southern Israel north through modern-day Syria, probably passing through Damascus and northeast into today's Turkey. He walked well over five hundred miles with very rustic accommodations. He journeyed back to Haran, where Abraham's brother had dwelled and where Rebekah's brother Laban was now in charge of the family. And Laban was every bit as sneaky and conniving as his nephew Jacob—Jacob would meet his match! But we are getting ahead of our story.

The journey was about twenty-five days of walking in the hot sun.[1] After living in the tents with a doting mother, Jacob was now alone traveling through rugged territory for the first time. No hotels or soft beds along the way. Having traveled these roads myself, I can testify that the terrain is rough and it can be *hot* and humid—the temperatures can exceed 100°. Jacob slept on the ground. When "he came to a certain place", he fell asleep under the stars. We learn that the "certain place" was Bethel, which is about fourteen miles north of Jerusalem; thus, Jacob had already been walking about four days (since it was three days' walk from Beersheba to Jerusalem [Gen 22:4]). Jacob

---

[1] "Using the distances between ancient stopping places, travel records, and comments in literary sources, scholars generally agree that a normal walking traveler could expect to cover twenty miles in a day. Peter's trip from Joppa to Caesarea (about forty miles) took two days (Acts 10:23–30). Travelers using beasts of burden generally covered the same distance." Tremper Longman III, Peter Enns, and Mark Strauss, eds., *The Baker Illustrated Bible Dictionary* (Grand Rapids, Mich.: Baker Books, 2013), 1656.

seemed unaware that his grandfather Abraham had stopped here himself and built an altar on his journey from Haran (12:8).

JACOB'S VISION OF THE STAIRWAY TO HEAVEN; GOD'S PROMISES (28:12–17)

The sun's setting made continued travel impossible, so he slept under the stars with a stone for a pillow (v. 11). Jacob had a dream of a ladder or stairway to heaven with angels ascending and descending.[2] God addressed him and reaffirmed the promise of the land that he had made to Abraham here many years before (12:7–8; 13:3; CCC 2573). He introduced himself as the "God of Abraham your father and the God of Isaac". It is important to note that God uses his name Yahweh, not just *El*, the name of God used by the Canaanites. The Lord God of Abraham made sure there was no confusion as to his identity. He stated that the very ground on which Jacob was sleeping would belong to his descendants, which would be like the dust of the earth spreading in every direction. He specifically promised to keep Jacob wherever he went and to bring him back to the land—never leaving him until the promises were fulfilled. Just as Jacob was preparing to leave the land, God said, in effect, "Don't worry, this land is yours, and after you start your family, I will bring you back—you own the deed to this land."

Jacob awoke with this amazing revelation filling his mind. It was his first encounter with God. He was afraid at the awesomeness of the place. It had appeared quite normal when he fell asleep, but now he saw it in a whole different light. He concluded that the Lord was in this place. It must be "the house of God, and this is the gate of heaven" (v. 17). When the sun came up, he erected his stone pillow, poured oil on it, and declared that the name of this place would be Bethel, which means "the house of God". We are not told where Jacob obtained the oil, but it was not unusual to carry a small jar or

---

[2] This is the only time the Hebrew word *sullam* is used in the Bible, and the meaning is unclear. It refers to a ladder, steps, stairway, or ramp as a connector between ascending levels. It may allude to the steps up the multileveled ziggurat pyramids of Mesopotamia (like the Tower of Babel, Gen 11:4). The ziggurat in Ur had four levels and reached over 100 feet into the sky, with steps leading to the top. Most translations render it *ladder*, and, due to artwork, we all have images of a wooden-type ladder going into heaven.

horn of olive oil (1 Sam 16:1). Oil had many uses in the Near East—practical, medical, culinary, and spiritual.

SPIRITUAL NOTE: *Understanding Jacob's Vision*

Do a biblical search for the phrase "angels of God descending and ascending", and you will find an enlightening passage in the New Testament. Jesus is certainly referring to Jacob's vision of the angels traversing up and down on the ladder or stairs. Speaking to Nathanael, Jesus says, "Truly, truly, I say to you, you will see heaven opened, and the angels of God ascending and descending upon the Son of man" (Jn 1:51). The ladder in Jacob's dream prefigures Jesus, the bridge or stairway between heaven and earth, between a holy God and sinful man (*CCC* 661). This illuminates the words of Saint Paul that there is one mediator between God and man, the man Christ Jesus (1 Tim 2:5; *CCC* 618), and John 14:6, where Jesus says, "I am the way, and the truth, and the life; no one comes to the Father, but by me." How will Jesus be lifted up to bridge the gap between heaven and earth (Jn 12:32–34; Acts 1:9; *CCC* 2795)?

A learned scholar, Saint Chromatius (d. 407), wrote concerning the ladder being the cross of Christ:

> Through the resurrection of Christ the way was opened. Therefore with good reason the patriarch Jacob relates that he had seen in that place a ladder whose end reached heaven and that the Lord leaned on it. The ladder fixed to the ground and reaching heaven is the cross of Christ, through which the access to heaven is granted to us, because it actually leads us to heaven. On this ladder different steps of virtue are set, through which we rise toward heaven: faith, justice, chastity, holiness, patience, piety and all the other virtues are the steps of this ladder. If we faithfully climb them, we will undoubtedly reach heaven. And therefore we know well that the ladder is the symbol of the cross of Christ. As, in fact, the steps are set between two uprights, so the cross of Christ is placed between the two Testaments and keeps in itself the steps of the heavenly precepts, through which we climb to heaven. (Sermon 1.6)[3]

---

[3] Mark Sheridan, *Genesis 12–50*, Ancient Christian Commentary on Scripture, OT 2 (Downers Grove, Ill.: InterVarsity Press, 2002), 188.

Old Testament types and images can often fulfill several realties. In the Eastern liturgy, they also acclaim the Blessed Virgin Mary as being foreshadowed by Jacob's ladder. "Hail, heavenly ladder, by whom God came down! Hail, bridge leading earthly ones to heaven" (*Akathist Hymn to the Theotokos*). I own an ancient icon showing Jacob looking at the Virgin Mary and holding a scroll with the words, "I beheld you in a dream as a ladder planted upon earth and reaching to the heights of heaven." In his encyclical *Ineffabilis Deus*, Pope Pius IX said, "The sublime and singular privilege of the Blessed Virgin ... these Fathers beheld ... in the ladder which Jacob saw reaching from the earth to heaven."[4]

UNDERSTANDING JACOB'S VOW (28:18–22)

Jacob's vow to make God his God can be interpreted in one of two ways. First, as his acceptance of God's promises and a vow to obey and follow through with his obligations, even including a tithe that he may have learned from his grandfather Abraham (Gen 14:20). Had Jacob suddenly "converted" and become virtuous? This view is suggested by Saint John Chrysostom, who writes, "Have you not read of Jacob, departing with nothing from his father's house? Have you not heard his prayer, when he said: *If God shall give me bread to eat, and raiment to put on* (Gen. xxviii.20), which was certainly not the prayer of one who was solicitous for his life, but rather of one who looked to God for all things."[5]

Or there is a second and different interpretation of Jacob's response to God. Jacob made a vow but added a few conditions. He started by saying *if* God is with me (we shall see), *and* if he keeps me in the way, *and* if he gives me food to eat and clothing to wear, *and* if he brings me back to my father's house—"*then* the Lord shall be my God." *If* God does this, *then* I will give him a tenth of everything he gives me. From this perspective, Jacob continued to be the negotiator and deal-maker. Jacob displayed his "jacob-ness". He learned to be humble

---

[4] Apostolic Constitution of Pius IX, *Ineffabilis Deus, Defining the Dogma of the Immaculate Conception* (Boston: Daughters of St. Paul, n.d.), 13, https://www.papalencyclicals.net/pius09/p9ineff.htm.

[5] M. F. Toal, ed. and trans., *The Sunday Sermons of the Great Fathers*, vol. 4 (San Francisco: Ignatius Press, 2000), 105–6.

and forthright only through all of his upcoming trials. At this point in his life, Jacob was still no paradigm of virtue.

Several commentators suggest this view:

> No prayer to *"my* God" had ever been heard from him. But now God was his God. But no! Rather God would be his God if he carried out his promise and accompanied him on his journey, seeing to his needs, and brought him back safely to this place. Are we hearing aright? I'm afraid we are. Jacob had met God for the first time personally and it had shaken him to the core, but being Jacob he was unable to prevent himself striking a bargain with him, saying in effect that he would only keep his side of it if God first kept his.[6]

> Paradox follows, however. He goes on to respond to God's commitment to him. And in so doing the author shows us that whatever transformations await us in Jacob's future, Jacob is still the Trickster. For the most prominent word in his response is the qualification "if".... If all of this happens, then—and one assumes this means *only* then—will Jacob serve the God who revealed himself at Bethel.[7]

For a man with only a walking stick to his name, seeing the angels between heaven and earth was consoling. He had a long and arduous journey ahead, with trials and conflicts, blessings and rewards. A lot of water would pass under the bridge before he returned to this land a changed man. An altar at this very spot would be his gesture of thanksgiving.

[6] John C. L. Gibson, *Genesis*, Daily Study Bible Series, vol. 2 (Louisville, Ky.: Westminster John Knox Press, 1981), 164.

[7] David W. Cotter, *Genesis*, in *Berit Olam: Studies in Hebrew Narrative and Poetry*, ed. Jerome T. Walsh, Chris Franke, and David W. Cotter (Collegeville, Minn.: Liturgical Press, 2003), 217.

Chapter 29

Jacob Meets Rachel; Laban's Treachery

INTRODUCTION

Once upon a time there was a cute young girl from Costa Mesa, California, who moved to Michigan. She was fifteen years old and had just become an Evangelical Christian—baptized in the Pacific Ocean by Chuck Smith, the pastor of Calvary Chapel, known as an organization made up of a large number of ex–Catholics. On the first day of high school in Plymouth, Michigan, she met a guy carrying a bunch of Bible study books. He was seventeen years old and had just "found Jesus" himself. She noticed the twinkle in his eye and his love for the Bible. She later divulged that this was the first time that God spoke to her, saying, "This is the man you will marry!" She was shocked and filed those words away in a file labeled "Strange, maybe, let's wait and see."

They were friends, and both joined a nondenominational church. Four years later, the young man took a romantic interest in the serious young woman. They fell in love, and time dragged by! He asked the question, and she responded "Yes"—deciding to spend the rest of their lives together serving God and raising a Christian family—proving to the world that a man and a woman could maintain a faithful monogamous marriage and raise a family for Jesus. The eight months between the question and wedding bells seemed like an eternity. By the way, the pretty young girl is now my wife. And it did not take long before both of us Evangelical Protestants found another love—the fullness of the Christian faith in the heart of the Catholic Church.

We will soon learn that Jacob and Rachel also fell head-over-heels in love but had to wait seven years! It is difficult to understand

how and why they thought the years flew by so quickly. They said
their love made the time fly (29:20)! Even in Scripture, that period
of time, the whole seven-year period, is encapsulated in only one
verse in the Bible!

JACOB ARRIVES IN HARAN (29:1–2)

For the next twenty years, Jacob lived in Haran away from his family
and the land of promise. Without modern communications, he was
completely cut off. The stay was expected to be short, and Jacob
would need to return to secure the promise of the land. Rebekah's
brother Laban was a trickster and more than a match for Jacob. He
was wily and disrupted everyone's plans and expectations. With great
irony, God made Jacob look in the mirror, and he saw himself in the
person of his deceiving and manipulating uncle who outsmarted and
out-deceived Jacob. God used the passage of time for two purposes:
(1) to teach Jacob a few lessons about life and (2) to raise up a family
for Jacob. In the end Jacob was vindicated.

In English, we read that Jacob "went on his journey", but the
Hebrew says, "he lifted up his feet." This is the only time this phrase
is used in the Old Testament and could mean that Jacob was light–
hearted after the encounter with God and the going was now easier, or that he directed his feet with a newfound determination and
purpose, or that he had to lift his feet to force himself to leave this
blessed place.

> *Be'er Mayim Chayim* explains that, as the Rabbis say, a living creature
> carries himself. When he is happy, and his mind is clear, his heart
> carries his feet even more buoyantly. *Rashbam* also explains: Since the
> Holy One, blessed be He, promised him [that He would protect him
> and bring him home safely], he walked joyfully and swiftly.[1]

The "land of the people of the east" (Gen 29:1) must refer to the
region east of Canaan and specifically the Semitic people of Abraham's family in Mesopotamia. Jacob arrived in Haran very differently

[1] Chayei Sarah, Toledoth, Vayetze, Vayishlach, *Genesis*, vol. 2 (New York: Judaica Press,
1994), 358.

from the way his grandfather's servant had years before. The servant had come with riches and gifts, camels and servants; Jacob, on the other hand, arrived tired and empty-handed. But God was with Jacob as he had been with Abraham's servant—both of whom arrived at the well.

Townspeople gathered at wells for obvious reasons. Water was essential and central to a community, and usually there was only one source. In the West, few of us have any concept of the long daily walk to a community well to share limited water with neighbors and animals. Here news was exchanged, children played, gossip was spread, marriages initiated, and visitors welcomed. Wells were often covered, as they are today in the Middle East, to safeguard the water and to keep animals or children from falling in. In this instance, the stone served as a control over water usage. There were formalities involved with ownership rights, and often the strong would restrict the weak (Ex 2:16–19). In Haran, the stone was removed periodically for flocks to be watered at the same time each day (29:8).

JACOB MEETS RACHEL AT THE WELL; STAYS WITH HIS UNCLE LABAN (29:3–14)

Seeing a well, but not realizing he had arrived at his destination, Jacob questioned the shepherds gathered to water their sheep. He learned he was in Haran and that his uncle Laban was alive and well. The timing was impeccable as they pointed to Laban's daughter, Rachel. Rachel was a shepherdess approaching with her father's flock. It seems Jacob violated the local laws or customs by removing the large rock from the well so Rachel could water her flock. The other shepherds were waiting patiently for all the flocks to gather according to the regulations—only then could the stone be removed. Even though the stone blocking the well was "large" and maybe to impress the beautiful young woman approaching, Jacob moved the large stone away single-handed. Rachel was probably shocked and pleased to receive such preferential treatment, especially at the hands of a total stranger (cf. Ex 2:16–19).

Discovering that the beautiful young maiden was his relative Rachel, Jacob kissed her and wept aloud for joy. There was nothing indecent about a customary kiss between relatives. Today much of the world, relatives and friends alike, greet each other with a kiss on each cheek (Gen 27:26–27; 29:13; 50:1). This is the only time in the Old Testament we read of a man kissing a woman who is not his mother or his wife.

Rachel rushed home to announce the arrival of Rebekah's son, which recalls Rebekah's running home with similar news many years earlier. Rachel's father, Laban, brother of Rebekah, rushed to meet Jacob. He embraced, kissed, and took Jacob to his house. The kiss of Laban was not far removed from the kiss of Judas and appears self-serving in the whole scheme of things. Jacob relayed the family news. After being warmly received as Laban's flesh and blood, Jacob stayed for a month.

LABAN AND JACOB'S AGREEMENTS (29:15–21)

Apparently, Jacob had been working for Laban as a gesture of grate-fulness for a relative and to cover his board and room. But family members did not work for each other as common laborers for hire, so Laban's question about wages cleverly disclaimed the formal family ties suggesting Jacob become a mere hireling. Not knowing Laban, it could be interpreted as an uncle's concern for his welfare and there-fore payment to him of a fair wage for his voluntary service. How-ever, there is another way of understanding this question that is much more in line with the devious nature of Laban. He suggested paying Jacob to continue receiving his services into the future, but also to distance Jacob as a relative and reduce him to merely a hired hand, an employee, giving Laban more latitude for his duplicity.[2]

And now for the irony! Jacob had grappled for supremacy all his life, and now *he* was the servant of a family member. Remember Isaac's blessing, "Let peoples *serve* you, and nations bow down to you"? (27:29) The Hebrew word used for *serve* is *abad* and—now for

---

[2] "Since a family member would work for nothing, Laban is degrading the blood relation-ship between himself and Jacob (29:14a) into an economic arrangement. What Laban should have done as a loving relative is to help Jacob get a start on building his own home, as Jacob asks of Laban in 30:25–34 (esp. vv. 26, 30, 33). Instead, Laban keeps Jacob as nothing more than a laborer under contract, as Jacob bitterly complains in 31:38–42." Bruce K. Waltke and Cathi J. Fredricks, *Genesis: A Commentary* (Grand Rapids, Mich.: Zondervan, 2001), 404.

the irony—the same word, *abad*, is used six times in fifteen verses, all referring to Jacob as the one who serves (29:15–30)! Jacob had to *serve* his uncle Laban—and *serve* and *serve* and *serve*! He was receiving his just desserts as God began to work in his soul.

NOTE OF INTEREST: *The Two Daughters of Laban*

Laban had two daughters. The older was Leah, and the younger Rachel. The name "Leah" is Hebrew for *wild cow* (others suggest *strong woman*) and for someone described as having "weak eyes". This is referring, not to her eyesight, but to her lackluster appearance, pale or dull—a polite way of saying she was physically unattractive. She was a stark contrast to the beautiful form and lovely features of Rachel. Jacob loved beautiful Rachel, whose name means *ewe*. The sisters had names appropriate for the pastoral life of Laban—the *cow* and the *ewe*. Similar descriptions are used of young David, "Now he was ruddy, and had beautiful eyes, and was handsome" (1 Sam 16:12). Beautiful eyes are mentioned again in Song of Solomon 4:1, 9.

Jacob came for a bride, and "Jacob loved Rachel." It was customary for the groom to compensate the family for the loss of a daughter. Jacob offered to work seven years in exchange for Rachel. Abraham's servant had brought gifts and payment for Rebekah. Since Jacob had nothing to offer except his labor, he offered to serve, and the years flew by because of his love for her—exemplified by the whole timespan covered in only one verse (v. 20). I have never understood this. The more I loved my fiancée, Janet, the more the time dragged. The more kids love Christmas, the longer it takes to arrive. Patient waiting is worth it, but—is the wait shorter for the depth of love or longing? Now there is another problem—it was also customary in their country for the eldest daughter to marry first. In the intervening years, no one had married the unattractive Leah.

THE DECEIT OF LABAN; JACOB SURPRISED BY LEAH (29:21–26)

After seven years, Jacob said to Laban, "Give me my wife." He did not say "my fiancée" or "my intended". Marriage was comprised of two parts: *betrothal*, and then the groom coming to take the wife. In our Western civilization, we get *engaged*, which is much less binding than the ancient custom of *betrothal*, which was a more formal transaction. When a couple was *betrothed*, they were pledged in marriage and were already considered man and wife, which became complete when the husband took the bride into his home and consummated the marriage. It is the same in much of the world today.

The day approached; Laban invited everyone to the feast. On the wedding night, the deceiver was deceived, the trickster was tricked. How ironic is the justice of God! As the younger son, Jacob had deceived his father into thinking he was the oldest—Laban now tricked Jacob into thinking the older daughter was the younger! Laban slipped his daughter Leah into unsuspecting Jacob's arms!

Jacob slept with Leah that night after the wedding celebration, and the text emphasizes his surprise in the morning, again using *behold*: "And in the morning, behold, it was Leah" (v. 25). How could Jacob have been so duped? First, such deception was never expected. Second, it was dark, and these feasts involved a lot of drinking, so he had likely been very inebriated. Lastly, the custom of veiling the face before marriage concealed her face. Remember Rebekah veiling herself when she met Isaac? God's ironic justice stings the supplanter. Leah's complicity in the ruse certainly did not inspire Jacob's love.

The maidservant Zilpah was given to Leah as a wedding gift from her father. We are shocked at the idea of human beings as property. To understand biblical times and Near Eastern cultures, we need to suspend our own expectations and enter their context—though of course that does not mean we must approve of their practices! A maidservant gives the bride prestige, assistance with daily chores, and provides offspring for the husband.

Leah knew she was unlovely and unloved and surely expected Jacob's shocked dismay and disdain in the morning. The tension in the tent was electric. Jacob confronted Laban with the fraud. Laban justified his actions and responded: "It is not the practice in our place to marry off the younger before the first-born." The seven-day period of the "bridal week" was probably based on the seven days of creation—a time for the bride and groom to be exempt from other activity to create new life. There was always the hope of children early in the marriage. As translated literally in the RSV-2CE "the week of this one", it indicates that the husband was to spend a week with his new bride (v. 27). It was a common practice (cf. Judg 14:12–17; Tob 11:19) and continues to this very day among the Jews.[3]

MARRIAGE TO RACHEL (29:27–31)

The seven days of the marital week with Leah must have been a stressful time, no less so for Rachel. After Leah had completed "her week", Rachel was given to Jacob as a wife. She received Bilhah the handmaid as a wedding gift. Jacob's days of bachelorhood were over—within a week he now had Leah and Zilpah, Rachel and Bilhah. Jacob went in to Rachel, and the text says he loved her more than Leah. He had to serve an additional seven years for Rachel. Laban was shrewd—he married off the homely older daughter and received an extra seven "free" years of servitude from Jacob. He outswindled the swindler!

Some translations render the Hebrew word *senu'ah* as "unloved" in verse 31. Hebrew lexicons define the word as hate, loved less than, unable or unwilling to put up with or to tolerate. Such a situation is mentioned in Deuteronomy 21:15. The stress in the tent was palpable; despised Leah lived with Jacob's hostility while watching her younger sister bask in the coveted love of their shared husband. The Lord took note that Leah was "hated", and providentially opened her womb, and in short succession she had four sons. Leah compensated by providing Jacob with sons, the most prized of possessions. Reuben

---

[3] "Following the ceremony, the wedding is celebrated at a reception and then by seven days of festive meals and a full year of private rejoicing. This follows biblical precedent, since Genesis refers to Laban's gathering all the people for the wedding feast of Jacob and Leah (Gen. 29:22). At Gen. 29:27, he asks Jacob to 'complete the week of this one'—understood to refer to a protracted wedding celebration—before continuing to work towards acquiring Rachel as a bride. The bridal week also appears at Judg. 14:12, where Samson allows the guests the seven days of the wedding feast to solve his riddle.... To take part in this communal celebration, traditionally, couples remained at home for at least the first week following marriage. During this entire week, the groom is required to stay with the bride, ensuring that he devotes all his energies to her. The couple remains in a state of private celebration for the next full year, exempting the groom from certain ritual obligations and, in ancient times, from military service." Jacob Neusner, Alan J. Avery-Peck, and William Scott Green, eds., *The Encyclopedia of Judaism* (Leiden, Boston, and Cologne: Brill, 2000), 803.

the firstborn, Simeon, then Levi, father of Israel's priestly line, and fourth, Judah, the father of the Kings of Israel from whom would come the Messiah, Jesus Christ. More were to follow.

THE FIRST FOUR SONS OF JACOB
THROUGH LEAH (29:32–35)

We now have a long procession of sons (and one daughter) birthed by the two competing sisters and their handmaids. These offspring were all born *outside* the land of promise! Only the last son of Rachel would be born in Canaan. Because Leah was unloved, God opened her womb. Rachel suffered barrenness like the matriarchs Sarah and Rebekah before her. She, too, resorted to her handmaiden to produce her offspring. The competition escalated. The sons of Leah had names related to her despised status and desire to be loved.

The following chart organizes the series of sons born to each woman in the sequence in which they were born, from the firstborn Reuben to the last-born Benjamin. It also gives the meaning of each name as explained in Scripture. God's blessing enabled Leah to bear more children than the other three women combined. There is only one daughter mentioned, Dinah, who played a significant role in a later conflict.

Mother	Offspring	Name's Meaning	Reference
Leah	Reuben	Because the LORD has *looked* upon my affliction; surely now my husband will love me	Gen 29:32
Leah	Simeon	Because the LORD has *heard* that I am hated, he has given me this son also	Gen 29:33
Leah	Levi	Now this time my husband will be *joined* to me, because I have borne him three sons	Gen 29:34
Leah	Judah	This time I will *praise* the LORD	Gen 29:35
Bilhah, Rachel's maid	Dan	God has *judged* me, and has also heard my voice and given me a son	Gen 30:1–6

Mother	Offspring	Name's Meaning	Reference
Bilhah, Rachel's maid	Naphtali	With mighty wrestlings I have *wrestled* with my sister, and have prevailed	Gen 30:8
Zilpah, Leah's handmaiden	Gad	Good *fortune*	Gen 30:11
Zilpah, Leah's handmaiden	Asher	*Blessed* am I! For the women will call me blessed	Gen 30:13
Leah	Issachar	God has given me my *hire* [wages] because I gave my maid to my husband	Gen 30:18
Leah	Zebulun	God has endowed me with a good dowry; now my husband will *honor* me, because I have borne him six sons	Gen 30:20
Leah	Dinah	A daughter: meaning *Judgment*	Gen 30:21
Rachel	Joseph	May the *Lord add* to me another son	Gen 30:24
Rachel	Benjamin	Rachel: Benoni: *Son of my sorrow* Jacob: Benjamin: *Son of my right hand*	Gen 35:18

CHAPTER 30

COMPETING WIVES;
JACOB'S SONS; AND PROSPERITY

RACHEL FRUSTRATED WITH INFERTILITY (30:1–13)

Reading Genesis chapter 30, we sense the intrigue, the bitterness, the envy, and the antagonism of two sisters in a bitter struggle to out-do each other for their husband's affection and in the sons they provide. The intrigue of these two sisters with the same husband may have influenced the later Mosaic Law that forbids a man from marrying sisters (Lev 18:18). It was a contest not just for their husband but also for the favor of God. It is not by coincidence that *God* is mentioned eight times in the next twenty-one verses. Envious of her sister's fertility, Rachel threatened Jacob as though it was his fault, "Give me children or I shall die!" He retorted in anger, "Am I in the place of God, who has withheld from you the fruit of the womb?"[1] Like Sarah before her, Rachel resorted to her servant. Bilhah bore two sons for Rachel, so Leah gave Jacob her servant Zilpah, and she bore two sons for Leah. Jacob now had eight sons.

Saint Ephraim the Syrian (ca. 306–373), a biblical scholar, hymn writer, and Doctor of the Church, provides an interesting perspective on Rachel's accusation against Jacob:

> Rachel was barren. Because she heard Jacob say that Abraham had prayed over the barren Sarah and was heard, and that Isaac had also prayed for Rebekah and was answered, she thought that it was because Jacob had not prayed for her that her closed womb had not

---

[1] The sorrow experienced by couples with infertility is discussed in the *Catechism* along with a discussion of medical procedures, both licit and illicit (CCC 2374–79), and of spousal relations in the absence of children (CCC 1654).

been opened. For this reason, she said in anger and in tears, "*Give me children, or I shall die!*" Although he was angry with her because she said, "*Give me children,*" instead of saying, "Pray that children be given me," Jacob persuaded Rachel that "even if my fathers were answered, nevertheless Abraham was heard only after one hundred years and Isaac after twenty." When she learned from him that she, who had become extremely despondent, ought to have great patience, she said to him, "*Then go into my handmaid, she shall bear on my knees and I shall be comforted by her,*" following [the example] of Abraham, who took Hagar and did the will of Sarah because he loved her.[2]

MATRIARCHS AND MANDRAKES (30:14–24)

Halfway through the account of these births there is a curious story of mandrakes and matriarchs. Mandrakes are mentioned twice in the Bible, here in Genesis 30 and again in the Song of Solomon 7:13. Due to the mandrake's properties, it is associated with Aphrodite, the goddess of love, who was also known as the "lady of the mandrake". It was put under the marital bed in regions of Europe.[3] The plant grows in the Mediterranean regions, and locals have considered the fruit to be exhilarating and aiding in the conception of children.

> The magical powers of the mandrake have been the subject of a mass of literature.... Mandrakes were used as aphrodisiacs in post-biblical times and are mentioned in later literature.... The Greeks, in whose country the mandrake is common and valued for its aphrodisiac powers, called it "love apple" and considered it effective as a love-potion when soaked in wine. They also believed it helped a barren woman

[2] Commentary on Genesis sec. 28.1, in Ephrem the Syrian, *St. Ephrem the Syrian: Selected Prose Works*, ed. Kathleen McVey, trans. Edward G. Mathews, Jr., and Joseph P. Amar, The Fathers of the Church, ed. Thomas P. Halton, vol. 91 (Washington, D.C.: Catholic University of America Press, 2004), 176.

[3] "On an Egyptian wall painting, dated c. 1340, an Egyptian queen is depicted holding two mandrakes and a lotus bud to her husband's nose.... Her open dress is suggestive of her amorous intentions. Moreover, the motif is a commonplace in Egyptian love poetry.... In the Greek world, the mandrake was an epithet of Aphrodite.... At Ugarit too, the plant is associated with love although the exact significance of putting the plant into the ground is a matter of debate." Jill M. Munro, *Spikenard and Saffron: The Imagery of the Song of Songs*, Journal for the Study of the Old Testament Supplement Series, vol. 203 (Sheffield: Sheffield Academic Press, 1995), 81n4.

to conceive.... Recent experiments have shown that the mandrake contains both sedatives and aphrodisiacs.... They are edible, but are said to be narcotic and purgative.[4]

Reuben found some mandrakes in the field. Knowing his mother would be pleased, he gave them to Leah. The rancor behind the tent flaps is revealed when Rachel requested some of Leah's mandrakes. Leah bitterly retorted, "Is it a small matter that you have taken away my husband? And would you take away my son's mandrakes also?" Rachel, who obviously kept Jacob to herself, made a deal, saying to Leah, "Then he may lie with you tonight for your son's mandrakes." Jacob did not argue when Leah announced the deal in the evening, "You must come in to me; for I have hired you with my son's mandrakes." The night he revisited Leah's bed, she again conceived.

Leah wanted mandrakes to buy her husband; Rachel wanted mandrakes to cure her infertility. This episode of the mandrakes breaks up the narrative and, for the reader, pulls back the curtain exposing the tension that was part of the sisters' daily existence. Jacob endured the friction and complied with the wishes of his wily wives—probably to keep peace in the tents.

Finally, God blessed Rachel with a son whom she named Joseph. The birth of Joseph and his growing family stirred a restlessness in Jacob and a desire to return home. Time to end his servitude in the distant land and become his own master. He had paid his debt; his obligations had been met. The exploitation of his uncle was galling, and the Promised Land was drawing him home. He was ready to establish his own household and fortune on the land.

LABAN AND JACOB RENEGOTIATE
JABOB'S EMPLOYMENT (30:25–36)

Laban did not relish the loss of an employee who had labored faithfully for him for fourteen years—one who had provided him with grandsons for additional labor and raised his status in the community. Jacob was blessed by God, and Laban thrived because of Jacob.

---

[4] Michael Zohary, *Plants of the Bible* (New York: Cambridge University Press, 1982), 188.

Laban was aware of God's blessing on Jacob and finagled to retain his services. The demands upon a shepherd, which Jacob had fulfilled with great ardor, were not easy nor without personal risk. "Shepherds were responsible to maintain the health and safety of the flock. They were to insure a minimum survival rate of 80% of all new births in the flock. It was assumed that 15% of the adult sheep and 14% of the adult goats would die during a normal grazing season. Anything above these percentages, and the hired herdsman was required to recompense the owner of the flocks."[5]

Jacob was not respected as family but as an indentured servant paying off a debt. When the debt was paid, Jacob decided it was time to leave with his large family and all he had earned. According to local customs, a master sent a servant away with provisions after his debt was paid. This law was later delineated in Deuteronomy 15:13–14. However, if a slave came to a master without a wife, was given a wife and had children, the wife and children remained the property of the master (Ex 21:2–4). This was not Jacob's situation. Nothing had been given to him. He had worked for his wives, and, along with the children, they were his.

Laban understood he was prosperous because God had blessed Jacob, so Laban offered to pay him to stay. Jacob saw his opportunity to "kill two birds with one stone"—to get even with Laban and to build his own flocks before leaving. A few more years to "steal" his own flock would be worth it. So he stayed. Jacob devised a strange scheme that worked to his advantage. Jacob's proposal was simple and easily verified. Black and spotted sheep along with streaked goats would be separated from Laban's flock and become the property of Jacob as his wages. With this deal consummated, Jacob divided the flocks between himself and Laban, delegating the speckled, spotted, and black ones to his sons, who moved them away a distance of three day's journey. He personally cared for Laban's flock himself. The "normal" sheep and goats remained in Laban's flock. "Not surprisingly, Laban accepts this very favorable deal; he did not anticipate

<hr />

[5] Vernon H. Alexander, "The 'Good Shepherd' and Other Metaphors of Pastoralism", in *Lexham Geographic Commentary on the Gospels*, ed. Barry J. Beitzel and Kristopher A. Lyle, Lexham Geographic Commentary (Bellingham, Wash.: Lexham Press, 2016), Mt 25:31— Jn 10:15.

Jacob making much out of it, certainly much less than the typical
20 percent of newborn lambs or kids that ancient shepherds usually
received as their wages."[6] With such a visible means of verification,
neither Jacob nor Laban could be accused of stealing or cheating—
which was a good arrangement since both were known swindlers.

JACOB PROSPERS AS FLOCKS INCREASE (30:37–43)

Jacob did something that strikes us as strange. He took branches from
trees and stuck them in the ground where the sheep and goats came
to drink. He used rods from poplar, almond, and plane trees. He
peeled back strips of the bark exposing "the white of the rods". The
sheep bred when they came to drink, and because they mated in front
of the rods with stripes showing, they gave birth to lambs and kids
with stripes, speckles, and spots. And when the strong were breeding, Jacob put the rods in front of their eyes in the water troughs.
Therefore, the strongest of the flock became Jacob's, and the weaker
became Laban's.

We can try to make sense of this rather obscure and strange passage. The ancients often had superstitious beliefs such as offspring
being altered by the visual input of a mother while mating. Folklore
was common in prescientific times and even continues today. But,
what happened probably *was* scientific, not due to sticks, but due
to genetics. If strong sheep breed with strong sheep, they tend to
produce genetically strong offspring. The opposite is also true. Col-
oration and spotting patterns are also achieved in a similar manner.
Ancient peoples knew *what* happened but did not understand DNA

[6] Gordon J. Wenham, *Genesis 16–50*, Word Biblical Commentary, vol. 2 (Dallas: Word,
Incorporated, 1994), 256. Also, "Archaeological records indicate that the ancient world placed
great importance on documenting sheep. Scribes kept records that included the type of animals in the flock and the production of wool or dairy products. These records provide insight
into government flocks, which were entrusted to shepherds. Written contracts included the
shepherd's payment in sheep products and newborn lambs. For example, Old Babylonian
contracts allowed shepherds to keep between 8 and 20 percent of newborn lambs as payment. The texts also indicate the proportion of breeding males (rams) to geldings (wethers)
and ewes. Once a year, the sheep would be brought in for shearing, and records would be
updated." Stephen Bennett, s.v. "Sheep", in *The Lexham Bible Dictionary*, ed. John D. Barry
et al. (Bellingham, Wash.: Lexham Press, 2016).

and genetics or *why* it happened. Regardless of superstition or careful breeding and genetics, God blessed Jacob and caused his flocks to grow and prosper.

Jacob became very rich with huge flocks of strong animals, plus many servants and camels and donkeys. Even with all Jacob's deviousness, God blessed him. At the same time, Laban received the just desserts of his unscrupulous behavior and foul play. Just as Jacob the trickster had earned his just recompense when he first came to Laban, Laban now paid the piper when Jacob left. Jacob successfully outsmarted and outwitted his crafty opponent. But he did not use deceit to accomplish his new goals. It was all done honestly, according to the agreement. This is drama at its best! And in the midst of this human sin and selfishness, God's providence worked all things well for his own purposes, not only to bless the seed of Abraham, but also to distribute reward and retribution justly to each participant in this saga. The definition of justice is giving to each man his due.[7]

---

[7] "Justice is a virtue which assigns to each man his due in conformity with the law; injustice claims what belongs to others, in opposition to the law." Aristotle, *The "Art" of Rhetoric*, ed. E. Capps, T. E. Page, and W. H. D. Rouse, trans. John Henry Freese, The Loeb Classical Library (London and New York: William Heinemann; G. P. Putnam's Sons, 1926), 91–93. See also *CCC* 1807.

CHAPTER 31

JACOB FLEES FROM HARAN; COVENANT WITH LABAN

TIME TO RETURN HOME TO CANAAN (31:1–16)

Rumors began to fly. Resentment, gossip, and hostility were spreading. The sons of Laban saw the results of Jacob's husbandry and God's blessing. They resented Jacob as they watched their flocks dwindle while Jacob's grew. "Jacob has taken all that was our father's; and from what was our father's, he has gained all this wealth." The Hebrew word translated "wealth" is used elsewhere to express *glory*, *honor*, and *reputation* as well. Jacob could see the change in Laban's demeanor toward him. The phrase "Jacob saw that Laban did not regard him with favor as before" is literally, "The face of Laban was not as before." The growing tension was not the only reason to leave. God told Jacob to return home. It was time to separate from his uncle and return to his father and the land. In fact, his father, Isaac, was still living though his mother Rebekah had died. We learn nothing of her death, but she was not there when Jacob finally returned.

God had not forgotten Jacob during his twenty years of exile. He had spoken to him personally on his way to Haran, and now God spoke to him again about returning to Canaan. Interestingly, Jacob consulted with his wives. This seems unusual for such patriarchal times. He "sneaked" his wives into the field with the flocks to assure no one was eavesdropping, and there he recounted in summary all that had taken place for the last twenty years (v. 4). He reminded them of his noble conduct with their father, Laban, even though he had cheated Jacob over and over again and changed his wages ten times. God had protected him and taken the flocks away from Laban and given them to him. We learn something new from his conversation with his wives—he told his wives an angel had visited him (v. 11) and confirmed that God himself caused the growth of the flocks and that Jacob was to leave and return to the land. God reminded Jacob that he was the God of Bethel, the place where Jacob had set up the stone as a pledge to God (v. 13).

Enlightened by God's renewed promise to their husband and the frustration of their father Laban's injustice, the two wives agreed that separation was essential. Leah and Rachel did not see eye-to-eye about much, but here they were in full agreement. Let's face it, they both said, "He has sold us, and he has been using up the money given for us." For them to have any inheritance, anything to pass on to their children, they must escape their father's dominance. In the field, Laban's daughters rejected any claim their father had on them and renounced any allegiance. They pledged allegiance to Jacob.

Here they seem to refer to the dowry given to daughters by rich fathers when they married. Poor families might sell their daughters to be slave-wives (cf. Exod 21:7–11), in which case no dowry would be given. However, it is clear from the story that both Leah and Rachel received handsome dowries, for they were given slave-girls on their marriage. So what are they referring to when they insist, "He has also wasted, yes wasted, our money"? Commentators often surmise that it was the marriage present given by the bridegroom to the bride's father, which might later be passed on to the bride in her dowry. But Jacob's marriage present was his fourteen years of service, so what they are referring to is elusive. It seems, rather, that they are agreeing that their father has indeed cheated.[1]

OUTWITTING LABAN; ESCAPING FROM HARAN (31:17–20)

There were no farewell dinners or going away parties. This was subterfuge again on Jacob's part; in fact, Scripture informs us that Jacob "outwitted Laban". He was "escaping" or sneaking away without notice. He waited until Laban had gone to shear his sheep. This was

[1] Gordon J. Wenham, *Genesis 16–50*, Word Biblical Commentary, vol. 2 (Dallas: Word, Incorporated, 1994), 273.

an extremely busy time for shepherds, who hired additional labor and often went far from home for extended lengths of time. Shearing took place in the spring so the sheep would not be too hot in the summer but would have time to grow back their wool for the cold winter months. This was the most inopportune time for Laban, but the best time to escape for Jacob. Moving quickly, he loaded his family on camels and drove his flocks and herds in the direction of Canaan.

Over one hundred years earlier, Abraham had saddled his camels and donkeys, gathered his sheep and goats, his wife Sarai, his nephew Lot and all his servants and headed off to a new land that God had promised him. He left Haran with no children. Now his grandson Jacob was saddling his camels and donkeys, gathering his sheep and goats, his wives, and all his servants and heading back to the land that God had given his grandfather Abraham and his descendants after him. But there was a big difference—Jacob was leaving for the Promised Land with a quiver full of sons.

The wording "Jacob outwitted Laban" is literally "Jacob stole Laban's heart." That was not all that was stolen; Rachel also stole Laban's household gods. The drama builds and the tension escalates not only because Jacob is covertly fleeing from Laban, but also because Rachel acting unilaterally had raided her father's house and stolen his household gods. We expect consequences for this theft. This brings up a new twist in the story. Did not Jacob serve the living God? If so, what were these "household gods"?

HISTORICAL NOTE: *The Household Idols*

The Hebrew word for the household gods is *teraphim*. They were figurines, idols of the gods that protected the family and were objects of worship. They were likely tied to some form of ancestral worship.[2] They were a kind of idol in the shape of a man but varying in size. They were placed in a household shrine. These idols, or gods, would often be the center of family religious life and were associated with divination (cf. Ezek 21:21; Zech 10:2). They could be small

[2] Jacob Milgrom, *Leviticus 17–22: A New Translation with Introduction and Commentary*, Anchor Yale Bible, vol. 3A (New Haven and London: Yale University Press, 2008), 1778.

enough to hide in a camel's saddle blankets (Gen 31:34) or sometimes as large as a man (1 Sam 19:13, 16). Maybe owning the family gods was thought to guarantee the family inheritance or blessing or gave the assurance of fertility or the supply of food. Laban's frantic attempt to retrieve the family gods demonstrates their importance. Jacob would eventually require everyone in his family to rid themselves of such idols (Gen 35:2).

Saint John Chrysostom wrote:

> This was included not by chance but for us to know how they still clung to their ancestral habits and showed great devotion to the household gods. I mean, consider how [Rachel] went to so much trouble as to steal nothing else of her father's than the household gods alone and did it without her husband noticing; Jacob would not have allowed it to happen, you see.[3]

THE ROUTE BACK TO CANAAN (31:21)

In verse 21, Scripture says they "crossed the Euphrates". In the Hebrew, it simply says "river", but in context it is the Euphrates River, which is often referred to simply as "the river" (Deut 11:24; Josh 24:3). Jacob fled south for the hills of Gilead, which are today in northern Jordan. The Euphrates is over 1,400 miles long and begins its flow in northern Turkey. It flows west around Haran and then turns southeast toward the Persian Gulf, through modern-day Iraq. It formed part of the Fertile Crescent along which travelers journeyed between Egypt, Canaan, and the East. Gilead is still on the map today—the mountains of Gilead are in Jordan, north of Amman. Jacob was heading south southwest, the way he had come.

LABAN PURSUES JACOB (31:22–42)

Word finally reached Laban out in the distant fields three days later— no cell phones back in those days, and news traveled slowly. He

[3] Homilies on Genesis 57.17, in Mark Sheridan, *Genesis 12–50*, Ancient Christian Commentary on Scripture, OT 2 (Downers Grove, Ill.: InterVarsity Press, 2002), 206–7.

assumed that Jacob had kidnapped his daughters at the point of a sword. He took off in hot pursuit for seven days and caught up with Jacob in the hills of Gilead. This time frame seems unlikely if these are the mountains of Gilead in northern Jordan.[4] Laban could travel more swiftly with just his men, whereas Jacob had family and flocks.

God warned Laban in a dream to say nothing good or bad to Jacob. Laban had his hands tied regarding the departure. The questions Laban asked after overtaking Jacob were comical. "What have you done, that you have cheated me, and carried away my daughters like captives of the sword? Why did you flee secretly, and cheat me …?" These two deserved each other and had cheated each other back and forth, so why was Laban surprised? He was probably angrier because he had been snookered and had lost the labor and services of Jacob and sons. And look at those huge flocks of sheep and goats that should be his! He had also lost his daughters, grandchildren, and his household gods. Ignoring God's caveat, he spewed out lengthy accusations against Jacob. Laban finally accused Jacob of the most serious crime—stealing his household gods. Jacob of course knew nothing of this theft, since Rachel had clandestinely stolen the *teraphim*.

Not knowing of Rachel's deception (what a deceiving, scheming family!), Jacob boldly spoke with great confidence, "Death to anyone who has your gods!" Jacob permitted him to search high and low. Laban had no luck, but the dramatic tension rose to a crescendo. After searching all the tents, he finally stepped into Rachel's tent. *We know the gods were there, but apart from Rachel no one else did.* We hold our breath as he began to search her tent. But Rachel had not lived with liars and swindlers without having learned a few tricks herself. She hid the gods in the camel saddle and then sat on the saddle, saying, "the way of women is upon me", which is a euphemism for menstruation. It worked. Rachel outwitted her father, and Laban did not search her or the saddle.

---

[4] "This is meant as a general figure indicating a distance of considerable length; cf. 2 Kings 3:9. Actually, Gilead could scarcely have been reached from Har(r)an in seven days, especially at the pace of Jacob's livestock." E. A. Speiser, *Genesis: Introduction, Translation, and Notes,* Anchor Yale Bible, vol. 1 (New Haven; London: Yale University Press, 2008), 246. This would mean that Jacob had sustained a pace of about forty miles a day as opposed to the usual six miles in a day. See Nahum M. Sarna, *Genesis,* The JPS Torah Commentary (Philadelphia: Jewish Publication Society, 1989), 217.

Scholars have posited three reasons for Rachel's successful ruse, and most hold to a combination of these reasons. First, menstruation was associated with religious impurity in the ancient world, and impurity was communicable, so Laban was preventing his own contamination (e.g., Sarna, *Genesis*, 219). Second, some ancient cultures believed menstruating women were vulnerable to demon possession—a danger that would also have deterred Laban (e.g., [John H.] Walton, ed., *Zondervan Illustrated Bible Backgrounds Commentary* [Grand Rapids, Mich.: Zondervan, 2009], 119). A third reason Laban may have left Rachel alone is that he could not have imagined that anyone would sit on his gods—especially someone in Rachel's condition (e.g., [Carl Friedrich] Keil and [Franz] Delitzsch [*Commentary on the Old Testament*, vol. 1 (Peabody, Mass.: Hendrickson 1996)], 191).[5]

Saint John Chrysostom comments on Rachel's deceit:

Wonderful is the shrewdness of Rachel, by which she succeeded in outwitting Laban. Let those heed it who are victims of deceit and give great importance to the worship of idols. "She put them under the camel saddles," the text says, "and sat on them." What could be more ridiculous than these people? Although endowed with reason and accorded such wonderful preeminence in God's loving kindness, they bring themselves to worship lifeless stone, and, far from being ashamed or having any sense of such absurdity, they even make a habit of it like dumb animals.[6]

LABAN'S COVENANT WITH JACOB (31:43–55)

Laban had been at the Prosecutor's stand accusing Jacob, but now Jacob took the offensive and Laban was on trial! Jacob had been double-crossed and cheated, lied to and taken for granted; now he was falsely accused of theft and kidnapping, and his privacy invaded. Laban had unjustly accused Jacob of theft and had rifled through all his tents and possessions—Jacob was rightly indignant. "Set [the gods]

---

[5] Douglas Mangum, Miles Custis, and Wendy Widder, *Genesis 12–50*, Lexham Bible Guide (Bellingham, Wash.: Lexham Press, 2013), Gen 30:25—31:55.
[6] Homilies on Genesis 57.28, in Sheridan, *Genesis 12–50*, 211.

here before my kinsmen and your kinsmen, that they may decide between us two" (v. 37). But of course, no material evidence of any crime had been uncovered. Rachel had outmaneuvered her father.

We now learn from Jacob that he had been in Haran serving Laban for *twenty years*—seven years working for Rachel, only to get Leah. Then working another seven years to pay for Rachel and another six years earning a wage working for Laban. As Jacob put it, "I served you fourteen years for your two daughters, and six years for your flock" (v. 41). Jacob recalled the twenty years nobly spent looking after Laban's best interests, even enduring the frigid cold nights and the sweltering hot days. He had served Laban loyally and flawlessly. "Feeling vindicated by Laban's failure to find the absconded god, Jacob then upbraids his father-in-law, laying it on pretty thick (vv. 43–54). It is a masterpiece of self-justification, in which the speaker is manifestly enjoying himself. Indeed, the author intends for the reader to enjoy it too."[7]

Jacob used a unique title for God found only here in Scripture (31:42, 53). We have heard the appellation "The God of Abraham and Isaac", but here there is an interesting twist. God is referred to as the "Fear of Isaac". It is the deity feared and worshipped by Isaac that causes awe. Jacob recognized that this God is no longer just the God of Abraham and his own father, Isaac, he is now Jacob's God as well. Jacob's closing statement against the scoundrel is essentially this: You, Laban, would have sent me away alone and penniless, but God has been my defense and has supplied me with everything; and *he* even rebuked you to your face! So—case closed!

Laban knew he was beat. The only thing left to do was to form a nonaggression pact, a covenant between them.

Laban still said his daughters, the children, the herds, and all Jacob owned were his. He could not mean that he had legal claim to them. What it seems to mean is that Jacob came to Laban with nothing but a walking staff. He is now leaving very wealthy with a large family—all of it acquired from Laban. But it was done fairly, honestly, cleverly, but mainly through hard work and integrity. Laban's last jab missed the target, and the covenant was made.

[7] Patrick Henry Reardon, *Creation and the Patriarchal Histories: Orthodox Christian Reflections on the Book of Genesis* (Chesterton, Ind.: Ancient Faith Publishing, 2008), 116.

Twenty years earlier, Jacob had raised a stone as a reminder as he fled Canaan. Now while fleeing Laban, he set up another stone on his way back to Canaan. The first had been for a witness before God, this one as a pledge before Laban. The stone was set as a pillar with smaller stones piled around it as a witness. Jacob called the heap *Galeed* ("the heap of witness" in Hebrew) and the pillar *Mizpah* ("the watchtower"); Laban called the heap *Jegar–sahadutha* ("the heap of witness" in Aramaic). Neither would pass this "heap" with intent to harm the other. At the "heap", they swore a pledge, made a sacrifice, and ate a ceremonial meal. This type of pledge and ceremony is common in the ancient literature from the time. They stayed all night on the mountain, and each went his separate way the next morning.

Jacob breathed a sigh of relief—one disaster had been averted. But he could not relax for long because another danger was looming dead ahead. Twenty years ago his angry brother Esau had pledged to kill him. Esau was now on his way to meet Jacob as he returned home. Jacob was out of the frying pan and into the fire!

CHAPTER 32

JACOB FEARS ESAU; WRESTLES WITH GOD

A VISION OF ANGELS (32:1–2)

Chapter 32 opens with Jacob realizing that even though Laban had left, he was not alone. He and his family were in the presence of angels. We might expect to hear of a few angels joining Jacob to protect him along the way, but the vision of the angels is surprising. The throng of angels revealed to Jacob is so large that Jacob exclaims, "This is God's army!" A similar description is used again in 1 Chronicles 12:22. Jacob had received a revelation of many angels upon his departure to Haran and now received a revelation upon leaving Haran.

As was his custom, Jacob named the place appropriately—*Mahanaim*, which means *two camps*, presumably a human camp and the angelic camp. The site retained its distinct identity and was significant in Israel's history (e.g., 2 Sam 17:24–27) and is mentioned thirteen times in the Bible. This vision of the angels is comforting for us. Short of divine revelation, we cannot see the angels encamped round about us. But in reality, there are two camps, those of Christians moving through their daily lives *and* the spiritual world around us. The unseen world is every bit as real as what we see with our eyes.

But even this vision of God's army did not allay the fear of the impending confrontation with Esau. Jacob sent messengers all the way to Seir where Esau dwelled. The Hebrew word for messengers is *mal'ak*, the word used for angels, who are, by definition, messengers. Jacob initiated contact with his estranged brother with hopes of directing the meeting in his favor. He was taking precautionary, preemptive action. There were six steps to his strategy: (1) send messengers ahead, (2) devise a plan of survival if attacked, (3) prepare gifts ahead to appease, (4) pray for God's deliverance, (5) prepare to be humble and obsequious, and (6) keep his family back until the last possible moment.

PREPARATION FOR THE IMPENDING MEETING WITH ESAU (32:3–21)

Jacob's main concern now was the reception he would receive from his brother Esau, who was coming from Seir. Seir and Edom are synonymous, though Edom generally refers to the country and Seir to the mountain range running through Edom (Ezek 35:15). Esau had settled in the rugged arid land east of the Dead Sea and south of Moab in southern, modern-day Jordan. It stretched from the southern tip of the Dead Sea to the Gulf of Aqaba. It was a long walk for the messengers and for Esau.

Jacob's messengers were instructed to call Esau "my lord", which was quite a change from Jacob's earlier attitude and the prophecy that said his brother would serve him. They were to inform Esau that his brother Jacob had amassed great wealth, subtly implying that if Esau was intent on murder, Jacob would "pay him off". Esau had pledged to kill Jacob after the death of their father, Isaac—but Isaac was still alive. The only update the messengers brought back was that Esau was coming to meet him with four hundred men. That is the size of a militia. David amassed four hundred men when Saul was out to get him (1 Sam 22:2; 25:13; 30:10). Was Esau coming with a large greeting party or an army to destroy him? The latter seemed more likely, and the response from the messengers was ominous and with no word of intent from Esau. The writer wanted the tension undiminished and Esau's approach was mentioned to keep the drama red hot.

Jacob was greatly afraid and distressed. He quickly divided the people and the animals into two companies, thinking, if Esau destroys one group, the second may survive. He poured out his heart to God and reminded him of his previous promises of protection and surety that Jacob would arrive safely back home. He was like an attorney presenting his case before God. He displayed an unusual humility, even though it was inspired by fear, but humility and submission nonetheless. With the whole caravan of people and flocks divided into two groups and bedding down for the night, Jacob prepared a present for Esau—many male and female sheep and goats, along with camels, cows and bulls, and donkeys. There were over 550 animals in total. He told his servants to take the animals ahead in droves and when meeting Esau to tell him these were gifts for him from his brother Jacob. They were to address him as *lord* and refer to Jacob as *your servant*.

Jewish scholar Ramban comments on Jacob's deference to Esau:

> Know that this respect which Jacob showed for his brother by fear-fully saying "my lord" and "thy servant" was due to it being the cus-tom of the younger brother to give recognition and respect to the firstborn as if he were his father, just as the Torah also hints to us on this matter: "This includes your oldest brother." Now Jacob had taken his birthright and his blessing, for which Esau hated him, and now he is acting towards Esau as if the effect of that sale was nil as far as he was concerned, and he is conducting himself towards him as to a firstborn and father in order to remove the hatred from his heart.[1]

The Hebrew word for "present" is *minhah*, which can suggest a trib-ute from a lesser to a greater person or a gift or offering. The anxiety heightens since we cannot anticipate how Esau would interpret the *minhah* or how he would respond. It is the birthright and Isaac's bless-ing that are the source of this great wealth through the providential hand of God fulfilling his promises to Abraham and Isaac. Jacob had "stolen" the birthright and the blessing from Esau, and now he was giving a portion back to the "rightful heir"—it seemed like the pru-dent thing to do. If Esau and his four hundred men were approaching with evil intent, then the gifts might placate them; if not, then the gift was an appropriate recompense considering the way Jacob had deceived Esau.

At night, his wives and children and all his possessions crossed the ford in the Jabbok River. I have visited the Jabbok River in Jordan many times, and it is not the Mississippi! It is a few feet deep along

---

[1] Rabbi Dr. Charles Chavel, *Ramban Commentary on the Torah* (New York: Shilo Publish-ing House, 1999), 395–96.

the edges with deeper areas around the curves. It is about thirty to forty feet across with stones along the shores and visible under the water. They could easily have crossed the river in the shallower areas. Jacob remained behind in the camp.

JACOB WRESTLES WITH GOD (32:22–26)

We are now introduced to a hugely significant episode in the history of Israel; in fact, we are about to hear the word *Israel* for the first time. Rarely does a passage of Scripture rise to the importance of the next eleven verses.

With his family and possessions safely across the river, Jacob was alone at night—or so he thought. A strange thing took place of which we have few details. Out of nowhere and for no apparent reason, a man began to wrestle with Jacob. We are not initially informed who it was, why he arrived, or *why* he attacked Jacob. The reason for the wrestling match is open to speculation. We do not know how long they wrestled, but the story implies it was all night, until the "breaking" of the day. According to the ages given so far, Jacob must have been nearly one hundred years old. When in high school, I was a pretty good wrestler, being young and strong. Even then, after thirty minutes or so of exertion, I would drop to the mat exhausted. Wrestling is very physically demanding, so to wrestle all night was a feat of strength, utter determination, and incredible persistence.

At one point the wrestler is called a "man" (v. 24) and at another point "God" (v. 30). The prophet Hosea refers to the wrestler as God and as an angel, saying, "In the womb [Jacob] took his brother by the heel, and in his manhood he strove with God. He strove with the angel and prevailed, he wept and sought his favor" (Hos 12:3–4). Jacob seemed to understand he was wrestling a heavenly being since he demanded a blessing and refused to release the wrestler until he *did* bless him. After wrestling with the "man", Jacob called the place *Peniel*, which means "the face of God". Just as the stranger who visited Abraham under the Oaks of Mamre was called Lord, so Christian tradition sees in the wrestler a theophany, a visible manifestation of God, even perhaps the pre-incarnate Word, sometimes called the

Angel of the Lord.[2] The tradition of the Church views this wrestling as a symbol of prayer, reminding us we need to battle in faith and triumph through perseverance (*CCC* 2573).

After the wrestling went on and on, the "man" realized he was not prevailing against Jacob, so he touched and dislocated Jacob's thigh (v. 25). Ancient Jewish tradition suggests that this was the sciatic nerve. This must have been extremely painful, but Jacob held on. Jacob would always fight for a blessing, and this case was no different. Through the pain, the fear, and the tiredness, he held on tenaciously. Jacob said, "I will not let you go, unless you bless me" (v. 26). He had grabbed Esau's heel at birth, now he was clutching this heavenly being with equal fervor.

At the conclusion of Gen 32, the text explains a food restriction that came out of the account of Jacob wrestling with "the man" (Gen 32:32). Because Jacob was injured in the "socket of the thigh at the sinew of the sciatic nerve," Israelites no longer ate the "sinew of the sciatic nerve" on the hip socket of animals. Nothing else in the Bible alludes to this restriction, but the food taboo continues in Judaism today.[3]

God did not demand this ritual observance in the Mosaic law, but the descendants of Israel of their own accord instituted the practice

---

[2] A theophany is a revelation or visible appearance of God such as at Mount Sinai, the visitors at Abraham's tent, the captain of the Lord with Joshua, the angel of the Lord in the burning bush, and here with Jacob and the wrestler. See *CCC* 707. The Angel of the Lord, or in this case the "man" who wrestles with Jacob, is seen by some to be an angel who mediates the words and presence of God, "*Mal'ak Yhwh* (Heb.): The 'angel' or 'messenger' of Yahweh. Sometimes this figure appears to be a messenger of God sent from heaven to speak in God's name (Gen 22:11–18; Judg 6:12). At other times, however, he appears to be an actual manifestation of God and a sounding forth of his own divine voice (Ex 3:2–6). For theological and other reasons, this messenger is most likely an angel who mediates the words of God to the world and manifests his divine presence in visible and audible ways." Scott Hahn and Curtis Mitch, *Genesis: With Introduction, Commentary, and Notes*, Ignatius Catholic Study Bible, Revised Standard Version, Second Catholic Edition (San Francisco: Ignatius Press, 2010), 38. "What matters is that there is an angelic medium by which God overrules his own transcendence and mercifully condescends to make himself known. For Justin Martyr, among other early Christian writers, the angel of the Lord is the pre-incarnate Christ, present in the Old Testament as the one in whom God's name and glory rest." Carol Zaleski, "Angels and Ministers of Grace. Review of No Ordinary Angel: Celestial Spirits and Christian Claims about Jesus by Susan R. Garrett", *First Things*, no. 193 (2009): 50.

[3] Douglas Mangum, Miles Custis, and Wendy Widder, *Genesis 12–50*, Lexham Bible Guide (Bellingham, Wash.: Lexham Press, 2013), Gen 32:1—33:20.

because they recognized how extremely important this experience of Jacob was for him and for themselves. Some interpret this *gidh han-nasheh* to be the sciatic nerve.[4]

WRESTLING CONTINUES; JACOB RECEIVES HIS NEW NAME OF ISRAEL (32:27–32)

The man asked Jacob his name, and he replied, "Jacob"—supplanter, cheat, conniver, swindler. It was like a confession, "OK, so I am a supplanter!" The man's reply hints at *his* true identity. He replied, "Your name shall no more be called Jacob, but Israel, for you have striven with God and with men, and have prevailed" (v. 28).

The last letters *el* in the word *Israel* mean *God*. Based on the context, the name *Israel* probably means "one who strives or wrestles with God", though others prefer the meaning of "seeing God". *Israel* was Jacob's new name, and it would be the name of the new nation God would form from Jacob's descendants. They would be known as the "children" or "sons of Israel", a phrase used 615 times in the Bible. If one thinks this name change is not significant, consider the fact that the name Israel is found over 2,700 times in Scripture. God had changed Abraham and Sarah's names; could it be less than a heavenly visitor who changed the name of this patriarch? Abraham's name had been changed at a significant moment of his life when taking on a new destiny, dignity, and status. Jacob was now in such a moment.

Yisra'el (Heb): Translates "Israel" and consists of a wordplay on the verb *sarah* ("strive, struggle, contend") coupled with the noun *'el* ("God"). Though compound names such as this are common in Hebrew and related Semitic languages, it is unusual for the divine name suffix to represent the object rather than the subject of the verbal element. But in Scripture the name Israel is taken to mean "he who strives with God" rather than the expected "God strives" (Hos 12:3). This is the new name given to Jacob after wrestling with God's angel (Gen 32:28; 35:10) and the national name given to the twelve tribes descended from Jacob (Gen 47:27; Deut 1:1).[5]

[4] H. C. Leupold, *Exposition of Genesis* (Grand Rapids, Mich.: Baker Book House, 1942), 883.
[5] Hahn and Mitch, *Genesis*, 60.

The divine visitor refused to divulge his name but blessed Jacob
on the spot. He asked Jacob, "Why is it that you ask my name?"
Almost as if to say, "I need not tell you, you already know."[6] The sun
rose, and the visitor vanished as mysteriously as he had appeared. The
result of the wrestling match would not be forgotten. Jacob painfully
limped away from the encounter knowing he had met God face to
face and lived to tell about it. This is the first time in the Bible we
see the word *Israelites* (RSV-2CE), though in the Hebrew it is not
Israelites but the *sons of Israel*.

After Jacob wrestled, was blessed, and received his new name of
Israel, he fully grasped with whom he had been wrestling. "So Jacob
called the name of the place Peniel, saying, 'For I have seen God face
to face, and yet my life is preserved.'" The word *peniel* means *the face
of God*.

As the Book of Wisdom has it, "When [Jacob's] oppressors were
covetous, [Wisdom] stood by him and made him rich. She protected
him from his enemies, and kept him safe from those who lay in wait
for him; in his arduous contest she gave him the victory, so that
he might learn that godliness is more powerful than anything" (Wis
10:11-12).

---

[6] "[T]he Angel answered the question with a question: *Why is it that you do ask after my
name?* The point was: 'Think on it, and you will know what My Name is.' And His Name
is *YHWH*. This was very similar to Manoah's question. Manoah was the father of Samson.
When Manoah had an encounter with the Angel of Jehovah, the Angel of God, he asked the
same question that Jacob did: *What is your name?* (Judg. 13:17-18). In that passage the Angel
also answered, 'Why do you seek after My Name?' However, in the Judges passage, the Angel
did not stop there but added: *seeing it is wonderful.* Moreover, the Hebrew word for *wonderful*
is *pele*, one of those words in the Hebrew text used only of God and never used of a man.
In this way, the Angel answered Manoah's question. By combining the two passages, there
is the same question on the part of man and the same answer with another similar question
on the part of the Angel. The additional answer given by the Angel in Judges indicates this
was clearly God Himself." Arnold G. Fruchtenbaum, *Ariel's Bible Commentary: The Book of
Genesis*, 1st ed. (San Antonio, Tex.: Ariel Ministries, 2008), 483-84.

Chapter 33

Jacob and Esau Meet

JACOB MEETS ESAU (33:1–11)

Jacob had just contended with Laban the scoundrel, followed by wrestling all night with God. Chapter 33 opens with another confrontation—two estranged brothers meet after twenty years of separation. The last Jacob remembered of Esau was his mother's warning, "Behold, your brother Esau comforts himself by planning to kill you" (27:42).

Jacob inched his way along slowly with his wives, children, servants, and flocks. As he crested the next hill, he lifted his eyes—"and behold, Esau was coming, and four hundred men with him" (v. 1). Jacob quickly divided his family into sections, the least important first, the most loved and important taking up the rear. The two slave women were placed on the front line with their children; then the unloved Leah with her children. The loved wife, Rachel, and her son Joseph were in the rear. Jacob then went on before them all. The one who grasped for supremacy by swindling his brother was now grasping for survival. As they approached each other on what could become a killing field, Jacob submissively bowed himself to the ground seven times, each time drawing nearer to his brother like a subject prostrating himself before a king. This is dripping with irony as the one who stole the paternal blessing through craftiness was now bowing to the one he had supposedly vanquished! In Genesis 27:29, Isaac's blessing had pronounced that Esau would bow to Jacob, not Jacob to Esau!

Either Jacob's plan worked splendidly, or Esau had abandoned his murderous intent. Esau ran to meet Jacob and embraced him, falling on his neck to kiss him. They wept together as the brothers reconciled. In this case the maxim proved true: "Time heals old wounds." Jacob must have shed tears of relief as well as joy. It was now Esau's turn to raise his eyes, and he spotted the wives and children (v. 5). Jacob explained that they were God's gracious gift. Each family group approached in order, prostrating themselves before Esau. While those in Jacob's troupe were calling Esau *lord*, Esau was referring to Jacob as *brother* (v. 9).

Esau followed the custom of Middle Eastern peoples by refusing the gift. I cannot tell you how many times even today my gift, payment, or tip to a friend in the Middle East has been rejected. However, with a little persistence, they "reluctantly" take the gift and smile as it enters their pockets. Esau refused the gift just enough to meet the quota of propriety, and then he "reluctantly" (gladly) accepted the gift. Should Jacob have stopped insisting too soon, it would have been bad manners on his part.

Jacob exclaimed that seeing Esau was like seeing the face of God. Guilt and regret welled up in Jacob. He earnestly requested that Esau accept his gifts. Jacob had used the Hebrew word *minhah* (tribute, present, or gift) five times and used it again in verse 10, but in verse 11 he referred to his offered *minhah* with the English word *gift*, the Hebrew word *beraka*, which means "blessing".[1] Was Jacob subtly acknowledging that he had stolen Esau's blessing (*beraka*) and was now trying to make amends, even reparation, by giving back a blessing (*beraka*)? And did Esau's acceptance of the *minhah*, the *beraka*, signal that old hostilities were settled and he forgave Jacob? It is apparent that Jacob's actions were motivated by fear as he repented and did penance by bowing to the one who was to serve him and "giving the blessing back" to Esau from whom he had stolen it.

It could be expected that Esau was happy with his current state in life. He was no longer angry about the blessing since his life had turned out well enough. Since he never seemed to grasp the whole idea of God's covenant and promises anyway, he just wanted to hunt and live life according to his passions and appetites.

---

[1] The Hebrew word *beraka* (blessing) is used six times in Genesis 27 in the context of the paternal blessing deceitfully received by Jacob, who stole it from Esau. Now it is used by Jacob for giving a "blessing" to Esau, presumably to make amends for his theft of the blessing twenty years earlier.

ESAU OFFERS TO ESCORT JACOB;
JACOB DECLINES (33:12–16)

After the amicable family reunion, Esau offered to escort Jacob home. Jacob expected that Esau and his men would move too swiftly for his family and flocks. Jacob reminded Esau that driving the flocks too hard even one day would kill them. Setting up camp each night, packing up the next morning, caring for the flocks, and securing water and food was time consuming. Young children or women could not be rushed through this rugged territory. Jacob declined Esau's assistance and insisted on traveling alone.

Jacob told Esau he would travel at his own pace, "until I come to my lord in Seir" (v. 14). He gave Esau the impression he was heading to Seir to visit him, if not to live with him. It seems this new deception was employed by Jacob to push Esau to move on and leave him alone. It was great to be reconciled, but he did not want Esau leading him, controlling him, or making demands of him. Esau conceded and returned home to Seir (Edom). From this point, except for one appearance at the burial of Isaac, Esau disappears from the story (35:29). His genealogy is provided in Genesis 36:1–5, and his descendants in Edom continued to play a significant role in biblical history.

In verse 14, we find an interesting word for travel. "I will *lead on* slowly, according to the pace of the cattle [livestock] which are before me and according to the pace of the children." This is a specialized word used among nomadic cultures. It is said that Eskimos have forty or more words for different kinds of snow because it is so elemental to their existence. Similar to that, nomads have various words related to walking or travel. According to Hebrew lexicons, the word *nahal* conveys the idea of "leading or guiding to a watering place or station and providing rest along the way".[2] Jacob would allow the sheep and goats to set the pace from one water hole to the next. *Nahal* is the word used in Psalm 23:2, "He *leads me* beside still waters."

---

[2] "Our root [word] ... denotes a shepherd's loving concerned leading of his flock, especially those with young (Isa 40:11).... The second passage (Gen 33:14) records Jacob's request to Esau that he be allowed to travel slowly and leisurely with his herds and children.... The root specifically is connected with what such a shepherd does in leading pregnant ewes." Leonard J. Coppes, "1312 נָהַל", in *Theological Wordbook of the Old Testament*, ed. R. Laird Harris, Gleason L. Archer, Jr., and Bruce K. Waltke (Chicago: Moody Press, 1999), 559.

300

JACOB SETTLES IN SUCCOTH (33:16)

After Esau's departure, Jacob journeyed to Succoth and built himself a house. He was free of hostile family relations and back on the land God had promised. But instead of heading south to follow Esau down to Seir, he turned northwest, re-crossed the Jabbok River, and settled at a lucrative major crossroads connecting Canaan and Damascus. He settled near the junction of the Jordan and Jabbok rivers. A large tell named Deir 'Allah is believed to mark the spot. He built a house for himself and booths for his animals—thus the place was named *succoth*, which means *huts* or *booths*. Building a house implies he lived here for some time.[3]

JACOB SETTLES IN SHECHEM (33:17–20)

Eventually Jacob crossed the Jordan River and moved to Shechem, where Abraham had built his first altar upon arriving from Haran (12:6–7).[4] Jacob may have chosen Shechem for its symbolism. He was now fully back in the land of Canaan, the land of his grandfather, Abraham, and his father, Isaac. Jesus would later request a drink from the Samaritan woman from "Jacob's well" here (Jn 4:5–7). On pilgrimages we frequently visit Jacob's well, which is in the lower level of a newly built Greek Orthodox church. The well is over 120 feet deep; the water itself is twenty-four feet deep. It is still fresh, cold, and sweet.

Jacob camped outside the city of Shechem and bought a parcel of land from Hamor, Shechem's father. The bones of Jacob's son

---

[3] Jewish tradition sets the time frame of Jacob's stays in Succoth and Bethel, "He left Aram Naharaim and arrived at Sukkot, and spent 18 months there, as is said, 'and Jacob traveled to Sukkot, and he built himself a house, and he made shelters [sukkot] for his cattle' (Gen. 33:17). And he spent 6 months in Beth El, and offered sacrifices" (Megillah 1:13). Jacob Neusner, *The Babylonian Talmud: A Translation and Commentary*, vol. 7b (Peabody, Mass.: Hendrickson, 2011), 87.

[4] The name Shechem means "shoulder" possibly because it is built on the slope or shoulder of Mount Ebal. "Also known as Tell Balâṭah; located 40 miles north of Jerusalem in the fertile valley between Mount Ebal and Mount Gerizim, just east of modern-day Nablus.... Shechem is the first place where Abram stops after entering Canaan (Gen 12:6). It is the location of the rape of Dinah (Gen 34), the covenant renewal (Josh 24), and the burial of Joseph (Josh 24:32)." Amy L. Balogh, "Shechem, City of", in *The Lexham Bible Dictionary*, ed. John D. Barry et al. (Bellingham, Wash.: Lexham Press, 2016).

Joseph would someday be brought to Shechem from Egypt and interred there (Josh 24:32). One can still visit the Tomb of Joseph there today, though the city is now named Nablus and the tomb is currently a bombed-out synagogue, destroyed in the *Intifada* of 2000. Jacob purchased the land from the sons of Hamor for 100 *qesitah*, a unit of money of unknown value. It is significant that he purchased the land; he was investing in the promises of God. Jacob was happy to be home, not only to have survived, but to have thrived. He would now serve the God of Abraham and Isaac. He had negotiated with God in Bethel after seeing the ladder or stairway to heaven. God had kept his end of the bargain—all of Jacob's *if*'s had been realized, so Jacob would now call Yahweh his God (28:20–21). Jacob—no, *Israel*—built an altar, and his new name was incorporated into the name of the altar. He named it *El-Elohe-Israel*, "God, the God of Israel" (v. 20).

CHAPTER 34

SHECHEM RAPES DINAH;
TREACHERY OF JACOB'S SONS

JACOB'S DAUGHTER DINAH GOES OUT TO
VISIT THE WOMEN OF THE LAND (34:1)

It seems Jacob was always in a quandary. Crawling out of the frying
pan with Laban, he fell into the fire with Esau. After crawling out
of that fire, he was embroiled in another mess in Shechem. This time
the trouble involved Jacob's only daughter, Dinah, and her protec-
tive brothers.

At this point in the narrative, we are aware that Jacob had eleven
sons and one daughter. If there are other daughters, we are not told.
Daughters are not usually mentioned unless significant to the story.
Dinah was probably a young teenager at the time. When Jacob
left Laban in Haran, his oldest son, Reuben, could not have been
more than thirteen years old. Considering the stated birth order to
be correct, Dinah was Leah's seventh and youngest child. We are not
told how many years they had lived in Shechem or Dinah's age. She
must have been at least a young teenager to wander off to visit the
Canaanite women in Shechem. That she was young is also implied
by the context of the story.

Dinah "went out to visit the women of the land". This has been
interpreted in various ways. Some suggest that Dinah was looking
for female companionship, being the only daughter among eleven
brothers. Rebekah and Rachel had freely mixed with the locals at
the well, but in both cases, it was among their own people and the
watchful eye of the family. One rabbi suggests that she was following her mother, Leah's, example, luring Jacob into her tent (30:16).
However, Leah was dealing with her husband, not a stranger from a
different tribe. There is no indication that Dinah went out to allure

302

men. The word in Hebrew is not *women* but *"daughters* of the land" and not to *visit* but to *see*. Canaanite women were shunned by the patriarchs, but Dinah seems intrigued. A visit to see the "daughters of the land" may be innocent enough, but the terms used may suggest improper motives. In their cultural context, it would be unheard of that a marriageable young maiden would go out from the family unaccompanied to visit the Canaanite women. Based on the wording of the text, and knowledge of the cultural norms, we can conclude that Dinah's actions were imprudent, risky, or even promiscuous.

Word Biblical Commentary has an interesting take on this passage:

> [T]he cognate Akkadian verb *wasû* describes a housewife who conducts herself improperly outside her home, and the targums [Jewish commentaries] translate "cult prostitute" as "one who goes out in the countryside." Furthermore, Genesis regularly condemns all intermarriage with women of the land (Gen 24:3, 37; 27:46; 28:1, 6, 8), so it may be doubted whether it totally approves of Dinah meeting the girls of the land, for they might have introduced her to one of the boys. Dinah was at least sailing close to the wind![1]

Using Dinah as a spiritual lesson, but also commenting on her actions, Saint Cyril of Alexandria writes:

> Those who want to avoid destruction must be careful not to leave the tabernacle of the father, that is, the house of God, in order not to be received into the herds of the heretics and other strangers. After moving out of the father's tabernacle, Dinah was brought to the house of Shechem. She would have never been reproached if she had stayed in the paternal houses and had lived constantly in the holy tabernacles.[2]

SHECHEM DEFILES DINAH (34:2–12)

Dinah went to see the women of the land, and in doing so, she was herself seen by Shechem, the aristocratic young prince, probably

[1] Gordan J. Wenham, *Genesis 1–50, Word Biblical Commentary*, vol. 2 (Dallas: Word, Incorporated, 1994), 310.
[2] Glaphyra on Genesis, 5.4–5, in Mark Sheridan, ed., *Genesis 12–50*, Ancient Christian Commentary on Scripture (Downers Grove, Ill.: InterVarsity Press, 2002), 226.

"spoiled rotten" and used to getting anything he wanted, any time
he wanted it. At first sight he wanted *her*. The prince "seized her and
lay with her and humbled her". Three verbs with escalating brutality
demonstrate the viciousness of Shechem's assault and rape. First, he
seized her. The Hebrew word is frequently used for grabbing and
carrying away, capturing and taking into one's possession. This is an
aggressive act of a stronger man grabbing a young female against her
will. Second, he *lay* with her. This is a common euphemism for sexual relations and, in this case, of forcible rape. Third, he "humbled"
or "shamed" her. The Hebrew suggests maltreatment and humiliation, especially regarding sexual offenses. That act alone was humiliating, though some rabbinic traditions suggest unnatural intercourse.[3]

If the Law of Moses had been in effect, and Shechem was a circumcised Israelite, he would have been forced to wed Dinah and give
to her father fifty shekels of silver and would subsequently have been
forbidden to divorce her (Deut 22:28–29). The Israelites were forbidden to marry the Canaanites under any circumstances (Deut 7:3–6).

A similar rape is recorded in 2 Samuel 13:15–17, but in that case
the young man Amnon expelled Tamar from his room after his
burning passion turned to a raging hatred. At least Shechem fell in
love and desired marriage. Shechem's "soul was *drawn* to Dinah"
("his soul stuck to Dinah") and "he *loved* the maiden and *spoke
tenderly* (reassuringly) to her." Notice the three verbs used to show
his love for Dinah corresponding to the three verbs used earlier of his
abuse. Even though the earlier wording severely condemned the
actions of Shechem, it now evoked an element of sympathy, since
his actions showed remorse and love, a desire to cherish the girl and
marry her.

After speaking *tenderly* to Dinah, he spoke rudely to his father,
"Get me this maiden for my wife." The word *maiden* refers to a marriageable girl. In those days, fathers arranged marriages, and Shechem

---

[3] "Said R. Pappa to Abbayye, 'Lo, [the] sexual relations themselves are classified as affliction, as it is written, "And he lay with her and afflicted her" (Gen. 34:2).' He said to him, 'In
that case, he afflicted her by means of other forms of intercourse'". Jacob Neusner, *The Babylonian Talmud: A Translation and Commentary*, vol. 5a (Peabody, Mass.: Hendrickson, 2011),
300. "[To] humiliate (a woman sexually), by rape or unlawful intercourse" (Gen 34:2). David
J. A. Clines, ed., *The Dictionary of Classical Hebrew* (Sheffield, England: Sheffield Academic
Press; Sheffield Phoenix Press, 1993–2011), 497–98.

expected his father to approach Jacob to secure the bride and arrange the wedding.

Jacob learned of the rape but kept his silence. The author likely expects us to be angry—why did the father fail to act? Scripture says he held his peace until his sons came in from the field. Their father's perceived lack of concern may have furthered the sons' strong reaction. Was it because she was the daughter of Leah? When the "sons of Jacob" returned from the fields, they ("the men") were furious. This kind of thing should *not* be done in Israel! Notice that the folly is said to have taken place in "Israel", which is either an anachronistic use of the term by the biblical writer, or people were already calling their tribe Israel (v. 7). Shechem offered to do whatever was necessary to secure Dinah as his wife.

DINAH IS AVENGED BY HER BROTHERS; THEY DECEIVE THE CITY OF SHECHEM (34:13–24)

The firstborn son Reuben was no longer a boy but a man; in fact, the sons of Jacob were now referred to as *men* (Gen 34:7). Jacob's silence in the face of treachery against his daughter does not bode well. Leah's sons considered their father's response to the egregious offense against their sister as inadequate. Hamor spoke with Jacob and his sons to negotiate for Dinah and the hoped-for wedding. It is amazing that Jacob said *nothing*—his silence continued. There was a long appeal from Hamor including an offer to pay whatever they asked and to join families through marriage and property. There was no apology or any recognition that a crime had been committed. All this time Dinah was still being held in Shechem's house (Gen 34:26). Only Jacob's sons responded to Hamor, but they replied with deceit.

Hamor suggested that the sons of Jacob marry his daughters and his sons would marry Jacob's daughters—planning for the long run when more daughters would be available for marriage, or maybe Jacob had other daughters not mentioned. Merging the families could never have worked because God had forbidden the sons of promise from marrying daughters of the land. Esau had brought grief to his parents by marrying Hittite women. Hamor's suggestion would have compromised the family line. The covenant would have been threatened.

Shechem chimed in, and his mercenary attempt to dismiss the immorality and reduce the matter to a financial transaction dishonored the
dignity of Dinah and the family.

The word "deceit" shows up again—like father, like sons. The
sons of Leah devised a plot to deceive and destroy Shechem and
all the men in retribution for their treachery. (Older brothers often
rush to their younger sister's defense.) The sacred writer hints of a
cunning plot without yet divulging the plot. He builds the suspense.
The sons of Jacob were not capable of confronting the whole city,
nor did they have the power to rescue their sister. Dinah was still
under the control of Shechem (v. 17). They resorted to subterfuge.
They considered it their obligation and duty to punish the crime and
vindicate their sister.

The first step in the plot was to raise the issue of circumcision. The
sons of Jacob were circumcised by the command of God (17:14). It
was impossible for their women to intermarry with uncircumcised
men. The trap was set.

Hamor and his son Shechem were cunning and diplomatic. They
took the news of the required circumcision to the city gate (the civic
center). It was discussed among the Shechemites. Because of the influence of Hamor and Shechem, the men all agreed. But it was really
about the acquisition of wealth. They enticed the men of the city with
the promise, "Will not their cattle, their property and all their beasts be
ours? Only let us agree with them, and they will dwell with us" (v. 23).
The men of the city all agreed to be circumcised (v. 24). Not only was
it to appease their prince—so he could marry Dinah—but primarily
because if they intermarried, what Jacob owned, they would own.

The circumcisions were done with crude flint knives. The men of
Shechem were in agony and physically incapacitated.

THE SECOND STAGE OF THE AVENGING OF DINAH;
TREACHERY OF HER BROTHERS (34:25–29)

Now for the second stage of the plot against the city. Dinah was the
daughter of Leah, and it was Leah's sons who perpetrated the deceit
and treachery. We hear nothing of Jacob; he continued his embarrassing silence. In pain and unable to resist, Shechem and the whole

city were ravaged and all cut down. Simeon and Levi avenged their sister with the edge of the sword. They killed Hamor and his son Shechem and all the males in the city. They rescued their sister as it says, "they took Dinah out of Shechem's house, and went away" (34:26). Then the brothers looted and plundered the city following Reuben and Simeon's ruse and slaughter.

Levi's descendants rose up centuries later in moral outrage when the children of Israel committed idolatry with the golden calf. At Mount Sinai, they pulled their swords to defend the honor of God, and three thousand fell that day (Ex 32:25–28). Because of their righteous indignation and prompt action, they were ordained for the service of the Lord (Ex 32:29). Another case of a Levite using the sword to purge Israel of sin was Phinehas. He, too, was honored for his action (Num 25:7–13; Ps 106:30–31).

The story began with Dinah *going out* and being *seized*. The story ends with the same two verbs used in reverse order—the brothers *seized* Dinah and *went away* (34:2, 6). The irony continues. The Shechemites had schemed to acquire ownership of Jacob's flocks and herds, but in the process lost all their own flocks and herds to Jacob's sons. The author ensures we understand that wealth or material gain was not the goal of the plunder—it was to punish evil and vindicate their sister. Except for mention in a list of Leah's offspring (46:15), Dinah disappears from the story, and we hear no more of her.

JACOB CENSURES HIS SONS SIMEON AND LEVI (34:30–31)

The righteous indignation of Jacob's sons is contrasted with their father's apathy. Only now did Jacob finally speak. But instead of condemning the Shechemites, Jacob berated Simeon and Levi. He was more concerned about his own safety and security than about the violation of his daughter. Were Simeon and Levi justified in their vicious response? The author does not tell us. There is no hint of judgment; no comment made for or against their actions. The fact that the author gives the brothers the final word may suggest he is sympathetic to their retaliation, whether or not he wholly agreed with the action.

However, because of their violence, Jacob later censured Simeon and Levi on his deathbed as he gave his final blessings (49:5–7). Referring back to this incident, Jacob pronounced:

> Simeon and Levi are brothers;
>   weapons of violence are their swords.
> O my soul, come not into their council;
>   O my spirit, be not joined to their company;
> for in their anger they slay men,
>   and in their wantonness they hamstring oxen.
> Cursed be their anger, for it is fierce;
>   and their wrath, for it is cruel!
> I will divide them in Jacob
>   and scatter them in Israel.

Though Jacob censures Simeon and Levi, the biblical book of Judith, through the prayer of Judith, praises the brothers for their action:

> Judith cried out to the Lord with a loud voice, and said, "O Lord God of my father Simeon, to whom you gave a sword to take revenge on the strangers who had loosed the girdle of a virgin to defile her, and uncovered her thigh to put her to shame, and polluted her womb to disgrace her; for you have said, 'It shall not be done'—yet they did it. So you gave up their rulers to be slain, and their bed, which was ashamed of the deceit they had practiced, to be stained with blood, and you struck down slaves along with princes, and princes on their thrones; and you gave their wives for a prey and their daughters to captivity, and all their booty to be divided among your beloved sons, who were zealous for you, and abhorred the pollution of their blood, and called on you for help—O God, my God, hear me also, a widow" (Jud 9:1–6).

The Twelve Patriarchs, a second-century Jewish document, written as from Levi himself on his deathbed, says:

> Levi was conceived in Haran and born there, and after that I came with my father to Shechem. And I was young, about twenty years of age, when with Simeon I wrought the vengeance on Hamor for our sister Dinah. . . . And the angel opened to me the gates of heaven, and I saw the holy temple, and the Most High upon a throne of glory.

And He said to me, Levi, I have given thee the blessings of the priest-hood until that I shall come and sojourn in the midst of Israel. Then the angel brought me to the earth, and gave me a shield and a sword, and said, Work vengeance on Shechem because of Dinah, and I will be with thee, because the Lord hath sent me. And I destroyed at that time the sons of Hamor, as it is written in the heavenly tablets (*The Testament of Levi concerning the Priesthood and Arrogance, 3.2, 5*).[4]

Political concerns appeared primary to Jacob. He was afraid again, this time of reprisals from the inhabitants of the land who might now rally against him. He used the pronouns "me" and "I" six times in two sentences. Forgetting the promises of God, he looked only to his own limitations.

The phrase "brought trouble on me" literally means to "muddy the water" (v. 30), which implies his reputation had been muddied and he was now taboo.[5] He feared he was now a social outcast. It is not too strong to define the phrase as his ruin or disaster. But what actually caused the social chaos: the slaughter of the Shechemites or the initial treacherous kidnapping and rape of Dinah? The phrase "making me odious" is interesting in the Hebrew. It literally means "you have made me stink" among the people, or, as understood by some Jewish commentators, you have made "my breath to stink".[6]

The last sentence makes it apparent where the sacred writer stood on the matter. After their father's angst-ridden lament, the sons had the last word: "Should he treat our sister as a harlot?"

Ironically, his sons preserved Jacob from contamination with the people of the land. The Shechemites had intended to take Jacob's daughters and flocks. Jacob appeared ready to compromise. Humanly

[4] "The Testaments of the Twelve Patriarchs", in *Fathers of the Third and Fourth Centuries: The Twelve Patriarchs, Excerpts and Epistles, the Clementina, Apocrypha, Decretals, Memoirs of Edessa and Syriac Documents, Remains of the First Ages*, ed. Alexander Roberts, James Donaldson, and A. Cleveland Coxe, trans. R. Sinker, The Ante-Nicene Fathers, vol. 8 (Buffalo, N.Y.: Christian Literature Company, 1886), 12–13.

[5] "Middle Hebrew and Jewish Aramaic use the root '*kr* with the basic meaning 'make (a liquid) turbid'." R. Mosis, "עָכַר", in *Theological Dictionary of the Old Testament*, ed. G. Johannes Botterweck, Helmer Ringgren, and Heinz-Josef Fabry, trans. David E. Green (Grand Rapids, Mich., and Cambridge, U.K.: Eerdmans, 2001), 68.

[6] The same Hebrew word for "offensive" is used in Exodus 5:21: "'*for making us loathsome*'. Literally, 'for causing our breath to be malodorous in the eyes of....' The mixed metaphor means 'brought us into contempt'." Nahum M. Sarna, *Exodus*, The JPS Torah Commentary (Philadelphia: Jewish Publication Society, 1991), 30.

speaking, it would seem God's plan could have been thwarted. Simeon and Levi's slaughter preempted the potential disaster. God again providentially used reckless human actions to further his plan. This episode may have been inserted to demonstrate the real threat and ease of contaminating the covenantal family line through intermingling with the Canaanites. Also, the muddying of the water in Shechem provided the impetus for Jacob to travel south to his father Isaac. They arrived too late for the death of Rebekah but in time for Jacob to show his father the realization of the promise before he died.

CHAPTER 35:

COVENANT RENEWED; BIRTH OF BENJAMIN
AND DEATH OF RACHEL; ISAAC DIES

INTRODUCTION

We have come a long way from the days of Abraham's testing and legendary faith and obedience. There is an old saying, "God has no grandchildren." Though Isaac and Jacob had not risen to the status of Abraham, God had worked in their lives with their unique personalities, strengths, and weaknesses. They had come to know him, rather than simply to know about him as the God of Abraham. There is another saying, "Grace builds on nature." God takes our human nature, the raw materials, and builds upon it with his grace. Time is marching on. God keeps working with his people, generation after generation, to fulfill his plans and promises. The patriarchs were stuck in the "now" of their own lives and experiences, but God sees the whole picture and providentially works his plan.

One way to view the story of salvation history is to envision God weaving a tapestry. He sees both sides at once, the finished surface and the back side with its loose strands and imperceptible patterns. For us, living in space and time, we see only the underside. It is difficult to comprehend what the finished tapestry will look like in the end. We see God working. At the end of time, when he flips the tapestry over for us to see, we will be speechless at the intricacy and sublime detail. Abraham and Sarah were gone. Death for Isaac was imminent. Rebekah had died. Benjamin would soon be born, Rachel would die, and God kept moving forward with each subsequent generation. It is sad for us say good-bye to these friends, but salvation history moves forward, progressing through the centuries to "when the time had fully come" (Gal 4:4) and to the coming of Christ through this very family line. Until the culmination of all things in Christ, God is providentially working through sinful men and women.

JACOB RETURNS TO BETHEL (35:1–8)

Chapter 35 opens with God speaking to Jacob in the midst of his muddled condition. We do not know how much time has elapsed since the plundering of Shechem, but God called Jacob away and sent him to Bethel. Remember Bethel? Abraham had stopped at Bethel and built an altar on his entrance to the land (12:8), and Jacob had seen the angels ascending and descending in Bethel over thirty years before. He had erected a stone pillar when he owned nothing but a walking stick, but now God commanded that he build an altar—an altar "to the God who appeared to you when you fled from your brother Esau" (35:1). Bethel, "the house of God", already had deep meaning for Jacob's clan.

God said "*Go up*" (v. 1). This can mean one of two things, or both. First, going to the house of God is always seen as *going up*, since the ancients often worshipped their deities from the highest points available. When the temple was eventually established in Jerusalem, travelers went "up to Jerusalem", which is a phrase used over twenty-six times in Scripture with many more variants of the phrase. It was *up to Jerusalem* no matter from which direction you were approaching. Second, it can also be a literal *going up* because Bethel is about 1000 feet higher in elevation than Shechem. God told him to dwell there, which was in contrast to his first visit to Bethel when he had been in a big hurry—fleeing from his angry brother Esau. His fortunes now reversed, he was in no hurry while at Bethel.

Before we approach the house of God on Sundays, we are to cleanse ourselves of sin. That is why Catholic churches normally offer confession on Saturday afternoons—so we can put away sins, idols, and anything that would encumber our worship of God at the altar. Jacob called his family together and instructed them to purify themselves. Rachel presumably still had her father's household gods, and others may have been added to the family's pantheon when they raided Shechem. Abandoning these gods made with hands was a way of saying, "We will put Yahweh at the center of our lives—God and God alone." They buried their pagan idols under the oak tree in

Shechem before leaving (v. 4). This cleansing was a sign of a renewed devotion to God. Abraham and Jacob had both named this site "the house of God". When Jacob arrived, he built another altar.

Eliminating the foreign gods is understandable, but the meaning of the removal of earrings in verse 4 is more elusive. Why earrings? In other passages, cleansing involved purifying and making donations from the spoils of war to the Lord (e.g., Num 31:19–20, 48–54). More likely the earrings may have been amulets used for magic or to honor the gods (Hos 2:13). They hid all the items, which probably made a big pile, under the "oak which was near Shechem". This tree is also referred to as a terebinth tree in other translations.

A great terror from God fell on the local people as Jacob journeyed from Shechem to Bethel as the means to preserve Jacob and his family (Gen 35:5). They arrived in Bethel (which we are reminded was also called Luz, *almond tree*), and Jacob built an altar. A point of curiosity: Was Abraham's altar still there, or the pillar Jacob had erected years before? Altars were built of rocks piled up with offerings placed on top. He named the altar *El-bethel*, "the God of Bethel". It was becoming a touchpoint for the chosen family to meet with God.

This chapter is about deaths and the progression of time, the falling of leaves from the tree as new leaves grow. The first death mentioned is that of Rebekah's nurse, Deborah. The memorialization of Deborah's death and burial is curious since Deborah was never introduced by name prior to her death (24:59) and we have not yet been told of Rebekah's own death. Could it be that Rebekah had promised to send for Jacob when "the coast was clear" and Esau was no longer a threat (27:43–45)? Might she have sent Deborah, who, then in her own hometown, helped raise Jacob's sons and was now returning with him, though there is no mention of it? If so, she would have been incredibly old—at least 130 years.

One commentary offers a summation, "Deborah had either been sent by Rebekah to take care of her daughters-in-law and grandsons, or had gone of her own accord into Jacob's household after the death of her mistress. The mourning at her death, and the perpetuation of her memory, are proofs that she must have been a faithful and highly esteemed servant in Jacob's house."[1] The Jewish sages have puzzled

[1] Carl Friedrich Keil and Franz Delitzsch, *Commentary on the Old Testament*, vol. 1 (Peabody, Mass.: Hendrickson, 1996), 203.

over this mystery for centuries, and the opinions are many.[2] In any case, Deborah was buried under the oak at Bethel, and it was named *Allon-bacuth*, which means *oak of weeping*.

GOD RENEWS HIS COVENANT
WITH JACOB (35:9–15)

Jacob was following in the footprints of Abraham, literally. He had left Haran to move to Canaan. He had passed through and built altars at Shechem and Bethel, and God spoke to him as he had to Abraham. Both received new names, and both were given the promise of the land and descendants beyond number. At the altar in Bethel, his name was changed for the second time, or it was reaffirmed here with great emphasis by God himself—while actually standing in the land. God appeared to Jacob, possibly again in a vision, and told him he was no longer to be called Jacob—his "supplanting" days were over. He would now be called *Israel* from that day. However, with the change from *Abram* to *Abraham*, we never hear the name Abram again, but with the change from *Jacob* to *Israel*, both names continued to be used an equal number of times through the end of Genesis and beyond.

God introduced himself to Jacob with a name he had used once each with Abraham and Isaac (17:8; 35:11). Jacob now heard this divine title with his own ears. "God Almighty" is literally *El Shaddai*. It is significant that God introduced himself to Jacob as he did to Abraham and Isaac, with a name used rarely in the Bible. This title was discussed in some detail in chapter 17.

As with Adam and Eve and Noah before him, God commanded Jacob to "be fruitful and multiply" (v. 11; Gen 1:28; 9:7). But Jacob already had eleven sons and a daughter. Yes, but God planned to give this land to Jacob and his descendants, so their numbers had to increase rapidly. They would be not only a nation, but a "company of nations" from which kings would spring forth. The promise of the land (the deed) was reaffirmed and extended beyond Abraham and Isaac, now to Jacob and his descendants. Jacob would refer to this

---

[2] For a thorough analysis of the various solutions to this conundrum, see Rabbi Dr. Charles Chavel, *Ramban Commentary on the Torah* (New York: Shilo Publishing House, 1999), 422–25.

important theophany at the end of his life (48:3–4). Scripture then says, "God went up from him."

The consolation from these words, not from men or angels, but directly from the mouth of God, was strengthening. Jacob's response was to set up a pillar of stone on which he poured a drink offering, followed by oil. He had used oil about thirty years before when he erected his stone pillar after seeing the angels on the ladder (28:18). There is an interesting anecdote in history that may shed light on this episode in Jacob's life: "[Jacob] is rehabilitating the original stela, which is now invested with new meaning. An interesting parallel may perhaps be drawn from an inscription by Sennacherib, king of Assyria and Babylonia (704–681 B.C.E.): 'When that palace shall have become old and ruined, may some future prince restore its ruins, look upon the stele with my name inscribed [on it], anoint it with oil, pour out a libation upon it, and return it to its place'."[3] Jacob reaffirms the name of Bethel, which, as we discussed earlier, means *the house of God*. Saint Cyril of Alexandria sees this pillar of Jacob as a prefiguration of Jesus Christ, the anointed cornerstone, demonstrating again how the Fathers of the Church discerned types and prefigurations in the Old Covenant.[4] He writes:

> When we ascend to Bethel, that is, to the house of God, we will know the stone, I mean, the elected stone, which was made into a cornerstone, that is, Christ. We will see the one who is anointed by the Father in joy and exultation for all the creatures that live under the sky. As I said, the Son is anointed by God the Father: "Joy of us all, universal exultation" according to the words of the psalmist. And you see how this is prefigured in the words that were just said to us: "And Jacob set up a stone and poured oil upon it." That action is a symbol of the mystery of Christ, through whom and with whom be glory to God the Father and the Holy Spirit, world without end. Amen.[5]

[3] Nahum M. Sarna, *Genesis*, The JPS Torah Commentary (Philadelphia: Jewish Publication Society, 1989), 242.

[4] The *Catechism of the Catholic Church* defines *typology* as, "The discernment of persons, events, or things in the Old Testament which prefigured, and thus served as a 'type' (or prototype) of, the fulfillment of God's plan in the person of Christ. The typology of the Old Testament which is made clear in the New Testament demonstrates the dynamic unity of the divine plan of salvation." Catholic Church, *Catechism of the Catholic Church*, 2nd ed. (Washington, D.C.: United States Catholic Conference, 2000), 902.

[5] *Glaphyra of Genesis*, 5.5, in Mark Sheridan, *Genesis 12–50*, Ancient Christian Commentary on Scripture, OT 2 (Downers Grove, Ill.: InterVarsity Press, 2002), 228–29.

BIRTH OF BENJAMIN AND THE DEATH OF RACHEL (35:16–21)

After leaving Bethel, we come to the second death in this chapter. Rachel, the beloved wife of Jacob, was pregnant with her second son. While presumably riding a camel, Rachel went into hard labor, mentioned three times. The Hebrew words refer to an unyielding, physical distress—unbearably heavy labor pains. Somewhere along the road toward Ephrath, she gave birth. As Rachel was dying ("her soul was departing"), the midwife exclaimed, "Fear not; for now you will have another son" (v. 17). With her last breath, Rachel called out his name *Ben-oni* (which means *son of my sorrow*). But Jacob renamed his son *Benjamin* (which means *son of my right hand*). Others suggest the name *child of my old age* (44:20) or *son of the south*, since he was the only son born in the land and toward the south near Hebron. Jacob now had twelve sons—the Twelve Tribes of Israel.

With no medical doctors or hospitals, the use of midwives was the common practice. "Midwives, who were generally older women, served as resources to teach young women about sexual activity and to aid in the birth of children. They were also a part of the naming ritual and may have helped teach new mothers about nursing and child care."[6] We encounter midwives again when the children of Israel were enslaved in Egypt (Ex 1:15–21).

How significant is the birth of a son in biblical times? Even though Rachel was in severe pain and breathing her last, the midwife said, "Fear not; for now you will have another son" (v. 17). Fear not? She is dying, but that is OK, as long as she has another son! We hear these exact words again in a very similar situation in 1 Samuel 4:20.

> Death in childbirth was tragically common, so doubtless Rachel's death did not have quite the same pathos for the ancient reader as it does for us. Yet it was undoubtedly tragic, for it was Rachel who had cried in desperation to Jacob, "Give me children, or I shall die" (30:1). It was ultimately the gift of children that killed her. And her choice of name, Ben-Oni, "son of sorrow" (cf. Ichabod in 1 Sam 4:21–22), reflects this. אוֹנִי "sorrow" is used of mourning for the dead in Deut 26:14;

---

[6] Victor Harold Matthews, Mark W. Chavalas, and John H. Walton, *The IVP Bible Background Commentary: Old Testament*, electronic ed. (Downers Grove, Ill.: InterVarsity Press, 2000), Gen 35:18.

Hos 9:4. But for Jacob, the child was the son of his favorite wife, so he "called him Benjamin," son of the right, the right-hand side being the favored lucky side (e.g., Deut 27:12–13; Mt 25:33).[7]

The *Catechism* includes Rachel as one of the holy women who kept alive the hope of Israel's salvation (*CCC* 64).

God had promised that kings would spring from Jacob's loins (35:11). From the lineage of this new baby Benjamin would come Saul the first king of Israel (1 Sam 9:1–2). Saul the Pharisee, who would eventually become the beloved Saint Paul, was also of Benjamin's line (Rom 11:1; Phil 3:5).

Ephrath was an ancient name for the city of Bethlehem, which is roughly five miles south of Jerusalem and fifteen miles north of Hebron. This is the first mention of Bethlehem (*house of bread*) in the Bible. But outside Scripture, it first appears in one of the Tell el–Amarna letters (fourteenth century B.C.) as *Bit-Lahmi*.[8] Today, Bethlehem is an Arab town in the West Bank, and just south of Bethlehem is an Israeli settlement called *Efrat* from Ephrath (Ephrathah) of the Old Testament. At one time, before the security fence (wall) was built to seclude Bethlehem, we drove past Rachel's Tomb every time we entered or exited Bethlehem. Today Rachel's Tomb is a synagogue walled off from view, quite extensive and heavily guarded. It has only been accessible to Jews since 1967. Almost four thousand years after her death, Jews still venerate her tomb and visit to pray. Almost one thousand years after Rachel's death, King Saul had lost his donkeys and inquired of the prophet Samuel, who directed him to the Tomb of Rachel (1 Sam 10:2).

We find the name *Ephrath* in several significant passages of Scripture, including Micah 5:2, which prophesies about the coming

---

[7] Gordon J. Wenham, *Genesis 16–50*, Word Biblical Commentary, vol. 2 (Dallas: Word, Incorporated, 1994), 326–27.

[8] "Little is known of the origin of the town, though in 1 Chr. 2:51 SALMA the son of CALEB is described as the 'father [i.e., founder ...] of Bethlehem.' The town is apparently first mentioned in one of the Tell el-Amarna letters of the 14th cent. B.C., where 'Abdu-Heba, the prince of Jerusalem, complains that Bit-*Lahmi* (if that is the correct reading of the ideogram) has gone over to the Apiru.... It was known first in the OT as Ephrath, but in general as Bethlehem Ephrathah or Bethlehem Judah.... Rachel's tomb was remembered (and still is) as being near Bethlehem (Gen. 35:19)." Moisés Silva and Merrill Chapin Tenney, *The Zondervan Encyclopedia of the Bible, A-C* (Grand Rapids, Mich.: Zondervan Corporation, 2009), 573.

Messiah, Jesus Christ: "But you, O Bethlehem Ephrathah, who are little to be among the clans of Judah, from you shall come forth for me one who is to be ruler in Israel, whose origin is from of old, from ancient days."

After burying Rachel and putting a pillar over her tomb, "Israel journeyed on and pitched his tent beyond the tower of Eder" (v. 21) (Hebrew: *Migdal-eder* or *watchtower of the flock* for the protection of livestock). The watchtower's exact location is unknown, but Saint Jerome, who lived many years in Bethlehem, located it about one mile from Bethlehem toward Hebron. Jacob's name had been changed earlier, but this is the first time in the text it is actually *used* as his name. Both names will be used interchangeably from this point on. We are told that Jacob "pitches his tent"—so he again lives in a tent, though he had built a "house" in Succoth earlier (33:17). He is still primarily a nomadic shepherd traversing the land like Abraham and Isaac. *Pitching his tent* is a Hebraism for "he settled in for a while."

REUBEN VIOLATES HIS FATHER'S CONCUBINE (35:22)

Before providing a list of Israel's sons, we are briefly told of a moral fault that had huge ramifications for the firstborn son, Reuben. He went in and lay with his father's concubine, Bilhah. Israel (Jacob) heard of it, but as in Shechem, he said nothing at the moment but later condemned Reuben on his deathbed, "Reuben, you are my first-born, my might, and the first fruits of my strength, pre-eminent in pride and pre-eminent in power. Unstable as water, you shall not have pre-eminence because you went up to your father's bed; then you defiled it—you went up to my couch!" (Gen 49:3–4; 1 Chron 5:1).

It is doubtful that Reuben would lie with Bilhah for passion or love, especially since she would have been considerably older than he. It was certainly more nefarious. Bilhah was the servant of Rachel, and Rachel had just died. If Bilhah had another son by Jacob, it would legally be Rachel's child, being through her servant. Reuben was the firstborn but treated as a second-class citizen as the son of the unloved Leah's womb. He feared additional sons of Rachel to stand in his way. Having sexual relations with Bilhah would pollute any of her future offspring. As one rabbi said, "Then how do I interpret, 'And he lay with Bilhah, his father's concubine' (Gen. 35:22)? He objected to the humiliation of his mother. He said, 'If my mother's sister was co-wife to my mother, should the bondmaid of my mother's sister be co-wife to my mother?' So he went and transposed her bed."[9] His fears were not ungrounded since Rachel's son Joseph ended up with the status of firstborn in the end since during the patriarchal age choosing the "firstborn" was the prerogative of the father.[10] Ironically, his misconduct with his father's concubine actually occasioned his worst fears.

Secondly, sexual relations with a father's concubine was a political move to claim the authority or inheritance of the father (cf. 1 Kings 2:13–25). Thus, it suggests a power grab on the part of Reuben. We can expect that he is defending his mother's rights and at the same time usurping his father's authority. Oftentimes a firstborn son would inherit the father's wives (though later outlawed in Deuteronomy 27:20). He was seizing his legitimate primacy knowing that the firstborn Ishmael and the firstborn Esau had both lost their pre-eminence—so he was staking his claim early. However, his power-grab plot backfired, and for the third generation in a row, the first son born was not the "firstborn". In all three cases, the office of the firstborn went to a younger brother. His actions rendered the tribe of Reuben politically insignificant.

LIST OF JACOB'S SONS; DEATH AND BURIAL OF ISAAC (35:22–27)

A brief list of Jacob's sons in conjunction with their mothers is provided at the end of Isaac's life. There is no need to elaborate. The author knows the reader is aware that Benjamin was not born in Paddan-aram as stated in verse 26. The list of sons is given again at the end of Jacob's major adventures, at Isaac's death, and right

---

[9] Shabbat 55b, in Jacob Neusner, *The Babylonian Talmud: A Translation and Commentary*, vol. 2 (Peabody, Mass.: Hendrickson, 2011), 236.

[10] "It was not always the biological firstborn who was designated chief heir: in some cases it was the son of the first wife, no matter when he was born; in others it was whichever son the father chose." Jeffrey H. Tigay, *Deuteronomy*, The JPS Torah Commentary (Philadelphia: Jewish Publication Society, 1996), 195.

before delineating the family line of Esau before he disappears from the picture.

Now we come to the third death in this chapter of transitions. While Jacob was away, his aged father, Isaac, remained living. We assume Rebekah preceded him in death, though she is not mentioned other than to say that she was buried in the cave of Machpelah with her husband, Isaac. Rebekah is one of three women in Genesis listed in the *Catechism* as holy women who helped keep alive the hope of Israel's salvation (*CCC* 64).

Isaac had lived long enough to see his son Jacob return along with his large family. The joy must have been overwhelming. We are not told about the reunion, only this short epitaph: "Now the days of Isaac were a hundred and eighty years. Isaac breathed his last; and he died and was gathered to his people, old and full of days; and his sons Esau and Jacob buried him" (35:28–29).

The reconciled twins of Rebekah met again after many years to bury their father. The cave of Machpelah where Abraham and Sarah were buried is not mentioned here, but it is clearly stated so later (Gen 49:29–32). The smooth twin, the mama's boy, the wily one was now a mature man imbued with worldly goods and a large family. The other, the hairy outdoorsman, was still a man on the hunt but matured. Still the weathered one living in the rugged land of Edom.

CHAPTER 36

ESAU'S DESCENDANTS

INTRODUCTION TO THE "ESAU CHAPTER"

Chapter 36 is the "Esau chapter" with a snapshot of his current situation and family line before he steps off the stage of salvation history. God said, "I have loved Jacob; but I have hated Esau" (Mal 1:2–3; Rom 9:13). Esau is set aside while the sons of Jacob now take center stage. At the end of Abraham's life, the Scriptures closed out the chapter on Ishmael by listing his genealogy. It was like saying "Goodbye, Ishmael." The same is happening again. Chapter 36 is concluding Esau's involvement. The twelve sons of Jacob would become the Twelve Tribes of Israel who would eventually occupy the land.

THE GENERATIONS OF ESAU (36:1)

The transition is again announced with the words, "These are the descendants of Esau (that is, Edom)" (36:1). Before Esau fades from the story, God wants us to know that his promises to Esau have been fulfilled (25:23; 27:39–40). The generations of Esau in the land of Edom, just like the tribes and success of Ishmael in Arabia, were promised and providentially fulfilled by God.

ESAU MOVES TO SEIR, THAT IS, EDOM (36:2–8)

Esau and Edom are synonymous. Edom is the name of the land where Esau's descendants lived. We are reminded of the Hittite wives taken by Esau—the wives who brought grief to Isaac and Rebekah and the two wives from the family of Ishmael. Now we are given more information about them and their children.

Some commentators think that Esau wandered throughout Canaan and Seir until he finally settled in Seir after the return of his brother Jacob. He was present with Jacob for the burial of their father, Isaac, in Hebron, and only *after* Jacob arrived back on the scene with his large herds and flocks did Esau finally settle in Seir. We detect an echo of the separation between Abraham, who stayed in Canaan, and his nephew Lot, who moved south by the Dead Sea to Sodom.

Edom lies south of the Dead Sea stretching to the Gulf of Aqaba. Later we hear God declaring, "I have given Mount Seir to Esau as a possession" (Deut 2:5; Josh 24:4). Deuteronomy 2:12 and 22 further describe the dispossession of the Horites and the people of Esau occupying the land of Edom.[1] An abundance of Edomite pottery from the early Iron Age confirms the region of Esau's progeny.

DESCENDANTS OF ESAU (36:9–43)

Verses 9–43 give detailed records of the generations of Esau and the chiefs and tribes and kings that were his descendants. This detailed information must have come from the recorded traditions and archives of the Edomites. The names are too many and not significant enough in the story of salvation for us to delve into the list with any detail. God had promised Esau that kings would spring from his loins, and in these detailed records we see that God remembered his promises.

Thus Esau and his family line are set aside as the sons of Jacob carry the story forward to the next generation. The great-grandsons of Abraham are now in the spotlight. We begin the next chapter with Joseph, the first son of Rachel. We will be following his adventures until the end of Genesis, and a fascinating story it is!

---

[1] In a recent article entitled "Archaeology Confirms Book of Genesis on Israel's Arch-nemesis, the Edomites", we read, "The team of American, Israeli and Jordanian archaeologists found that people at different sites in the Aravah [part of Edom] were producing metal using the same standardized techniques, which improved and advanced in parallel, more than 3,000 years ago. This, the archaeologists say, is a sign that there was a strong, centralized entity that coordinated copper production over vast distances: in other words, a state.... The hypothesis dovetails with the biblical claim that there were 'kings who reigned in the land of Edom before any king reigned over the children of Israel' (Genesis 36:31)." Ariel David, "Archaeology Confirms Book of Genesis on Israel's Arch-nemesis, the Edomites", *Haaretz*, Sept. 18, 2019, https://www.haaretz.com/archaeology/2019-09-18/ty-article-magazine/.premium/archaeology-confirms-book-of-genesis-on-israels-arch-nemesis-the-edomites/0000017f-f90b-ddde-abff-fd6fcd1a0000.

CHAPTER 37

JOSEPH'S DREAMS;
SOLD INTO SLAVERY IN EGYPT

INTRODUCTION TO THE FOURTH GENERATION

"*OK, children, take your seats. Sunday school is ready to begin. Quiet down please. Today we are going to learn the story of Joseph and the coat of many colors.*" I leaned over to the kid with the bow tie next to me, "Oh, brother, not that one again. We learned all this last year in Sunday school." Well, there are only so many exciting Bible stories you can read to kids, so we learned them over and over again each year. We sang songs about Noah and the Ark, David and Goliath, and Daniel in the Lion's Den. We never sang about Abraham trying to kill his son with a knife.

"*Now children, pay attention. Here is Joseph and here is his beautiful coat of many colors his father gave him.*" As she talked, the teacher put the colorful felt figures up on the felt board, which was indispensable for a Sunday school class. "*Now, let me find it, oh, yes, here is the well.*" She snatched Joseph off the felt board and put him upside down in the well. "*See, this is what his brothers did; they got jealous and threw him in the well.*"

I tell this story tongue in cheek, but I am grateful for learning these stories and thankful for those faithful teachers who voluntarily suffered through a whole hour with us rambunctious kids. Even though Scripture was often trivialized, misunderstood, and poorly applied, it provided me with a familiarity that has served me well in later life.

But now I find out that the "coat of many colors" may not have actually been a "coat of many colors", but only an ornamental full-length robe with long sleeves. But let's back up and return to Hebron to rejoin the great-grandsons of Abraham, the itinerant shepherds living the pastoral life in tents with camels and wells—with treachery and intrigue.

"THESE ARE THE GENERATIONS OF JACOB ..."
(37:1–2)

Chapter 37 opens with the typical start of a whole new beginning in the narrative. For some reason the RSV renders the words differently here ("This is the history of the family of Jacob"), whereas it is actually the same formula used repeatedly in Genesis to mark a shift in the story. Verse 1 begins, "These are the descendants of Jacob." This is the last time this phrase is used, which informs us that we are embarking on the last generational cycle in Genesis.

Specific details about where Jacob actually settled down are not given. Jacob dwelt in the land of his father's sojourning, in the land of Canaan, which means around the Negev desert between Hebron, Beersheba, and Gerar. Notice in the opening few verses the names *Jacob* and *Israel* are used interchangeably and seemingly arbitrarily.

TEXTUAL NOTE: *Introducing Jacob's Beloved Son Joseph*

Abraham's story took up fourteen chapters in Genesis; now Joseph will take up an equal number. Until this point we have never been introduced to Joseph. He has simply been a name in a list, the only son of the loved Rachel (before Benjamin) and the last son born to Jacob in Haran. What follows will be "the history of the family of Jacob", though Joseph becomes the main protagonist. This section of the book is frequently referred to as the "Joseph cycle". God gave Joseph dreams and the ability to interpret them, but it is never recorded that he had a theophany or visit from God like his forefathers. He is mentioned four times in the New Testament (Jn 4:5; Acts 7:9–14; Heb 11:21–22; Rev 7:8), and Joseph, the foster father of Jesus, was certainly named after this Old Testament saint.

We first meet him when he is seventeen years old, and trouble is brewing right from the start. His brothers hated him with a vicious jealousy because their father demonstrably loved Joseph more than his other sons. If that was not bad enough, he spoke ill of his half-brothers to their father. They hated him with such passion that they could not speak amicably with him. Joseph was shepherding the sheep with the sons of Bilhah and Zilpah. While tending the flocks, their younger brother Joseph was apparently helping them but also acting as a liaison between them and their father back home, as explained in Genesis 37:12–14. He was serving them in the fields, as David the youngest son of Jesse had served his brothers by running back and forth between home and his older brothers on the battlefront (cf. 1 Sam 17:13–18).

JOSEPH'S "ILL REPORT" AND HIS BROTHERS' ANIMOSITY (37:2)

The "ill report" that Joseph brought back to his father could range from honest concern to manipulative gossip. The author is purposefully ambiguous. To report a misdeed was not a sin or crime. In any work setting, the employer wants to know how things are faring on the job. As Joseph shuttled back and forth, Jacob would certainly ask him how the work was faring. Maybe the brothers were neglecting the sheep, involved in misconduct, or disloyal to their father. If Joseph had given an honest report about offenses of his brothers, then his "evil report" could actually have been an honest concern (though he would still have been perceived as a sycophant tattletale). No matter what Joseph did, their hatred caused them to see everything he did in the worst possible light.

Every time this particular Hebrew word is used, it is in a negative sense, as in gossip or false tales (cf. Num 13:32; 14:36–37). It is further enhanced by the adjective "evil". So if he were lying about his brothers, and his father believed his lies or exaggerations, then we could understand the increased tension and hatred against Joseph. However, the hatred would not have been diminished if Joseph's reports had been true, exposing evil on the part of his brothers. Truthfully reporting to his father on the negligent, irresponsible, or evil conduct of his brothers might also have been regarded as an "evil report". However, in the whole course of the narrative, we see no deceit or animosity clouding Joseph's character. In fact, we never see any moral shortcomings in his conduct.

The real root of the problem and animosity was his "favored son" status. This was manifested visibly, which only fanned the flame of their hatred. Jacob made Joseph a unique and special robe, in this case an outer garment. This would be analogous to giving all of your sons cheap sneakers but giving your youngest child a pair of $500 designer sports shoes.

JOSEPH'S ORNAMENTAL ROBE (37:3–4)

There is much discussion about this "coat of many colors"; specifically, about what made it so exceptional and noticeable. The exact type of this exceptional robe is disputed; the Hebrew phrase *kethoneth passim* is difficult to translate with certainty. The Hebrew word *kethoneth* means more than just your average robe. It refers to a "special tunic, i.e., long robe with long sleeves, with a special focus that this garment is not 'work clothing' (Gen 37:3, 23b, 32a; 2 Sam 13:18, 19+), note: good argument can be given that tunic was special because it was a richly ornamented robe."[1]

The *Septuagint* renders it "many-colored tunic" and the Latin *Vulgate* translates the phrase as a "tunic woven of many colors". However, many modern translations and lexicons—both Catholic and Protestant—have leaned away from the emphasis on colors. The *New International Version* translates it "richly ornamented robe", The AMP translates it as "a [distinctive] long tunic with sleeves", the NAB renders it "a long tunic" and the RSV-2CE "a long robe with sleeves".[2]

The Hebrew adjective *pas* causes the problem. It literally means *palm* (of the hand) or *sole* (of the foot); therefore, by implication, it describes a robe that goes all the way to the hand and the foot. The above Hebrew lexicon also states, "special tunic, distinctive robe, i.e., a tunic or robe unique in design for showing special favor or

---

[1] James Swanson, *Dictionary of Biblical Languages with Semantic Domains: Hebrew (Old Testament)* (Oak Harbor: Logos Research Systems, 1997), ref. no. 4189.

[2] "The richly ornamented robe is probably more than just a symbol of favoritism. The term is used elsewhere only for the garment of the princess Tamar (2 Sam. 13:18–19). Many commentators suggest it has something to do with royalty. If so, it may foreshadow Joseph's royal rule in Egypt. By this regal apparel (see 2 Sam. 13:18) Jacob publicly designates Joseph as the ruler over the family. Jacob wants to pass on the rule to godly Joseph; in the end, he will pass it on to Judah." Bruce K. Waltke and Cathi J. Fredricks, *Genesis: A Commentary* (Grand Rapids, Mich.: Zondervan, 2001), 500.

relationship; note: either the robe was very long-sleeved and extending to the feet, or a richly ornamented tunic either of special color design or gold threading, both ornamental and not suitable for working." This exceptional robe could not be missed when Joseph strolled out to his brothers in the field.

Regardless of the debate on the nature of the robe, the Fathers saw a deeper meaning to the story. The *Catechism* teaches that in Scripture we pay attention to the literal meaning of a text, but there is also the spiritual (*CCC* 115–18). Saint Caesarius of Arles wrote of the father's love for Joseph and how it prefigured God the Father's love for his Son Jesus Christ:

> When the Christian people devoutly come to church, of what benefit is it that they hear how the holy patriarchs took their wives or begot their children, unless they perceive in a spiritual sense why these things happened or what the facts prefigured? Behold, we have heard that blessed Jacob begot a son and called his name Joseph, and that he loved him more than the rest of his sons. In this place blessed Jacob prefigured God the Father; holy Joseph typified our Lord and Savior. Therefore, Jacob loved his son because God the Father loved His only-begotten Son, as He Himself said: "This is my beloved Son."[3]

Jacob failed in wise parenting. There is nothing sons need more than a father's love and approval, but they did not get it. Joseph was the son loved by Jacob. There are four reasons the brothers hated Joseph: (1) he was the youngest but the one their father loved; (2) he was the pampered son of the loved wife; (3) he gave their father "evil reports" about them; and (4) he apparently flaunted the contemptible robe. Now we are told about the final straw that broke the camel's back, the fifth and final "insult" that pushed them to treachery.

JOSEPH'S DREAMS (37:5–11)

God gave Joseph a dream. When he explained the dream to his brothers—maybe not a wise thing to do—they hated him even more.

---

[3] Sermon 89.1, in Caesarius of Arles, *Saint Caesarius of Arles: Sermons (1–238)*, ed. Hermigild Dressler and Bernard M. Peebles, trans. Mary Magdeleine Mueller, The Fathers of the Church, vol. 2 (Washington, D.C.: Catholic University of America Press; Consortium Books, 1956–1973), 38–39.

He dreamt that he and his brothers were binding sheaves of wheat in the field. His sheaf rose from the ground and stood upright, while his brothers' sheaves all bowed to Joseph's sheaf. How would *you* react to such a dream if you were one of his older brothers? Not only was Joseph wearing a special—even a "royal"—robe, but now he has dreams about his older brothers bowing to him. So his brothers said, "Are you indeed to reign over us? Or are you indeed to have dominion over us?" So they hated him more than ever for his dreams (v. 8).

To make matters worse, Joseph had another dream. Joseph's second dream was more pretentious than the first because this one had his father, Jacob, bowing to him with his brothers! The sun, moon, and stars were all bowing down to Joseph! Even his father rebuked him, saying, "Shall I and your mother and your brothers indeed come to bow ourselves to the ground before you?" But Jacob did not dismiss these dreams entirely. Scripture says, "his father kept the saying in mind." This reminds us of Mary, who heard marvelous things, "pondering them in her heart" (Lk 2:19, 51).

Saint Ambrose wrote, concerning the dreams of Joseph:

> God's grace shone on Joseph even in his boyhood. For he had a dream that when he was binding sheaves with his brothers—so it appeared to him in the vision—his sheaf rose up and stood straight, while the sheaves of his brothers turned and bowed down to his sheaf. Now in this the resurrection of the Lord Jesus that was to come was revealed. When they saw Him at Jerusalem, the eleven disciples and all the saints bowed down; when they rise, they will bow down bearing the fruits of their good works, just as it is written, "Coming they shall come with joyfulness, carrying their sheaves (Ps. 125(126): 6)."[4]

Dreams were highly esteemed in the ancient world. They were usually thought to be from God and taken very seriously. The repetition of Joseph's dream would normally give it added veracity, authenticating its legitimacy and seriousness. But these dreams appeared to be a pampered boy's delusion of grandeur—his brothers scoffed at young Joseph's egocentric aspirations. Three times we are told of

---

[4] *On Joseph*, in Ambrose of Milan, *Seven Exegetical Works*, ed. Bernard M. Peebles, trans. Michael P. McHugh, The Fathers of the Church, vol. 65 (Washington, D.C.: Catholic University of America Press, 1972), 191.

their hate (vv. 4, 5, 8), and in Scripture three is emphatic—hatred has escalated. These dreams would prove genuine. And these prophetic dreams were not the last dreams that God would bestow upon Joseph. But we the readers are not supposed to know the whole story yet. These two dreams add anticipation to this intriguing drama.

From Joseph's perspective, he did not ask for the robe or the dreams, and, though a bit naïve at times, he was not doing anything extraordinary to be hated by his brothers. From God's perspective, it was all ironically prophetic of events soon to explode. The robe and the dreams represented the impending role reversals.

SPIRITUAL NOTE: *Joseph and Typology*

This is a bit of a spoiler, but it will help us as we read through the "Joseph cycle". The Fathers of the Church delighted in the story of Joseph as a marvelous prefiguration of Jesus Christ. Jacob prefigures the Father who begot a Beloved Son. Jesus was royal, and the stately robe given by father Jacob represents Jesus as king standing apart from his brothers though at the same time one of them, in the flesh. Jesus came to his own people with revelation from God, and his own people rejected him. They hated him and could not speak civilly with him or listen to him—the Jewish leaders despised Jesus and debated with him. Envy caused the brothers to sell Joseph to the pagans, and they showed the blood to the father. Jesus was handed over to the Romans because of jealousy and killed. The sacrifice and blood of Jesus was presented to the Father. Eventually all on the earth and in heaven would bow to him. Joseph is a picture of Christ who is rejected by his brothers but is ultimately raised up to save them all.

We will revisit this typology as the story of Joseph develops, but this sample just opens the door a crack to whet our appetites for a deeper understanding of the beautiful multilayered fabric of Scripture.

JOSEPH IS BETRAYED BY HIS BROTHERS (37:12–25)

Jacob sent some of his sons to the grassy hills of Shechem about fifty miles north as the crow flies from Hebron. The terrain is hilly and rocky. Jacob sent his son Joseph to check on his brothers. Joseph's response to his father's request is echoed many times in Scripture. "Here I am." They are the words of submission and obedience. It was a long way for the seventeen-year-old boy to traverse alone. He could not find his brothers and ended up wandering around in a field. He knew their general location within a radius of ten to twenty miles. A man approached young Joseph and asked "What are you seeking?" and then pointed him to Dothan (meaning "two wells"), another twenty miles to the north.

Dothan is located between the modern cities of Nablus (Shechem) and Jenin.

> Dothan has been identified since the mid-nineteenth century with Tell Dotha ..., an imposing mound of some 25 acres 14 miles N of Shechem. The mound presents a classic *tell*-formation, rising steeply nearly 200 feet above the surrounding terrain. It is situated along the E reaches of the broad fertile Dothan Valley, on the main route N from Samaria to En-gannim (modern Jenin) and the pass leading into the Jezreel Valley.[5]

Artifacts have been found in Tell Dothan from 1900 B.C., the time of the patriarchs.

Imagine Joseph's older brothers in the heat of the sun, sleeping on the ground, tending their father's sheep seventy miles from home. And who should appear but their "self-important" little brother who stayed at home with dad most of the time. Joseph suddenly crested the hill "sporting" his beautiful robe, which was a dead giveaway as they saw him approaching. "Here comes this dreamer!" They hastily hatched a plan to kill him and threw him in one of the nearby pits. This probably referred to an artificial water reservoir called a cistern (especially since they later commented on the cistern being dry).[6]

---

[5] William G. Dever, "Dothan (Place)", in *The Anchor Yale Bible Dictionary*, ed. David Noel Freedman (New York: Doubleday, 1992), 226.

[6] "Although 'pit' could refer simply to a hole in the ground, generally it was a cistern several meters deep, carved in rock to collect and store precious water. Building a cistern involved a great deal of work (Deut 6:11). A cistern usually had a small access near the top into which groundwater flowed. Dark, damp, rocky and isolated, the pit provided a near-death experience for anyone hapless enough to fall in and be stranded inside. Despair quickly followed the realization that there was no escape. The metaphor of pit as prison stems from actual use. A nearly dry cistern could function as a handy prison (Zech 9:11). The Hebrew

Two of Jacob's sons had slain men and plundered Shechem only a short time before, so it is not unthinkable that killing was in the realm of possibility. But this time the victim would be their younger brother. The Hebrew word for *kill* is the same used to describe Abel's murder, "Cain rose up against his brother Abel, and *killed* him" (Gen 4:8). The plan was to kill Joseph, toss him in one of the pits (a cistern), and then tell their father he had been devoured by a wild beast. No one would ever find out. The dishonor of killing and depriving him of a proper burial expressed their hatred. Ancient cisterns have been discovered in Israel containing men's bones, so this practice of throwing someone into a cistern to die or to dispose of a body was not uncommon.[7] It was an evil deed perpetrated not only on the victim but also on those living nearby because the source of water would be contaminated and rendered unclean.

The brothers would explain to their father that Joseph had probably been mauled by a wild animal. In this way, Jacob would be the *guilty party* for having sent Joseph on such a dangerous mission. "The wild carnivores of Palestine included the wolf, the lion, the leopard (both spotted and black varieties), the cheetah, the jackal, and the bear. Recent archaeological excavations have uncovered remains of both the lion and the bear in Iron Age levels. While the lion appears to have disappeared before modern times, the bear survived until early in this century."[8] It would not be unusual for a boy to be attacked by one of these carnivores (see 2 Kings 2:24).

Reuben interceded to save Joseph's life. He said "Let us not take his life.... Shed no blood" (Gen 37:21–22). He asserted his authority

---

designated the dungeon as *bēt habbôr*, literally, 'house of the pit' (Ex 12:29). Joseph (Gen 37:22) and Jeremiah (Jer 38:6) are doubtless only the most famous of many prisoners kept in dark holes (Is 24:22; Ps 107:10)." Leland Ryken et al., *Dictionary of Biblical Imagery* (Downers Grove, Ill.: InterVarsity Press, 2000), 646.

[7] "Another burial at Gezer that must have been connected with some unusual circumstance led to the deposit of fifteen bodies in a cistern, and a number of spear heads were found with them. The skeletons were all males except one, which was that of a girl about sixteen years old, whose spine had been severed and only the upper part of the skeleton deposited in the cistern." George A. Barton, *Archaeology and the Bible* (Philadelphia: American Sunday-School Union, 1925), 196. "The place to which Bacchides withdrew and where he slew several Jews ... where a cave-cistern is pointed out as the 'great pit' into which the bodies of the murdered Jews were thrown." R. E. W. Bason, "Beth-Zaith", in *The International Standard Bible Encyclopedia, Revised*, ed. Geoffrey W. Bromiley (Wm. B. Eerdmans, 1979–1988), 480.

[8] Edwin Firmage, "Zoology (Fauna): Animal Profiles", in *The Anchor Yale Bible Dictionary*, ed. David Noel Freedman (New York: Doubleday, 1992), 1143.

as the eldest; the brothers did not argue with him. To save Joseph's life, Reuben suggested tossing the boy into a cistern and leaving him there. Why be guilty of outright murder with his blood on our hands? Just leave him in the pit to die. But Reuben planned to sneak back later, rescue Joseph, and deliver him back to Jacob.

All of this was devised as Joseph approached across the field. Instead of the expected greeting, Joseph was grabbed and stripped of his robe, the "long robe with the sleeves that he wore", and he was tossed into a dry cistern with no water. I have climbed into many cisterns in Israel, some with water and others dry. It would be terrifying to be dropped in and left to look up at the small hole knowing you could never escape. We are not immediately told of Joseph's reaction to his brothers' abrupt treachery. Much later, the truth came out, "In truth we are guilty concerning our brother, in that we saw the distress of his soul, when he begged us and we would not listen'" (42:21).

In verse 23, the text mentions stripping the robe from Joseph, but the writer does not just mention it briefly—he amplifies it by describing it again in detail. This emphasizes how much they hated that robe. It symbolized their father's favoritism toward Joseph and his apathy toward them.

What did the older brothers do after they dispensed of their younger brother? They sat down to eat lunch—maybe even eating food that Joseph had just brought for them (cf. 1 Sam 17:14–18). They looked up from their meal and saw an Ishmaelite caravan arriving. They were coming from Gilead with a load of gum, balm, and myrrh on their way down to Egypt. You may be familiar with the traditional spiritual hymn "There Is a Balm in Gilead" that mentions this balm, taken from Jeremiah 8:22. The words are "There is a balm in Gilead to make the wounded whole, there is a balm in Gilead to heal the sin-sick soul."

SELLING JOSEPH INTO SLAVERY (37:26–30)

Dothan was located on a major trade route between Egypt and Mesopotamia. The caravans would pass through Syria and Gilead, into Canaan along the coast of the Mediterranean, through the Sinai Peninsula and into Egypt. This was the great trade route for the transport of spices, fabrics, incense, medicinals, and perfumes, many of which were in great demand in Egypt for embalming. Obviously from this passage, we learn that slaves were also traded along this route. The spices and aromatics carried by this caravan into Egypt were very symbolic, for these gifts would later be given to the sons of Jacob to carry back to Canaan from Egypt.

The traders in the caravan were called both Ishmaelites (vv. 25, 27, 39:1) and Midianites (vv. 28, 36). Ishmaelites were the descendants of Abraham's eldest son, Ishmael, and Midianites were also the sons of Abraham though his later wife Keturah (Gen 25:1–6). That Joseph was treated so egregiously by his brothers and other descendants of Abraham made his betrayal all the more devastating. There has been much ink spilled over the two apparently different groups involved with the sale and transport of Joseph to Egypt: the Ishmaelites and the Midianites.

> The interchange of these two names in the story probably reflects a close affinity between the two groups. Some suggest that the Ishmaelites were considered a subtribe of the Midianites. Others suggest the Midianites simply purchased Joseph from the Ishmaelites. However, based on the intermingling of the names in Judges 8:24, it would appear that the biblical writer either assumed they were related or is reflecting a known kin tie between them.[9]

Why let Joseph die in the cistern when they could make a profit? They quickly plotted to sell their brother into slavery and deceitfully infer to their father that Joseph was killed by wild beasts. Who would ever know? Joseph would be forever a slave in a far-off land, and no one would be the wiser for it; plus, Jacob would die soon anyway. They pulled Joseph up out of the pit and were paid twenty shekels of silver.[10] "The twenty shekels paid for Joseph was about normal for a slave in this time period, as attested in other literature of this time (for instance, the laws of Hammurabi). It would constitute approximately two years of wages."[11]

---

[9] Victor Harold Matthews, Mark W. Chavalas, and John H. Walton, *The IVP Bible Background Commentary: Old Testament*, electronic ed. (Downers Grove, Ill.: InterVarsity Press, 2000), Gen 37:29–36.

[10] In the Hebrew there is no word "shekel" in the text. It just reads "twenty of silver". Assuming the measurement was close to a shekel, then the "twenty of silver" would have been about ½ pound of silver.

[11] Matthews, Chavalas, and Walton, *IVP Bible Background Commentary*, Gen 37:28.

He would be forced to walk all the way to Egypt, be treated like an animal, made to work, and all he had to look forward to was miserable slavery in a foreign land. The Psalmist wrote, "[God] had sent a man ahead of them, Joseph, who was sold as a slave. His feet were hurt with shackles, his neck was put in a collar of iron" (105:17–18). Saint Ambrose comments on the parallels with Christ:

> Here too, so that you may note the symbolic representation of the Lord's passion, the patriarch Juda says, "Let us sell Joseph to the Ishmaelites and let not our hands be laid upon him," and earlier he had done well to say, "Do not lay hands upon him," which is what the Jews said in the Lord's passion, "It is not lawful for us to put anyone to death." Thus the word of Jesus could be fulfilled, signifying by what death He was going to die.[12]

Saint Caesarius concurs and sees Christ as the true Joseph:

> Upon seeing Joseph, his brothers discussed his death; just as when the Jews saw the true Joseph, Christ the Lord, they all resolved with one plan to crucify Him. His brothers robbed Joseph of his outside coat that was of divers colors; the Jews stripped Christ of His bodily tunic at His death on the cross. When Joseph was deprived of his tunic he was thrown into a cistern, that is, into a pit; after Christ was despoiled of human flesh, He descended into hell. Afterwards, Joseph is lifted up out of the cistern and is sold to the Ishmaelites, that is, to the Gentiles; when Christ returns from hell, He is bought by all nations at the price of faith. Upon the advice of Juda, Joseph is sold for thirty pieces of silver; Christ is sold for the same amount upon the counsel of Judas Iscariot.[13]

The Mother church of the world—which contains the Chair of Saint Peter—is Saint John Lateran in Rome. Among its many treasures are the sculptured reliefs running along both sides of the church's nave, starting in sequence from the apse to the rear of the church. They are typological images demonstrating the parallels between the Old

---

[12] *On Joseph* 3.14, in Ambrose of Milan, *Seven Exegetical Works*, ed. Bernard M. Peebles, trans. Michael P. McHugh, The Fathers of the Church, vol. 65 (Washington, D.C.: Catholic University of America Press, 1972), 197–98.

[13] Sermon 89.2, Caesarius of Arles, *Saint Caesarius of Arles*, 2:39–40.

Testament and the New, starting with the Garden of Eden and ending with the Resurrection of Christ. In the middle of the sequence is a set that corresponds to our story of Joseph's betrayal by his brothers. On the one side are Joseph's brothers selling and handing him over as a slave to the Midianites. Correspondingly on the opposite side is Judas kissing Jesus in the Garden of Gethsemane as all of his "brothers" abandon him, handing him over to be crucified. Touching parallel, indeed.

It was all downhill from here. The hatred and betrayal were now capped off with a bold and cruel lie. Judah had decided to sell Joseph. Apparently, Reuben was not with the brothers at the time. He went back to the cistern to retrieve Joseph only to find him gone. He tore his own clothes in dismay. This was an act of grief and sorrow. Now they had to decide upon a new twist to their plot. They dipped Joseph's special robe in the blood of a male goat.

THE BROTHERS TREACHEROUSLY DECEIVE THEIR FATHER ABOUT JOSEPH (37:31–36)

Joseph's brothers took his bloodied robe back to their father with a wicked lie—actually, they tried to sidestep the lie like they tried to evade the murder. They told their father they had found the robe and then asked if he recognized it, which of course he did. They "avoided" lying by letting their father draw the tragic conclusion that Joseph had been "torn to pieces" and "a wild beast [had] devoured him." The brothers remained silent in their deceit, which was a lie in itself.

"There is a certain poetic justice to the brothers' cruel deception of their father, since Jacob had used kids [young goats] to deceive his own father (27:5–23)."[14] And not only that, the brothers used the clothes of Joseph to deceive their father like their father, Jacob, had used the cloths of Esau to deceive his father (27:15–27). "The beginning of the story of Joseph still stands under the shadow of Jacob-Israel's guilt, which had clung to the old man since his youth. Just as

[14] Adele Berlin, Marc Zvi Brettler, and Michael Fishbane, eds., *The Jewish Study Bible* (New York: Oxford University Press, 2004), 76.

he had once deceived his father and robbed the brother whom his father had preferred, so Jacob is now in turn deceived by his sons who have sidetracked his favorite son."[15] Like father, like sons!

Jacob drew the intended conclusions: Joseph had been devoured by a wild animal. He tore his clothes following the customary rituals of mourning—rending the clothes, weeping and wailing, putting dust or ashes in the hair, and wearing coarse sackcloth made of camel or goat hair. Many saints, like Saint Thomas More, wore "hair shirts" under their outer garments as a means of penance or mortification of the flesh. Many traditions and practices in the Catholic Church find their origins in Scripture and the practices of God's people through the centuries. Mourning was a very solemn ritual and would often last for thirty days or more.

"All his sons and all his daughters rose to comfort him", but he was inconsolable. Interestingly the text refers to *daughters*. Up until now, we have only heard of one daughter, Dinah. This may refer to additional daughters hitherto unmentioned or, more likely, to Dinah and Jacob's daughters-in-law (cf. Gen 46:15; Ruth 1:11). In the meantime, Joseph was taken to Egypt and sold to Potiphar, an officer of Pharaoh (literally "a eunuch" or "high official"), the captain of the guard. Now there is a parenthetical story inserted—about Judah—before the drama with Joseph continues.

[15] Otto Procksch, as cited in W. Gunther Plaut, "Genesis", in *The Torah: A Modern Commentary* (New York: Union of American Hebrew Congregations, 1981), 248.

CHAPTER 38

JUDAH AND TAMAR

INTRODUCTION

Any experienced writer knows how to break the tension in a story and increase the tension at the same time. For example, if a story brings a character right to the edge of the cliff and his feet slip, the tension is at its peak. Quickly breaking from the story at this point is called a "cliff hanger". An author may move to another simultaneous plot leaving the reader to wonder what happened to the guy tumbling off the cliff—anxious to return and discover his fate. During the "breather" or "distraction", the writer may be giving information crucial to the whole story, possibly even to make the slip and fall more significant.

Many commentators think the Judah-Tamar episode in Genesis chapter 38 was a later addition to the Book of Genesis or that it is completely out of place. But the unity of Scripture created by the Holy Spirit working through the various human authors means that the placement of the new sordid episode is certainly intentional, at least as far as the Spirit is concerned (*CCC* 112, 304). It is important to see the integrity of the main characters juxtaposed against each other in chapters 38 and 39.

THEOLOGICAL NOTE: *The Significance of Judah*

A new storyline is being developed that supersedes Joseph, not only in the current narrative, but in the salvation story as a whole. This "interlude" introduces us to Judah, from whom the kings of Israel will arise—eventually even Jesus Christ. Joseph and his sons play the primary role as he receives the birthright stripped from Reuben (see 1 Chron 5:1–2), but in the big picture, Judah plays a much more important role than Joseph.

We embark now on a seedy episode in the family that demonstrates again God's superintendence of historical events using sinful people and unfortunate situations to fulfill his own divine plan as Judah's family line carries the ball toward the goal line. Some of the names appearing in this unsavory tale show up in the genealogical line of Jesus Christ, including Tamar, one of five women mentioned in Jesus' family tree.

Judah was only a name on a list until the last chapter, when he suggested selling rather than killing Joseph. Judah was the fourth son of Jacob following Reuben, Simeon, and Levi. He was a son of Leah, the unloved wife, and his name meant "praised". When the children of Israel eventually possessed the Promised Land, the area surrounding Jerusalem, Bethlehem, Hebron, and Beersheba would be allotted to the tribe of Judah—an area named Judea at the time of Jesus (Mt 3:5). The words "Jew" and "Judaism" derive from the name Judah, which is *Yehuda* in Hebrew. Today the word "Jew" refers to anyone ethnically a Jew, since after the exile of the Ten Tribes into Assyria, it was only the tribe of Judah that remained as a tribe, although many people knew their ancestral tribes and identified with them. Jew also refers to those who follow the Jewish religion. From Judah comes the royal line of the kings of Israel through David (Gen 49:9–10; 1 Chron 5:1–2; 28:4; Ps 60:7; Heb 7:4; Rev 22:16). Jesus Christ will be known as the "lion of the tribe of Judah" (Rev 5:5).

It is time we met Judah, who is not known for his virtue, but God would use him providentially to fulfill his covenant with Abraham. Knowing that this story is inserted here for a reason, let's meet Jacob's fourth son, who is somewhat a skeleton in Jesus' genealogical closet.

JUDAH'S MARRIAGE AND SONS (38:1–2)

The story begins abruptly with the words "It happened at that time." In Hebrew, this could mean a few days or many years. After Jacob mourned for Joseph, it appears that Judah broke off on his own. The period of time was between the sale of Joseph and the family's exile into Egypt. Jacob "turned in to a certain Adullamite, whose name was Hirah". Adullam is west of Bethlehem and Hebron, and near there is the Cave of Adullam where David would later hide from King Saul (1 Sam 22:1–2; 2 Sam 23:13). Judah married the daughter of Shua of whom we know nothing other than that she was a Canaanite and she bore Judah three sons before she died "in the course of time" (v. 12). Only later in 1 Chronicles 2:3 do we learn her name was Bath-suah the Canaanitess. The three sons were Er, Onan, and Shelah. Judah scorned his ancestors by taking a wife from among the idolatrous Canaanites.

TAMAR AND THE LAW OF *LEVIRATE MARRIAGE* (38:6–10)

When the oldest son, Er, was able to marry, Judah took a wife for him. Her name was Tamar, meaning "palm tree". God did not approve of Er, for no specific reason divulged other than that he was wicked in God's eyes, so God slew him (v. 7). Rabbinic opinion suggested that Er wanted no children, therefore refusing to consummate the marriage. Others suggested Er did not want to mar Tamar's beauty with a pregnancy.[1] This, of course, is speculation, though the next son, Onan, was also killed by God, this time definitely for refusing to impregnate Tamar, so the speculation about Er is not without merit.

Tamar was now a young widow with no sons. There were laws accommodating widows, orphans, and the poor. Through the law of *levirate marriage*, as it later came to be codified, brothers were compelled to preserve the family name of their brother who died childless. The law stated that if a man died leaving a widow with no son, the brother of the deceased man was required to impregnate his brother's widow, thus providing a son for his brother; and, in addition, the widow would be cared for by that son (see Deut 25:5). The son would legally be the heir of the dead brother, inheriting his deceased father's estate. In the Mosaic Law, the only exception to a man

[1] "We have no problem knowing why Onan did what he did, because he knew, 'that the seed would not be his' (Gen. 38:9). But why did Er do it? D. [says] It was so that she would not become pregnant and lose her looks." Jacob Neusner, *The Babylonian Talmud: A Translation and Commentary*, vol. 8 (Peabody, Mass.: Hendrickson, 2011), 171–72.

marrying his brother's wife was the levirate marriage—otherwise, the marriage would be considered incest (Lev 18:16; 20:21). The practice that would later be enshrined as *levirate marriage* can also be found in the writings of the Hittites (similar time period) as they dealt with the same issue of a brother-in-law or father-in-law sleeping with the widow to procure a son.[2]

Judah told his second son, Onan, to go in to Tamar, Judah's firstborn's widow, and do his duty to raise up offspring for his deceased brother. But knowing the offspring would not be his, Onan spilled his semen on the ground. Because he did this, God was displeased and killed Onan, too (38:8–10).

The son of the *levirate marriage* would be the dead man's firstborn son, which could decrease the inheritance and authority of the dead man's living brother—which is why he refused to do his duty. An example of this in practice is found in the relationship between Ruth and Boaz in Ruth, chapter 4. In the Mosaic Law, there was an "escape clause" where the brother could refuse, but he would be publicly shamed by the brother's widow (Deut 25:7–10).

THEOLOGICAL NOTE: *The Sin of Onan*

Judah demanded that his son Onan perform his family duty and impregnate his deceased brother Er's wife. Onan proved disobedient, disloyal to the family, and selfish. He pretended to do his duty but practiced *coitus interruptus*—a primitive form of birth control—or, as described in the Bible, he "spilled the semen on the ground". The Hebrew text emphasizes that he did this on every occasion, not just once or twice. His refusal to fulfill his duty was "displeasing in the sight of the LORD", so God killed Onan, too.

---

[2] "Thus we have seen that the Hittite laws have the same devolution along the line of agnates from brother-in-law to father-in-law as Genesis 38, which shows us that the case of Judah was not an unprecedented deviation from the normal law. Again, Hittite law shows the same tension between incest and levirate, and makes a distinction between a brother's wife and widow, which internal evidence had already suggested to be the resolution of the contradiction between the Levitical and the Deuteronomic law." Raymond Westbrook, *Property and the Family in Biblical Law*, Journal for the Study of the Old Testament, Supplement Series, vol. 113 (Sheffield: Sheffield Academic Press, 1991), 87.

Onan's actions have been named *onanism*, the spilling of the semen outside of intercourse to avoid impregnation. It has been argued that God was displeased for one of two reasons: (1) that for reasons of greed, Onan refused to fulfill his duty to his brother's wife and/or (2) that Onan spilled his semen on the ground, thus practicing a form of birth control. That Onan's sin is his refusal to fulfill a moral obligation seems primary to the text, but this is not an *either/or* proposition. Jewish and Christian scholars have seen it as *both/and*. In Scripture, the refusal to impregnate the brother's wife did not rise to a capital offense, so there must have been more to it. It must be a case not only of what Onan did, but of how he did it.

Utilizing this form of primitive contraception was a grave offense, not just in Catholic teaching, but also with first-century Jewish sages. In the Jewish Talmud it is written, "And why all this? It is because he purposelessly emits semen. For, said R. Yohanan, 'Whoever emits semen purposelessly is liable to the death penalty, as it is said, "And the thing that he [Onan] did was evil in the sight of the Lord, and he slew them also" (Gen. 38:9)'."[3]

> The more plausible interpretation is that Onan is killed for *the deliberately contraceptive sexual act* of spilling his semen on the ground and thereby willfully rendering procreation impossible. This is supported by the fact that elsewhere in the Pentateuch, sexual acts that render procreation impossible are also capital crimes punishable by death (e.g., Lev 20:13, 15–16).
>
> In the eighteenth century, the term "onanism" was coined and sometimes misleadingly used as a euphemism for masturbation. This led to some confusion in interpreting this text, since what is in view in Genesis 38 is not masturbation but a deliberately interrupted sexual act (Latin *coitus interruptus*).[4]

In *Casti Connubii* (*On Christian Marriage*), Pope Pius XI wrote:

> But no reason, however grave, may be put forward by which anything intrinsically against nature may become conformable to nature

[3] Babylonian Talmud, Tractate Niddah, folio 13a, chap. 2, in Neusner, *Babylonian Talmud*, 22:50–51.

[4] John Bergsma and Brant Pitre, *A Catholic Introduction to the Bible*, vol. 1, *The Old Testament* (San Francisco: Ignatius Press, 2018), 145.

and morally good. Since, therefore, the conjugal act is destined primarily by nature for the begetting of children, those who in exercising it deliberately frustrate its natural power and purpose sin against nature and commit a deed which is shameful and intrinsically vicious.

Small wonder, therefore, if Holy Writ bears witness that the Divine Majesty regards with greatest detestation this horrible crime and at times has punished it with death. As St. Augustine notes,[5] "Intercourse even with one's legitimate wife is unlawful and wicked where the conception of the offspring is prevented. Onan, the son of Juda, did this and the Lord killed him for it." (54–55).[6]

The *Catechism* discusses the positive regulation of births and the illicit acts of contraception (2351–52, 2370, 2399).

TAMAR TAKES THINGS INTO HER OWN HANDS (38:11–30)

After having two "husbands", the unfortunate Tamar still had no sons. Both men had been punished with death by God for evil conduct. Judah had one son remaining, so he promised Shelah to Tamar. Because he was young, Tamar was to wait until he was older. Under the authority of her father-in-law, Judah, Tamar remained a widow and moved back to her father's house. Judah feared losing his last son if he gave Shelah to Tamar, assuming God would kill him, too. Time passed, and Judah's wife died (38:12). He went up to visit his sheepshearers, along with his friend Hirah the Adullamite.

After Judah refused to fulfill his obligation to Tamar by giving her his last son, Shelah, Tamar decided to take matters into her own hands, hoping to teach her father-in-law a humiliating lesson and to acquire a son at the same time. Shelah had reached a marriageable age and had been denied to her, contrary to the promise of Judah. Learning her father-in-law's plans of going to Timnah for the sheepshearing, she removed her "widow's garments" and "put on a veil,

[5] Bk. 2, chap. 12, Augustine of Hippo, "Adulterous Marriages", in *Treatises on Marriage and Other Subjects*, ed. Roy Joseph Deferrari, trans. Charles T. Huegelmeyer, The Fathers of the Church, vol. 27 (Washington, D.C.: Catholic University of America Press, 1955), 116–17.

[6] Pius XI, *Casti Connubii* (Vatican City: Libreria Editrice Vaticana, 1930), nos. 54–55.

wrapping herself up". Judah quickly passed his time of mourning
for his deceased wife, but Tamar many years later was still dressed for
mourning in her widow's garments. Tamar dressed as a prostitute
and covered her face with a veil to conceal her identity. The term in
Hebrew is *sacred woman*: a woman who served a pagan deity by pros-
titution (also in verse 21).[7] She sat in the gate of the city as though
soliciting men as they passed in and out.

Judah noticed her sitting on the side of the road. He drew the
intended conclusion, that she was a harlot, and quickly propositioned
her. Judah would never have lain with Tamar if he had known she
was his daughter-in-law. It was a casual affair; he never got her
name. This sexual fling was obviously done on a whim; if Judah had
intended to solicit a prostitute, he would have brought a means of
payment. Judah realized he had no gold or silver to pay the prostitute in advance, so he promised a young goat from his flock. Being
shrewd, Tamar requested a pledge be given her until the goat was
delivered. He left his personal signet, his cord, and his staff. The
signet was a cylinder with his personal seal or symbol (cf. *Catechism*
1295). When rolled on wet clay or wax, it left an impression, much
like a signature today. He left these items with the "prostitute".

After giving the pledge, he went in to Tamar, and she conceived.
After he left, Tamar quickly removed her disguise, redressed as
a widow, and returned home. The prostitute had disappeared to
Judah's great dismay. When he returned with payment, she was gone.
This was a serious problem! This was legally dangerous and could be
very embarrassing. He decided to drop the search lest he be made a
public fool.

Three months later, Tamar's pregnancy became apparent, and it
was reported to Judah that his daughter-in-law was pregnant. He
assumed she must have been playing the harlot unaware that it was
with *him*! The drama heated up; he demanded she be brought out and
burned publicly. Any sexual intercourse outside the *levirate* arrangement would be punishable by death (cf. Lev 20:10; Deut 22:22).

---

[7] "In Genesis 38:15–24, Tamar, disguised as a 'sacred' woman, is also called a prostitute.
Sexual relations evidently transpired around sanctuaries (cf. Hos 4:13–15; Amos 7:17) and
were perhaps sponsored by them in order to generate revenue (cf. Lev. 19:29; 21:9)." Mark
S. Smith, *Exodus*, The New Collegeville Bible Commentary, ed. Daniel Durken, vol. 3 (Collegeville, Minn.: Liturgical Press, 2011), 131–32.

Stoning was the usual form of execution. But the *real* crime committed was a father-in-law lying with his daughter-in-law after refusing to obey and enforce the *levirate law* (Lev 20:12). Tamar flipped Judah's world upside down when she produced his personal signet, cord, and staff, announcing it was the owner of these items that was the father of her child. She confronted him with unimpeachable evidence, and the light of retributive justice swung away from her and fully shone in the face of Judah.

In due time, Tamar's twins were born. A tiny left hand slipped out of the womb first, and the midwife tied a scarlet thread around the wrist to mark the firstborn. But the little hand was withdrawn, and the other baby emerged first. The hand belonged to the second-born, Zerah; the firstborn was Perez. *Perez* means "breach", since the midwife had exclaimed, "What a breach you have made for yourself!" Zerah disappeared from the story, but Perez the firstborn was the link to future generations and, ultimately, to King David and to Jesus Christ. For the genealogy of Judah and these boys, read 1 Chronicles 2:3–8. Tamar and Perez are included in the genealogy of Jesus (Mt 1:1–3). Tamar won a "moral" victory over her deceitful and immoral father-in-law, Judah, who admitted his fault. She now had two sons, had paid Judah back for his evil, and was included in Jesus' lineage. This sordid account of Judah interrupts the flow of Genesis to connect the dots in God's plan.

One last interesting note before we move on to chapter 39. Even today many Jews wear a "red string" on their left wrist supposedly to ward off the "evil eye". An elderly Jewish woman offers them for a small donation as we enter the Western Wall in Jerusalem. It is a tradition that recalls the scarlet thread tied to the little hand that reached out from Tamar's womb. Today this tradition is often associated with the Kabbalah movement of Judaism and is also a superstitious practice in the wider population.[8]

---

[8] https://www.myjewishlearning.com/article/ask-the-expert-red-string-bracelet.

CHAPTER 39

JOSEPH'S SUCCESS IN EGYPT; POTIPHAR'S WIFE

JOSEPH'S JOURNEY TO EGYPT;
SOLD AS A SLAVE (39:1-6)

Returning to the main narrative in Egypt, we focus on Joseph, who had been sold as a slave to the high official of Pharaoh. Leaving the pastoral life in Canaan behind, we now enter the upper echelons of cultured life in the palaces of Egypt.

> The Joseph Cycle is a well-integrated, discrete narrative that has been described by some scholars as a kind of short novel (*novella*) and recognized by many as a masterpiece of world literature. It is largely set in Egypt, and, as one might expect, it reflects Egyptian culture and literature, sharing themes with classic Egyptian literary works from the second millennium B.C., notably the *Tale of Sinuhe*.[1]

In fetters, Joseph trudged over three hundred miles through inhospitable territory from Dothan in northern Canaan, through the Negev, through the Sinai wilderness into Egypt. The pyramids of Giza had been standing proudly for over six hundred years (built 2570 B.C.) before Joseph passed them in misery, clueless as to his future. The kings of Egypt were called *pharaohs*, which means "big house", originally referring to their palaces, but became their title as well. They were religious and political kings, thought to be the incarnation of the Egyptian god *Horus*, the god of the sky.[2]

---

[1] John Bergsma and Brant Pitre, *A Catholic Introduction to the Bible*, vol. 1, *The Old Testament* (San Francisco: Ignatius Press, 2018), 145.

[2] "In Egyptian religion the living king of Egypt was the god Horus or the 'son of Re,' making his edicts inviolate. His chief role as the mediator between the gods and society was to maintain *maat*, that is, order in the land." K. A. Mathews, *Genesis 11:27–50:26*, The New American Commentary, vol. 1B (Nashville: Broadman & Holman, 2005), 763.

Title meaning "great house" for the ancient kings of Egypt. Every ancient pharaoh had five "great names" which he assumed on the day of his accession. Since it was not deemed proper to use such powerful names in direct fashion, a polite circumlocution developed; he came to be called Pharaoh.... An ancient pharaoh was an absolute monarch, supreme commander of the armies, chief justice of the royal court, and high priest of all religion. His absolute power may be seen in that justice was defined as "what Pharaoh loves"; wrongdoing as "what Pharaoh hates." An example of his divine power was that he daily conducted "the Rite of the House of the Morning," an early morning ritual in which he broke the seal to the statue of the sun god, waking him up with a prayer. This act brought the sun up and started every day for the people.[3]

Potiphar was an official of Pharaoh and the captain of the guard. He purchased Joseph as his slave. The Lord was with Joseph so that everything he put his hand to was very successful. His new master was quite impressed with young Joseph and noticed the Lord made him successful in all he did "in house and field". The Hebrew word *successful* is used seven times in Genesis: four times related to Abraham's servant who was successful on the journey to find the bride for Isaac (Gen 24:21, 40, 42, 56) and three times in this present chapter (vv. 39:2, 3, 23). It means effective, prosperous, able to exceed the goals. As a result, "Joseph the slave" was promoted to "Joseph the overseer". He became Potiphar's personal attendant—the same word used of Joshua serving Moses, and Elisha serving Elijah (Ex 24:13; 2 Kings 6:15). He was placed over everything in the master's house, so much so that Pharaoh's officer had no concerns except the food he ate. Joseph was trusted completely, and God blessed Potiphar's house for the sake of Joseph.

PERSONAL NOTE: *God's Grace Builds on Joseph's Nature*

Joseph's success and blessing from God is not apart from Joseph's own character and integrity. There is a Latin phrase, *gratia supponit naturam*

---

[3] Chad Brand et al., eds., "Pharaoh", *Holman Illustrated Bible Dictionary* (Nashville, Tenn.: Holman Bible Publishers, 2003), 1285–87.

et perficit eam, or, in English, "grace builds on nature and perfects it."—I alluded to this phrase earlier. God's grace does not replace human nature, traits, dispositions, or talents, much less destroy these things. Grace sanctifies, elevates, and renews our natures. Joseph is attractive not only in his character but also in outer form and appearance—in other words, he was "handsome and good-looking" (v. 6). His inner qualities only enhanced the outer. The Jewish historian Josephus wrote, "When Jacob had his son Joseph born to him by Rachel, his father loved him above the rest of his sons, both because of the beauty of his body, and the virtues of his mind; for he excelled the rest in prudence."[4]

In Genesis 49:22, where Jacob blesses his twelve sons before his death, part of Joseph's blessing has been translated differently in the English than in Saint Jerome's Latin *Vulgate* and the D-R. The English translation in the RSV-2CE reads, "Joseph is a fruitful bough, a fruitful bough by a spring; his branches run over the wall." The D-R renders it, "Joseph is a growing son, a growing son and comely to behold: the daughters run to and fro upon the wall."[5]

Elsewhere Jerome, translator of the Vulgate, explained this passage's meaning: "And the sense of this section is: O Joseph, you who are thus called because the Lord added you to me, or because you are to be the greatest among your brothers ... O Joseph, I say, you who are so handsome that the whole throng of Egyptian girls looked down from the walls and towers and windows."[6]

---

[4] *The Works of Josephus: Complete and Unabridged,* trans. William Whiston, updated edition (Peabody, Mass.: Hendrickson, 1987), 53.

[5] *The Holy Bible, Translated from the Latin Vulgate* (Bellingham, Wash.: Logos Bible Software, 2009), Gen 49:22.

[6] Jerome's *Hebrew Questions in Genesis* 49:22, quoted in James L. Kugel, *The Bible As It Was* (Cambridge, Mass.: The Belknap Press of Harvard University Press, 1997), 256. Though not all Jewish commentators agree with Rashi's understanding of this passage, Rashi explained, "His charm is evident to the eye. *Wild colts on a hillside.* Rather, 'girls marched in order to look.' The Egyptian girls walked along the wall to gaze on Joseph's beauty. 'Girls' is plural, but 'march' is singular; each and every one of them found a place where she could look at him. 'Look' here is related to the verb in 'what I *behold* will not be soon' (Num. 24:17). There are many midrashim about this phrase; the explanation I have given is intended to settle the meaning of the words in context." Michael Carasik, ed. and trans., *Genesis: Introduction and Commentary,* The Commentators' Bible (Philadelphia: Jewish Publication Society, 2018), 437. Other Jewish commentators disagreed with Rashi.

In an ancient document entitled *Joseph and Aseneth*, written between 100 B.C. and A.D. 100, a Jewish elaboration of Genesis reads:

> And looking up with his eyes, Joseph saw Aseneth leaning through
> (the window). And Joseph said to Pentephres and his whole family,
> saying, "Who is this woman who is standing in the upper floor by
> the window? Let her leave this house," because Joseph was afraid,
> saying, "This one must not molest me, too." For all the wives and the
> daughters of the noblemen and the satraps of the whole land of Egypt
> used to molest him (wanting) to sleep with him, and all the wives and
> the daughters of the Egyptians, when they saw Joseph, suffered badly
> because of his beauty.[7]

We read of other biblical characters with eye-catching physical
appearances such as Saul (1 Sam 9:2), David (1 Sam 16:18), Esther
(Esther 2:7), Judith (Jud 10:7), and Joseph's own mother, Rachel
(Gen 29:17). Joseph's pleasing appearance is introduced here to set
the stage for the next scene in the drama.

POTIPHAR'S WIFE DESIRES JOSEPH (39:7–11)

Potiphar's wife, we may suppose, noticed Joseph as he went about
the house—her eyes followed him. She saw his muscular body and
his handsome features, and she wanted him. Some translations render
the words "she longed for him" or "she looked at him with desire"
or "looked fondly on him". She was the mistress of the house, the
wife of the master! She cooed no soft words, no emotional entice-
ments, just the lustful command of a mistress to a slave, "Lie with
me!" Notice the wry twist of depravity—the lady of the house was
a slave of her lusts and lusted for the slave of her husband. Nowhere
else in the Bible do you see a woman with such shameless conduct.
In her lasciviousness, she used her appeal and power to command
him into her bed.

---

[7] James H. Charlesworth, *The Old Testament Pseudepigrapha and the New Testament: Expan-
sions of the "Old Testament" and Legends, Wisdom, and Philosophical Literature, Prayers, Psalms and
Odes, Fragments of Lost Judeo-Hellenistic Works*, vol. 2 (New Haven; London: Yale University
Press, 1985), 210.

Joseph was noble and moral; he refused to acquiesce to her demands. He wisely defended himself, reminding her that her husband had put him in charge of everything in the house except her, since she was his wife. His refusal was based on a knowledge of sin and the righteousness of God (vv. 8–9). She remained aggressively unabashed in her pursuit. She may have done it successfully before. Joseph was single, lonely, and away from home, lacking the moral constraints of family and friends—yet, he demonstrated great virtue in the face of the direct command of his master's wife. Joseph was as wise and self-controlled as he was handsome and successful. Consider the warnings against falling for the adulteress in the book of Proverbs (5:5–22; 6:24–33; 7:5–23; 9:13–18).

This was a slave society, and one did not dare refuse a direct order! Without preaching or criticizing her, he resisted every advance. She came at him day after day, attempting to wear him down; looking for a momentary weakness. She was unsuccessful. He would not listen to her or even *be* with her. He was avoiding every appearance of evil. He feared the mistress, but he feared God more. He practiced what Saint Paul wrote later to young Timothy, "So shun [flee] youthful passions and aim at righteousness, faith, love, and peace, along with those who call upon the Lord from a pure heart" (2 Tim 2:22; cf. 1 Cor 6:18). We have in Joseph an exemplary character. Consider the stark contrast between Joseph and his morally compromised older brother Judah.

TREACHERY OF POTIPHAR'S WIFE; JOSEPH IMPRISONED (39:11–20)

Once while alone in the house, Potiphar's wife grabbed Joseph to force a sexual encounter. She demanded, "Lie with me!" but he turned and fled, leaving his garment in her hand. Out of vindictive rage, she called the other men of the household, accusing Joseph of attacking her. She showed his garment as evidence. "See, he [my husband] has brought among us a Hebrew to insult us; he came in to me to lie with me, and I cried out with a loud voice ... and [he] fled and got out of the house" (vv. 14–15). She accused him of attempted rape. She told the same story to her husband, Potiphar, using the garment again as her evidence.

Joseph's obedience to God's law and his honorable escape, without accusing Potiphar's wife or making a scene, has always been recognized as heroically virtuous. Scripture comments on Joseph's obedience to God's prohibition against adultery, "Remember the deeds of the fathers, which they did in their generations; and receive great honor and an everlasting name.... Joseph in the time of his distress kept the commandment, and became lord of Egypt" (1 Mac 2:51–52).

Garments are significant in this story of Joseph. His special robe was stripped from him before he was sold as a slave, and now his garment was ripped from him by Potiphar's wife immediately before Joseph was sent to prison. Both times, the garment was used as evidence—the first time as evidence of his faked "death" and the second time as evidence of his faked "rape attempt". Jesus also had a robe stripped from him when he was falsely accused and killed.

Potiphar's wife was brilliant in her accusations—a study in manipulation and psychological maneuvering. Potiphar responded with a burning anger. Joseph did not defend himself. As a type of Christ, he did not utter a word. In prophetic words related to Jesus, we read, "He was oppressed, and he was afflicted, yet he opened not his mouth; like a lamb that is led to the slaughter, and like a sheep that before its shearers is silent, so he opened not his mouth" (Is 53:7; Mt 27:12–14). Might it be that Joseph looked to God's providence to vindicate him and defend him from his enemies?

GOD PREPARES JOSEPH THROUGH HIS PRISON EXPERIENCE (39:21–23)

Potiphar "took and put" Joseph in prison. It had gone from bad to worse. First, he had been betrayed by his brothers and sold into slavery; now he was betrayed by his master's wife and thrown into prison and forgotten. We read, "And he was there in prison" (v. 20). God did not quickly deliver Joseph from prison. God had his plans and his own timing.

> But Potiphar was also the Governor of the State prison ... transferred him to the prison to make himself useful there as he had been in his house, and so he became an inmate there. This would presuppose that in his heart he was really convinced of Joseph's innocence, and only

for the sake of his honor did he have to take the action that he did.... This was a prison to which both those condemned and those committed for trial were brought. The sequel, too, bears this out. Through that Joseph could come into contact with men who were only temporarily interned, and who, when acquitted returned to important position. As in fact the Lord High Baker and His Highness the Butler also seem to have been in the prison only awaiting trial.[8]

The Hebrew word for *prison* used here means just that, a jail or prison, but in Genesis 40:15 and 41:14, a different Hebrew word is used that means a dungeon or a pit, implying subterranean in nature—the same word in chapter 37, meaning a pit or cistern. The prison seems to have been within Potiphar's own compound (cf. Gen 40:3, 7; 41:10), in which case Joseph would have been the administrator of the very prison in which he was now confined—making the situation all the more poignant. His former employee, "the keeper of the prison", would now be his "warden". Even though God did not immediately deliver Joseph from the dungeon, he continued to be "with Joseph and showed him mercy, and gave him favor in the sight of the keeper of the prison" (39:21) as he had done for Joseph as he had served Potiphar. The jail keeper might have remembered the good management and blessing of God upon Joseph in his former position of being over the house of Potiphar.

> Prison (*sohar*), which appears in the Bible only in Genesis, was probably a special place where important prisoners were confined. Joseph was put in prison rather than punished in the usual way, by death; perhaps Potiphar was aware of his wife's roving eyes and not at all sure of Joseph's guilt.[9]

St. John Chrysostom explains how God was with Joseph even in prison:

> What is the meaning of "The Lord was with Joseph"? Grace from on high stood by him, it is saying, and smoothed over all his difficulties. It arranged all his affairs; it made those traders well disposed to him

[8] Samson Raphael Hirsch, *The Pentateuch*, vol. 1, *Genesis* (Gateshead: Judaica Press, 1999), 564.
[9] W. Gunther Plaut, "Genesis", in *The Torah: A Modern Commentary* (New York: Union of American Hebrew Congregations, 1981), 258.

and led them to sell him to the chief steward so that he should advance gradually and, by proceeding through those trials, manage to reach the throne of the kingdom. But you, dearly beloved, hearing that he endured slavery at the hands of the traders and then experienced the slavery of the chief steward, consider how he was not alarmed and did not give up hope or debate within himself in these terms: How deceitful were those dreams that foretold such prosperity for me! I mean, look, I have gone from slavery to harsh slavery and a range of masters, from one to another, forced to associate with savage races. Surely we haven't been abandoned? Surely we haven't been passed over by grace from on high? He said nothing of the sort; he gave it not a thought; on the contrary, he bore everything meekly and nobly. "The Lord was with Joseph," after all, "and he became a man of means."[10]

God showed him steadfast love (extended kindness) and again granted him favor in the eyes of those around him, namely, the keeper of the prison. Just as Potiphar had made Joseph overseer of his whole house, now the keeper of the prison put Joseph in complete charge of the prison. Very similar language is used of the delegation of Potiphar and the warden, who "paid no heed to anything that was in Joseph's care, because the LORD was with him; and whatever he did, the LORD made it prosper" (v. 23). We recall Romans 8:28 with personal confidence in God's providential hand, "We know that in everything God works for good with those who love him, who are called according to his purpose."

[10] Homilies on Genesis 62.13, in John Chrysostom, *Homilies on Genesis 46–67*, trans. Robert C. Hill, The Fathers of the Church, ed. Thomas P. Halton, vol. 87 (Washington, D.C.: Catholic University of America Press, 1992), 204.

CHAPTER 40

JOSEPH INTERPRETS DREAMS IN PRISON

INTRODUCTION: *Dreams and Dreaming*

Dreams have always been a great mystery. "What is the purpose of this odd state called sleep? Scientists are still not sure, but they have discovered some fascinating information about it.... Dreaming, like sleep, has been studied extensively but still remains a mystery."[1] We have been mystified by dreams from the dawn of time—are dreams random, or do they mean something?

The word *dream* is used around 125 times in the Bible. Of these occurrences, forty-two are in the book of Genesis alone, and of these, thirty-five occur in the story of Joseph! God used dreams to communicate to the patriarchs. The prophet Joel prophesied, "I [God] will pour out my spirit on all flesh; your sons and your daughters shall prophesy, your old men shall dream dreams, and your young men shall see visions" (Joel 2:28). Peter quoted Joel's words on the day of Pentecost so we would know God continues using dreams and visions to communicate as he wills.[2]

---

[1] E. L. Hillstrom, "Sleep and Dreaming", in *Baker Encyclopedia of Psychology & Counseling*, ed. David G. Benner and Peter C. Hill, Baker Reference Library (Grand Rapids, Mich.: Baker Books, 1999), 1130, 1131.

[2] While most of our dreams are random and surreal, Janet and I *have* experienced numerous instances when dreams were clearly from God—giving us instruction, informing us of things to come, and specifically encouraging and directing us. Some of the most important decisions in our lives started with God revealing his plan for us in dreams. Of course, not all dreams are from God or to be taken seriously. Scripture teaches, "As one who catches at a shadow and pursues the wind, so is he who gives heed to dreams.... Divinations and omens and dreams are folly.... Unless they are sent from the Most High as a visitation, do not give your mind to them. For dreams have deceived many, and those who put their hope in them have failed" (Sir 34:2, 5, 6–7).

God had spoken to Joseph's forebears through dreams and visions. Joseph was now dreaming dreams as well. As with his forefathers, the dreams were generally about the patriarchs and their immediate circumstances, with promises of future blessings. But with Joseph, dreams took on a broader significance—to prophesy of future events. Dreams needed interpretation! Joseph was gifted with dreams and with their interpretation. God spoke *to* Joseph and *through* Joseph. One Protestant commentary went so far as to say that "God endowed Joseph with the gift of infallible interpretation."[3]

IMPRISONED ROYAL SERVANTS
HAVE DREAMS (40:1–8)

Now we descend into the dungeon to join Joseph as we begin this chapter of dreams. Verse one gives a very indefinite time frame, "Some time after this", but we can draw some conclusions based on the text. In another two years, Joseph would be thirty years old (41:46), so Joseph must now have been twenty-eight years old. Eleven years have passed since he was sold into slavery at the age of seventeen (Gen 37:2). We do not know how long he had been in prison before these two significant prisoners arrived.

The text reminds us that the Pharaoh was indeed the king of Egypt (40:1). As the king, he had servants to provide his every need, two of which were the royal cupbearer (cf. Neh 1:11—2:1) and the baker (cf. 1 Sam 8:13). The RSV-2CE translates the Hebrew word *masqeh* as "chief butler", but the word specifically relates to drink. The "cupbearer, wine taster, i.e., a person in charge of many aspects of the drink of a ruler, including tasting and quality control ... often a person in favor and close contact with the king".[4] Most modern translations, including the Catholic translations ESV-CE, NAB and the NJB, render the word *cupbearer*. In the royal echelons, good food was expected. The cupbearer was the *sommelier* of his time; the

---

[3] Carl Friedrich Keil and Franz Delitzsch, *Commentary on the Old Testament*, vol. 1 (Peabody, Mass.: Hendrickson, 1996), 226.

[4] James Swanson, *Dictionary of Biblical Languages with Semantic Domains: Hebrew (Old Testament)* (Oak Harbor: Logos Research Systems, 1997), ref. no. 5482.

chief baker was also a master at his art, our equivalent of a three-star Michelin chef. "The Egyptians were renowned gourmets and knew fifty-seven varieties of bread and thirty-eight different kinds of cakes."[5]

The cupbearer and baker were trusted officials who served the king. To ensure the safety of the royal family, such officials would often test the king's food and drink to protect him from poisons. Due to their close contact with the Pharaoh, they had to be unimpeachable and had the possibility of becoming rich and influential. We have no clue what offense these two officials committed. According to Eastern custom, the prison would usually be part of the dwelling of the chief of the guard or the executioner. The prisoners were kept "in custody in the house of the captain of the guard, in the prison where Joseph was confined" (v. 3). They shared Joseph's ignominious fate—going from riches to rags.

Throughout, these narrative dreams came in pairs. Back in Canaan, Joseph had a pair of complementary dreams about sheaves and stars. The cupbearer and the baker each had matching dreams. Pharaoh would also have two related dreams. Joseph was given the ability to *know* the dream and to *explain* its significance. Joseph said that the doubling of Pharaoh's dream "means that the thing is fixed by God, and God will shortly bring it to pass" (41:32). The sets of dreams demonstrated their import.

> Throughout the Joseph narratives, dreams come in pairs in order to demonstrate their seriousness, as noted in 41:32. The possibility of an idle dream was recognized by the ancients. From the literature of the ancient Near East we have accounts of double, triple, and even sevenfold repetition of dreams in which one symbol is successively substituted for another, although the basic meaning and central theme remain the same throughout the series.[6]

Two dreams by two officials with two accurate interpretations established Joseph's ability and credibility. Joseph's two dreams in Canaan

[5] W. Gunther Plaut "Genesis", in *The Torah: A Modern Commentary* (New York: Union of American Hebrew Congregations, 1981), 258.

[6] Nahum M. Sarna, *Genesis*, The JPS Torah Commentary (Philadelphia: Jewish Publication Society, 1989), 257.

brought him misery; two sets of two dreams in Egypt would bring him majesty.

During their incarceration, and on the same night, the cupbearer and the baker both had vivid dreams of great significance, but they had no clue what the dreams meant—there was no one to interpret their dreams. Joseph noticed their downcast faces and asked why they were dismayed. He offered to interpret their dreams. He asked the rhetorical question, "Do not interpretations belong to God? Tell them to me, I beg you" (v. 8).

JOSEPH INTERPRETS THE DREAMS (40:9–23)

The chief cupbearer went first and told his dream associated with his profession. A vine grew with three branches and produced grapes, and he squeezed the grapes into Pharaoh's cup and placed the cup in Pharaoh's hand. Joseph quickly interpreted the dream. The three branches were three days, so the cupbearer would be released in three days and back in the employ of the Pharaoh. Joseph asked a favor, and I paraphrase: Mr. Cupbearer, speak a kind word to the king for me, OK? I think he has forgotten about me in this prison. Help me get out! I was kidnapped from the land of the Hebrews. I did nothing worthy of my treatment there and nothing worthy of my imprisonment here. Joseph considers himself innocent of wrongdoing among his brothers back home and innocent here.

Encouraged by this good report, the baker in turn disclosed his dream to Joseph. He told of three cake baskets on his head with the top basket full of baked goods for the king, but birds were eating out of the basket. Without hesitating, Joseph said the three baskets represented three days after which the baker will lose his head and be hung on a tree for birds to feast on his flesh!

As a side note: in the dream, the baker is carrying baskets of bread on his head. We do not usually see this sort of thing in the United States, but in other parts of the world, especially in the Middle East, it is common for baskets or large flat boards of bread to be balanced on the head. It is quite entertaining to watch a man with a large flat board balanced on his head stacked high with bread running through the streets dodging traffic, sometimes simultaneously talking on his mobile phone.

Here is another interesting fact: the dream mentioned "all sorts of baked food". From ancient sources in Egypt, we learn about the office of the royal baker:

> As court baker he is not content with the usual shapes used for bread, but makes his cakes in all manner of forms. Some are of a spiral shape like the "snails" of our confectioners; others are coloured dark brown or red, perhaps in imitation of pieces of roast meat. There is also a cake in the shape of a cow lying down. The different cakes are then prepared in various ways—the "snails" and the cow are fried by the royal cook in a great frying pan; the little cakes are baked on the stove.[7]

In the prescribed times, the dreams came true, just as Joseph had said. On the third day, the cupbearer was restored to his position with the Pharaoh, and the baker was hanged. But the cupbearer forgot Joseph's kindness and forgot to mention Joseph to the king, so Joseph languished in the prison. But he continued to trust God and had to wait for two more years before the next scene of the drama. God is not always in as big a hurry as we are.

[7] Adolf Erman, *Life in Ancient Egypt*, trans. H. M. Tirard (New York: Dover Publications, 1971), 192.

CHAPTER 41

JOSEPH INTERPRETS PHARAOH'S DREAMS; MADE RULER OF EGYPT

PHARAOH'S DREAMS (41:1–13)

Chapter 41 opens a full two years later. Joseph had been forgotten and still endured his imprisonment. He was now thirty years old, the same age as Jesus when he came out of obscurity to begin his earthly ministry (Lk 3:23). Pharaoh had a dream. He was standing by the Nile River, which was Egypt's source of fertility, the symbol of Egypt's greatness, and one of its many gods. It also competed with the Amazon as the longest river in the world, at 4,132 miles. Out of the river came seven fat cows eating reed grass along the river's edge. Behind them emerged seven gaunt and thin cows who ate the seven fat cows. Pharaoh awoke from his terrifying and mysterious dream. The Hebrew word for *gaunt* is used twenty-six times in Genesis and is usually translated as evil or bad. It is the same word used for the "ill" report Joseph gave of his brothers (37:2). The word suggested a ghastly and evil sight even before the grotesque creatures ate the fat cows.

It is not surprising that cattle appeared in the dream. They were sacred symbols of Egypt; the Egyptian god Hathor was represented as a cow. In a hymn to Hathor, we see Egypt's reverence for "the queen of gods".

> O beauteous one, O cow, O great one,
> O great magician, O splendid lady, O queen of gods!
> The King reveres you, Pharaoh, give that he live!
> O queen of gods, he reveres you, give that he live!

> Behold him, Hathor, mistress, from heaven,
> See him, Hathor, mistress, from lightland,
> Hear him, flaming one, from ocean![1]

All of the images seen by the king conform to Egyptian motifs of life and the sacred.

> So seven-year famines are not something merely recorded in Scripture but also in Egyptian documents. This famine would affect indeed the gods of Egypt. For example, it would affect Osiris, a god who had the form of a bull [and] was the god of the Nile. It would also affect Isis, also known as Hathor, who was a goddess in the form of a cow; and she was the goddess of fertility.[2]

Pharaoh fell asleep again and had the second dream (remember that a *set* of dreams is significant). Seven ears of grain were growing on one stalk. They were plump and good. After them sprouted another seven ears, but these were thin and blighted (scorched). The seven thin ears ate up the plump ears. Again, Pharaoh woke up!

Egypt was the breadbasket of the Roman Empire, famous for its grain production along the bountiful Nile River, especially in the northern delta. But the powers of nature can devastate the grain harvest. In verse 6, the second batch of grain was "thin and blighted by the east wind". "*The east wind* is almost a technical term for the desert wind, whether its quarter is strictly east or not. This scorching blast, in Palestine the sirocco, and in Egypt the khamsīn, can be devastating to crops (cf. Ezek. 17:10; Hos. 13:15f.)."[3]

The wording of the text implies Pharaoh thought his dream was real. "And Pharaoh awoke, and *behold* it was a dream" (emphasis added). It could be worded, When he awoke he was amazed it had only been a dream. Troubled by these parallel ominous dreams, he called his magicians and wise men. They were clueless; none could interpret the dreams. The same term is used of the *magicians* who opposed Moses

[1] Miriam Lichtheim, *Ancient Egyptian Literature*, vol. 3, *The Late Period* (Berkeley: University of California Press, 1973–), 108.

[2] Arnold G. Fruchtenbaum, *Ariel's Bible Commentary: The Book of Genesis*, 1st ed. (San Antonio, Tex.: Ariel Ministries, 2008), 567.

[3] Derek Kidner, *Genesis: An Introduction and Commentary*, Tyndale Old Testament Commentaries, vol. 1 (Downers Grove, Ill.: InterVarsity Press, 1967), 206.

during the Exodus (see Ex 7:11). The wise men were a more general category of learned men who answered the Pharaohs' questions.

> Magicians refers to a class of Egyptian priests who had special powers and knowledge. The Hebrew term is found only in passages related to Egypt; for example, Exo 7:11, 22; 8:18–19; 9:11. Most English translations call them "magicians," but [REB: Revised English Bible] prefers "dream-interpreters." Interpreting dreams, however, was probably only one of their functions. A magician is a person skilled in magic or the control of secret forces in nature. Wise men refers to another class of Egyptian priests or people with special knowledge or wisdom.... "These 'priests' (magicians) were the head 'reader priests' according to Egyptian terminology. They are here the highest in the hierarchy. The 'wise men' are the top level civil servants educated in the scribal schools. These two groups were the scholars of their day and were responsible to answer the Pharaoh's questions."[4]

Suddenly the chief cupbearer remembered his negligence and confessed his offense to Pharaoh. He reminded Pharaoh that, two years before, a young Hebrew prisoner had accurately interpreted dreams for the cupbearer and the baker. He had promised to mention him to Pharaoh and had neglected to do so.

JOSEPH INTERPRETS PHARAOH'S DREAMS (41:14–32)

Joseph was hastily brought out of the dungeon, shaved, and given a change of clothes. Egyptians were clean shaven, unlike other ancient peoples. Joseph probably shaved his head, too, which was a common practice among Egyptians. Pharaoh, the king of Egypt, a world superpower of the time, had summoned Joseph. After explaining his dreams to Joseph, the Pharaoh mentioned that his magicians (dream-interpreters) had failed to interpret his dreams and he had been informed that Joseph could interpret dreams. Joseph humbly admitted that it was not *he* who could interpret dreams, but that God would provide Pharaoh with a favorable answer.

---

[4] William David Reyburn and Euan McG. Fry, *A Handbook on Genesis*, UBS Handbook Series (New York: United Bible Societies, 1998), 919.

Verses 17–24 are a detailed recap of the "dream"—singular—since Pharaoh was already viewing the two dreams as one message, which Joseph confirmed, saying, "The dream is one." Joseph immediately began to decipher the dream and reveal God's message. The seven fat cows and the seven good ears were seven years of great plenty. After that would come seven years of severe famine; so grievous that Egypt would forget the bounty of the seven good years. The doubling of the dream "means that the thing is fixed by God, and God will shortly bring it to pass" (v. 32).

For the Egyptians, the Nile River was a god. As the Greek historian Herodotus (ca. 484–ca. 425 B.C.) said, "Egypt is the gift of the Nile." It brought prosperity to the desert land as only water can do. As soon as you step away from the Nile, the land is dry and arid. On a current map you see the cities hug the Nile and its tributaries. The Pharaohs installed "Nile meters" (or Nilometers) to measure the depth of the Nile during the rainy seasons so they could anticipate the yield of crops that year to assess taxes—more water meant more crops and more taxes. The flooding covered the croplands with rich fertile silt. Egyptians had three seasons each year, one of which was called the "Season of the Inundation".[5]

But for the Nile and its inundation, Egypt would be as desolate as the deserts on either hand; wherever the Nile waters reach, vegetation can grow, life can exist. So sharp is the change from watered land to desert that one can stand with a foot in each. Egypt's agriculture depended wholly on the inundation, whose level was checked off against river-level gauges or Nilometers. A high flood produced the splendid crops that made Egypt's agricultural wealth proverbial.[6]

JOSEPH OFFERS A PLAN IN RESPONSE TO PHARAOH'S DREAMS (41:33–36)

Pharaoh did not even have time to respond before Joseph launched into a concrete proposal. He proved to be not only an interpreter

[5] Ed. Hershel Shanks, *BAR* (Biblical Archaeology Society), Nov./Dec. 1992, 18:06.
[6] K. A. Kitchen, "Nile", ed. D. R. W. Wood et al., *New Bible Dictionary* (Leicester, England; Downers Grove, Ill.: InterVarsity Press, 1996), 824.

of dreams, but also a civic engineer and manager. Had Joseph just *interpreted* the dreams, he would have been a celebrated hero, but he did not stop there; he courageously advised the Pharaoh. God gave Joseph wisdom right on the spot. He proceeded boldly, yet humbly, to suggest a course of action for Pharaoh. He should appoint a man discreet and wise (hmm? Who might that be?) to administer the land of Egypt. Then overseers should collect a fifth of the yearly produce of the land during the seven abundant years; gather and store the food for the lean years.

This plan would require a massive government project—setting laws and officials in place to increase the crops, impose and collect a tax of 20 percent on all landowners, and to build huge warehouses to store the mountains of grain. Transportation of grain from the outlying areas to the central warehouses itself would be a massive undertaking. But that was not all. Implementing the distribution of the grain during the famine would be enormous as well! Not only would grain be sold to Egyptians, but the surrounding nations would come to Egypt to buy food. Such an enterprise covering fourteen years and tens of thousands of square miles preserving millions of tons of grain would require remarkable management skills. Find a discreet and wise man, indeed!

JOSEPH APPOINTED MASTER OF EGYPT (41:37–45)

Pharaoh recognized the wisdom of the interpretation and the brilliance of the proposal. He asked his servants, "Can we find such a man as this, in whom is the Spirit of God?" Pharaoh looked at Joseph and said, "Since God has shown you all of this, there is none so discreet and wise as you are." In the morning Joseph had been an unshaved, unkempt prisoner in the dungeon. By dinnertime, he was the master of all of Egypt, second only to the king!

Scripture comments on Joseph's fall and rise and how wisdom was always at his side:

> When a righteous man was sold, wisdom did not desert him,
> but delivered him from sin.
> She descended with him into the dungeon,
> and when he was in prison she did not leave him,

> until she brought him the scepter of a kingdom
> and authority over his masters.
> Those who accused him she showed to be false,
> and she gave him everlasting honor. (Wis 10:13–14)

Pharaoh put Joseph over his entire house, and all of Egypt was under his command. Only on the throne would the king be greater than Joseph. Joseph's title would be Vizier or Prime Minister of Egypt. Pharaoh took the signet ring from his finger and put it on Joseph's hand—a sign of his delegated authority. The signet ring was used to sign official documents with the seal of the king. When impressed onto a soft wax or clay surface, it left the seal or the mark of the Pharaoh, which was unique in all the kingdom. Engraved in the signet was the king's *cartouche*—his name spelled out in hieroglyphics. It was his personal seal! With this seal, the Grand Vizier of Egypt, the second in command in all of the kingdom, would authenticate the royal decrees. Wearing the signet ring meant that Joseph possessed the authority of the king. (For more, see Numbers 31:50; Esther 3:10; Tobit 1:22; 1 Maccabees 6:15.) Joseph was also given garments and a golden chain as part of the royal vestments.

In the context of Joseph as the Vizier of Egypt, Roland de Vaux, a Dominican scholar, writes:

> In Israel the powers of the master of the palace were far more extensive and the similarity between his functions and those of the Egyptian vizier is even more important than the verbal resemblances. This vizier used to report every morning to the Pharaoh and receive his instructions.... All the affairs of the land passed through his hands, all important documents received his seal, all the officials were under his orders. He really governed in the Pharaoh's name and acted for him in his absence. This is obviously the dignity which Joseph exercised, according to Genesis.... The master of the palace had similar functions at the court of Judah.... One is reminded of our Lord's words to Peter, the vizier of the Kingdom of Heaven (Mt 16:19).[7]

Joseph as Vizier of Egypt is also instructive when compared to the delegated office of Peter in the Catholic Church. The king gave his

[7] Roland de Vaux, *Ancient Israel: Its Life and Institutions* (New York: McGraw-Hill, 1961), 130.

signet ring to Joseph, and King Jesus gave a like sign of delegated authority to Peter with the keys of the kingdom.

> The king leaves the administration of his kingdom in the hands of his delegated majordomo. The parallels are too striking to be mere coincidence. To understand Christ's words in light of the biblical history is to see that Jesus is establishing his Church with a majordomo in place to rule and govern in his absence. Scripture interpreting Scripture gives us the background so that we can rightly understand the full intention of our Lord Jesus when he gave Peter the keys to the kingdom of heaven. . . .
>
> Referring to Matthew 16 and the "keys", Protestant commentator Matthew Henry sees the clear correlation and writes, "The power here delegated is a spiritual power; it is a power pertaining to the kingdom of heaven, that is, to the Church. . . . It is the power to bind and to loose, that is (following the metaphor of the keys), to shut and open. Joseph, who was lord of Pharaoh's house, and steward of his stores, had power to bind his princes, and to teach his senators wisdom (Psa 105:21, 22)."[8]

In his autobiography, an ancient Vizier of Upper Egypt in the days of Thutmose III (fifteenth century B.C.) described how he "went forth . . . clad in fine linen":

> I was a noble, the second of the king and the *fourth* of him who judged the Pair. . . . It was the first occasion of my being summoned. All my brothers were in the outer *office*. I went forth . . . clad in fine linen. . . . I reached the doorway of the palace gate. The courtiers bent their backs, and I found the masters of ceremonies clearing the way [before me]. . . . My abilities were not as they had been: my yesterday's nature had altered itself, since I had come forth in the accoutrements [*of the vizier, having been promoted*] to be Prophet of Maat.[9]

Isn't it interesting that a special robe had gotten Joseph in trouble with his brothers back home, and now he was given a new royal robe of fine linen by the king, along with a gold chain around his

---

[8] Stephen K. Ray, *Upon This Rock: St. Peter and the Primacy of Rome in Scripture and the Early Church*, Modern Apologetics Library (San Francisco: Ignatius Press, 1999), 287–89.

[9] James Bennett Pritchard, ed., *The Ancient Near Eastern Texts Relating to the Old Testament*, 3rd ed. with supplement (Princeton: Princeton University Press, 1969), 213.

neck. What the first robe had signified, the second robe fulfilled. His boyhood dreams were starting to make sense! Ancient documents of Egypt confirm these steps of investiture in detail. The sacred writer intimately knew the culture of the Egyptians (remember, Moses was born and trained in the royal house in Egypt). History and archaeology continue to confirm the accuracy of Scripture. Joseph received a chariot that was "second" only to the Pharaoh's, an indication of his high office. This is the first mention of a chariot in the Bible. As the horses of Joseph galloped through Egypt, the royal heralds and charioteers would shout *"Abrek"*, which has been variously translated as "Attention, make way!" or "Bend the knee!" (v. 43). This is the only time the word is used in Scripture. Everyone had to bow to the ground as Joseph passed.[10]

The investiture process continued. Next Pharaoh changed Joseph's name. This should immediately get our attention. We discussed the significance of name changes with Abraham (from Abram), Sarah (from Sarai), and Jacob (to Israel). Joseph was given the new name *Zaphenath–paneah*, which means "God speaks, he lives." The *Septuagint* renders it "the creator and sustainer of life", which would fit the

---

[10] Roland de Vaux writes, "In retrospect, Joseph's installation in his high office of state in Egypt is an event that we can visualize in all its details as very few others in the Bible. Every detail of the ceremony has been passed down to us in Egyptian representations, even down to the almost transparent linen garments. We can view the rings, the golden chains, and the war chariots in the museums." Claus Westermann, *Genesis 37–50*, trans. John J. Scullion, S.J. (Minneapolis: Fortress Press, 1986), 97. I confirm this statement having seen ancient Egyptian chariots in the Egypt Museum many times along with signet rings and other spectacular items.

"Some of these Semites who rose to a high position in the Egyptian hierarchy are fairly well known to us. A tomb discovered at Tell el-'Amārna was that of a man called Tûtu, who acquired a great number of titles during the reign of Amen-hotep IV (Akh-en-Aten)—he became the first servant of the king in the temple of Aten, the first servant of the king in the boat, the inspector of all the king's undertakings, the inspector of the treasure of the Temple of Amarna and finally 'highest mouth' in the whole country. This last title meant that he had total authority in the special tasks he was given and was responsible only to the Pharaoh. It is one of the titles that Joseph is supposed to have had. The wall paintings on the tomb at Tell el-'Amārna show Tûtu's appointment by the Pharaoh, who is putting the golden necklace of office around his neck. They also show him leaving the palace, getting into his chariot and riding off as the people prostrate themselves before him in acclamation. This is altogether an excellent illustration of what must have taken place when Joseph was appointed chancellor in Egypt, in charge of the Pharaoh's household (Gen 41:41–43). Similar scenes are illustrated elsewhere, but what is particularly interesting in this case is that the person whom the Pharaoh is honoring is a Semite." Roland de Vaux, *The Early History of Israel*, trans. David Smith (Philadelphia: Westminster Press, 1978), 299.

mission of Joseph as head over all of Egypt to sustain them during the impending famine.

A wife also came with the elevation to vizier—Joseph married into the elite of the Egyptian nobility—her name was Asenath, meaning "belonging to the goddess Neith". She was the daughter of Potiphera, priest of On. On was the city known as *Heliopolis*—city of the sun, built about seven miles from modern Cairo in honor of *Ra*, the sun god. The name On comes from an Egyptian word meaning *column*. Today an immense obelisk from On stands in the center of Saint Peter's Square in Vatican City.

> A large pink granite obelisk can be admired in the center of the square. It was hewn from a single block and stands 25.31 m. high on a base 8.25 m. wide. The obelisk which comes from Heliopolis, Egypt, where it was built by the Pharaoh Mencares in 1835 B.C. in honor of the sun, was brought to Rome in 37 B.C. by the Emperor Caligula (37–41) and erected in the circus he built. Here it was silent witness of the martyrdom of Saint Peter and of many other Christians.[11]

Abraham, along with Joseph and Moses, must have seen this column. If this obelisk had had a video cam attached from the beginning, you would have seen much of the story of salvation history, including possibly Joseph galloping past in his chariot. Remember that next time you see the obelisk in St. Peter's Square!

JOSEPH PREPARES EGYPT FOR THE FAMINE (41:46–57)

Joseph was thirty years old at his meteoric rise from prison to the royal household. He wasted no time in familiarizing himself with Egypt and implementing the program Pharaoh had approved. Joseph's strategy worked, and he carried out the plan with precision, with the help of God. The years of plenty yielded more grain than could be counted—"like the sands of the sea". He stockpiled it in preparation for the famine.

Before the disaster struck, Joseph and Asenath had two sons. The first was named Manasseh ("making me forget", my hardships and

---

[11] Nicolò Suffi, *St. Peter's, Guide to the Square and the Basilica* (Vatican City: Libreria Editrice Vaticana, 1998), 16–17.

my father's house). The name of the second son was Ephraim (*fruit-fulness*, as in, God has made me fruitful in the land of my affliction). These two sons would play a *huge* role, constituting two of Israel's twelve tribes to possess portions of the land.

The seven years of plenty came to an end, and the seven years of famine commenced. Joseph was vindicated. The famine was not limited to Egypt but extended to all the surrounding nations. When food ran out in Egypt, the people cried out to Pharaoh for bread, and Pharaoh said, "Go to Joseph and do what he says to do." Joseph opened the granaries and sold the grain to the Egyptians. Then they started getting requests from all the other lands. "All the earth came to Egypt" (v. 57). Egypt had grain when the rest of the world was without food.

God had used Joseph to save the Egyptians, but his plan was much grander. There were nomadic shepherds tending their flocks in Canaan who had no forewarning of the famine. They had sold their young brother into slavery intending it for evil. But God had intended it for good (*CCC* 312). In the next lesson we begin to see how God works all things for his glory.

Psalm 105:16–24 poetically recounts Joseph's exploits and virtue:

> When he summoned a famine on the land,
>   and broke every staff of bread,
> he had sent a man ahead of them,
>   Joseph, who was sold as a slave.
> His feet were hurt with shackles,
>   his neck was put in a collar of iron;
> until what he had said came to pass
>   the word of the LORD tested him.
> The king sent and released him,
>   the ruler of the peoples set him free;
> he made him lord of his house,
>   and ruler of all his possessions,
> to instruct his princes at his pleasure,
>   and to teach his elders wisdom.
> Then Israel came to Egypt;
>   Jacob sojourned in the land of Ham.
> And the LORD made his people very fruitful,
>   and made them stronger than their foes.

CHAPTER 42

JOSEPH'S BROTHERS TRAVEL TO EGYPT; RETURN HOME DEVASTATED

INTRODUCTION

With this chapter we open what is one of the most exquisitely written, redemptive, and poignant stories in all the Bible and in literature in general. Not only because of the elegant storytelling, but because it is deeply human, stirring, and emotional—even the protagonist weeps six times.[1] The drama is profound and tender as it reveals the heart of God as he condescends to work among his people in space and time. It has every element of spectacular theatre: suspense, love, and betrayal, disaster and redemption, irony and surprise. The author invites us into the saga in the subtlest of ways. The plot has been intricately arranged from the beginning. Affliction and misery hang like a dreadful cloud. Guilt, shame, and recriminations lurk behind every page. They are all in prisons of different sorts—some of their own making and some through the treachery of family members.

Just as with any great story, we are now poised for the unknown. We long for punishment and revenge. We hope for redemption and resolution—and the author does not disappoint. The curtain is pulled back, and the story continues as we switch scenes from Egypt back to Canaan.

THE DROUGHT BEGINS (42:1–2)

The rains failed in Canaan just like the rains deserted Egypt. The grass withered; the dry ground cracked and sent dust into the air.

---

[1] Genesis 42:24; 43:30; 45:2, 14–15; 46:29; 50:1.

The herds and flocks panted in the heat, and the shelves gave up their last scraps of goods. Caravans passed back and forth through Canaan on their way between Egypt and the East. It is no wonder that news spread quickly about an abundance of grain in Egypt. Jacob and his family became frantic in Canaan.

Chapter 42 opens with a somewhat humorous line. We can imagine Jacob and his eleven sons looking around with expectations of starvation. Jacob surveyed the bunch of them and chided them for their inaction. "Why do you look at one another?" or "Don't just stand around staring at each other; do something!" Jacob told them they must find food, "that we may live, and not die".[2]

Jacob had learned there was grain in Egypt. In Hebrew, the word "learned" is actually "saw". He saw camels and donkeys loaded with grain passing through from Egypt. Since bread was mentioned in regard to the famine, the stored grain was most likely wheat for which Egypt was famous, but there were other grains as well.[3]

JACOB SENDS HIS SONS TO EGYPT FOR GRAIN (42:3–6)

Assuming Jacob was living in Hebron, the last location mentioned (37:14), it would have been for him about 250 miles to the Nile Delta region of Egypt, called Lower Egypt. Caravan routes passed

[2] "The phenomenon and the motif of seven-year famines are well documented in Egyptian and other ancient Near Eastern texts (cf. 2 Sam. 24:13, but see 1 Chron. 21:12). One Egyptian text speaks of a famine where 'the entire Upper Egypt was dying because of hunger, with every man eating his (own) children'." Bruce K. Waltke and Cathi J. Fredricks, *Genesis: A Commentary* (Grand Rapids, Mich.: Zondervan, 2001), 536.

[3] "The most frequently mentioned food in the Bible is bread. The term refers in a general sense to all foods but also to food prepared from grain. In biblical times bread was prepared from several grains. Wheat, barley, and spelt were grown in Egypt (Ex 9:31, 32)." Hazel W. Perkin, "Food and Food Preparation", *Baker Encyclopedia of the Bible* (Grand Rapids, Mich.: Baker Book House, 1988), 802.

"Alexandrian grain ships, upon one of which Paul traveled to Rome, played a key role in the ancient world. The wheat of Egypt supplied at least a third of the grain necessary to feed the population of Rome. Rome needed to import annually between 200,000 and 400,000 tons to feed its population of about a million." Edwin M. Yamauchi, "On the Road with Paul", *Christian History Magazine*, issue 47: *The Apostle Paul & His Times* (Carol Stream, Ill.: Christianity Today, 1995).

along the Via Maris, the *Way by the Sea* around the Mediterranean
through the Sinai Peninsula and into Egypt. Remembering again
that caravans covered roughly twenty miles per day, it would easily
have taken twelve to thirteen days traveling in each direction. Having passed this way by car and bus many times, I can attest that it
is rugged territory. Water is scarce along the way, and you cannot
drink from the salty Mediterranean.

Keeping his youngest son, Benjamin, home, Jacob sent his ten
sons to Egypt to purchase grain. The last time Jacob had sent a
favored son on a journey, he was thought to have been "ravaged
by beasts". Jacob was taking no chances with Benjamin, who had
replaced Joseph as the favorite son, the other one born of Rachel.
The brothers now had families of their own, and the amount of food
to purchase made it necessary to send all ten sons. It was also a pre-
caution against brigands and thieves along the way. Notice how we
read "ten of Joseph's brothers", not "Joseph's ten brothers", since
one stayed home. In the past they would have been referred to as the
"sons of Jacob" (e.g., Gen 34:7; 35:5), but the anticipated meeting
had changed that—they were now referred to as "the brothers of
Joseph". In verse 5 for the first time they were now called the "sons
of Israel". Rarely are they ever again called the "sons of Jacob" (only
a mere seven times).

JOSEPH RECOGNIZES HIS BROTHERS;
THE BROTHERS' FIRST ORDEAL (42:7–17)

Joining the throngs of foreigners who had come to buy grain, the
ten brothers approached Joseph, who is described as the "seller" and
the "governor" of Egypt (v. 6). His brothers did not recognize him,
which is not surprising, having not seen him for twenty years; he
had matured, was dressed as an Egyptian official with face and head
shaven, and elevated above them. But Joseph recognized his brothers. They were adults, and they were relatively unaltered in their
appearance and mannerisms. The last time he had seen their faces
he had been begging for mercy and they had scoffed. But now the
tables had turned. According to custom, they bowed with their faces to
the ground. One immediately senses the bitter irony here, recalling the
dreams of Joseph as a boy with the sheaves of grain all bowing to

him (37:7–9). The sheaves were bowing as they came to buy sheaves. Joseph remembered his two dreams. The text says Joseph "treated them like strangers and spoke roughly to them", though other translations suggest he disguised himself and spoke harshly with them. Why? He seems to be testing them, but also justly punishing them—tweaking their consciences and teaching them a lesson.

Joseph asked them (roughly), "Where do you come from?" They told him, but he pretended not to trust them; he accused them of being spies who had come to look at the undefended parts of the land. Spying out a land was not uncommon (Josh 2:1; 7:2; Judg 18:2; 1 Sam 26:4). Moses had sent the twelve spies to reconnoiter the Promised Land (Num 13:1–25). The ten brothers profusely denied they were spies, insisting they are "honest men", sons of one father with a younger brother back home. *Honest men?!?!* Even while they were there, their consciences were riddled with guilt and self-accusations for the treachery and lies they had lived with for twenty years. They told Joseph that they had one brother who "was no more"—referring of course to Joseph! This implied he was dead; as far as they were concerned, he *was* dead.

Joseph may have known that both Reuben and Judah had saved his life on that fateful day and that it might have been Simeon, the second oldest who had already proved his treachery in Shechem, who pushed for his death. He continued to insist they were spies, tossing them in prison for three days. They had put him in a dungeon pit, and now they were in prison. He demanded they all remain as prisoners and one would be released to bring back their younger brother. After leaving them in prison for three days, Joseph decided that Simeon would remain as a prisoner, as hostage, until they proved that they were not spies. He sent the others home with orders to fetch the youngest brother, Benjamin, who was his only brother through their beautiful mother, Rachel.

You cannot read this story without wondering how you would have responded to your ten brothers who were in desperate need, approaching you for help after they had callously sold you into slavery. Imagine the swirling conflict of emotions! Unpleasant memories, nostalgia for home, desire to exact revenge, a love for the foolish older brothers, looking for any sign of remorse, sorrow for the agony of his father—the immediate impulse to reveal your identity, all controlled by the wisdom of restraint.

St. John Chrysostom reflects on Joseph's looking for any signs of affection:

> See how he takes every means of putting fear into them so that, on seeing Symeon's bonds, they may reveal whether they manifested any sympathy for their brother. You see, everything he does is to test their attitude out of his wish to discover if they had been like that in dealing with Benjamin. Hence he also had Symeon bound in front of them to test them carefully and see if they showed any signs of affection for him. That is to say, concern for him led them to hasten Benjamin's arrival, which he was anxious for, so as to gain assurance from his brother's arrival.[4]

JOSEPH SENDS THEM HOME WITH ORDERS TO BRING BENJAMIN; SIMEON HELD HOSTAGE (42:18–25)

After three days in prison, Joseph brought them out. Assuming he could not understand them—since he had been communicating through an interpreter—they began to accuse each other and reveal their inner guilt and regret. They attributed their calamity here in Egypt to the fact they had sold their younger brother into slavery in Egypt. They vividly recalled "the distress of his soul, when he begged us and we would not listen, therefore is this distress come upon us" (v. 21). Reuben chided them for refusing to listen to him when he tried to release Joseph: "Did I not tell you not to sin against the lad? But you would not listen. So now there comes a reckoning for his blood" (v. 22). Back in Dothan, the brothers would not listen to Joseph's pleading. Now he was not listening to them as they pleaded for their lives. They had no idea he could understand them as they reflected back on their culpability and sin.

Joseph's reaction revealed the soul of this righteous man. He quickly left their presence and wept. He was emotionally moved by their apparent remorse and distress. He was a man of immense power who could exact justice with just a word. He could have executed them on the spot, but he wept. He would later weep over them

[4] "Homilies on Genesis", 64.11, in John Chrysostom, *Homilies on Genesis 46–67*, trans. Robert C. Hill, The Fathers of the Church, ed. Thomas P. Halton, vol. 87 (Washington, D.C.: The Catholic University of America Press, 1992), 230.

again. Simeon was bound in front of their eyes. The others were sent home with grain to feed their families—with the strict command that they not show their faces in Egypt again without their youngest brother. Then, unbeknownst to them, Joseph had their money replaced inside the sacks of grain.

Why did Joseph select Simeon as the lone brother to stay behind in imprisonment? Two Jewish rabbis and scholars, Rashi (1040–1105) and Ibn Ezra (1089–1167), suggest answers. Rashi: "Simon [was] the one who had thrown him [Joseph] into the pit, the one who had told Levi, 'Here comes that dreamer!' (37:19)." Ibn Ezra: "When a group sins, the oldest of them is punished the most. In this case Reuben was skipped, since he had tried to save him."[5]

St. Caesarius of Arles comments on the righteousness of Joseph's actions and motives:

> If we notice carefully, dearly beloved, we will realize that Joseph did to his brothers what we believe God did to blessed Jacob. Truly, he was so holy that he could not have hated them. Therefore, we must believe that he wearied them with so many tribulations, in order to arouse them to a confession of their sin and the healing of repentance. Finally, with great grief, they said they suffered those ills deservedly, because they had sinned against their brother, "whose anguish of heart they witnessed." Since blessed Joseph knew that his brothers could not be forgiven their sin of murder without much penance, once, twice, and a third time he worried them with salutary trials as with a spiritual fire. His purpose was not to vindicate himself, but to correct them and free them from so grave a sin.[6]

THE BROTHERS TRAVEL HOME AND DISCOVER THEIR SILVER RETURNED TO THEIR SACKS (42:26–38)

Verse 27 mentions a "lodging place". Travelers would often sleep on the ground, but on heavily traveled routes, there were periodic

[5] Michael Carasik, ed. and trans., *Genesis: Introduction and Commentary*, The Commentators' Bible (Philadelphia: Jewish Publication Society, 2018), 378.

[6] Sermon 91.6, in Caesarius of Arles, *Saint Caesarius of Arles: Sermons (1–238)*, ed. Hermigild Dressler and Bernard M. Peebles, trans. Mary Magdeleine Mueller, The Fathers of the Church, vol. 2 (Washington, D.C.: Catholic University of America Press; Consortium Books, 1956–1973), 52.

lodging places to rest and restock water and supplies. Protection from robbers and wild animals was a benefit. It was usually a resting place or night encampment. It can be imagined as a camp full of black tents to protect from the sun, places to water the animals, and mats to sleep for the night.

At the encampment, one of the nine brothers traveling back to Canaan opened his sack and noticed the silver buried in the grain. They trembled and looked at each other, then groaned, "What is this that God has done to us?" They professed to be honest men, but now it appeared they had rustled their silver to defraud the king. Things could not be worse! Simeon was imprisoned; they had to answer for the silver in their bags; Benjamin had to go to Egypt; they had to distress their father with all this bad news—and any resolution was weeks away. When they unloaded their sacks, *all* of them discovered their silver buried in the grain. What would the Lord of Egypt do when they returned, knowing they went home with the silver? The tension builds!

> Coined money was not invented and put into common use until the sixth century B.C. Thus precious metals, gems, spices, incense and other luxury items were bartered by weight. Their relative value would also depend on scarcity. Silver was used throughout antiquity as a common item of exchange. Since Egypt lacked native silver deposits, this metal was particularly desirable as a standard for business transactions.[7]

Precious metals were weighed out and used for payment. "Shekel" is a unit of measurement, only later referring to a coin because it contained a "shekel's worth" of silver or gold. Shekel weights have been discovered from ancient times. There are different-size stones ("weights") with varying weights engraved in the smooth surface. The merchant would place gold or silver pieces of various sizes on one side of the scale and the various "weight" stones on the other to balance out 1, 5, 10, or 20 shekels of silver. The weights would be standardized so no one could cheat, though sometimes they did (cf. Is 46:6; Jer 32:10; Lev 19:36; Prov 16:11; Ezek 45:10; Hos 12:7;

[7] Victor Harold Matthews, Mark W. Chavalas, and John H. Walton, *The IVP Bible Background Commentary: Old Testament*, electronic ed. (Downers Grove, Ill.: InterVarsity Press, 2000), 77.

Amos 8:5; Mic 6:11). The bags of money the brothers used to pay for the grain, and which they found returned to their sacks, were not coins like we know them but rather bags of weighed silver.

The brothers recounted the whole story to their father, Jacob, except that the king had threatened their lives (v. 20). Jacob was informed that Pharaoh considered them spies and required the proof of a young brother to test their honesty. Jacob couldn't bear the thought of losing his only remaining son of Rachel. He said Joseph was gone, Simeon was gone, and now you want me to lose Benjamin as well? He retorted that Benjamin would *not* go to Egypt! If harm befell Benjamin, Jacob said his gray hair would go down to Sheol in sorrow. *Gray hair* is literally "a head that is old and gray", synonymous with old age. *Sheol* was the underworld or the abode of the dead.

Little did Jacob know that God was sitting in his heaven providentially directing history to save the whole family and fulfill his promise to Abraham. As the *Catechism* powerfully reminds us, God in his universal power is called the "Mighty One of Jacob" and the "Lord of Hosts" and "the strong and mighty". He is not only the lord of heaven but also the master of history, governing hearts and minds to do his will (see *CCC* 269).

Joseph had spoken correctly—the horrendous famine continued unabated. They were in the second year of the famine with five years to go (Gen 45:6)! Farmers scraped the last of the seeds from the storage room floors—no seeds were left to plant next year. If you eat your sheep and goats, where will the new baby lambs and kids come from? If a famine ravages the land for years, not only do crops die but there is no food for the flocks.

We are not told how many donkeys the ten brothers took, though it appears they had one donkey per man (see Gen 44:11–13). Donkeys can carry an amazing amount of weight—up to one-third of their body weight for fifteen to twenty miles a day. If a small donkey weighs three hundred pounds, it can carry one hundred pounds of weight, though many are larger and expected to carry much more. They are sturdy, rugged animals that can do a prodigious amount of work. They could conceivably have brought home over a thousand pounds of grain combined. Used as the main staple for ten growing families and all the animals, it would not last long (Gen 42:27).

CHAPTER 43

JOSEPH'S BROTHERS BRING BENJAMIN
BACK TO EGYPT

FAMINE RAGES; JACOB REFUSES TO
SEND BENJAMIN (43:1–10)

The famine dragged on; the grain ran out. Israel refused to send Benjamin, but hunger was an unrelenting motivator. The sons refused to go without Benjamin, saying, "The man solemnly warned us, saying, 'You shall not see my face, unless your brother is with you' (43:5)." Israel was forced to relent, and he sent Benjamin with his sons back to Egypt. Israel was furious that they had revealed the existence of Benjamin. But the brothers explained that the man had asked many questions as if he knew the family. "[C]ould we in any way know that he would say, 'Bring your brother down'?"

Judah stepped forward and warned that all of them, including their little ones, would starve if they did not act quickly. Here we learn that many grandchildren had been added to the clan. Judah used legal terminology to convince his father. He accepted the legal responsibility and promised to be personally accountable for the return of Benjamin. Israel finally acquiesced and sent Benjamin along with his brothers. Israel was grieved and asked for God's mercy to bring them all back, along with Benjamin and "your other brother". He did not call Simeon by name or even say "my son". "Judah's plan succeeds where Reuben's had failed (42:37–38). This is another indication that one function of the Joseph story is to explain why Joseph (the dominant tribe of the North) and Judah (the royal tribe of the South) became more important than Reuben (the first-born)."[1]

[1] Adele Berlin, Marc Zvi Brettler, and Michael Fishbane, eds., *The Jewish Study Bible* (New York: Oxford University Press, 2004), 86.

JACOB RELENTS AND PREPARES GIFTS FOR EGYPT (43:11–14)

Israel surely recalled preparing gifts to appease his brother Esau years ago and now shrewdly sent gifts to "the man", but this time it was not from his flocks because it would have been too difficult and time-consuming to move the flocks over 250 miles. The gifts were "choice fruits of the land" (cf. Ezek 27:17). The word is found four times in Scripture, here translated as "fruits of the land" and the other three times as "song" (Ex 15:2; Ps 118:14; Is 12:2). As some rabbis taught, "they are items whose praises are widely sung" or "products that themselves 'sing the praises' of the land".[2] Others translate it *strong* (the best or strongest).

The list of gifts is interesting. The first on the list is honey, commonly found in Israel. Hives can be seen across the countryside. Samson found honey in the carcass of a lion (Judg 14:8), and John the Baptist ate "wild honey" (Mt 3:4). Israel is described as "the land of milk and honey" twenty-three times. The gifts included gum, myrrh, pistachio nuts, and almonds—a list similar to the transport of the Ishmaelites when Joseph was sold into slavery (37:25).

With double the silver, the special gifts, and their brother Benjamin, they journeyed back to Egypt. They intended to prove their honesty by returning the silver and by bringing their brother. In verse 14, Israel again appealed to *El Shaddai*, God Almighty (Gen 17:1; 28:3; 35:11).

THE BROTHERS ARRIVE BACK IN EGYPT (43:15–30)

When Joseph saw his brothers, especially Benjamin—his one and only full-blooded brother from the same mother, Rachel, the only one not involved in the treachery perpetrated against him—he was deeply moved. Joseph commanded his steward to slaughter an animal for a feast at noon, to bring the men into the house, have their feet washed, and their donkeys tended (v. 24). The men were to dine with him.

[2] Michael Carasik, ed. and trans., *Genesis: Introduction and Commentary*, The Commentators' Bible (Philadelphia: Jewish Publication Society, 2018), 382.

The brothers just wanted to get more food, get Simeon, and head home with Benjamin. But now it was getting inexplicably more complicated. They thought it was a setup to ensnare them. The brothers were terrified that they were being unjustly accused to force them into slavery and confiscate their donkeys (v. 18). Before entering, they secretly confided in the steward of Joseph's house (they address him as "my lord") and tried to enlist him in their defense, explaining their plight. He amazed them by telling them the money was from God since he himself had received their payment in full on their last trip. Simeon was then released and brought to them.

St. Ambrose discerns spiritual parallels:

> And they began to desire to plead their case to the man who was steward of the house at the door of the house. They still hesitate to enter in and prefer to be justified from their works, for they desire to prove a case rather than to receive grace and so they are refuted at the gates. But the man who awaits the fruit of the virgin's womb and the inheritance of the Lord is dealing in the goods of the Son and is not ashamed at the gate.[3]

JOSEPH PREPARES A FEAST (43:31–34)

They were taken to Joseph's private dwelling. With extreme nervousness, they prepared to present their gifts. This is the same word *minhah* used for the gift, present, or "tribute" Jacob prepared for his brother Esau when leaving Haran (33:10). When Joseph arrived home, they presented the gifts and immediately "bowed down to him to the ground". Again, the irony of the brothers bowing to Joseph in accord with the "dreamer's" dreams back in Canaan. In Eastern lands, respect for a sovereign required prostration with face to the ground. "Bowing himself to the ground seven times: according to the Tell El-Amarna tablets (government documents sent from Syria and Palestine to Egypt some thirteen centuries before Christ), local chiefs were required to bow seven times before the kings of Egypt."[4]

---

[3] *Joseph*, 9.48, in Ambrose of Milan, *Seven Exegetical Works*, ed. Bernard M. Peebles, trans. Michael P. McHugh, The Fathers of the Church, vol. 65 (Washington, D.C.: Catholic University of America Press, 1972), 221.

[4] William David Reyburn and Euan McG. Fry, *A Handbook on Genesis*, UBS Handbook Series (New York: United Bible Societies, 1998), 772.

Joseph—to them the mighty Vizier of Egypt—asked about their welfare, requesting specific information about their father. They answered, then bowed to the ground again. What a contrast between uncultured shepherds from the desert in the regal home of the Vizier of Egypt presenting their paltry gifts and quaking in their sandals. Joseph held back his emotions while gazing on his brother Benjamin. Joseph had not seen his younger brother for twenty-five years. One short sentence to Benjamin sent him rushing from the room to weep in his chamber. Joseph had a godly and tender heart.

As an aside, I would note that a number of the Church Fathers saw Benjamin as a type or prefiguration of Saint Paul, not least of all because Paul was from the tribe of Benjamin (Rom 11:1). The original apostles went out into the world first to gather the harvest of the Gentiles back home, but it was Paul who was the latecomer (1 Cor 15:8), not going with them at first but only later in the ministry. Saint Quodvultdeus (fl. 430) was a Carthaginian bishop and friend of Augustine who delighted in illuminating the New Testament using the Old.

> Hearing people talk about his brother, Joseph longed for him and said, "I will prove in this manner that you are not spies, if your younger brother comes along with you." And taking Simeon from them he had him bound before him and sent him to prison. If you want to know who is Benjamin, our younger brother, desired by our Joseph, that is, Christ, he is Paul, formerly Saul, from the tribe of Benjamin according to his testimony, who asserts to be the least among the apostles. In Simeon we can recognize Peter bound by the threefold chain of denial, that Peter whom fear has bound and love has untied.[5]

Joseph washed his face and, "controlling himself", said, "Let food be served." The feast prepared by the culinary chefs of Egypt was like nothing they had ever seen or tasted before. Joseph sat apart from the brothers, as was the custom of the Egyptians. Foreigners were loathsome to Egyptians—much like Gentiles were loathsome to the Jews (cf. Acts 10:28). Joseph's separation was a matter of custom since "Egyptians might not eat bread with the Hebrews, for that is an

---

[5] "Book of Promises and Predictions of God", 1.30.42, in Mark Sheridan, *Genesis 12–50*, Ancient Christian Commentary on Scripture, OT 2 (Downers Grove, Ill.: InterVarsity Press, 2002), 277.

abomination to Egyptians" (v. 32). Joseph's separation was also due to rank.

Joseph had prepared a seating arrangement, from the oldest to the youngest. The brothers were aghast—how could he know the order of their births? They were served portions from Joseph's table. They ate the food of royalty prepared by the cupbearer and royal baker. Benjamin received five times more food than the others. They ate, and the last line of chapter 43 says, "they drank and were merry with him." That is, they drank wine and made merry with the Vizier, who had, for unknown reasons, shown such an interest in these rustic Hebrew shepherds. The Hebrew word for *merry* is literally "to drink freely, become drunk or intoxicated". When the evening was over, they were completely unprepared for what would happen the next morning after their hangovers wore off.

CHAPTER 44

JOSEPH TESTS HIS BROTHERS
AND DETAINS BENJAMIN

JOSEPH SENDS HIS BROTHERS HOME BUT
PREPARES A FINAL TEST (44:1–13)

After dinner was over, Joseph commanded the steward of his house
to set up his brothers for the worst scenario they could possibly have
imagined. His instructions were to fill the men's sacks overflowing
with grain, put their silver back in each sack, and, most incriminating
of all, he was to put Joseph's silver cup in Benjamin's sack—the special silver cup used for divination (44:5).[1] Their earlier treachery with
Joseph broke their father's heart. Now his remaining cherished son is
poised for the slaughter which would, as Jacob had said, "bring down
my gray hair to Sheol". They would anguish over Benjamin as they
should have grieved over Joseph. He would see if they had learned
virtue or if they remained callous rogues. The next day, they finally
embarked on the journey home with food, Simeon and Benjamin,
and their freedom.

Concerning the returned silver, as mentioned before, "silver
money" was actually silver small pieces, or even coin-like shapes. The

---

[1] "The cup that Joseph plants in Benjamin's sack is identified as being used for divination.
Just as tea leaves are read today, the ancients read omens by means of liquid in cups. One
mechanism involved the pouring of oil onto water to see what shapes it would take (called
lecanomancy).... Lecanomancy was used in the time of Joseph, as is attested by several Old
Babylonian omen texts concerned with the various possible configurations of the oil and their
interpretations." Victor Harold Matthews, Mark W. Chavalas, and John H. Walton, *The IVP
Bible Background Commentary: Old Testament*, electronic ed. (Downers Grove, Ill.: InterVarsity
Press, 2000), Gen 44:5. This kind of divination was later forbidden by God in the Law of
Moses (Lev 19:26; Deut 18:10).

last time *keseph* was used for silver money was when the brothers sold
Joseph to the Ishmaelites for twenty pieces of "silver money" (*keseph*)
in Genesis 37:28. It is *very* interesting that during the brothers' interaction with Joseph on their trips to Egypt, the word *keseph* was used
exactly twenty times! They had sold him for twenty pieces of silver,
and now the silver used to ensnare and convict them was mentioned
twenty times! But there is a similar interesting observation.

> The first time, when ten brothers come to Egypt, Joseph imprisons
> Simeon, and he has their silver placed back in their *nine* sacks. The
> second time, when they return with Benjamin, Joseph releases Sim-
> eon, and he has their silver placed back in their *eleven* sacks. The total
> number of portions of silver returned is *twenty*, corresponding to the
> price that was paid for Joseph (37:28). It is yet another case of a hidden
> link between acts of deception and their payback in later events.[2]

Joseph instructed his steward to pursue his brothers and accuse them
of returning evil for good! His soldiers overtook and surrounded
the brothers, while the steward looked disdainfully at them all. Very
dramatic scene for the brothers! He accused them of stealing Joseph's
silver cup with these words, "Why have you returned evil for good?
Why have you stolen my silver cup? Is it not from this that my lord
drinks, and by this that he divines? You have done wrong in so
doing" (vv. 4–5). They were stunned and vociferously denied the
accusation. Knowing they did not steal the cup, they offered that
if the cup were found in any sack, the owner of that sack would
die and the remaining ten would become slaves. They were confident. The sons of Israel lowered each man his bag for the steward
to search. There is no mention of the silver that must have been
found in each sack. You can imagine the collective sighs of relief
after each subsequent sack from the oldest to the youngest failed to
produce the silver cup—until lastly, and suddenly, utter shock and
devastation as the cup was pulled from young Benjamin's sack. After
tearing their clothes in grief (cf. Gen 37:29, 34), they returned *again*
to the city.

---

[2] Richard Elliott Friedman, *Commentary on the Torah* (San Francisco: HarperSanFrancisco,
2003), 145.

BENJAMIN IS DETAINED AS A THIEF (44:14–17)

The next twenty-one verses relay in detail Judah's impassioned appeal, and a sense of empathy is unavoidable. Judah stepped forward to take responsibility for Benjamin, even offering his own servitude in exchange for the young man—all the more poignant since Judah was the one who had suggested they sell Joseph, their other younger brother, as a slave (37:26–27). Likely Joseph remembered watching on as Judah negotiated his own sale to the Ishmaelites. Now Judah was willing to become a slave himself to defend his *new* youngest brother.

Joseph accused Benjamin of theft, and they expected death or slavery as Joseph had promised earlier. Before his imposing regalia, they melted and fell on their faces. Before they could speculate on how the Vizier could have known about the cup, Joseph said, "Do you not know that such a man as I can indeed divine?" (v. 15). The suggestion is that divination informed him of their subterfuge. He had them right where he wanted them. He watched their faces to learn if they were just afraid or had genuine contrition, taking personal responsibility for their evil.

JUDAH MAKES AN IMPASSIONED PLEA FOR HIS BROTHER BENJAMIN (44:18–34)

In the longest speech contained in Genesis, Judah poured out his heart to "the man" who was presumably sitting on his raised throne looking down at them. The scene begins with "Judah and his brothers", no longer just "the brothers". Judah acted as the supplicating defense attorney with all the circumstantial evidence against him. He took the responsibility (he had promised himself as surety to his father regarding Benjamin) and now acted as the spokesman for the ten. Judah acknowledged that "God has found out the guilt of your servants", which in the immediate context would be interpreted as culpability for the stolen cup (v. 16). But we and Joseph know the admission regards the dark and unmentionable family secret— the suppressed treachery against their never-mentioned but never-forgotten brother Joseph. Joseph refused Judah's offer to all become slaves, ruling that only the implicated brother become a slave. The rest could return to their father in peace.

What was going through their minds, offering themselves as slaves? Were they putting two and two together—was this finally payback for their maltreatment of Joseph? And what about the promises of God to Abraham, Isaac, and their devastated father, Israel? How would the promise now be fulfilled? Their sin weighed heavy. Judah used the title "lord" nine times in addressing Joseph.

A few chapters ago, we were disgusted with these brothers and wanted to see them severely punished, especially Judah, who had come up with the idea of selling Joseph. Now they were receiving the just desserts for their wickedness. But the newfound humility is appealing; it softens our hearts—and the heart of Joseph and God. God responds to the contrite and repentant soul (Lk 18:13–14).

Judah was willing to sacrifice himself for his father and younger brother. Judah poured out his soul, but fell short of a full confession of their crime. It was buried in their souls and too painful and dangerous to confess. Judah began with an appeal for his aged father. Unbeknownst to him, nothing could have touched the heart of the Grand Vizier more deeply. He told of the father's son who was dead (unaware that Joseph knew every detail and that he was not dead). He recounted the earlier interviews with Joseph and how Benjamin became part of the negotiations and how even the thought of losing Benjamin was inconceivable to their old father. He divulged the words of his father, "You know that my wife bore me two sons; one left me, and I said, Surely he has been torn to pieces; and I have never seen him since. If you take this one also from me, and harm befalls him, you will bring down my gray hairs in sorrow to Sheol" (vv. 27–29). Judah did not tell the full story of what befell Joseph.

Like an impassioned and terrified defense attorney, Judah concluded his desperate closing remarks by informing his judge that he was surety for Benjamin and offered his life in exchange for the lad. He humbly pleaded, "Now therefore, let your servant, I beg you, remain instead of the lad as a slave to my lord; and let the lad go back with his brothers. For how can I go back to my father if the lad is not with me? I fear to see the evil that would come upon my father."

What a change of heart from their younger days. He had been quite willing to return home to his bereaved father with Joseph's bloody robe twenty-five years earlier. Was it by chance that it would be Judah's future descendant Jesus Christ who would offer his life to save his brothers, and the world? "The Son of man did not come to be served, but to serve, and to give his life as a ransom for many" (Mt 20:28). St. Paul, a descendant of Benjamin, wrote, "Christ Jesus, who, though he was in the form of God, did not count equality with God a thing to be grasped, but emptied himself, taking the form of a servant, being born in the likeness of men. And being found in human form he humbled himself and became obedient unto death, even death on a cross" (Phil 2:5–8).

CHAPTER 45

JOSEPH REVEALS HIMSELF AND DEALS KINDLY WITH HIS BROTHERS

JOSEPH MOVED TO TEARS AGAIN (45:1–2)

We have reached the climax of this epic saga. We have been let in on the secret of Joseph's identity, but his brothers are still in the dark. The brothers await the outcome—will the Vizier of Egypt forgive and accept, or enslave and kill? Joseph does not find it easy to chide his brothers.

> Mercy takes over Joseph when he sees his innocent brother; but he contrives to keep a stern face, in order to cleanse them of their evil.... What sufferings does mercy not bring with it! It punishes yet it loves. That holy man pardons and punishes his brothers' crime: clemency is contained in the punishment; though he has mercy, his brothers who have sinned do not go unpunished; and though he is just, they are not left without mercy. This is a good example of how to exercise authority: it shows how to pardon faults and yet punish them mercifully.[1]

Joseph could not control himself. He cleared the chamber to be alone with his unwitting brothers. For the third time, the great leader of Egypt was overcome with emotion and wept, this time in the presence of his brothers and so loudly that even the Egyptians outside could hear him. The medieval Jewish scholar Ramban believed Joseph removed everyone from the room to prevent them from hearing the awful truth about his brothers:

---

[1] Saint Gregory the Great, *Homiliae in Ezechielem*, 2, 9, 19, in James Gavigan, Brian Mc-Carthy, and Thomas McGovern, eds., *The Pentateuch*, The Navarre Bible (Dublin and New Jersey: Four Courts Press; Scepter Publishers, 1999), 206.

He cried out. Out loud, angrily. Have everyone withdraw from me! Except for these men. He did not want them to hear when he reminded his brothers about how they had sold him, which could make trouble for his brothers and for himself, too. Pharaoh's servants and the other Egyptians would say, "These treacherous men must not stay in our country nor 'tread upon our fortresses' [Mic. 5:4]. They betrayed their brother and their father, too. What will they do to our king and our people?!" They would not believe in Joseph any longer, either.[2]

Joseph wanted his family to be accepted, not despised. Or maybe he wanted the intimate family reunion to be private.

JOSEPH REVEALS HIS IDENTITY TO HIS BROTHERS; EXPLAINS GOD'S PLAN (45:3–8)

Joseph's courtiers, fan-wavers, attendants, cupbearer, scribes, steward— his whole entourage, all those who waited on him hand and foot would not share this private moment and the impending revelation. They quickly rose and left the room. This was the pinnacle moment. The emotional tension had been building! During the months leading up to this moment, he had tested his brothers. He had searched their souls, their motives, and their honesty. The emotion could no longer be contained. The Grand Vizier of Egypt, "the man" who had caused dread in their lives, while saving their lives, said through his tears, "I am Joseph; is my father still alive?"[3]

How long did they stand frozen in disbelief and utter fear? The English word "dismayed" is the Hebrew word *banal*, which means terrified, horrified, out of one's senses, bewildered, panicked, trembling with fear. They had had no clue how serious this *really* was.

---

[2] Michael Carasik, ed. and trans., *Genesis: Introduction and Commentary*, The Commentators' Bible (Philadelphia: Jewish Publication Society, 2018), 394.

[3] In October 1960, Pope Saint John XXIII used this passage to greet a Jewish delegation of 130—Joseph being the pope's baptismal name, "I am Joseph, your brother", said Pope John XXIII to Jewish visitors. But even earlier, on September 6, 1938, Pius XI had asserted, "Anti-Semitism is unacceptable. Spiritually, we are all Semites." Stephen Ray and R. Dennis Walters, *The Papacy: What the Pope Does and Why It Matters* (San Francisco: Ignatius Press, 2018), 112.

Their whole world collapsed at these three short words—"I am Joseph!" The scene back at Dothan rushed back, their ghastly memories were like a horrible nightmare—Joseph pleading for his life. They remembered his pleas, the blood, the tears, the guilt, their dismayed father, the decades of suppressed memories, the constant fear of God's retaliation. This was *Joseph!* Never in their wildest imagination did they dream he was still alive, much less the Ruler of Egypt!

And now what? He had every right to get his revenge, to torture them, kill them, or make them slaves. He had every power and authority to punish them. God had found them out. Now their father would learn the awful truth they had kept buried while perpetuating the lie, with fears that someday one of them would slip and the awful truth would spill out to condemn them all. The truth was out; the tragic sin was finally revealed. They had been dying inside for twenty years. Those few moments must have seemed like a lifetime as conflicting thoughts and fears, relief and terror all rushed them at once.

Joseph asked in the same breath about his father. They did not answer. They stood there dumbfounded in the presence of their brother. He called them to come close. He said, "I am your brother, Joseph, whom you sold into Egypt." He obviously saw the terror on their faces. Now we see mercy and love richly displayed as from the heart of God. Joseph, probably still weeping, surprised them with his gentle forgiveness and blessing—"Do not be distressed, or angry with yourselves, because you sold me here; for God sent me before you to preserve life" (cf. Gen 50:20). God is able to make all things work together for his purposes (Rom 8:28). God in his almighty providence can bring good out of evil. Where sin abounds, grace does even more abound (Rom 5:20–21). The *Catechism* reminds us of this truth:

> In time we can discover that God in his almighty providence can bring a good from the consequences of an evil, even a moral evil, caused by his creatures: "It was not you," said Joseph to his brothers, "who sent me here, but God.... You meant evil against me; but God meant it for good, to bring it about that many people should be kept alive." From the greatest moral evil ever committed—the rejection

and murder of God's only Son, caused by the sins of all men—God, by his grace that "abounded all the more," brought the greatest of goods: the glorification of Christ and our redemption. But for all that, evil never becomes a good (*CCC* 312; see also *CCC* 313–14).[4]

Jesus was sold into bondage, too, sent to the cross, and killed as less than a slave. The Jewish leaders and the Romans killed him, not realizing the magnitude of their actions. Even at the time of his execution, Jesus said, "Father, forgive them; for they know not what they do" (Lk 23:34). At the end of time, those who have sinned grievously (all of us) and who have been transformed by grace will be tested, too, but afterward, if we are genuinely transformed by God's grace and repentant, we will have shown to us the same mercy and kindness experienced by these guilty brothers of Joseph. The outcome with Joseph may have been very different had there been no remorse or humility on their part. Had they been unrepentant, callous toward their father and brother Benjamin, Joseph might have responded differently.

St. Ambrose elucidates:

And lifting up his voice with weeping he said, "I am Joseph. Is my father still alive?" This means, He stretched out His hands to an unbelieving and contradicting people, for He did not seek an envoy or messenger but, as their very Lord, desired to save His own people. "I myself who spoke, I am here," and "I was made manifest to those who sought me not, I appear to those who asked me not." What else did He cry out at that time but "I am Jesus"? ... "[H]ereafter you shall see the Son of Man sitting at the right hand of the Power and coming upon the clouds of heaven." This is what he means when he says, "I am Joseph" (*On Joseph*, 12.67).[5]

After Joseph's emotional revelation, he revealed the plan for the survival of the family. Joseph, the wise steward of Egypt's survival, was

---

[4] Catholic Church, *Catechism of the Catholic Church*, 2nd ed. (Vatican City: Libreria Editrice Vaticana, 1997), 82–83.

[5] *On Joseph* 12.67, in Ambrose of Milan, *Seven Exegetical Works*, ed. Bernard M. Peebles, trans. Michael P. McHugh, The Fathers of the Church, vol. 65 (Washington, D.C.: Catholic University of America Press, 1972), 228–29.

now saving the progeny of Abraham, Isaac, and Jacob. This was the ultimate purpose of his rise to power in Egypt in the first place. Notice the partner phrases, "You sold ...but God sent" (v. 5). During Joseph's long explanation, the dumbstruck brothers did not say a word. Only after eleven long verses (vv. 3–13) did his brothers dare to speak (v. 15).

JOSEPH INVITES HIS WHOLE FAMILY TO LIVE IN EGYPT (45:9–15)

It was only the second year of the seven-year famine. Things would get far worse. Joseph would send them back to their father with news of "all my splendor in Egypt" and with orders to come to Egypt. Jacob and the families would settle in Goshen in northern Egypt, called Lower Egypt. The Nile River originates from Lake Victoria in Kenya, Uganda, and Tanzania. Today it runs through or along the borders of ten eastern African countries and north through Egypt until it spreads into the distributaries of the Nile Delta before emptying into the Mediterranean Sea. The Nile Delta is fertile and well-watered, lush and green. While visiting this delta, we have been impressed with the crops, the water canals, the greenery, and the ubiquitous donkey carts still moving grain and food back and forth in the streets. Joseph gave his family the finest land in Egypt. He fell on Benjamin's neck and wept, and Benjamin wept on his neck. He embraced them all. Now for the first time since the revelation, they spoke with Joseph.

JOSEPH SENDS HIS BROTHERS HOME TO GET JACOB AND THEIR FAMILIES (45:16–28)

Pharaoh wondered what the commotion was all about—his Vizier weeping so loudly everyone could hear him. He was pleased when he learned that Joseph's family had come from Canaan. He confirmed Joseph's promise even more, commanding them to take wagons from Egypt to transport back the little ones and the wives—and to bring their father as well. They would need nothing. The best of the land would be theirs (vv. 19–20). In Hebrew the emphasis is on "You are commanded." What an astounding turn of events!

They were all dressed in "festal garments" (v. 22). In days gone by, Joseph alone wore a festal garment given to him by his father. Not resenting his brothers for deceiving his father with his blood-ied robe, Joseph now gave all of his brothers their *own* festal robes. Benjamin received five! They had stripped off Joseph's special robe before sending him a slave *to* Egypt; now he stripped off their beg-garly clothes, dressing them royally to send them *from* Egypt. He gave Benjamin "three hundred of silver" remembering that the word *shekel* is not in the Hebrew text (v. 22). If we calculate a piece of sil-ver as roughly a shekel of weight, it would equal 7.6 pounds of silver. Joseph had been sold for only twenty pieces of silver. Three hundred pieces was enough to buy fifteen slaves.

Joseph sent his father ten donkeys loaded with good things from Egypt. The brothers had speculated that Joseph was plotting to steal *their* donkeys (43:18), but now he gave them additional don-keys loaded with grain, bread, and provisions to bring their father back. Knowing his brothers all too well, he told them not to quarrel among themselves along the way. He was now acting as their "elder brother" and warning them about their conduct. A lot of blame and accusations could be flung around.

Their return home was glorious, as they informed Jacob that Joseph was still alive and ruler of all Egypt. There is no mention of their confessing to their father their earlier treachery. Joseph perhaps knew. Jacob could not believe it, and his heart fainted literally, his heart froze, turned cold, was paralyzed or numb. When he had heard all they reported and seen the wagons Joseph had sent, his spirit revived. Israel said, "It is enough; Joseph my son is still alive; I will go and see him before I die" (v. 28).

The family secret had been exposed (between Joseph and his broth-ers), the "dead" brother found, starvation averted, and the elderly father would see his long-lost son before he died. Comparing Joseph the ruler with Jesus Christ, St. Ambrose writes:

> Scripture says that He is alive and ruler of the whole land, for He opened His storehouses of spiritual grace and gave the abundance to all men.... [I]t is written of Jacob, "He was greatly frightened

in heart," for he did not believe his sons. He was greatly frightened
from love of an unbelieving people, but afterward he came to recognize Christ's deeds; won over by the mighty benefactions and mighty
works, he revived and said, "It is a great thing for me, if my son
Joseph is still alive. I will go and see him, before I die." The first and
greatest foundation of faith is belief in the resurrection of Christ. For
whosoever believes Christ has been restored to life, quickly searches
for Him, comes to Him with devotion, and worships God with his
inmost heart. Indeed, he believes that he himself will not die if he has
belief in the Source of his resurrection. (*On Joseph*, 13.79–80)[6]

---

[6] Ibid., 234–35.

CHAPTER 46

JACOB AND FAMILY MOVE TO EGYPT;
JACOB AND JOSEPH REUNITED

INTRODUCTION

We near the end of the Age of the Patriarchs. Abraham and Isaac
were buried in the cave of Machpelah in Hebron, and the last of
the patriarchs was packing to leave the Promised Land. A short visit
it was not. It was the beginning of four hundred years in a land not
their own; oppression would overtake them as foretold to Abraham
(15:13). Abraham had fled to Egypt to survive a famine at the beginning of his sojourning (Gen 12:10); his grandson Jacob was now fleeing to Egypt during a famine at the end of his sojourning. Abraham's
saga had begun with a divine revelation and promise; Jacob's ended
the same way. God would speak to Jacob as he left the Promised
Land for Egypt. His people would not hear from God again until he
introduced himself by name to Moses four hundred and thirty years
later (Ex 12:40–41). These last five chapters of Genesis close the curtain on the Age of the Patriarchs and open a whole new chapter in
God's work among his people.

Jacob's father, Isaac, had been forbidden to go into Egypt (Gen
26:2) or to set foot out of Canaan. Jacob was leery of leaving. He may
have recalled his grandfather's words of enslavement for four hundred
years (Gen 15:13). "As the [Jewish] Passover *Haggadah* puts it, 'Our
father Jacob did not come down to strike roots in Egypt but only to
sojourn there'."[1] Jacob's family would sojourn in Egypt, but God
would bring them back (Gen 15:13–14; Hos 1:11; Mt 2:15). It was

---

[1] Adele Berlin, Marc Zvi Brettler, and Michael Fishbane, eds., *The Jewish Study Bible* (New
York: Oxford University Press, 2004), 91.

393

too soon for God to deliver Canaan over to the sons of Israel. First, the iniquity of the Amorites (Canaanites) was not yet complete (Gen 15:16). Second, the sons of Israel were too few in number to conquer the land. In Egypt they would become a mighty people.

JACOB OVERCOMES HIS HESITANCY
AND LEAVES FOR EGYPT (46:1)

Jacob packed all his belongings and family in the carts and on the donkeys provided by Joseph to travel twenty-five miles from Hebron southwest to Beersheba toward Egypt (Gen 37:14; 46:1). Some suggest hesitancy restrained him. An ancient Jewish document entitled the *Book of Jubilees* ("The Little Genesis"), written about 200 B.C., suggests Jacob hesitated:

> Israel set out from Hebron, from his house, on the first of the third month. He went by way of the well of the oath [Beersheba] and offered a sacrifice to the God of his father Isaac on the seventh of this month. When Jacob remembered the dream that he had seen in Bethel, he was afraid to go down to Egypt. But as he was thinking about sending word to Joseph that he should come to him and that he would not go down, he remained there for seven days on the chance that he would see a vision (about) whether he should remain or go down.... On the sixteenth the Lord appeared to him and said to him, "Jacob, Jacob." He said, "Yes?" He said to him, "I am the God of your fathers—the God of Abraham and Isaac. Do not be afraid to go down to Egypt because I will make you into a great nation there. I will go down with you and will lead you (back). You will be buried in this land, and Joseph will place his hands on your eyes. Do not be afraid; go down to Egypt."[2]

According to the medieval Jewish scholar Ramban:

> This verse contains a secret, which the Rabbis revealed to us.... When Jacob was about to go down to Egypt he saw that the exile was

---

[2]James C. VanderKam, *Jubilees: A Commentary on the Book of Jubilees, Chapters 1–50*, ed. Sidnie White Crawford, Hermeneia—A Critical and Historical Commentary on the Bible, vols. 1 & 2 (Minneapolis, Minn.: Fortress Press, 2018), 1087.

beginning for him and his children, and he feared it, and so he offered many sacrifices to *the Fear of his father Isaac* and in order that Divine judgment should not be aimed against him. This he did in Beer-sheba which was a place of prayer for his father, and from there he had taken permission when he went to Haran.[3]

GOD APPEARS TO JACOB IN A VISION (46:2–4)

Jacob offered sacrifices to "the God of his father Isaac". It does not say he built an altar, which lends support to the idea the altar may have been built earlier by Isaac (26:25). God spoke to Jacob in a vision; he responded like his grandfather Abraham (22:1) and like he had earlier, "Here I am!" (Gen 31:11). God permitted Jacob to go to Egypt without fear. God promised to go with him and make his descendants a great nation. "Go with" does not simply mean to shadow him but that he would escort, protect, and be present to him. He affirmed that Jacob would die in Egypt, which is stated in a compassionate manner, literally, "Joseph will put his hand upon your eyes." Even today it is the custom among Jews for a family member to close the eyes of the dead. There are many examples of this custom in classical literature.[4]

Jacob would die in peace with Joseph and his family around him. God also promised, "I will also bring you up again" (v. 4). God would bring the whole people out of Egypt and back up to Canaan. Jacob's bodily remains would be buried in the cave of Machpelah with Abraham and Sarah, Isaac and Rebekah, and Leah (Gen 50:12–14). Their six tombs can be visited to this day.

Origen (ca. 185–ca. 254), the great biblical scholar, sees deep spiritual meaning in God's announcement that he would recall Israel from Egypt in the end:

---

[3] Rabbi Dr. Charles Chavel, *Ramban Commentary on the Torah* (New York: Shilo Publishing House, 1999), 542.

[4] One negative example is found in Homer's *Iliad*, "And he fell with a thud, and goodly Odysseus exulted over him: 'Ah Socus ... poor wretch, thy father and queenly mother shall not close thine eyes in death, but the birds that eat raw flesh shall rend thee'" (Hom. *Il.* xi. 453). Homer, *Iliad*, ed. G. P. Goold, trans. A. T. Murray, Loeb Classical Library, vol. 1 (Cambridge, Mass.; London: Harvard University Press; William Heinemann, 1924), 515.

But regarding the statement: "I will recall you from there in the end," I think this means, as we said above, that at the end of the ages his only begotten Son descended even into the nether regions for the salvation of the world and recalled "the first-formed man" from there. For what he said to the thief, "This day you shall be with me in paradise," understand not to have been said to him alone, but also to all the saints for whom he had descended into the nether regions. In this man, therefore, more truly than in Jacob the words "I will recall you from there in the end," will be fulfilled. But each of us also, in the same manner and in the same way, enters Egypt and struggles and, if he be worthy that God should always remain with him, he will make him "into a great nation."[5]

God promises to go down to Egypt with Jacob. In those days, "gods" were considered territorial; that is, they were thought to belong to an area of land. The gods of Egypt were territorial to that land, the gods of Moab and Ammon ruled over their particular kingdoms. Baal was the god of Phoenicia and Canaan. Even the God of Israel was thought to be the God "in Israel". But Yahweh is not limited to any particular territory—he is the eternal God who created and owns the whole world![6] He was with Abraham in Mesopotamia, with Joseph in Egypt, with Moses in Sinai, and with Elijah in Phoenicia. The Israelites kept limiting their God; failing to realize Yahweh is the God above all gods, the Creator of the universe and not territorially restricted.

THE JOURNEY TO EGYPT (46:5–7)

Jacob had walked thousands of miles in his lifetime, but now "the sons of Israel carried Jacob their father" along with their little ones

---

[5] Homily 15.5–6, in Origen, *Homilies on Genesis and Exodus*, ed. Hermigild Dressler, trans. Ronald E. Heine, The Fathers of the Church, vol. 71 (Washington, D.C.: Catholic University of America Press, 1982), 211–12.

[6] "This choice of the land contrasts significantly with the predominant ideas of other peoples in the ancient world, in which the deity or divinities were usually bound to a particular parcel of ground outside of which they lost their effectiveness or reality. Although some such concepts may very well have crept into Israelite thought during the period of the kings (from Saul to Jehoiachin), the crisis of the Babylonian Exile was met by a renewal of the affirmation that the God of Israel was, as Lord of all the earth, free from territorial restraint, though he had chosen a particular territory for this chosen people." *Encyclopedia Britannica* (Chicago, Ill.: Encyclopædia Britannica, [1981] 2016), 10:288.

and their wives. With them were his sons, his daughters, and all of his offspring. They rode in bumpy four-wheeled carts with wooden wheels and no suspension system usually pulled by slow-moving oxen. Earlier we had surmised that families with flocks and children could cover six miles in a day. Even if we stretch it to ten miles a day, it would have taken the large family over twenty-five days to arrive in Goshen, Egypt.

Imagine the logistics of finding water, preparing food, caring for the animals, setting up and tearing down camp each morning and night, dealing with sandstorms and heat, flies and toiletry needs. There were no rest stops, hotels, showers, laundromats, diapers, toilet paper, baby wipes, air conditioners, sunscreen, sunglasses, or any modern conveniences we take for granted. It was a rigorous journey.

THE DESCENDANTS WHO TRAVELED WITH JACOB TO EGYPT (46:8–27)

Verses 8–27 detail all of those who journeyed to Egypt with Jacob. Each son is listed with children born to him. Wives, daughters, granddaughters, and daughters-in-law are not named unless there are special reasons to name them, such as with Dinah. They are broken down not only by son, but also by which wife of Jacob they came from. The direct descendants of Jacob are summarized as follows: "All the persons belonging to Jacob who came into Egypt, who were his own offspring, not including Jacob's sons' wives, were sixty-six persons in all; and the sons of Joseph, who were born to him in Egypt, were two; all the persons of the house of Jacob, that came into Egypt, were seventy" (vv. 26–27; cf. Ex 1:5; Deut 10:22).

LOGISTICAL NOTE: *How Many Actually Traveled from Canaan to Egypt?*

Questions are raised about the actual number of people who traveled to Egypt. St. Stephen mentions, "And Joseph sent and called to him Jacob his father and all his kindred, seventy-five souls" (Acts 7:14). St. Stephen's name is Greek, which suggests he was a Hellenic Jew and more familiar with the Greek *Septuagint* translation of the Old

Testament (seventy-five persons) than with the Hebrew *Masoretic* text (which states seventy people). Many suggestions have been offered to explain the disparity of numbers. We do not have time to discuss them all in detail, but we will mention two solutions: one simple explanation, the other more complex.

> Seventy-five, according to the Septuagint, but seventy according to the Masoretic Hebrew text (Genesis 46:27, Exodus 1:5). Genesis 46:20 accounts for the discrepancy. In this verse the Septuagint names four grandsons and one great-grandson of Joseph, whereas the Masoretic text does not.[7]

> The difference arises from the difference in the way the totals are calculated. Jacob has twelve sons. Adding Jacob's grandsons and great-grandsons, the total was 66. Adding Ephraim and Manasseh who were born to Joseph in Egypt, the total is 68. When you add Jacob and his wife the total is 70, as the Hebrew records. The Septuagint, however, starting with Jacob's 12 sons, added Jacob's grandsons and great-grandsons for a total of 66. Then, it added the seven additional descendants of Joseph who were probably sons of Ephraim and Manasseh who were born to Joseph's sons some time after the migration of Jacob to Egypt, but before Jacob died. The Septuagint also omitted Jacob and his wife. This makes a total of 75 as Stephen mentions in the Acts passage.[8]

However, before we conclude there were only seventy persons traveling to Egypt, think again. The list comprises only direct descendants of Jacob. If you count the unnamed females, the sons-in-law, and all those *not* of direct descent, it is likely that there were more than three hundred.

> This figure [of seventy] also excludes all the wives and husbands of daughters or granddaughters, and so the number was actually far

---

[7] David H. Stern, *Jewish New Testament Commentary: A Companion Volume to the Jewish New Testament*, electronic ed. (Clarksville: Jewish New Testament Publications, 1996), Acts 7:14.

[8] Norman L. Geisler and Thomas A. Howe, *When Critics Ask: A Popular Handbook on Bible Difficulties* (Wheaton, Ill.: Victor Books, 1992), 432–33. For Saint Augustine's extensive discussion on the numbers, see *Questions on the Heptateuch, First Book: Questions on Genesis 152*, in Saint Augustine, *Writings on the Old Testament*, ed. Boniface Ramsey and Joseph T. Lienhard, trans. Joseph T. Lienhard, Sean Doyle, and Joseph T. Kelley, The Works of Saint Augustine: A Translation for the 21st Century, vol. 14, no. 152 (Hyde Park, N.Y.: New City Press of the Focolare, 2016), 74–75.

greater than just seventy. Therefore, the figure *seventy* includes only Jacob and his immediate descendants: Jacob, twelve sons, fifty-one grandsons, two great grandsons, one daughter, one granddaughter, one unnamed daughter of Leah, and one unnamed granddaughter. If one begins to add the servants and wives plus the women and children absorbed from Shechem (Gen 34:29), probably the entire figure would be about three hundred or more.[9]

JACOB AND JOSEPH REUNITED (46:28–30)

Judah was sent ahead to discover the route up to Goshen so he could guide the family when they arrived. It is becoming evident that Judah was taking precedence among the sons of Jacob. Joseph mounted his royal chariot and rode up to Goshen to meet his family; it had been over twenty years since he had last seen his father.

All that time, Jacob thought Joseph was dead, and Joseph had no idea if his aged father was still alive. Now Joseph weeps again! Presented to Jacob, he "fell on his neck, and wept on his neck a good while". To "fall on one's neck" is a Hebrew idiom for a full hug and embrace with the face snuggled into the other's neck. The phrase "for a long time" is another Hebrew idiom and means "extended up to and beyond the expected point".[10] The Greek *Septuagint* translates this very graphically, "they wept a flood of tears." This was certainly an embrace that both had not expected and was long overdue. Jacob was so overjoyed to see Joseph, he exclaimed, "Now let me die, since I have seen your face and know that you are still alive."

DECIDING WHERE TO DWELL IN EGYPT (46:31–34)

In order to secure the desired response from Pharaoh, Joseph coached his brothers how to answer questions. However, it is not entirely clear what Joseph was coaching them to do or why. He informed them that Egyptians loathed shepherds. Consider three possibilities.

[9] Arnold G. Fruchtenbaum, *Ariel's Bible Commentary: The Book of Genesis*, 1st ed. (San Antonio, Tex.: Ariel Ministries, 2008), 610.

[10] James Swanson, *Dictionary of Biblical Languages with Semantic Domains: Hebrew (Old Testament)* (Oak Harbor: Logos Research Systems, 1997), ref. no. 6388.

First, knowing they would be despised as shepherds, hopefully Pharaoh would assign them to their own private location in Goshen away from the Egyptians, or second, to convince Pharaoh that they had not come with ulterior motives to eventually acquire power or possess the land. There would be no nepotism; they intended to mind their own business, survive the famine, and return to Canaan. A third possibility is that the Egyptians, mainly an agricultural people, were threatened by flocks and herds that endangered their crops and, therefore, did not want the Israelites to intermingle with the Egyptian population.

Various commentators offer several reasons why the Egyptians loathed shepherds:

> Their antipathy is probably an example of the widespread distrust and fear of nomadic peoples by settled urban dwellers (cf. modern attitudes towards gypsies and hippies). By drawing attention to their life-style, Joseph hoped that Pharaoh would assign them land on the margin of Egypt, e.g., in an area like Goshen. As the next scene describes, his ploy succeeded.[11]

> The reason for this is not specified, but it seems the Egyptians despised shepherds as offenders against their religion. This is because several herding and grazing animals were revered as symbols of Egyptian deities. Shepherding, which entailed eating these beasts for food and using their hides for various domestic purposes, was probably thought to profane and desecrate these sacred representations of the gods.[12]

Whatever the reasons, God used the ethnic and occupational prejudices of the Egyptians to preserve the Israelites' distinct identity and separation both ethnically and spiritually. Genesis 38 reveals Jacob's sons were already intermarrying with Canaanite women. Soon their bloodline, and therefore their religious commitment, would be polluted, causing them to lose their distinction, disappearing into Canaanite society. Egyptians hated shepherds, so the shepherd clan

[11] Gordon J. Wenham, *Genesis 16–50*, Word Biblical Commentary, vol. 2 (Dallas: Word, Incorporated, 1994), 445.

[12] Scott Hahn and Curtis Mitch, *Genesis: With Introduction, Commentary, and Notes*, Ignatius Catholic Study Bible, Revised Standard Version and Second Catholic Edition (San Francisco: Ignatius Press, 2010), 75.

would be secluded, therefore keeping their identity as the Hebrews, the people of God.

St. John Chrysostom praises Joseph's wisdom in counseling their response to Pharaoh:

> Note the shrewdness with which he advises them, not idly or to no purpose making these suggestions but anxious to put them in a more secure position and at the same time to ensure their assimilation among the Egyptians. You see, since they loathed and despised those who tended flocks for having no time for Egyptian wisdom, consequently he counsels them to make a pretense of their occupation so that he may plausibly apportion them the most attractive land and cause them to live in considerable prosperity.[13]

---

[13] Homily 65.9, in John Chrysostom, *Homilies on Genesis 46–67*, trans. Robert C. Hill, The Fathers of the Church, ed. Thomas P. Halton, vol. 87 (Washington, D.C.: Catholic University of America Press, 1992), 248.

CHAPTER 47

ISRAEL AND SONS SETTLE IN GOSHEN

SELECT BROTHERS MEET PHARAOH (47:1–4)

Chapter 47 opens with Jacob being ushered in to meet Pharaoh. From his eleven brothers, Joseph selected only five to meet Pharaoh. Rashi, the medieval Jewish scholar, suggests why the five were chosen, "Literally, 'five' of them—five of the less formidable of them, those who did not look particularly powerful. For if Pharaoh saw how powerful they were, he would have made them soldiers. He presented them to Pharaoh. And here are the five he presented: Reuben, Simeon, Levi, Issachar, and Benjamin."[1]

The Pharaoh, as Joseph had predicted, immediately asked their occupation, and they were prepared with an answer. Like their fathers before them, they were shepherds—arriving in Egypt because there was no pastureland in Canaan. They humbly pled that Pharaoh allow them to dwell in the land of Goshen. The Nile Delta provided water for the family and the flocks. They were near the river since they had freely eaten fish while in Egypt: "We remember the fish we ate in Egypt for nothing, the cucumbers, the melons, the leeks, the onions, and the garlic" (Num 11:5). The fresh water was ideal for raising animals and growing crops. The Israelites dwelled there for 430 years until Moses led them out of Egypt (Ex 4–13). It was close enough for Joseph to care for them, yet far enough from the Egyptians to remain separate and inoffensive due to their flocks.

---

[1] Michael Carasik, ed. and trans., *Genesis: Introduction and Commentary*, The Commentators' Bible (Philadelphia: Jewish Publication Society, 2018), 407.

PHARAOH GRANTS JACOB'S REQUEST
TO SETTLE IN GOSHEN (47:5–6)

Pharaoh granted their request, but he did not answer the brothers directly; he turned to Joseph to authorize the settlement. He then said to Joseph: put any good men from your family in charge of my cattle—meaning any kind of grazing animal. Maybe this was why Joseph coached them to tell Pharaoh that they were keepers of livestock. Since Egyptians were not inclined to such an occupation, the king might hire Joseph's brothers to do the work shunned by Egyptians.

> Hebrew *sarei mikneh*, literally "officers of cattle," that is, superintendents of the royal cattle. This office is mentioned frequently in Egyptian inscriptions since the king possessed vast herds of cattle. Ramses III is said to have employed 3,264 men, mostly foreigners, to take care of his herds. The appointment of some of Joseph's brothers to supervise the king's cattle means that they are to be officers of the crown and thus will enjoy legal protection not usually accorded aliens.[2]

After the five brothers, Jacob arrived in the court of Pharaoh. The gray-haired, weather-beaten old shepherd approached the mighty Pharaoh, King of Egypt. The wording "set him before Pharaoh" might better be translated "stood him before Pharaoh". However, bowing or prostration before the king would have been expected, but Jacob stood and took the bold initiative—he blessed the king. We are not sure what this blessing entailed, maybe a salutation as in "May God bless and prosper the king" or something of that nature. The word "bless" (*barak*) in Hebrew has the meaning of invoking or enacting divine favor, a positive disposition or kind actions toward a person. It has a sense here of the *lesser* being blessed by the *greater*. We have other samples of "blessings" of kings later in the kingdom of Israel (cf. 2 Sam 16:16; 1 Kings 1:31).

[2] Nahum M. Sarna, *Genesis*, The JPS Torah Commentary (Philadelphia: Jewish Publication Society, 1989), 319.

PHARAOH INTERVIEWS JACOB; JACOB BLESSES PHARAOH (47:7–12)

Pharaoh asked Jacob his age. Jacob replied 130 years old and the years had been "few and evil" compared to Abraham, who lived to 180 years (Gen 35:28) and Isaac who lived to 175 (Gen 25:7). Egyptians believed 110 years was the ideal life-span and in the end Joseph himself died at 110.³ By *evil*, he was probably referring to the unsettled nature of his life, his unbroken string of conflicts and misfortunes. But one could argue that Jacob's trouble was reaped because of what he sowed—he made selfish and deceitful choices that brought grief to himself and those around him. He would live another seventeen years before his death at the age of 147 (Gen 47:28).

Jacob again blessed Pharaoh and departed. Everything was now arranged for the family to settle "the land of Ramses", another name for Goshen. "The new Pharaoh, who knew nothing of Joseph, was—in our reckoning—Seti I. With his successor in the 19th Dynasty, Ramses II, this monarch moved the royal throne from Thebes in Upper Egypt to the delta area and inaugurated a vast building program. The excavations at Tell er-Retabeh (ancient Pithom) and Tanis indicate the plausibility of the slave labor imposed upon the Israelites."⁴ The new king built cities in the northeastern section of the Nile Delta (cf. Ex 12:37). When filming our documentary *Moses: Signs, Sacraments and Salvation*, we worked in Qantir and Tanis and were shown amazing remains of statues of Ramses II along with other archaeological finds including massive carved stone feet of Ramses in the fields among the crops. Jacob's future generations were enslaved in the land of Egypt, where they built cities for Ramses. In Exodus 1:11, it states, "Therefore they set taskmasters over them to afflict them with heavy burdens; and they built for Pharaoh store-cities, Pithom and Ra-amses." But before their enslavement, the family lived happily in Goshen

³ "Abundant records from Egypt show that 110 years were considered an ideal lifetime." Raymond Edward Brown, Joseph A. Fitzmyer, and Roland Edmund Murphy, *The Jerome Biblical Commentary* (Englewood Cliffs, N.J.: Prentice-Hall, 1996), 1:46. "It is hardly a mere coincidence, but rather an instance of the Egyptian affinities of the narrative, that 110 years is at least three times spoken of as an ideal lifetime in Egyptian writings." John Skinner, *A Critical and Exegetical Commentary on Genesis*, International Critical Commentary (New York: Scribner, 1910), 539–40.

⁴ Brown, Fitzmyer, and Murphy, *Jerome Biblical Commentary* 1:49.

with plenty of area to graze their flocks and herds and a generous supply of food and provisions granted them by Joseph.

THE FAMINE RAGES; PHARAOH ACQUIRES ALL THE LAND OF EGYPT (47:13–26)

Verses 13–26 are an interlude to the story and demonstrate the wisdom and power of Joseph. The famine raged on with no food available in Egypt or Canaan. People were increasingly desperate to buy the grain so wisely stored in advance by Joseph. When their money was depleted, the people came with their livestock to barter for food, then they bartered their land, and soon they sold themselves and became servants of Pharaoh.

According to the Jerome Biblical Commentary:

> Despite the obvious oversimplifications indicated by the universal statements ("all the money," v. 14; "all the Egyptians," v. 15; "all their cattle," v. 17 [Masoretic Hebrew text]; "all the land," v. 20), the general background is historically accurate. The process of centralization in Egypt, from which the priests' holdings were exempt (cf. vv. 22 and 26), gained momentum in the new kingdom (ca. 1570) and was fostered by the belief that the Pharaoh, as a divinity, was absolute master of both land and people.[5]

In verse 17, horses are first mentioned in the Bible. Being listed first seems to indicate their newly acquired importance. Their popularity spread rapidly, which would be expected if one considered the difference between a chariot drawn by a donkey and one by a fleet-footed horse.

> Several Hebrew words are translated "horse" in the Bible. The terms usually used are *sus* and *parash*, of which the former were chariot horses, and the latter cavalry horses and of a lighter build for riding.... The Land of Promise was too hilly and rocky to be much benefited by their services, and the occupations of the people being agricultural they neglected to breed animals whose uses were mainly warlike.[6]

---

[5] Ibid., 1:44.

[6] Henry Chichester Hart, *The Animals Mentioned in the Bible* (London: Religious Tract Society, 1888), 128–29.

The people became servants in exchange for food. This was a common practice to pay off a debt or support families. In the Mosaic Law, indentured servitude was institutionalized, but one Hebrew could not keep another Hebrew indentured as a slave more than six years (Ex 21:1–11). The Egyptians had no such limitations. Joseph wisely organized the whole land of Egypt and distributed grain for sowing, and every Egyptian had to provide Pharaoh with one-fifth of the produce. Egyptian priests were exempt and could keep their land according to the customs in place prior to the famine (v. 22). The people all became tenant farmers. But Jacob and his family fared well and prospered.

Scripture scholar and Church Father Origen (third century) explains how Israel remained near to God even while dwelling in Egypt, and how we as believers can do the same:

> Let us see what Moses says after these words: "And Israel dwelt," the text says, "in Egypt, in the land of [Goshen]." Now [*Goshen*] means "proximity" or "nearness". By this it is shown that although Israel dwells in Egypt it is, nevertheless, not far from God, but is close to him and near, as he himself also says: "I will go down with you into Egypt, and I will be with you."
>
> And, therefore, even if we appear to have gone down into Egypt, even if placed in the flesh we undergo the battles and struggles of this world, even if we dwell among those who are subject to Pharao, nevertheless, if we are near God, if we live in meditation on his commandments and inquire diligently after "his precept and judgments"— for this is what it means to be always near God, to think the things which are of God, "to seek the things which are of God"—God also will always be with us, through Christ Jesus our Lord, "to whom belongs glory forever and ever. Amen." (*Homilies on Genesis*, 16.7)[7]

ISRAEL FARES WELL IN EGYPT (47:27–28)

God was faithful—the Israelites fared well in Egypt, and God was with them. They acquired property, their flocks and herds grew,

[7] Homily 16.7, in Origen, *Homilies on Genesis and Exodus*, ed. Hermigild Dressler, trans. Ronald E. Heine, The Fathers of the Church, vol. 71 (Washington, D.C.: Catholic University of America Press, 1982), 224.

and in spite of the famine, they were fruitful and became numerous. Jacob lived another seventeen years to 147 years old—dwelling near his powerful son surrounded by his family. He was the first of the patriarchs to die on foreign soil, but God had promised that his descendants would return and possess Canaan. Jacob's focus now was on his impending death, and he planned carefully for his end.

JACOB MAKES JOSEPH SWEAR TO RETURN
HIS BONES TO CANAAN (47:29–31)

Knowing his time was drawing near, Jacob called Joseph to his side. Like Abraham did with his servant, Jacob requested that his son put his hand under his thigh and promise. As described earlier, *thigh* is likely a euphemism for the male genitals (Gen 24:2), marking a solemn pledge. The master of Egypt swears with his hand under his aged father's "thigh". Jacob makes Joseph swear, and again the sacred number seven is used, as in "to seven oneself" (see Gen 21:22–31). The request is simple: Do not bury me in Egypt; rather, carry me up out of Egypt and bury me with my fathers in the cave of Machpelah in Canaan—bury me on our land! (Joseph's bones will also eventually be carried back to Canaan and buried in Shechem near Jacob's Well; Ex 13:19; Josh 24:32.) Joseph agreed and solemnly swore to do as his father had charged. The oath ensured that Pharaoh would allow Joseph to travel to Hebron with the body of his father as he had sworn to do (Gen 50:6).

"Then Israel bowed himself upon the head of his bed" (v. 31). The *Septuagint* translates this, "And Israel did obeisance upon the top of his staff", which corresponds to Hebrews 11:21, "By faith Jacob, when dying, blessed each of the sons of Joseph, bowing in worship over the head of his staff." This seems more likely since the staff represented authority, and he was the patriarch who was now to bless and curse. He was old and fragile, too weak to stand on his own. King David in his old age bowed the best he could from his seated or inclined position on the bed (1 Kings 1:47). Jacob's bow could be a gesture of thanks to Joseph, but more likely a sign of his full trust and confidence in God that all would be accomplished according to the divine will.

CHAPTER 48

JACOB BLESSES JOSEPH AND HIS TWO SONS

The change brought about by death can be daunting. My father died at ninety-four years of age. During his last days, I visited him regularly. He was my hero; he had loved the outdoors, and as I looked down at his sun-browned, wrinkled, emaciated body, it was difficult to maintain my composure. He still had a ready smile and bright eyes, and I could still see the strong and loving man who had raised me, who read me stories instead of buying me a television, and who bought me a pony and taught me to ride. Dad and Mom had courageously become Christians in 1954 and raised us boys to be good Baptist Christians.

The same day I was writing the rough draft of this chapter about Jacob calling his sons to his deathbed—I received a call to come quickly to Dad. He had not slept and was struggling to breathe. We drove to the house of my childhood to visit him. Memories flooded me as I looked down the hall past my old bedroom door to Dad's room. I remembered thunderstorms rumbling at night and how Dad would call us to jump in bed with him and Mom because he knew we were afraid.

Dad was slowly slipping away. My grown children came with their young kids, and we all visited Dad (Grandpa and Great-Grandpa). He summoned his strength and sat up to talk with us. Before we left, I kissed him and said I would be back tomorrow. I returned home to write this study and was again struck by the passage of time and the similarity of my situation with the history of Jacob calling his sons to his bedside. I felt I was writing about my own beloved father, not Jacob. Going to be with his Lord Jesus in heaven was all Dad talked about during his last days. My dad went to be with his Lord, and we buried his body on resurrection morning. Change is hard; death is hard.

JOSEPH VISITS DYING JACOB, WHO REVISITS
HISTORY WITH HIM (48:1–7)

Jacob had advanced in years and knew his time had come to be "gathered to his fathers". Joseph was informed and rushed to Goshen. This is the first time the word *illness* is mentioned in the Bible signifying weakness, affliction, sickness, or the feeling of pain. Joseph took his two sons, Manasseh and Ephraim, to visit their grandfather Israel. Jacob summoned his strength and sat up in his bed to greet them. Israel desired to recount to them his life and God's promises. This was *the* most important thing. He began all the way back in Luz (which he had renamed Bethel; 28:19), where God Almighty (*El Shaddai*) had graciously given him a vision of the angels ascending and descending on the stairway between heaven and earth and twice made promises to him there (Gen 28:10–22; 35:6).

Jacob reminded Joseph of his great-grandfather and the great, great-grandfather of Manasseh and Ephraim—Abraham, and all of his descendants after him, which included Joseph and his sons, to whom God had given the land of Canaan. The most important words were again drilled into their heads. God had promised, "Behold, I will make you fruitful and multiply you, and I will make of you a company of peoples, and will give this land to your descendants after you for an everlasting possession" (Gen 17:8; 48:4). Egypt was serving a special purpose in preserving the family, but it was not their home. They were sojourners in this foreign land—Canaan was their destiny and their everlasting possession. (This is, by the way, why Jews consider the land of Israel their inheritance and possession even to this day.)

Joseph had been in Egypt long before Jacob arrived. He was the ruler of the land and the son-in-law of the priest of On. His children were born to Asenath the Egyptian, daughter of On. Yet Israel had the audacity to say "your two sons, who were born to you in the land of Egypt before I came to you in Egypt, *are mine*; Ephraim and Manasseh shall be mine." He was the *patriarch*! God had spoken to him and revealed the plan! He claimed these two boys as part of that divine plan. This could imply that Joseph had or might soon have other sons who could remain in Egypt, but more likely, Jacob meant that any other sons would not receive separate tribal inheritances but would be subsumed within the tribes of their older brothers Ephraim and Manasseh. He then recounted the death and burial of his beloved wife, Rachel, the mother of Joseph.

JACOB BLESSES JOSEPH'S SONS (48:8–11)

Like his father, Isaac, Jacob was losing his eyesight (Gen 27:1; 48:10). Joseph had brought his two sons, but Israel could not see them, but presumably he could hear them or see shadows. (One wonders if his mind went back to deceiving his own blind father, Isaac.) "Who are these?" Jacob asked. Joseph said it was his two sons Ephraim and Manasseh. Jacob called them closer; he kissed and embraced them. Jacob said he never expected to see Joseph, and now he had the great blessing of seeing Joseph's sons, too. Then Joseph, the great Vizier of Egypt and head of the world's superpower, bowed his face to the earth before his father!

JACOB BLESSES JOSEPH'S TWO SONS (48:12–20)

Chapter 48 features the blessing of Joseph and his sons Manasseh and Ephraim; chapter 49 details Jacob blessing his other sons. After introducing Manasseh and Ephraim, Joseph removed them from his knees (v. 12). Translators have struggled to determine whose knees they were removed from: Jacob's or Joseph's. Though many translations use Joseph's knees, it appears more likely to be Jacob's knees as a sign of adoption. Putting a child on or between the knees is part of adoption rites in Eastern cultures. It is a symbol of receiving or adoption into the family. Joseph claimed these two boys as his own, equal to Reuben or Simeon (v. 50).[1]

[1] "The Hebrew literally reads, 'from with his knees.' It is highly unlikely that a bedridden, dying old man had twenty-year-old boys on his knees. More probably they were 'at/ near Israel's knees.' In any case, it is a legal gesture symbolizing their adoption." Bruce K. Waltke and Cathi J. Fredricks, *Genesis: A Commentary* (Grand Rapids, Mich.: Zondervan, 2001), 598. "To set a child upon the knees was to symbolize reception or adoption into the family.... From this passage it would appear that Joseph had set Ephraim and Manasseh upon, or against, the knees of their grandfather, so that they might receive the formal symbol (not

Joseph had not presented his sons to Jacob in any particular order, but he now arranged them in the proper order for the patriarchal blessing, with his eldest son, Manasseh, on Jacob's right and the second born, Ephraim, on his father's left side, positioned so Jacob's right hand would be on the eldest Manasseh's head and his left hand on Ephraim's. But suddenly Jacob surprisingly crossed his hands, placing his right hand on Ephraim who was the younger! Before Joseph could stop him to rearrange his hands, Israel blessed Joseph, by blessing his sons, making the younger the greater with the words, "God make you as Ephraim and as Manasseh."

Eastern cultures firmly believed that the patriarchal blessing was irrevocable (exemplified with Isaac's blessing of Jacob over Esau); and that the right hand is more powerful in blessing than the left. Being born first does not insure the standing as "firstborn". The blessing of the "firstborn" is determined by God and the patriarch, not by nature and birth order. Neither Isaac nor Jacob was the first son born. The younger Ephraim would become a greater tribe than Manasseh (cf. Deut 33:17) and would have prominence in the future Northern Kingdom. The blessing beautifully summarizes God's promises and passes it to the future generations.

In verse 15, the RSV-2CE translates the word *ra'ah* as "who has led me". *Shepherd* is used in most modern versions including the Catholic NAB and NJB. The Hebrew word *ra'ah* is the same as used in Psalm 23, "The Lord is my *shepherd*." This seems more appropriate as the elderly shepherd portrayed God shepherding him. Jacob blessed the boys with Ephraim being blessed as the "firstborn". Jacob claimed them for the covenant and prayed that his name would live on through them. Joseph was displeased and tried to place Israel's right hand on Manasseh's head. Israel insisted on blessing Ephraim, but he said he knew that Manasseh would also be a great people, but the younger would be first and the greater. The precedent had been set, and the younger again took precedence over the elder: Isaac over Ishmael, Jacob over Esau, Judah over Reuben, and now Ephraim over Manasseh.

---

here described) of adoption. This being done, he then removes them from between the knees of Jacob." Herbert E. Ryle, *The Book of Genesis in the Revised Version with Introduction and Notes*, The Cambridge Bible for Schools and Colleges (Cambridge: Cambridge University Press, 1921), 422.

412

ISRAEL'S WORDS TO JOSEPH (48:21–22)

Israel promised Joseph two things: (1) He would be brought back to Canaan, the land of his fathers, and (2) He would exclusively be given *shekem*, which means *portion* or *shoulder* or *mountain slope* or *ridge* (v. 22). There is ambiguity concerning the words of this blessing, but it is likely that he incorporated a wordplay, meaning several things. The Hebrew word *shekem* is taken to mean *shoulder* and could refer to the shoulder of a mountain in Shechem, especially since the words sound similar. This is likely because the area is associated with both Jacob and Joseph since Jacob bought land there (Gen 33:19). It is the location of Jacob's Well (Jn 4:5–6), and Joseph would eventually be buried there.[2] Shechem would also lie within the territories allotted to Joseph's sons, very near the border between the two. St. John's Gospel seems to confirm that this prophecy referred to the geographical area of Shechem: "[Jesus] had to pass through Samaria. So he came to a city of Samaria, called Sychar, near the field that Jacob gave to his son Joseph" (Jn 4:4). Sychar is only a "stone's throw" from Shechem. The identification with the city of Shechem is held by the *Septuagint* and ancient Jewish interpretation.

However, others conclude *shekem* means a double portion. Joseph had two sons included in the twelve tribes, and it could mean that God was giving Joseph a double portion through his two sons. 1 Chronicles 5:1–2 informs us of Joseph's double portion. It reads, "[Reuben's] birthright was given to the sons of Joseph the son of Israel … the birthright belonged to Joseph." The other brothers received one portion each, but Joseph received two portions through his two sons. The *Vulgate* renders this as *portion*, emphasizing the double inheritance given to Joseph.

---

[2] "The reference is to Genesis 48:22, where Israel (= Jacob) on his deathbed tells Joseph, 'And to you, as one who is over your brothers, I give the ridge of land [Heb. *šᵉḵem*, lit. "shoulder" of a mountain] I took from the Amorites with my sword and my bow.' When the Israelites conquered and settled Canaan, they brought with them out of Egypt the bones of their ancestor Joseph, and buried them 'at Shechem in the tract of land that Jacob bought for a hundred pieces of silver from the sons of Hamor, the father of Shechem. This became the inheritance of Joseph's descendants.' Sychar (if it is to be identified with 'Askar) lies about a mile from the ancient town of Shechem (modern Balata). Joseph's tomb lies but a few hundred yards north-west of Jacob's well." D.A. Carson, *The Gospel according to John*, The Pillar New Testament Commentary (Leicester, England; Grand Rapids, Mich.: Inter-Varsity Press; Eerdmans, 1991), 216–17.

We are not told when Jacob took the land from the Amorites, especially with bow and arrows. Amorite is used as a generic name for the Canaanites. This is either an unrecorded event, or he is taking credit for his sons' massacre of the Shechemites, which is unlikely since he criticized them for their cruel despoiling of the city. His final words to Joseph were intended to tie him inexorably to the land of the Amorites (Canaan) that would be their future, not Egypt.

CHAPTER 49

JACOB'S BLESSINGS AND
LAST WORDS TO HIS SONS

JACOB CALLS HIS SONS TO HIS BEDSIDE (49:1–2)

Chapter 49 moves forward with the final blessing of all Israel's sons. Until now, the covenant has been promised serially: to Abraham, then Isaac, then Jacob. The covenant now passes collectively to the twelve tribes of Jacob who become heirs of the promise. All through history, many heirs have been surprised and even dismayed at the reading of hitherto unknown content in a family will. Here, too, there will be surprises and disappointments with Israel's "last will and testament". Reuben, the firstborn of the twelve, lost the status of the "firstborn" for violating his father's concubine (Gen 35:22). The next oldest, Simeon and Levi, were jointly censured due to their treachery in Shechem (Gen 34:25–30).

Judah as fourth born was next in line. He was not chastised, and he received the kingly line, and "the scepter shall not depart from Judah" (49:10).

On the other hand, Joseph, the eldest son of Jacob's beloved wife Rachel, also obviously exercises leadership in the family and receives the most profuse blessing (Gen 49:22–26). Remarkably, it is upon the heads of his sons—who bear the blood of an Egyptian mother—that the covenant blessings are conferred (Gen 48:15–16). In this way, Jacob's blessing sets up a tension between these two brothers and the tribes that will come from them by granting the "scepter" (kingship) to Judah (Gen 49:10) and yet calling Joseph the "prince" among his brothers (Gen 49:26 NABRE). It is from these two tribes, Judah and Joseph (= Ephraim), that the kings of southern Judah and northern Israel, respectively, will be provided.[1]

Israel gathers his sons to this bedside knowing the end has come. It is described as the family blessing in verse 28—the word "blessing" (*barak*) being used three times in the one verse. The blessings are given in the form of poetry; this is the first passage in the Bible where poetry extends for more than a few verses. His words are historical and prophetic. The blessing or censure of each brother is not personal only but applies to the future of each individual tribe. This may be one of the more difficult passages to interpret within Genesis due to frequent vagueness, illusive language, and ambiguity. A similar list of tribal blessings is given by Moses prior to his death (Deut 33:1–29).

The order of the sons is laid out in the literary style of parallelism: Leah's sons first, followed by Bilhah's, Zilpah's, Bilhah's, and ending with Rachel's sons. From Leah, one son is predominant; from Rachel one son is predominant. Of the twenty-five verses total, five each are allotted to Judah and Joseph. Together they make up ten of the twenty-five verses.

JACOB'S BLESSINGS, CURSES, AND PROPHECIES (49:3–27)

Not all the blessings were positive, in the usual sense of a blessing— some of Israel's "blessings" were curses and rebukes; some were promises or prophecies. Some of the "blessings" were related to the past; others looked to the future. These were prophetic oracles. There were messianic allusions in Judah's, while others were short and ambiguous. The choices of individuals had affected their destiny and that of their children.

Jacob specifies that he is prophesying about the future with the words, "That I may tell you the things that will befall you in the last days" (v. 1). This is clearly not just referring to their immediate

[1] John Bergsma and Brant Pitre, *A Catholic Introduction to the Bible*, vol. 1, *The Old Testament* (San Francisco: Ignatius Press, 2018), 147–48.

situations but to their descendants as well. "By saying, '*in the last days*,' he implies that he is about to speak about the mysteries of Christ and about the things that would be fulfilled at his coming."[2]

Jewish commentator Nahmanides affirms that "in days to come" refers to the days of the Messiah:

> *In days to come.* Messianic times, to which Jacob alludes with these words (see v. 10). Our Sages say he wished to reveal the end of the exile to them, at which point the Shekhinah departed from him. For everyone agrees that the "days to come" described here are the days of the Messiah.[3]

St. John Chrysostom in his commentary on Genesis concurs:

> Come along, [Jacob] says, and learn from me, not the immediate future, but what will happen in the last days. This I foretell to you not of myself but under the inspiration of the Spirit; hence I predict ahead of time what will occur after many generations. You see, as I am on the point of departing this life, I want to imprint it on the memory of each of you as if on some bronze pillar.[4]

REUBEN (49:3–4)

We have discussed Reuben's violation of his father's concubine Bilhah and his grasping for his father's authority (35:22). He was firstborn through Leah. Jacob uses the word "preeminent" twice before telling him he will *not* be preeminent. He should have been the "firstborn" in the full sense of the term, but his flawed character and moral shortcomings haunted him. He was deemed unworthy to

[2] Denis the Carthusian, "Exposition on Genesis (Genesis 47–50)", in *The Book of Genesis*, ed. Joy A. Schroeder et al., trans. Joy A. Schroeder, The Bible in Medieval Tradition (Grand Rapids, Mich.; Cambridge, U.K.: Eerdmans, 2015), 242.

[3] Michael Carasik, ed. and trans., *Genesis: Introduction and Commentary*, The Commentators' Bible (Philadelphia: Jewish Publication Society, 2018), 424.

[4] Homily 67.4, in John Chrysostom, *Homilies on Genesis 46–67*, trans. Robert C. Hill, The Fathers of the Church, ed. Thomas P. Halton, vol. 87 (Washington, D.C.: Catholic University of America Press, 1992), 267.

lead the family. He was as unstable as water—an apt description (cf. Is 57:20). His birthright was given to the sons of Joseph (1 Chron 5:1). Moses pronounced a similar "blessing" as well: "Let Reuben live, and not die, and let his men be few" (Deut 33:6).[5] Reuben's tribe decided to stay on the east side of the Jordan when Joshua led the people into the Promised Land. They disappeared after the Assyrian Exile around 732 B.C.

SIMEON AND LEVI (49:5–7)

These brothers were the second and third born to Jacob by Leah, and they are grouped together in the "blessing" because they collaborated to slaughter the men of Shechem (34:25–31). Scripture did not specifically condone or censure their actions, and though Jacob said nothing at the time, disapproval was expressed in Jacob's judgment. Their swords were not used for peaceful purposes but as "weapons of violence"—they slew men because of their anger and hamstrung oxen because of their wantonness. To "hamstring oxen" means to cripple them by cutting the large tendon in their legs, causing great pain and rendering the oxen useless. There is no particular instance of hamstringing, so it may be a metaphor for unnecessary destruction. They were cursed for their anger, wrath, and cruelty—they would be divided and scattered in Israel (Josh 19:1, 9).

With Reuben disqualified, Simeon should have been next in line, followed by Levi, but their moral shortcomings had now disqualified them both as well. Simeon's tribe became absorbed into the more vigorous tribe of Judah. Levi's numbers diminished during the wilderness wandering but were appointed the priestly tribe (Aaron and Moses were from the tribe of Levi) based on their heroic efforts to

---

[5] "'Nor let his men be few': as some commentators say, this is a wrong translation. The Hebrew text [Vulgate also] has 'and his people be few'.... This is actually a request that the tribe of Reuben will never become strong and dominant; see Gen 49:3–4. A possible alternative translation model for this verse is: 'May you never die out; but may you always be few in number'". Robert G. Bratcher and Howard A. Hatton, *A Handbook on Deuteronomy*, UBS Handbook Series (New York: United Bible Societies, 2000), 577. The tribe of Reuben would fall to the Moabites and those remaining be taken captive to Assyria (1 Chron 5:26) and have no importance in the future of Israel.

defend the honor of God—also done with swords when they slew three thousand Israelites who worshipped the golden calf at Mount Sinai (Ex 32:26–28). In both cases, they slew men with the sword, but the difference is this: at Sinai they obeyed the command of God to defend his honor; in the earlier case at Shechem, it was a personal vendetta. Levi's tribe *was* eventually scattered among Israel as prophesied, but not in a bad sense. They were the priests who owned no tribal territory—their inheritance was the Lord and throughout the land served God as priests in specified cities (Josh 21:3). Levites would later receive a blessing and special privilege from God (Deut 33:8–11). St. Matthew the Apostle was also named Levi, which may indicate he was of that tribe (Mt 9:9; Lk 5:27; Mk 2:14). Other famous Levites were Barnabas (Acts 4:36), Zechariah and Elizabeth, and their son John the Baptist (Lk 1:5; 1 Chron 24:1, 10)—and by virtue of being a close relative of Elizabeth, maybe Mary, the mother of Jesus, as well (Lk 1:36).

JUDAH (GEN 49:8–12)

From Judah, the fourth son, would come the royal line of kings starting with David and concluding with Jesus Christ. Jacob's blessing of Judah was effusive, taking up five full verses, and he was the only one praised. The poetic wording was rich with kingly and messianic allusions: his brothers would praise him, he would grasp his enemy's necks, and his brothers would bow to him. He was a young lion (first time lions are mentioned in the Bible), the scepter and the ruler's staff would not depart from him; the people would obey him. The promise was fulfilled in King David of the tribe of Judah and ultimately with Jesus the "Lion of the tribe of Judah" (Rev 5:5). Jesus was adopted by Joseph into the family line; "Abraham was the father of Isaac, and Isaac the father of Jacob, and Jacob the father of Judah and his brothers.... And David was the father of Solomon ... and Jacob the father of Joseph the husband of Mary, of whom Jesus was born, who is called Christ" (Mt 1:2, 6–7, 15–16).

Around 1,800 years after Jacob's blessing, Gabriel announced, "Do not be afraid, Mary.... You will conceive in your womb and bear a son ... and the Lord God will give to him the throne of his father David, and he will reign over the house of Jacob for ever; and of his kingdom there will be no end" (Lk 1:30–33). Jesus inherited the lineage of Judah when adopted by his foster father, Joseph.

Notice *lion* is used three times in verse 9. David defended his sheep against lions (1 Sam 17:34–35). Lions inhabited Canaan until hunted into extinction around the thirteenth century. Even today, the lion is a symbol of Jerusalem, the royal city of David. The word *Jew* comes from the word *Judah* as does *Judaism*. Judah was the tribe that survived the exiles and returned to Israel after the Babylonian captivity—after the other tribes had disappeared, although many people retained their tribal identities.

Verse 10 contains wording much debated, "The scepter shall not depart from Judah, nor the ruler's staff from between his feet, *until he comes to whom it belongs*; and to him shall be the obedience of the peoples" (RSV-2CE, Vulgate, D-R). Other translations render the third clause as "until Shiloh comes" (Hebrew *Masoretic*, KJV, NASB), or "until tribute is brought to him" (NAB, ESV-CE). Obviously with such a diversity of translations we will not untie the knot here. However, a few thoughts are required since it is such a significant messianic prophecy.

"*So that tribute shall come to him.*" The straightforward sense of the Hebrew is actually "until Shiloh comes"; [New Jewish Publication Society] adopts a midrashic reading—not "Shiloh" but *shailo*, "tribute to him," as in "all who are around Him shall bring *tribute* to the Awesome One" (Ps. 76:12). But Shiloh refers to the King Messiah, for kingship is *shelo*, "his." [Targum] Onkelos indeed translates it as "Messiah".[6]

This may contain an immediate reference to David and his successors, but the text itself points to a descendant of Judah who will be universal king. The Hebrew term used to describe this descendant (*siloh*) has been interpreted by Jewish and Christian tradition in a messianic sense, linking it to other oracles about the dynasty of David (cf. 2 Sam 7:14; Is 9:5ff; Mic 5:1–3; Zech 9:9). In the light of the New Testament we can see what the oracle means: with David royalty in Israel will emerge from the tribe of Judah and will extend until the coming of the "Son of David", Jesus Christ, in whom all the prophecies find fulfilment (cf. Mt 21:9).[7]

[6] Carasik, *Genesis: Introduction and Commentary*, 430–31.

[7] James Gavigan, Brian McCarthy, and Thomas McGovern, eds., *The Pentateuch*, The Navarre Bible (Dublin and New Jersey: Four Courts Press; Scepter Publishers, 1999), 224.

In verse 11, the Church Fathers perceived another reference to Jesus Christ. St. Cyprian of Carthage (died A.D. 258) wrote:

> In the blessing of Judah also this same thing is signified, where there also is expressed a figure of Christ.... To which things divine Scripture adds, and says, "He shall wash His garment in wine, and His clothing in the blood of the grape." But when the blood of the grape is mentioned, what else is set forth than the wine of the cup of the blood of the Lord?[8]

St. Irenaeus (120–200) wrote:

> Now let these, who are said to search out all things, see what was the time wherein the Prince failed, and the Leader out of Judah, and who is the Hope of the Gentiles, and who the Vine, and who his foal, and what is the garment, and what the eyes, and what the teeth, and what the wine, and every particular above mentioned; and they will find that no other Person, but our Lord Jesus Christ, is proclaimed.[9]

There is a parade of biblical images in these five verses: lions, foals, donkeys, prey, scepters, staffs, vines, wine, milk, eyes, teeth, and garments. They are rich in meaning, and much discussion swirls around their interpretations.

ZEBULUN (49:13)

Leah's sixth son, Zebulun, is listed prior to her fifth son, Issachar. His blessing is enigmatic since the blessing says he will dwell at the shore of the sea and become a haven for ships with his border toward Sidon. The territory of Zebulun lay between the Mediterranean and the Sea of Galilee but bordered neither—it was landlocked. It

---

[8] Epistle 62.6, in Cyprian of Carthage, "The Epistles of Cyprian", in *Fathers of the Third Century: Hippolytus, Cyprian, Novatian, Appendix*, ed. Alexander Roberts, James Donaldson, and A. Cleveland Coxe, trans. Robert Ernest Wallis, The Ante-Nicene Fathers, vol. 5 (Buffalo, N.Y.: Christian Literature Company, 1886), 360.

[9] *Against Heresies*, bk. 4, chap. 10, in St. Irenaeus, Bishop of Lyons, *Five Books of S. Irenaeus against Heresies*, trans. John Keble, A Library of Fathers of the Holy Catholic Church (Oxford, London, Cambridge: James Parker and Co.; Rivingtons, 1872), 334.

would be like praising Kansas, to exaggerate a bit, for its expansive seashore and beaches. Moses' blessing in Deuteronomy also mentions Zebulun and Issachar as drawing wealth from the sea. It possibly suggests that Zebulunites were employed along the coast by the Phoenicians, who were shipbuilders and seafaring folks. But the blessing is ambiguous, and its fulfillment is unknown. Zebulun's territory was also about sixty miles south of the city of Sidon in Phoenicia (today's Lebanon). Because of Sidon's prominence, the name of the city is often used as a synonym for the country (see Deut 3:9; Judg 3:3; 1 Kings 17:9).

Jewish sages tried to harmonize the prophecy of Zebulun with the fact that they were not dwelling by the sea. Rashi wrote:

> His land would be on the shore of the sea, the "district" of the sea.... He will be frequently found in the shipping district, the port where ships bring their cargo. For Zebulun was engaged in trade, providing sustenance to the tribe of Issachar, who were engaged in Torah study. As Moses put it, "Rejoice, O Zebulun, on your journeys, and Issachar, in your tents" (Deut. 33:18)—Zebulun would journey forth to trade and Issachar would stay in their tents engaged in Torah study.[10]

ISSACHAR (49:14–15)

Leah's fifth son is now blessed by his father, Jacob. Imagine two sheepfolds with a donkey lying down between them. The donkey has a load on its back but does not rise to do its work. It prefers to lie down and become a slave. The tribe of Issachar seemed to take a passive role in the conquest of Canaan, lying down between sheepfolds rather than heroically fighting. As shown above, some rabbinic tradition suggests that Issachar studied the Torah while Zebulun was busy with commerce and supporting Issachar. In Judges, chapter 1, Issachar is not listed in the catalogue of tribes that fought to conquer the land. They may have desired peace more than possession of their allotted land. Like the donkey, they likely preferred servitude to exertion.

---

[10] Carasik, *Genesis: Introduction and Commentary*, 433.

DAN (49:16–18)

Dan is the first concubine son to receive a blessing, the seventh son of Jacob, the first born to Bilhah. Jacob prophesies that "Dan shall judge his people." This is a wordplay, since Dan means *judgment* (Gen 30:6). They lived in a "camp city" (*Mahaneh–dan*) in the south instead of settling in their allotted territory (Judg 18:11–12). Their allotment was along the Mediterranean, but the Amorites and Philistines pushed them out, so they went to the far north and conquered Laish (Judg 18:27). One of their claims to fame is Samson, who is a type of Christ (Judg 13:1–25). The image of the serpent may be due to Dan as a tough fighting force in spite of its size (cf. Judg 18). A little snake lurching at a horse can unseat a rider as quickly as an armed opponent. Dan is not listed in the twelve tribes sealed by God at the end of time (Rev 7:4–8).[11] It is suggested that Dan's exclusion was a penalty for its rampant idolatry. Even today you can see the remains of a huge pagan altar at the 120-acre Dan National Park in northern Israel. Though Israel was prohibited from intermarriage with Canaanites, the Danites violated the prohibition, including Samson (Judg 14:1–3; 16:4), the blasphemer (Lev 24:11), and Huram–abi (2 Chron 2:12–13).

An intermission interrupts Jacob's prayer (v. 18). "I await your salvation, O LORD." This prayer may have been uttered for Dan, foreseeing his dismal future. But more likely Israel is catching his breath halfway through his blessings, realizing the importance of the moment and asking for strength and wisdom to continue.

GAD (49:19)

Gad is the first son of the concubine Zilpah. Gad's blessing is a long pun with four of the six words containing the consonants *gd*. Gad sounds like the words *raid* and *raiders*. His descendants settled in trans-Jordan, east of the Jordan River. Tribes to the east such as the

---

[11] "Ezekiel names Dan in his vision of the apportionments of land (Ezek. 48:1), but the tribe is excluded from John's vision of the 144,000 servants of God (Rev. 7:4–8), perhaps because Dan actively promoted idolatry under King Jeroboam (1 Kgs. 12:29)." Allen C. Myers, *The Eerdmans Bible Dictionary* (Grand Rapids, Mich.: Eerdmans, 1987), 256. The tradition that the antichrist would come from the tribe of Dan emerged early in the Church with Church Fathers Irenaeus and Hippolytus.

Ammonites, Moabites, and the Arameans often attacked Gad. But Gadites were known as famed warriors (Deut 33:20; 1 Chron 5:18) and proved to be brave. In 1 Chronicles 12:8 we learn that the Gadites went over to David's forces and were "mighty and experienced warriors, expert with shield and spear, whose faces were like the faces of lions, and who were swift as gazelles upon the mountains".

ASHER (49:20)

The second son of Zilpah occupied the land in the north along the Mediterranean coast up to the border with modern Lebanon. He was named Asher because he made Leah happy. He was now promised a happy future in the fertile and beautiful lands along the Sea, encompassing the Carmel mountain range. However, their tribe was insignificant in the history of Israel, and they were among those taken into exile by the Assyrians. St. Luke mentions the prophetess Anna from the tribe of Asher, a widow eighty-four years old who never left the Temple. She recognized Jesus the Messiah when he was presented in the Temple as an infant (Lk 2:36–38).

NAPHTALI (49:21)

Naphtali is the second son of Bilhah, Rachel's servant, and the sixth son of Jacob. We know next to nothing about Naphtali. The territory of Naphtali encompassed some of my favorite land in Israel—the Upper Galilee area bordering the Sea of Galilee north along the Jordan River up to its source in the foothills of Mount Hermon along today's Israel's northern border with Lebanon. They were slow in conquering their territory from the Canaanites (Judg 1:33) but served gloriously in the war led by Deborah at Mount Tabor (Judg 4:10). Naphtali is said to be a deer let loose. "The interpretation of this verse is quite uncertain. Each line can be understood in about three different ways, which has given rise to a great variety of interpretations."[12] Some translations render the words "bears comely

---

[12] Gordon J. Wenham, *Genesis 16–50*, Word Biblical Commentary, vol. 2 (Dallas: Word, Incorporated, 1994), 482.

fawns" while others render them "gives beautiful words". Who had more "beautiful words" than Jesus, who lived in the land of Naphtali (though he was from the tribe of Judah). The territory of Naphtali is where Jesus spent most of his time during his earthly ministry, where he lived in Capernaum, and where he preached his Sermon on the Mount. Might this be a hint referring to Christ? Notice what St. Matthew writes:

> Now when he heard that John had been arrested, he withdrew into Galilee; and leaving Nazareth he went and dwelt in Capernaum by the sea, in the territory of Zebulun and Naphtali, that what was spoken by the prophet Isaiah might be fulfilled:
>
> > "The land of Zebulun and the land of Naphtali,
> > toward the sea, across the Jordan,
> > Galilee of the Gentiles—
> > the people who sat in darkness
> > have seen a great light,
> > and for those who sat in the region and shadow of death
> > light has dawned."
> > From that time Jesus began to preach, saying, "Repent, for
> > the kingdom of heaven is at hand." (Mt 4:12–17)

JOSEPH (49:22–26)

Joseph, like Judah, receives five verses of blessings and accolades. However, unlike Judah, his tribes (those of his two sons Manasseh and Ephraim) would not survive the Assyrian conquest and deportation. Their massive land allotment disappeared after the fall of the Northern Kingdom of Israel. The wording and allusions in this blessing are some of the most difficult to interpret and understand. Jacob expresses love and pride for Joseph the firstborn of his beloved wife, Rachel, and savior of his family who inherits the birthright and the double portion. There is an interesting list of names for God: Mighty One of Jacob (used only four other times in Scripture and always in poetic texts, Ps 132:2, 5; Is 49:26; 60:16), the Shepherd (appropriate name used by a shepherd; see Ps 23:1; 80:1), the Rock of Israel (actually *stone*, used only here as a name for God), God of your fathers, and God Almighty (*El Shaddai*) (see *CCC* 269). Each is rich with meaning. Verse 22 was discussed earlier in regard to the handsome appearance of Joseph (Gen 39:6).

BENJAMIN (49:27)

One would expect Benjamin to receive an effusive blessing, but not so; it is one of the shortest bestowed. Far from resembling a ravenous wolf, he seems more lamblike, needing protection. The blessing obviously refers to his descendants. The territory allotted to Benjamin was located just north of Judah and encompassed Jerusalem. They were known for military exploits. The tribe of Benjamin could muster 26,000 troops that drew the sword, among whom there "were seven hundred picked men who were left-handed; every one could sling a stone at a hair, and not miss" (Judg 20:15–16; 1 Chron 8:40). Other famous Benjamites were Ehud, who delivered Israel from the Moabites (Judg 3:15–30); King Saul, the first king of Israel, with exceptional military prowess and the tallest, most handsome man in Israel (1 Sam 9:1–2); and Saul of Tarsus, who ravaged the Church (Phil 3:5–6) before converting to become the defender of the faith called St. Paul, sometimes pictured with sword in hand.

JACOB FINISHES HIS BLESSINGS AND DIES; PLANS FOR HIS BURIAL AT MACHPELAH (49:28–33)

In verse 28, we find the first mention of the "twelve tribes of Israel". Jacob concluded his blessings for his twelve sons, "blessing each with the blessing suitable to him". Joseph stood at Jacob's bed with his brothers, as a son, not as a ruler—the former being more important in the big picture. Though Jacob's next command was directed to them all, it was obviously Joseph who would implement it. Joseph had sworn an oath to bury Israel in Canaan (47:30–31), now specified as the cave of Machpelah purchased by their great-grandfather Abraham from Ephron the Hittite (see Gen 23:8–17; 25:9). In a way, that burial cave represents the family's down payment on God's promise of the land. We knew that Abraham, Sarah, and Isaac had been buried there

(Gen 23:19; 25:9; 35:29), but now we learn that Rebekah and Leah were also buried there (49:31). The last we heard of Rebekah was when she had quickly sent Jacob away to Haran (Gen 27:42–46). The last mention of Leah was during the flight from Haran before meeting up with Esau (Gen 33:2–7). Four thousand years later, we can still visit the mosque or the synagogue inside the massive walls built by King Herod the Great between the years 31–34 B.C. It is the last existing "intact" building of King Herod the Great.[13] In A.D. 700, Bishop Arculf traveled through the Holy Land and kept a journal, "written from his dictation, by Adamnan, Abbot of Iona":

Hebron, which is also called Mamre, has no walls, and exhibits only the ruins of the ancient city; but there are some ill-built villages and hamlets scattered over the plain, and inhabited by a multitude of people. To the east is a double cave, looking towards Mamre, where are the tombs of the four patriarchs, Abram, Isaac, Jacob, and Adam the first man. Contrary to the usual custom, they are placed with the feet to the south, and the heads to the north; and they are inclosed by a square low wall. Each of the tombs is covered with a single stone, worked somewhat in form of a church, and of a light colour for those of the three patriarchs, which are together. The tomb of Adam, which is of meaner workmanship, lies not far from them, at the furthest extremity to the north. Arculf also saw poorer and smaller monuments of the three women, Sarah, Rebecca, and Leah, who were here buried in the earth. The hill of Mamre is a mile to the south-west of these monuments, and is covered with grass and flowers, with a flat plain at the summit; on the north side of which is a church, in which is still seen, rooted in the ground, the stump of the oak of Mamre, called also the oak of Abraham, because under it he received the angels (*The Travels of Bishop Arculf in the Holy Land* [A.D. 700]).[14]

Between A.D. 1160 and 1173, Rabbi Benjamin of Tudela witnessed the cave of Machpelah and the tombs of the patriarchs and matriarchs:

[13] In my *Footprints of God* documentary series, in the episode *Abraham: Father of Faith and Works*, we take you into the synagogue and mosque inside the cave of Machpelah under tight security to see the resting place of the patriarchs and matriarchs Abraham, Sarah, Isaac, Rebekah, Jacob, and Leah.
[14] Thomas Wright, ed., *Early Travels in Palestine* (London: Henry G. Bohn, 1848), 6–7.

But if any Jew come, who gives an additional fee to the keeper of the cave, an iron door is opened, which dates from the times of our forefathers who rest in peace, and with a burning candle in his hands, the visitor descends ... [and reaches] six sepulchres, those of Abraham, Isaac, and Jacob, and of Sarah, Rebecca, and Leah, one opposite the other. All these sepulchres bear inscriptions, the letters being engraved: thus, upon that of Abraham, we read, "This is the sepulchre of our father Abraham, upon whom be peace;" and so on that of Isaac and upon all the other sepulchres. (*Travels of Rabbi Benjamin of Tudela* [A.D. 1160–1173])[15]

After following this intriguing patriarch Jacob for so many years (and fourteen chapters), it is sad to read 49:33: "When Jacob finished charging his sons, he drew up his feet into the bed, and breathed his last, and was gathered to his people."

CHAPTER 50

JACOB EMBALMED; BURIED IN MACHPELAH; DEATH OF JOSEPH

JACOB EMBALMED FOR BURIAL (50:1–3)

Joseph has wept many times on the necks of his brothers and his father, but now he falls on the weather-beaten old face and weeps over him one last time. Joseph then commands his physicians to embalm his father. This is the first occurrence of the words *physician* (literally "healers", including morticians) and *embalming* in the Bible. Embalming was an Egyptian practice based on the cult of Osiris and the Egyptian view of the afterlife. Embalming took forty days.[1] With Jacob, it was certainly not done for religious reasons, as it was among the Egyptians, but for practical reasons to prevent putrefaction and prepare his body for the long journey to the burial site in Canaan. Joseph would also be embalmed for the same reasons, and that would be the last time embalming is mentioned in the Bible. The Egyptians and Jacob's family wept for Israel for seventy days.

JOURNEY TO CANAAN FOR THE BURIAL OF JACOB (50:4–14)

With the time of mourning complete, Joseph requested permission of Pharaoh to bury his father in Canaan, as he had sworn he would do.

---

[1] "[Embalming] was an elaborate and ritual-filled procedure performed by a trained group of mortuary priests. It involved removing the internal organs and placing of the body in embalming fluids for forty days. The idea behind this is based on the Egyptian belief that the body had to be preserved as a repository for the soul after death." Victor Harold Matthews, Mark W. Chavalas, and John H. Walton, *The IVP Bible Background Commentary: Old Testament*, electronic ed. (Downers Grove, Ill.: InterVarsity Press, 2000), Gen 50:1–3.

Pharaoh granted permission. It was no average caravan traveling to Canaan with the embalmed body of Israel but a procession of dignitaries, elders of Egypt, and Pharaoh's household, along with Jacob's family. They were a "very great company" accompanied by chariots and horsemen. It was certainly something Hebron had never seen before.

The Canaanites were alarmed by such an impressive retinue of Egyptians crossing their borders with a military escort. Jacob's sons carried his body to the cave of Machpelah, where they buried him. Joseph and the whole group returned to Egypt. The route they took is unknown, and the two sites mentioned, "the threshing floor of Atad" and "Abel-mizraim" are both uncertain. "Beyond the Jordan" is a matter of the perspective of the speaker. After they buried Jacob with his fathers, the whole retinue returned to Egypt. It must have been nearly a two-month journey there and back.

JOSEPH REASSURES HIS BROTHERS (50:15–21)

After their father was buried and unable to intercede for them, Joseph's brothers became apprehensive that Joseph might inflict vengeance on them for their treachery when he was a boy. Their apprehension was misdirected after all that Joseph had done for them. He had never hinted at being vengeful, but they were so fearful they contrived a lie about their father to secure their safety. Joseph wept when he heard their unfounded fears. His brothers fell before him again, at the end of the story, like the dream had predicted at the beginning—and they said, "We are your servants."

Joseph responded, "Fear not!" Joseph closed out the book of Genesis with a statement that had been proven true over and over again—"you meant evil against me; but God meant it for good" (CCC 312). Joseph was looking at the big picture, not consumed with petty, vindictive emotion. He saw the providential hand of God in the life of his fathers and in his own circumstances. His brothers had always been shortsighted—Reuben with grasping for his father's authority, Simeon and Levi for their vengeance against the men of Shechem—all of them for their petty hatred of Joseph and his elegant robe. Genesis paints the big picture of God's overarching control of history and mankind's destiny.

JOSEPH'S DEATH; PROMISE TO RETURN
HIS BONES TO CANAAN (50:22–26)

Joseph assured his brothers of his fidelity and care. They all lived peacefully and prosperously in Egypt until Joseph died at the age of 110 years old. Joseph saw his great-grandsons. In a funerary inscription from Syria, it is recorded that righteousness is rewarded with seeing your future generations: "Belonging to Agbar, priest of Sahr, in Nerab. Because of my righteousness before him, he gave me a good name and prolonged my days. On the day I died, my mouth was not closed to words, and with my eyes, what do I see? Children of the fourth generation."[2] Regarding the birth of Joseph's great-grandsons of Machir, in Hebrew it literally reads they were "born on his knees" which implies he adopted them as his own, as Jacob had done with Ephraim and Manassah. Joseph summoned his brothers; though it is surprising he would die before them, and told them of his impending death.

Joseph reminded them that God would visit them in Egypt and eventually bring them back to the land of Abraham, Isaac, and Jacob. It is all about the *land* and the promise of God for a people to live on the land. God's plan would not be thwarted by Egypt, any more than it was thwarted by sin, indifference, or evil. As the Vizier of Egypt, he would have been expected to abandon the distant thoughts of Canaan when his family had such a bright future in Egypt. After all, his wife was the daughter of the high priest of Egyptian gods, and he was in the highest echelons of Egyptian culture and society, but the insistence of both Joseph and Jacob to be buried in Canaan implies that they had resisted all devotion to Egyptian deities and remained faithful to the God of their fathers. Joseph had his eyes on the long game. Ruler of Egypt, yes, but his future was the covenant with God in the land of Canaan. The biblical book of Sirach summarizes, "And no man like Joseph has been born, and his bones are cared for" (49:15).

His brothers swore an oath that Joseph's bones would be carried to Canaan. We see this fulfilled in Exodus 13:19 and Joshua 24:32.

---

[2] James Bennett Pritchard, ed., *The Ancient Near Eastern Texts Relating to the Old Testament*, 3rd ed. with supplement (Princeton: Princeton University Press, 1969), 661.

Joseph died, was embalmed according to the custom of the Egyptians, and he was put in a coffin in Egypt. After four hundred years of the sons of Israel being in Egypt, Joseph's embalmed body would be carried through the Red Sea, through the wilderness of Sinai, across the Jordan River into the Promised Land—to its final resting place in Shechem, where you can visit his tomb today.[3]

St. John Chrysostom comments on Joseph's age, the span of his life, and the rewards for his virtue:

> The text goes on: "Joseph passed away at one hundred and ten." Why did it indicate to us his age, too? For you to learn how long he had been entrusted with the control of Egypt. He was seventeen when he went down to Egypt, and it was when he reached the age of thirty that he appeared before Pharaoh and interpreted his dreams. He then held complete control of Egypt for eighty years. Do you see how the rewards were greater than the hardships and the recompense manifold? For thirteen years he struggled with temptations, suffering servitude, that illicit accusation, ill-treatment in prison. Since he nobly bore everything with thankfulness, accordingly he attained generous rewards even in the present life. Consider, after all, I ask you, that as a result of that short period that he endured servitude and imprisonment he occupied a royal position for eighty years. For proof that it was by faith that he did all this and for the same motive gave directions about the transfer of his bones, listen to Paul's words: "It was by faith that at the point of death Joseph gave a reminder about the exodus of the sons of Israel." Instead of stopping there, he went on so that you might learn the reason why he ensured the transfer of his bones: "and gave directions about his bones."[4]

At the death of Joseph, no weeping or mourning is recorded like the lamenting at the death of Jacob. His bones were placed in a coffin, which was characteristically Egyptian; coffins are never again

---

[3] For a marvelous overview of Genesis and the lives of Abraham, Isaac, Jacob, and Joseph, the Exodus—and much more leading up to God coming to earth as a man, read Saint Stephen's inspired defense before he was stoned to death. The whole dramatic summary can be read in Acts 7:1–53.

[4] Homily 67.22, in John Chrysostom, *Homilies on Genesis 46–67*, trans. Robert C. Hill, The Fathers of the Church, ed. Thomas P. Halton, vol. 87 (Washington, D.C.: Catholic University of America Press, 1992), 277–78.

mentioned in Scripture.[5] The Israelites simply wrapped dead bodies
and placed them in tombs.

And so the book of Genesis ends. We could say we have reached
the end of the beginning. But it is also the beginning of everything
else that is to come. It lays the foundation for the rest of Scripture
and the whole story of salvation. The nation of Israel has begun, and
what a thrilling journey it has been. We already sense the impending darkness of Egyptian slavery on the horizon, in accordance with
Abraham's vision (Gen 15:12–14), yet there is hope of redemption
with God's promised visitation, like a silver lining to the ominous
cloud approaching.

LOOKING TO THE FUTURE

The story of Israel continues in Exodus, where we are immediately
confronted with a menacing verse that sets the stage for their impending bondage, "Now there arose a new king over Egypt, who did not
know Joseph" (Ex 1:8). The children of Israel would multiply greatly
and become prosperous, which would be seen as a threat. The vast
number of foreigners within his kingdom was intimidating. It was
also obvious that their God was blessing them, a God other than the
gods of Egypt. The new king would enslave them with forced labor
seven days a week for hundreds of years before God "remembered"
his promise to Abraham, Isaac, and Jacob. The death of the patriarchs
did not impede God's promises.

After about three hundred years of slavery, God would raise up
Moses to deliver the people, and a whole new saga and adventure
would begin as God carried out his promises and covenant. Then, two
thousand years after Abraham, "When the time had fully come, God
sent forth his Son, born of woman, born under the law" (Gal 4:4).

---

[5] "The word for *coffin* is *'ārôn*, the word used for the 'ark' (i.e., chest) of the covenant.
Perhaps it is best to understand *'ārôn* as a sarcophagus here (the only time *'ārôn* has this
nuance in the OT); the use of the definite article on coffin (*the coffin*) may be a way of
specifying that the coffin in which Joseph was placed was similar to a sarcophagus used
in Egypt for a high-ranking Egyptian." Victor P. Hamilton, *The Book of Genesis, Chapters
18–50*, The New International Commentary on the Old Testament (Grand Rapids, Mich.:
Eerdmans., 1995), 711–12.

Jesus established his Church, which marches through history until the end of time.

Genesis is not just for reading pleasure or academic study, although it is for both. It is written primarily for *our* instruction on how to live. St. Paul writes, "For whatever was written in former days was written for our instruction, that by steadfastness and by the encouragement of the Scriptures we might have hope" (Rom 15:4). And referring to Abraham's justification, Paul tells us, "But the words, 'it was reckoned to him,' were written not for his sake alone, but for ours also. It will be reckoned to us who believe in him that raised from the dead Jesus our Lord" (Rom 4:23–24).

Even when institutions fail and leaders fall short, we learn to stay firmly rooted in the covenant people of God and to cling without flinching to God and his promises—like the patriarchs did. As Mother Saint Teresa is famous for saying, "God does not require that we be successful only that we be faithful." And in the midst of our striving, though stumbling and falling, "We know that in everything God works for good with those who love him, who are called according to his purpose" (Rom 8:28; *CCC* 312–14). Looking beyond our own finite situations and experiences, we begin to perceive the big picture of God's work in history.

OLD TESTAMENT SAINTS

In our liturgical year, we celebrate the saints, and there are hundreds of them, from Saints Peter and Paul to Saint Maria Faustina and Pope Saint John Paul II. But what about the virtuous patriarchs and heroes from the Old Testament? Are they enjoying the glory of God's presence in heaven?

The *Catechism* reminds us that many Old Testament figures are saints, "The patriarchs, prophets, and certain other Old Testament figures have been and always will be honored as saints in all the Church's liturgical traditions" (*CCC* 61). Some of them have their state revealed to us in Sacred Scripture. We get a sneak peek behind the curtain to view the blessed lives of the patriarchs in the glory of heaven. In the Gospels, Jesus chides the unbelievers among his people with these words, "There you will weep and gnash your teeth, when you see Abraham and Isaac and Jacob and all the prophets in the kingdom of God and you yourselves thrust out. And men will come from east and west, and from north and south, and sit at table in the kingdom of God" (Lk 13:28–29). The fact that Moses and Elijah appear alive with Jesus on the Mount of Transfiguration certainly gives us a hint as to their saintly status.

By studying the lives of the saints in Genesis, we can learn about our own conversion of heart and salvation. Much was required of these heroic men and women in Genesis. Nothing less is required of us. We have more at our disposal than they could have ever hoped to have. We have been given the fullness of the truth in the revelation of Christ and the institution of his Church. We have the indwelling Holy Spirit and the sacraments that impart grace to strengthen us to live as saints. Jesus says to us, "Every one to whom much is given, of him will much be required" (Lk 12:48).

Saints Abraham and Sarah, Isaac, Rebekah, Jacob, and Joseph, pray for us! All holy men and women—heroes of God, pray for us!

GENERAL INDEX

Melchizedek, 140, 141–46
Meshberger, 59n19
Mesopotamia, 55, 94, 118, 124–26,
    128–29, 133, 139, 157, 185, 212,
    257, 261, 268, 332, 396. *See also*
    Haran (city); Ur; ziggurats
Messiah
    Elijah and, 166
    Ephrath (Bethlehem) and, 317–18
    genealogical lines and, 85
    Gentiles and, 166–67, 246
    line of Jacob and, 246
    line of Judah and, 274
    line of Seth and, 83
    line of Shem and, 113, 114
    Melchizedek and David as
        foreshadowing of, 142, 144
    Nahmanides on, 416
    Revelation on, 71
    Shiloh and, 419
Methuselah, 87
Michelangelo, 59, 109
Midrash, 48, 143, 211, 347n6, 419
Mitch, Curtis, 21–22
Moab (person), 191
Moab, land of, 138, 187, 191, 238,
    291, 396
moon, creation of, 34, 37–38
moral law
    conscience and, 14–15
    Lewis on, 15
Moriah, 214–16, 218–23
Mosaic Law
    ban on eating blood in, 103
    ban on marrying sisters, 276
    capital punishment and, 104
    indentured servitude in, 406
    levirate marriage law, 339–40
Moses
    authorship of Genesis and, 19–22
    death of, 21
    God speaks to, 393
    God's relationship with, 24
    at Transfiguration, 434
    typology of, 26

Mount Ararat, 99
multiverse, atheists on, 15–16
murder, Cain's punishment for, 81–82
The Mystery of Mary (Haffner), 87

Nahmanides, 143, 416
Nahor
    family of, 225
    father of, 123, 125
    in Haran, 225, 231–32
    as pagan, 125
    sons of, 232, 261
    wife of, 232
nakedness, 107
    of Adam and Eve, 18, 61, 67, 76,
        107, 153
    of Noah, 107, 108, 109, 116
    shame over, 70, 107, 153
Nanna/Sin (Chaldean god), 124, 125,
    217
Naphtali
    Jacob's blessing for, 423–24
    as son of Jacob through Bilhah, 275
    territory of, 424
Nathanael, 258–59
nature, God as transcending, 37
Navarre Bible, 38
Nebuchadnezzar, King of Babylon,
    64
Nephilim, 89–91
New Testament
    concealed in Genesis, 25–26
    typology and, 25–26, 315n4,
        334–35
Newman, John Henry Cardinal Saint,
    207–8, 208
Nimrod, 115, 119–20
Nineveh, 115, 119
Noah. *See also* ark; the Flood
    after the Flood, 99–102
    blessing of, 93
    blessing of Japheth, 114
    blood prohibition, 103–4
    building of ark, 92–94
    capital punishment, 103–4

SCRIPTURE INDEX

1 Samuel (*continued*)
   10:3, 142
   14:15, 258n5
   15:22, 79
   16:1, 264
   16:12, 242, 271
   16:18, 348
   16:20, 142
   17:13–18, 325
   17:34–35, 419
   17:42, 242
   19:13, 16, 285
   22:1–2, 339
   22:2, 291
   25:13, 291
   26:4, 371
   30:10, 291

2 Samuel
   6:12–14, 142
   13:15–17, 304
   13:18, 19+, 326
   16:16, 403
   17:24–27, 290
   18:18, 140
   23:1, 257
   23:13, 339
   24:2, 140
   24:13, 369n2

1 Kings
   1:31, 403
   1:47, 407
   2:13–25, 319
   11:1, 5, 7, 33,
       191
   11:1–8, 194
   11:3, 194
   12:29, 422n
   17:9, 421

2 Kings
   2:9, 244
   2:24, 331
   3:9, 286n
   6:15, 346

1 Chronicles
   1:32, 238
   2:3–8, 344
   5:1, 318, 417
   5:1–2, 338, 412
   5:18, 423
   8:40, 425
   12:2, 106
   12:22, 290
   21:12–14, 369n2
   24:1, 10, 418
   28:4, 338

2 Chronicles
   2:12–13, 422
   3:1, 215
   12:8, 423
   20:7, 169
   36:16, 254n

Nehemiah
   1:11–2.1, 354
   9:7–8, 20–22, 151
   9:7–17, 129n

Tobit
   1:22, 363
   11:19, 273

Esther
   2:7, 348
   3:10, 363

1 Maccabees
   2:51–52, 224, 350
   6:15, 363

2 Maccabees
   7:27, 200n3
   7:28cf, 30

Job
   1:6, 91
   1:6–7, 64
   2:1, 91
   38:7, 91

Psalms
   7:13, 106
   8:3–7, 40–41
   8:5, 53
   19:1, 38
   23:1, 424
   23:2, 299
   29:1, 91
   50:5, 154
   51:18, 142
   52:8, 100
   60:7, 338
   76:1–2, 141
   76:3, 143
   76:12, 419
   78:35, 147
   80:1, 424
   90:10, 155
   104 cf, 38
   104:2, 34
   105:16–24, 367
   105:17–18, 334
   105:21, 22, 364
   105:23, 27, 115
   106:22, 115
   106:30–31, 153, 307
   110, 143–44, 145
   110:1–4, 143
   110:4, 141
   118:14, 377
   125(126):6, 328
   132:2, 5, 424
   148:4, 36

Proverbs
   5:5–22, 349
   6:24–33, 349
   7:5–23, 349
   9:13–18, 349
   16:11, 374
   23:3, 6, 253
   31:23, 180

Ecclesiastes
   3:20, 73
   12:7, 73

INDEX OF *CCC* REFERENCES